The Promise of America

SÆTESDALSLAGET

M'INTOSH, MINN. J

The Promise of America

A History of the Norwegian-American People

Odd S. Lovoll

UNIVERSITY OF MINNESOTA PRESS   MINNEAPOLIS
in cooperation with
THE NORWEGIAN-AMERICAN HISTORICAL ASSOCIATION

The University of Minnesota Press gratefully acknowledges the publication assistance provided by Northwestern National Life Insurance Company.

Published by the University of Minnesota Press,
2037 University Avenue Southeast, Minneapolis MN
55414

Printed in the United States of America

Translation of *Det løfterike landet* © Universitetsforlaget.
Oslo. 1983.

Library of Congress Cataloging in Publication Data

Lovoll, Odd Sverre.
  The promise of America.
  Translation of: Det løfterike landet.
  Bibliography: p.
  Includes index.
  1. Norwegian Americans—History. I. Title.
E184.S2L6913 1984   973′.043982   83-27350
ISBN 0-8166-1331-1
ISBN 0-8166-1334-6 (pbk.)

The University of Minnesota
is an equal-opportunity
educator and employer.

To my wife, Else

Contents

Preface

The Norwegians who built an immigrant community on American soil brought with them a strong awareness of Norwegian history. They defined themselves in terms of their ethnic background and found unifying symbols in their national cultural heritage and traditions.

Norwegian Americans—in the manner of other ethnic groups in America—were pulled between two cultures, the one they had left behind and the one they had to gain a foothold in. They tried to embrace both while moving inexorably toward integration with American society. They felt a strong need to clarify national identity, to preserve traditions, and to explain the circumstances surrounding their lives. The urge to examine and to articulate their varied emotions and experiences produced a rich literary activity. It included works of fiction, nostalgic accounts, chronicles, narrative records of many kinds, and historical studies of high quality that describe and interpret the subculture created by Norwegian immigrants and their descendants. The role of the immigrant in American life and history in general was thereby elucidated, for Norwegian-American participation in the making of America was similar to that of the many other nationalities who sought economic security and social order within the boundaries of this diverse and complex society. Few immigrant peoples have, however, produced a more complete record of their presence in America than the Norwegian Americans. The heightened sense of their own history may to some degree be attributed to a surge of patriotism in the homeland during the main era of Norwegian emigration. It was a quest for national expression in language, in literature, and in history that made Norwegians in America become more sensitive to their common immigrant past, to the merits of their national heritage, and to a vista of a shared future in the new land.

The Promise of America was written with great humility toward the task and with affection for the people and circumstances dealt with. The point of departure was to a large extent my own personal search for a place in this complicated, but fascinating, historical process. In my efforts I drew on extensive historical literature, and I am indebted to earlier scholarship. My investigations took me to archival collections and libraries, to local museums and historical societies from coast to coast in America, and to research institutions in Norway. I also visited Norwegian areas of settlement—in the cities as well as in the country—interviewed numerous Norwegian Americans, received advice and information, and enjoyed the hospitality and assistance of many friends. Colleagues gave generously of their time and shared with me their insights into immigration history. They are too numerous to mention individually here, and I thank them all most heartily. I wish to express a special word of gratitude to my academic institution, St. Olaf College, for granting me a one-year leave of absence, and to the Minnesota Historical Society and Universitetsforlaget in Oslo for providing the needed financial support so that the work could be undertaken. It was a pleasure to cooperate with the University of Minnesota Press in the publication of this English-language edition of the book, which originally was prepared in Norwegian.

Odd S. Lovoll

St. Olaf College
Northfield, Minnesota

The Promise of America

A History of the Norwegian-American People

Norway and Europe

"The inhabitants of Norway are among the few fortunate ones in Europe," wrote Johan Christian Fabricius at the University of Kiel following a journey through the country in the 1770s. He based his flattering judgment on the assumption that "separated from other nations by impenetrable mountain ranges, they live in happy solitude, far from the debauchery and vices of recent times."

Norway was a remote province of the Danish-Norwegian kingdom. Ruled from the distant capital city of Copenhagen, it was isolated from the great cultural centers of that day and apparently unaffected by the dramatic events, new ideas, and profound changes in other parts of Europe. Casual outside observers might therefore think that they had found lost virtues there and an unspoiled natural state.

The idyllic description Fabricius gives of Norway, with people who have "preserved ancestral virtues," was in part determined by the fact that the Danish-Norwegian government had financed his travels, and he therefore found it expedient to reassure his readers that the Norwegians were "the faithful and worthy subjects of their king." His views were, however, not original. Fabricius expressed common conceptions and attitudes that were advanced by his contemporaries and which were maintained later in historical accounts. These emphasize the country's remoteness, its untouched condition, and its isolation. As a consequence, it is thought, Norway developed a distinctive folk life and a unique social order.

To be sure, Norway was located in the far North and its population was small and scattered. But even though Norway together with other Nordic states lay on the outskirts of the continent, it formed a part of northwestern Europe. In the eighteenth and nineteenth centuries this was the most dynamic and expansive region of the world. Commercial interests linked Norway to the two great European powers, France and Great Britain, and especially from the mid-1700s the country enjoyed a continuous period of economic growth. It was based on Norway's traditional export industries in mining, lumbering, fishing, and shipping. The country was able to take advantage of the favorable economic conditions produced by wartime demands to expand its foreign trade. A separate Norwegian merchant fleet developed, and the transportation of goods between Norway and France and most of the export of lumber to Great Britain was in Norwegian hands. Norway thereby was pulled more firmly into European and overseas commercial connections.

Nordic neutrality, largely dictated by trade interests, collapsed after 1800, and the Nordic states became directly involved in the war policies of the great powers. The consequences were dramatic and decisive. Economic growth came to an end in 1807 when Denmark-Norway became allied with France and adopted the continental system with a blockade of all British exports to the continent of Europe.

Norwegian society can hardly be described as ideal even before 1807. The rapid rise in prices in the preceding decades had caused suffering and distress in a large portion of the population. During the years of hardship between 1807 and 1814 the country's economic life became paralyzed. Shortages of grain and other foodstuffs created a devastating situation, which most severely affected the lower classes in the cities, the workers in logging operations, and the landless classes in the countryside. The misfortunes that befell Norwegian foreign trade also undermined the basis for both the social prestige and the pretentious life-style of the commercial elite. During the European depression following the Napoleonic Wars Norwegian economic life went through a lengthy process of adaptation and readjustment.

The good economic times before 1800 had brought increasing prosperity to the Norwegian bourgeoisie, which had become a style-setting group. It constituted one of the two leading social classes; the second was the official class of civil servants, or "the thousand academic families," as the historian Jens Arup Seip described it. When the political bonds with Denmark were severed in 1814, both these groups took part in formulating Norway's new government, but the official class had more than half of the representatives in the constitutional assembly that convened at Eidsvoll. The constitution adopted by that body on May 17, 1814, established a governmental structure that assured the official class a dominant position in both the executive and the legislative branches of government. Seip compared what happened in Norway to developments in many colonial areas: "The colonists tore themselves away from the motherland and on their own assumed rule over the natives." It was an epoch in Norwegian history that lasted more than fifty years, and that has been called *embetsmannsstaten*, or government by elite.

From as early as the 1760s a growing self-assertion and dissatisfaction with the Danish-Norwegian state's policy of centralization in economic and cultural affairs had prepared Norwegians for independence. Nevertheless, it was forces outside the country that caused the final dissolution of the Danish-Norwegian union, which had lasted more than four hundred years. External interests were also decisive in forging the union Norway entered into with Sweden on November 4, 1814, this time as an independent kingdom. Norway emerged with a separate national identity; in an incredibly short time the nation had moved from royal absolutism to liberal constitutional rule. And Norway guarded and increased its independence and secured a place among the nations of Europe, although in the shadow of its mightier partner.

Nationalism, which became a powerful movement in the nineteenth century, had developed in opposition to the forced internationalism of the Napoleonic Era. In nation states like Great Britain, France, and Spain it produced a new patriotism and a will to defend national interests; in other parts of Europe, like Italy, Germany, and Poland, the idea of nationalism stimulated powerful movements toward national unification and political independence. The strength and prosperity of the French and British examples inspired efforts toward unification in western as well as eastern Europe.

Great Britain held the lead in the process of industrialization that had begun in the previous century; in the years after Napoleon's fall it became the workshop and the financial center of the world. The industrial revolution spread from Great Britain, first to western Europe and only after 1870 to eastern Europe and to overseas areas. British industry was thus spared serious foreign competition until the 1870s.

Throughout the nineteenth century Great Britain continued to develop its colonies of white settlers and to secure its empire in India and its scattered possessions elsewhere. At the same time it founded and expanded a new empire in Africa. France also established an empire on the African continent and fortified its position in southeastern Asia. Overseas regions, both those administered by the motherland and those not directly controlled by the colonial powers, as well as underdeveloped parts of Europe, provided vast opportunities for investment and construction.

A necessary condition for the economic growth that occurred was improvement in the system of transportation and communication. The nations of northwestern Europe invested in great undertakings both within Europe itself and overseas. From the 1840s railway construction expanded rapidly. During this decade steamships began to replace sailing ships in the transatlantic trade, and from the 1860s steamships gradually gained the upper hand in the overseas transport of goods and people. The telegraph began in the same period to link distant regions and to create a unified economic system whereby the industrialized parts of the world might easily communicate with regions that provided them with raw materials. The rate of growth and expansion in underdeveloped areas naturally fluctuated, and investment was not consistently high, but by and large the areas of the world that received the majority of European emigrants experienced a rapid transformation and a strong economic growth.

Overseas emigration from Europe was tied both to developments created by European economic activity and to the trade patterns and commercial interests that held together the world's economic system. The emigrants populated new and underdeveloped regions; they gave life and content to new societies and had a marked influence on older civilizations.

Of the world's underdeveloped nations, the United States was obviously the most advanced and progressive, and, fueled by European, especially British, investments, it showed a vigorous growth. In the nineteenth century the United States had a nearly limitless need for new citizens to settle the country's empty regions and utilize its enormous resources, although the need rose and fell with changing economic conditions.

When the mass emigration from Europe to all parts of the world began after 1815, the United States became the most important destination. Of the fifty million emigrants who went to overseas regions between 1815 and 1915, as many as thirty-five million came to the United States, and of the remaining fifteen million nearly ten million settled in Canada, South America, Australia, and New Zealand. It was an unparalleled migration in size and probably also in significance. With a pronounced feeling for the individual in this dramatic tale of "mankind in motion," the pioneer historian of immigration Marcus Lee Hansen described the emigration as "fifty million epics." Until the mid-1840s, however, the migration was just beginning; the majority of emigrants left Europe in the course of the seventy years from about 1846 to World War I.

Impersonal economic forces may of course be viewed as prime causes of emigration, but they provide an inadequate explanation of the complicated process that made millions of people seek a better life in other parts of the world. It is important to bear in mind the expectations and the uncertainty the individual emigrant harbored as he or she made the fateful decision to depart from the homeland, and the many personal motives that affected the emigrant's resolution.

The circumstances that induced emigration varied from place to place, and they changed in the course of time. But common to all nations of Europe was a doubling of population between 1750 and 1850. Although this population explosion was hardly a direct cause of emigration, it had great and searching social consequences. Industrialization, modernization of agricultural production, and the growth of cities liberated millions of people from traditional modes of livelihood tied to agriculture and the crafts and made them mobile and receptive to better prospects elsewhere. The rising expectations, which progress in the homeland created, spurred people on to seek even greater happiness outside the confined conditions at home.

Political and religious motives were also important. People left autocratic forms of government and religious oppression. And the advent of liberalism, which encouraged greater toleration and freedom in the different European countries—in the northwestern part of the continent from the 1840s—became in itself a source of dissatisfaction and impatience with local conditions. Possibilities were always greater and institutions freer on the other side of the Atlantic. Still, it was the acceptance of liberal philosophy by European states that gave the individual freedom of movement and made emigration a matter of personal choice.

Norway and the other Nordic countries were early pulled into an Atlantic economy and pattern of trade. Emigration from these countries was therefore a response to economic circumstances that affected northwestern Europe in general. From the 1840s emigration became ordinary in the North.

Toward the end of the century, from the 1880s, southern and eastern Europe came under the influence of the economic and commercial developments that had begun in Great Britain, France, and the other nations of northwestern Europe. These regions now were pulled into the overseas migratory pattern.

The shifting intensity of emigration was determined by an interplay of economic forces, by the tempo and level of investment, demand, and production. Before the century had ended, these factors affected all the European continent and linked it to a worldwide economic system.

Seen in this context, Norwegian emigration falls into a larger European pattern, but with a unique development and special national manifestations. Norway, with a marked tradition of emigration, was until well into the twentieth century one of the principal countries of emigration. In a certain sense Norway became a colonial power, although the emigrants settled in regions that were beyond Norwegian jurisdiction. Their fate in the new land is worthy of scholarly attention and must be viewed as part of both Norwegian and American history and social development.

5576
Eneret Wilse
Emigrantreisens begyndelse.
5576
Eneberettiget 1906
Wilse Christiania

The Emigration

The exodus from Norway began in 1825, gained momentum in the 1840s, and fluctuated throughout the era of emigration. During the fifty years following the American Civil War there were three distinct waves. Large contingents of Norwegians left the homeland to seek a new life in America. They were encouraged to leave by difficult economic and social conditions, coupled with an irrepressible faith in the opportunities for a better life in a different part of the world.

The journey to America begins.

Those Who Left

The great migration of the nineteenth century radically expanded the area of Norwegian settlement, experience, and influence. It was a movement of people that is unrivaled in Norwegian history, except perhaps for the explosive westward sweeps of conquest and exploration during the Viking Age. Norwegian immigrants to America were well aware of the similarities between their own wanderings and their ancestors' forays to the west, and they treasured the comparison. The Viking past has in fact served as an effective symbol in Norwegian-American history up to the present time. "Because we are reminded of sagas of old/And are proud of the land we forsook/Can it be that the blood of the Vikings still flows/In our veins like a still-running brook?" the Norwegian-American poet Franklin Petersen wrote around 1900.

Cultivation of the Viking image among Norwegian Americans is, however, more interesting in a different connection, for it reveals more about patterns of adjustment and efforts at self-assertion in an immigrant population than it does about actual historical parallels a thousand years apart. Unlike the Viking expansion, the initial emigration from Norway in the nineteenth century can hardly be described as explosive, even though it seemed alarming and incomprehensible at the time. After the first group emigration in 1825 there followed a long pioneer phase—a founding period—of forty years. Annual emigration did not get under way until 1836, and it gained momentum only in the 1840s. The mass exodus began in the mid-1860s. After that time three major waves of emigration can be identified, the first one from 1866 to 1873, the second from 1880 to 1893, and the final mass crossing during the first decade of this century. There was also considerable emigration in the 1920s. From the first emigration up to 1980 more than 900,000 Norwegians moved overseas. Of course, not all these people were lost to the homeland. A smaller countercurrent took many of them back to Norway again. A fact that should be underscored is that of all those who emigrated, 780,000—87 percent—left during the period from 1865 to 1930. Like the Viking expansion, this movement trans-

The resolution to leave the homeland was frequently a painful decision, and the departure therefore a somber occasion. The first stage of the long journey became a favorite motif for Norwegian artists. Above: "The Emigrants" by Gustav Wentzel.

ferred Norwegian people and culture to other parts of the world, although in other respects the comparison is lame.

During the nineteenth century the United States was the destination of nearly all the Norwegians who moved overseas, and it has continued to be the main receiving country. Only after 1900 did Norwegians begin to settle to any extent in Canada; in the years up to World War I Canada received 10 pecent of all Norwegian emigrants and in the 1920s 24 percent. Other overseas regions such as Australia, South Africa, and South America have attracted only statistically insignificant numbers of emigrants from Norway.

As a result of the emigration, there evolved on American soil an immigrant community, a Norwegian America. It has never constituted a large percentage of the American population—well under 2 percent even at its peak during the period of World War I—but concentrations of Norwegians in certain regions of the United States have made this ethnic group an influential and dominant element in some parts of the country. It is not unreasonable to assume that the combined number of present-day Americans of Norwegian birth or ancestry approaches in size Norway's own population.

Norwegian Society

The country the emigrants left had a population of 883,487 in 1801. Norwegian society consisted of clearly separated social strata. The upper class —the people of condition—consisting of officials, great merchants, operators of mines and mills, and wealthy landowners, made up at most 2 percent of the country's inhabitants. About half of all Norwegians belonged to the middle class of farmers, craftsmen, and petty bourgeois of various kinds. The rest of the people formed a lower class of servants, day laborers, cotters, and a large number of paupers.

More than 91 percent of the population lived in rural areas, and of the 304,804 individuals listed in the 1801 census in specific occupational groups, more than half were directly involved in the production of raw materials as farmers, cotters with land, lumberjacks, and fishermen. If cotters without land and servants are included, one finds that 83 percent of the working population made a living in these basic modes. The facts indicate that Norway was economically an underdeveloped region at the beginning of the nineteenth century.

The cities were small. In 1801 Bergen, with 17,000 people, was Norway's largest urban center and Oslo's population was less than 11,000. But because Oslo was the nation's capital, it grew rapidly after 1814, and by 1830 it had passed Bergen in population. Oslo had become a city of 30,000 inhabitants, with more officials than shop clerks.

The men who in 1814 formulated Norway's constitution and secured its rebirth as an independent kingdom were familiar with the political thought of the Enlightenment, and the new constitution, like the American one, was based on the principles of popular sovereignty and the separation of powers. The officials formed a distant and exalted governing elite that administered the country according to the letter of the constitution as conscientious and incorruptible bureaucrats. The constitution provided for greater political participation by the people; the existence of freer political institutions was one of several new forces that affected Norwegian society. It required time, however, for the people to learn to exercise their rights.

The culture of the official class belonged in an urban setting, and peasant society was more or less untouched by it. The local community existed independently of the larger national society, and their contact with it was frequently limited to the parish priest and the sheriff, the local representatives of the official class.

Great differences were evident not only between the cities and the countryside, but also between one part of the country and another. In eastern Norway the social distance between the wealthy farmer and his cotters was insurmount-able, whereas western Norway, with its smaller independent farms, had greater social equality. In northern Norway fishing was given more importance than farming.

Norway's inhabitants in 1814, as later, were concentrated in two or three major areas of the country. The most important region consisted of both sides of the Oslo fjord and a broad belt northward toward Lake Mjøsa. Another large area of settlement was the middle and inner regions around the Trondheim fjord; a third major area was Jæren, the lowland district between the Bokna fjord and the town of Egersund. Otherwise most people lived in the narrow valleys, with some settling even above the timberline, and on the strip of land along the country's immensely long coastline.

Norwegian society was moved by a spirit of change and transformation, and new influences and ideas affected old customs and a traditional way of life. But a barter economy, in which almost all consumer goods were produced on each individual farm, continued. According to the Norwegian historian Sverre Steen, a money economy was limited to the cities. Even though such an economic division was present to a great extent, some trade did occur in the countryside, and there was production for barter or sale. In his history of the Norwegian fisheries, Trygve Solhaug emphasized the direct participation of the fishing population in the export industry, both in catching the fish and in preparing it for export by drying or salting.

On the whole, Norwegian society experienced gradual economic growth until the 1830s, although with crises and recessions in individual branches of the economy, especially in those relating to lumber. The cities grew, and urban industries increased. At the same time the old peasant society was slowly dissolving, weakened by the impact of the cities, new consumer goods, and an expanding money economy, as well as by political reform brought about by financial self-interest and influenced by economic liberalism and the ideas of the Enlightenment. Sweeping religious revivals were also strong forces for change. The activity of Hans Nielsen Hauge and his many followers, called Haugeans, had a great impact. They did not leave the Norwegian Lutheran State Church but worked for a renewal of Norwegian Christian life within its framework.

It all began with the Restauration, *a small sloop of about 39 tons, 54 feet long and 16 feet wide.*

The pietistic lay movement that came out of the Haugean revival indicated a general resistance to authority and the dominance of the officials and reflected a growing class consciousness. Behind all these developments lay the rapid increase in population that Norway experienced after 1814.

The Restauration

Norwegian emigration in the nineteenth century began dramatically on July 4, 1825, with the sailing of the sloop *Restauration* from Stavanger on the southwestern coast of Norway. On board were fifty-two persons, crew and passengers, who all intended to emigrate. The *Restauration* reached the port of New York on October 9, after an adventurous voyage of fourteen weeks across the Atlantic. During this time a child was born, so that on arrival there was an additional passenger. This tiny vessel of about thirty-nine tons was only fifty-four feet long, and both it and its daring voyagers aroused curiosity. *The New York Daily Advertiser* of October 15, 1825, informed its readers in an article entitled "A Novel Sight" that "those who came from the farms are dressed in coarse cloths of domestic manufacture, of a

Conditions were crowded for the 52 pioneer emigrants on board the Restauration. *This full-size replica of the sloop was built for the centennial of Norwegian immigration in 1925.*

fashion different from the American; but those who inhabited the town wear calicos, ginghams, and gay shawls, imported, we presume, from England."

The Sloopers, as the pioneers of Norwegian emigration are called, have been the subject of historical research and of literary treatment. Their journey and their destiny in the new land provide an exciting first chapter to an important historical movement. Who were these Sloopers? Why did they opt for an uncertain future in new surroundings? What conditions made their actions possible?

There was a strong strain of religious motivation in the pioneer emigration, and because religious considerations were not significant in the later exodus they have tended to overshadow the economic concerns that also influenced the Sloopers' decision to emigrate.

Lars Larsen Geilane was the leader of the expedition. He was a member of the little Society of Friends in Stavanger and the only declared Quaker among the Sloopers. But many of the others sympathized with the teachings of the Friends and joined them after they arrived in America. Quakerism had come to Norway by way of Norwegian prisoners of war in England between 1807 and 1814, and the Friends formed societies in Stavanger and in Oslo.

Haugeans must have made up a second group among the emigrants, a group designated "the holy." The Haugean movement had many adherents in Stavanger and surrounding districts. There were, to be sure, important differences in belief and religious practice between them and the Quakers, but the two groups shared a pietistic conviction and an experience of conversion. They were both in opposition to the authorities; they were dissatisfied with the powerful position of the Norwegian Lutheran State Church; and they desired complete religious freedom and the right of lay people to preach the Word of God. These circumstances brought them together. Lines of communication must surely have existed.

The idea of emigrating no doubt matured slowly, and scholars have debated how it first arose and was communicated. In this regard it is important to bear in mind the international character of the Quaker society and the lively contact that existed with English Quakers. Even though few Norwegian peasants knew anything about America, the Quaker Lars Larsen Geilane was certainly aware of the existence of the United States and probably knew something about the country's free institutions. America's War of Independence and the American constitution had of course inspired the men who gave Norway its constitution at Eidsvoll, but in the country as a whole most Norwegians were ignorant of the new society that was being created in America.

Something else that should be mentioned in this connection is an event that took place outside Bergen in September, 1817. A Dutch ship with about 500 German emigrants from Württemberg, who were fleeing religious and political oppression, was shipwrecked. Most of these dissenters stayed in Bergen for a year before they could continue to America. Their story was no doubt known in Stavanger, and the resoluteness of the German pietists could easily have planted the idea of emigration.

In addition, knowledge of America was likely to be more general in a port city like Stavanger, with sailors and a growing merchant fleet, than elsewhere in Norway. By 1821 plans had in any case developed to the point where the Stavanger Quakers sent two agents to America to investigate conditions there. These two were Cleng Peerson from Tysvær and Knud Olsen Eide. Cleng Peerson is an enigmatic figure in the emi-

gration drama who at various times has been called "the father of emigration," "the pathfinder," and "Peer Gynt on the prairie," but there is no doubt about his role in the early emigration. Peerson returned to Norway alone in the summer of 1824 to report on his findings. After a short stay there he went back to America to prepare for the arrival of the Norwegian dissenters, who now made arrangements to leave the country.

With a group of American Quakers Cleng Peerson met the Sloopers when they landed in New York. All of them were in good condition after the long and dramatic voyage across the Atlantic by way of Madeira, where they had been received by the Norwegian-Swedish consul. Among the immigrants there were ten couples and nineteen children, in addition to the Slooper child born on the way, the daughter of the leader Lars Larsen and his wife, Martha. She was named Margaret Allen after a well-known English Quaker. There were twelve single men and one unmarried woman in the group.

Most of the Sloopers came from rural communities in Rogaland, especially from the communi-

More than anyone else, it was Cleng Peerson (1782 or 1783-1865) who served as pathfinder for Norwegian emigration. This "Peer Gynt of the prairie" came from Tysvær, a community near the town of Haugesund.

ty of Tysvær, and a few from Stavanger. They had been encouraged to leave Norway both by prospects of material improvement and by a desire for religious freedom. Quakers and Haugeans generally did not belong to the wealthy classes; still, the Sloopers cannot be described as poor, for they had purchased the vessel in which they made the crossing and also a cargo of iron bars and plates. They hoped to realize a profit by selling both the ship and the merchandise in America. After a conflict with American authorities because they had overloaded the *Restauration*, and after a petition to President John Quincy Adams who annulled the fine they had been given, they sold the sloop at a loss for $400. With assistance from American Quakers they moved to northern New York state and settled in Kendall township on land Cleng Peerson had bought. There on the shores of Lake Ontario they struggled through the hardships of pioneer life. The settlement became a way station to the Middle West, where most of the Sloopers, along with newcomers from Norway in the mid-1830s, established a colony in the Fox River valley in Illinois. It was again Cleng Peerson who like a Moses led his people to the Promised Land.

The America Fever Spreads

Because many years passed before emigration became a yearly phenomenon, it is easy to regard the pioneer venture as a mere episode, isolated from the later crossings. In fact, though, the Kendall settlement formed a bridgehead, a point of contact in the New World. The group emigration that got under way more than a decade after the daring voyage of the *Restauration* is directly related to the Kendall settlement.

Mention must be made of the letters Gjert Gregoriussen Hovland, who had come to Kendall in 1831, wrote home about the "pleasant and fertile land," and about the greater freedom and equality to be found in America. These circulated widely in Norway and created interest in America. This favorable information, coming at a time when Norwegian agriculture had experienced a number of poor harvests, encouraged people to leave. In the summer of 1836 two brigs, *Den norske klippe* and *Norden*, sailed from Stavanger with a total of 167 people destined for America. Knud Andersen Slogvig, who like Hovland had emigrated in 1831, had returned to Norway the previous year and served as leader for the emigrants on board *Norden*. His return created a great stir, and people from all over Rogaland and Hordaland came to hear about America. Almost without exception the emigrants were peasants from Ryfylke and Jæren, and a few from Hordaland. Most of them went to the Fox River settlement and surrounding areas.

A striking feature of the emigration, or "America fever," as people called it as early as 1837, was how unevenly it affected various districts as it moved like a dangerous disease from the southwestern coastal regions to fjord settlements farther north and to the valleys of East Norway. The spread of information might determine when emigration from a specific district occurred. Knowledge about the new land, with its promise of personal advancement and freedom, became a decisive factor for those who already were inclined to leave. The idea of emigration was often planted by certain individuals; these were the innovators, and in Norwegian emigration history they came mainly from the peasants themselves. They were often persons who had broken with their environment and as a consequence were less bound by traditional norms in the peasant community.

In the period from 1836 to 1845 – the first decade of regular emigration – the impulse to go to America spread to nine of Norway's nineteen counties, or *fylker*, including the two cities of Bergen and Oslo (in 1866 Troms became the twen-

Adolph Tidemand, "The America-Travelers Bid Farewell." It was common to have an auction before the departure. "The cow, the calf, and the sheep, and the modest personal belongings were auctioned off." ("En Amerikareise i 1872," in Samband, *November, 1916.)*

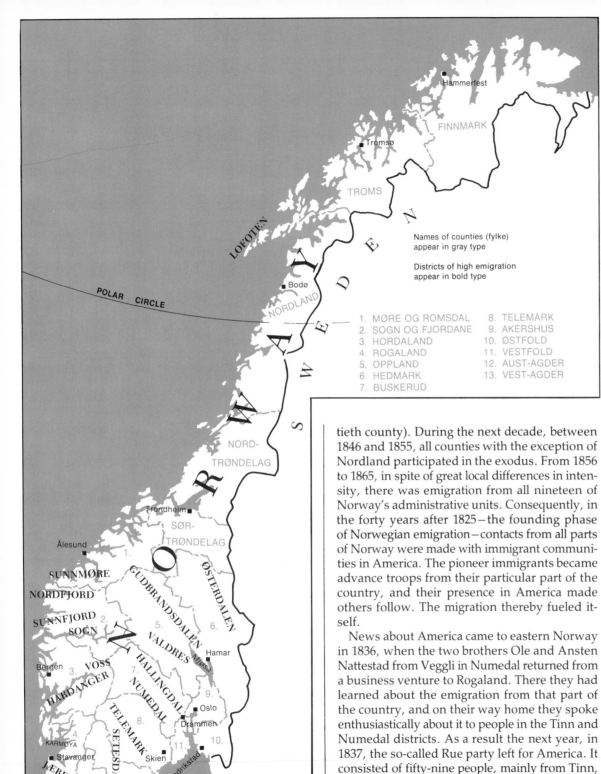

tieth county). During the next decade, between 1846 and 1855, all counties with the exception of Nordland participated in the exodus. From 1856 to 1865, in spite of great local differences in intensity, there was emigration from all nineteen of Norway's administrative units. Consequently, in the forty years after 1825—the founding phase of Norwegian emigration—contacts from all parts of Norway were made with immigrant communities in America. The pioneer immigrants became advance troops from their particular part of the country, and their presence in America made others follow. The migration thereby fueled itself.

News about America came to eastern Norway in 1836, when the two brothers Ole and Ansten Nattestad from Veggli in Numedal returned from a business venture to Rogaland. There they had learned about the emigration from that part of the country, and on their way home they spoke enthusiastically about it to people in the Tinn and Numedal districts. As a result the next year, in 1837, the so-called Rue party left for America. It consisted of fifty-nine people, mainly from Tinn, and was the first group emigration from East

Norway. The Nattestad brothers joined the group. The next year, Ansten created a sensation when he came back from America. His accounts accelerated the movement overseas, especially from his home district of Numedal.

During the founding phase, from 1825 to 1865, 77,873 Norwegians crossed the Atlantic to make a home for themselves in America, more than half, or 39,350, in the decade 1856-65. The whole country was represented, but most of the emigrants had come from the inner fjord districts in West Norway and the mountain valleys in East Norway. It was emigrants from these regions of Norway who first shaped a Norwegian immigrant community and gave it a content and a direction that reflected the traditions, mores, and religious as well as secular values of their Norwegian home districts. The reasons these areas of Norway dominated the early emigration must be sought in common circumstances that will be discussed later.

How Did People Learn about America?

The arrival of news about America was a prime factor in starting immigration from specific districts. As has been underscored earlier, knowledge of America frequently supplied the final incentive to leave. When Norwegian Americans returned to the homeland for a visit, for instance, they told about the opportunities in America and were by their own example evidence of the advancement that was possible there, even for poor people. Some of the visiting Norwegian Americans took groups of emigrants with them when they departed for America and served as guides for their fellow Norwegians.

"America letters"—letters that Norwegians in America wrote home to relatives, friends, and acquaintances in Norway—were the most common source of information. These immigrant letters created a positive picture of the new land. They told about freedom and equality; in America common people need not bow to officials and their "betters" in society. "As soon as a man is known to be decent and honest, then one is as

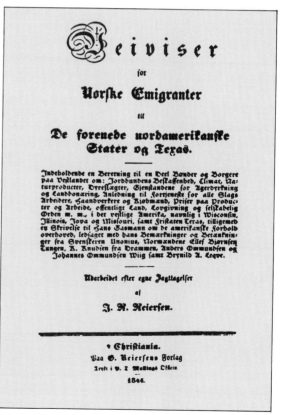

An "America letter" from 1842 in the collection of the Norwegian-American Historical Association. *Sigdalslagets aarbok* for 1941 relates the following about one Mother Braatelien: "Many people came to her to get her to write letters to America for them, and to read the letters they received. Yes, even young girls came to her to ask her to write to their boys who had gone to America. They consequently had to reveal the secrets of their hearts for mother."

1842, and his reason was that "any poor person who will work diligently can become a well-to-do man here in a short time."

Most letters of course were written by more anonymous men and women, and they flowed into Norway in a steady stream. A few of the writers were scouts or agents for organized groups of emigrants. Such a person was Johan R. Reiersen, editor of the reform newspaper *Christianssandsposten*; he spoke enthusiastically about America and encouraged emigration. In 1843 he set out for America to study conditions there as the representative of some people who wanted to emigrate, and upon his return to Norway in 1844 he published *Veiviser for norske emigranter til De forenede nordamerikanske stater og Texas* (Pathfinder for Norwegian Emigrants to the United States and Texas). Immigrant guides of this kind, or "America books" as they were called, provided more complete and systematic information than the letters, though these guides

A guide was like an expanded America letter.

much respected as the other, peasants and craftsmen just as much as merchants and officials," an immigrant wrote from Wisconsin in 1845. The letters became an indictment of Norwegian class distinctions and other social and political, as well as economic, conditions that were at the root of the decision to emigrate. But they also described toil and hardship, and they gave advice and guidance to people who had in mind to come to America. The combined effect of the America letters was to promote wanderlust and increase the number of emigrants. The letters were copied and sent from farm to farm, from community to community; many of them were printed in newspapers. The influence of Gjert Hovland's letters on the first regular emigration has been noted, and Hovland continued to be a productive letter

writer. Other immigrants also were able and well-known correspondents.

The progressive reformer Hans Barlien, who had emigrated at age sixty-five in 1837, wrote glowing accounts of America in which he contrasted the superior conditions there with those he disliked in the homeland. In a letter from 1839 he concluded, "Tell all who would like to know that I am as contented as any human being can be, and anyone who wants to come over will with little effort become just as happy." Johannes Nordboe from Ringebu in Gudbrandsdalen was another capable letter writer, and he also sharply criticized conditions in Norway. Ole K. Trovatten from Telemark and Gunnul Vindegg from Numedal were both famous for their letters. "I in no way wish to return," Trovatten wrote in in a certain sense may be regarded as expanded America letters, and they were eagerly read by people who intended to emigrate.

The first guidebook was Ole Rynning's *Sandfærdig beretning om Amerika til oplysning og nytte for bonde og menigmand* (True Account of America for the Enlightenment and Benefit of the Peasant and the Common Man). Ansten Nattestad brought the manuscript with him when he visited Norway in 1838, and the book appeared the same year. Like later America books, it described the country, explained its institutions, and gave practical advice about the journey and adjustment to American life. Rynning did not conceal the difficulties the emigrants would face in the new land; nevertheless his conclusion was that "from everything I have seen so far, the industrious farmer or craftsman as well as the respectable merchant will soon acquire a sufficient income in America."

The effect of personal contacts and information may be illustrated by looking at the genesis of the emigration from the parish of Vik in Sogn. Emigration was initiated by the departure of Per Iversen Unde in 1839, after he had talked to relatives in Voss farther south, where emigration already had commenced, and after he had studied Rynning's guide. Letters from Unde and his brother, who emigrated in 1841, attracted others from the community to America. In 1845 the county governor (*amtmann*) complained that the emigration, from there as elsewhere, was "partly caused by exaggerated accounts of the happiness and prosperity that might be anticipated there."

The Authorities' View of Emigration

Norwegian authorities had been aware of the sailing of the Sloopers, and in 1825 as well as from 1836 on they investigated the departure of Norwegian citizens, but there was never a question of restricting emigration to America. The ideas of liberalism were gaining acceptance, and the government had no desire to interfere with individual freedom of mobility. Such an attitude

would have been inconceivable under the reign of absolute monarchs before 1814.

But the authorities did not view emigration with favor; to the contrary, they deplored it and could not grasp its causes. The information they collected about the emigration and about Norwegians in America was as a result mainly intended to discourage people from leaving. Many opponents of the disturbing increase in the number of travelers to America thought that the emigrants left because of erroneous and misleading reports. The newspaper *Morgenbladet* (Morning Post) insisted in 1866 that "the imprudent, ignorant, and poor part of our population . . . is enticed to emigrate by false accounts from America of easy access to extraordinarily high wages."

Many people thought that America fever, which possessed its victims with infatuation, explained the emigration. In a pastoral letter of 1837, "A Word of Admonition to the Peasants in the Diocese of Bergen who Desire to Emigrate," Bishop Jacob Neumann pictured the desire to emigrate as a contagious disease. The bishop warned the peasants not to believe the news from America, and his advice was: "Stay in the land and support yourself honestly."

Official published reports about Norwegian settlers and letters and tracts written by dissatisfied emigrants were used to agitate against emigration. The effect of these publications is difficult to assess; negative reports were quickly repudiated on both sides of the Atlantic. The pioneer pastor J. W. C. Dietrichson was probably right when he contended that "those in Norway who wish to emigrate care less about what the public newspapers warn them against than about what their relatives write to them." The latter information was considered to be more trustworthy; it was the experience and judgment of relatives and friends that people relied on when they resolved to seek America.

The First Decades

Emigration between 1825 and 1865 involved, as has been seen, almost 80,000 people. The annual rate after regular emigration began in 1836 varied

greatly. In 1838 only about 100 people departed, whereas the number was 1,600 in both 1843 and 1847. As many as 4,000 emigrated in 1849. Emigration remained at about this level through 1854, after which there was a decline up to 1861. That year there was a dramatic jump, a foretaste of mass emigration, as 8,900 Norwegians crossed over to America. The number of emigrants fell rather quickly, however, until the great exodus of 1866 heralded the era of mass emigration.

An interplay of domestic and international circumstances affected emigration, and the fact that the emigrants were sensitive to shifting economic conditions and events in America illustrates the efficiency of the system of communication created by personal correspondence and an increased dispersal of news about America. The depression in America beginning in 1837 explains the disillusionment expressed in letters written to those still in Norway and as a consequence the decline in the number of emigrants. The American Civil War and Indian uprisings in regions of Norwegian settlement were both clear factors in reducing the stream of emigrants in the 1860s. At the same time, improved economic conditions in Norway in the 1850s and the sense of optimism they produced must have made the desire to emigrate less urgent.

Still, there existed a constant encouragement to emigrate, a pressure which was especially strongly felt in those regions that had the highest rates of emigration. It was created by a population growth that outstripped available resources and a lack of alternative employment outside the home district. As a whole, however, the Norwegian economist Fritz Hodne has shown that the country's rate of production was higher than its increase in population. Norway experienced a strong economic growth in the nineteenth century, albeit with many recessions and crises that were intensified by the population explosion. The distribution of the new wealth was in addition uneven. Both in the cities and in the rural areas a process of impoverishment occurred which caused many people to sink down into lower social classes. The bottom stratum of Norwegian society therefore grew faster than the other social groups. This development sharpened class tensions and increased social distance.

These demographic changes resulted from a

drop in the mortality rate beginning in the late 1700s; Norway's population rose from 883,487 in 1801 to 1,194,827 in 1835, and to 1,701,756 in 1865. It is impossible to give a complete explanation of the falling death rate. Some scholars have called attention to vaccination as a factor, although its significance is now in doubt. Others have referred to an improved nutritional base, with increased cultivation of potatoes after their widespread acceptance in 1809 and the introduction of potatoes and herring as the staple food for poor people. There was also a public health service that could combat epidemic diseases better, and there was improvement in sanitary conditions, especially in housing. All these changes contributed to making it possible for more children to live to adulthood.

Investigations of Local Emigration

Regions that experienced emigration in the period before 1865 had certain similarities: social, economic, and demographic. These parallels can be seen in two typical districts, Vik in Sogn, examined by Rasmus Sunde, and Tinn in Upper Telemark, studied by Andres A. Svalestuen, the first a fjord community and the second a mountain valley. The historian Andreas Holmsen stated that "overpopulation had progressed further in the inner communities of Sogn than elsewhere in Norway." A contemporary witness agrees: in the 1840s, according to the county governor, there was "overpopulation in the district of Sogn which presumably will make emigration from this district necessary also in the future."

The Fjord Community of Vik in Sogn

A crisis was averted for a generation or more by the introduction of the potato toward the end of the 1700s, but by 1845 all resources had been utilized to the maximum and something had to give. As the production of potatoes increased in Vik, grain cultivation and animal husbandry at the same time decreased, so that

There were many people and crowded conditions on the small farms in the Norwegian fjord districts and mountain communities. A tradition-bound agricultural system based on impractical strip farming was unable to increase production in pace with the rapid growth in population. These agrarian communities were bursting their economic bonds, and a solution had to be found.

the supply of foodstuffs did not become appreciably greater. With the falling mortality rate, the number of people in Vik rose from 2,270 in 1801 to 3,230 in 1845, an increase of 42.7 percent. An agricultural system bound by tradition and hampered by impractical strip farming was incapable of expanding production to keep pace with demand. The authorities complained that the system of strip farming was a hindrance to rational management; in addition Vik was isolated, and new agricultural methods arrived late.

Emigration did not get under way in earnest before 1841, although the first emigrants from Vik had left two years before. After people had learned about opportunities in America, the

floodgates opened. Between 1844 and 1846—in the course of only three years—417 persons left Vik, and of these 244 went to America. Emigration was a safety valve that reduced an acute strain on resources. The pressure to leave was felt not only by the landless rural classes, but also by independent farmers in straitened circumstances who, as the county governor explained in 1845, "have sold their property and afterward emigrated to North America or in some cases gone to Nordland and Romsdalen." America eventually became almost the exclusive destination for those who moved from the community.

But during the 1840s people went both to

America and to North Norway. The northern part of the country offered new opportunities; in those sparsely populated regions there was still land to be had. Some people also found a livelihood in the rich fisheries along the coast. Financial resources became the deciding factor; those who were unable to raise money for the ticket to America went to northern Norway.

Other circumstances than economic ones partly determined the local differences in geographic mobility. There are, for instance, striking contrasts between the overseas movement from the district of Sogn and that from the district of Sunnfjord and Nordfjord to the north; in the latter region emigration was insignificant during the entire period. Vik continued as the major area of emigration in Sogn. Economic conditions were, to be sure, somewhat more favorable in the northern district, and as a consequence population pressures were less pronounced there than in Sogn. This circumstance, however, does not provide an adequate explanation of the great difference that existed between the two districts in their respective rates of emigration. A general rule appears to be that an established internal migration might resist the call from America, and from the areas north of the Sogn district there seems to have been a strong tradition of moving to Bergen, which was the largest urban center in western Norway. The presence of relatives and acquaintances from the home community made the city an attractive alternative to going to America.

Similar forces attracted people overseas from specific parishes, communities, and districts. The pull from America became stronger for people who had grown up in areas with a tradition of leaving Norway.

The Mountain Community of Tinn

Tinn in Upper Telemark had early established contact with the New World, and a self-generating migration had come to exist there. As in Sogn, the district had utilized and exhausted all the resources that a primitive and tradition-bound agricultural system could muster. In Tinn the population increased by 37 percent between 1801 and 1835, from 1,810 to 2,481. Even though one can find communities with a great-

er population growth, it must be recognized that a mountain community such as Tinn was especially vulnerable. The natural basis for agricultural production was limited. For a time in Tinn, as in Vik, the introduction of the potato, which generally gave reliable annual yields, made it possible to feed more people and thus delayed the inevitable crisis. Natural resources were put to more intensive use, as far as agricultural methods of the time permitted. Farms were divided among brothers; new land was put under the plow in marginal agricultural areas, as high up as possible; and pastures in outlying fields and in mountain grazing areas were fully exploited. As in Sogn, the largest increase in population occurred among the lower, landless classes, and it was the cotters who took the lead in this cultivation. The increase in population created a reservoir of mobile people, on the lookout for opportunity wherever it might be found, who, once the initial contact had been made in 1837, would consider America a realistic alternative.

The Mass Exodus Begins

During the initial phase of emigration, circumstances at home had pushed people out of the country; the same forces continued to produce emigration during the first mass exodus after 1865. In addition, social ferment and political impulses from the Continent acted on the emigration. Helge Tveiten, a historian of the region, uncovered a clear connection in the district of Nedenes in southern Norway between the socialistic movement headed by the reformer Marcus Thrane and departures for America during the early 1850s. Still, it is important to bear firmly in mind that the resolve to emigrate represented for the individual a personal decision. The number of people who chose America jumped from 4,000 in 1865 to 15,727 in 1866, and in the course of only eight years, through 1873, 110,896 Norwegians emigrated, an annual average of 13,862. The number then fell to 4,601 in 1874. The first great wave of migration

had deprived Norway of 63.4 percent of its natural increase in population.

The mass exodus that was heralded by the emigration of 1866 created both excitement and deep concern. A contributor to *Morgenbladet* who had visited the emigrant vessel *Nordlyset* in the port of Oslo reminded the authorities that "one could no longer be satisfied with the claim that it was only duped fools or sanguine adventurers who leave the fatherland." *Nordlyset*, which was then ready to sail for Quebec in Canada, carried 176 passengers, most of them from the farming areas north of Oslo. Seventy-one of them were twelve years old or younger; six had passed sixty, the oldest being seventy-two; and there were approximately twice as many men as women. "Most of those who leave Oplandet this year," one of the emigrants said, "are either cotters, farm laborers, or servants, and the majority of these have received passage money from America."

The emigration of the 1860s must be considered in relation to the earlier one, but its intensity can only be explained against the background of specific economic conditions in Norway. Many potential emigrants had no doubt postponed their departure because of the Civil War in America, but the most significant cause of the emigration was an agricultural crisis that followed the good times of the 1850s.

During the period of prosperity farmers had invested heavily in modernizing production and making the transition from self-sufficiency to commercial agriculture. This process had come farthest in the good agricultural districts of East Norway; the crisis of the 1860s was therefore most acute there. It was caused by a loss of domestic markets to cheap imported grain, and farmers were forced to change to cattle raising. Where this could be done quickly, the crisis was short-lived, but in less favorable areas it dragged on because of a lack of capital. During the 1860s there was in addition a severe debt problem, with many bankruptcies, and several poor harvests, and the entire agricultural sector suffered.

The depression affected all social classes, but those who had the least were of course the worst off. The number of people on the public dole rose from 40 per one thousand inhabitants to 45 in the course of the year 1866. Relief for the poor and other taxes were an extra burden on economic life. The transition to a money economy in rural areas had reached a critical point. Large numbers of people had been made superfluous, and prospects at home were dim. People were ready to leave, and domestic conditions, as well as established migratory patterns, determined how many went and where.

The Social Background of the Emigrants

The emigrants on board *Nordlyset* reflected the general situation. They left because of lack of prospects; they belonged to the cotter and laboring classes in the countryside; and they had been encouraged to emigrate by earlier emigrants. But the contributor to *Morgenbladet* had also been told that "a few smaller farmers who have fallen on hard times are also leaving, provided they have any money left over or have family either in this country or in America who can pay for their passage." Small farmers and sons of independent farmers constituted a large emigrant group, and in communities such as Vik in Sogn and Tinn in Telemark, by far the largest percentage of emigrants belonged in the early years to this stratum of rural society. The younger son who could not count on inheriting the family farm or finding employment there was socially in an exposed position. Both for him and for the independent farmer, work in a city might seem like a fall in social status, and moving to America became an attractive alternative. The proximity of the city also influenced the decision. It was easier for people in the vicinity of a city to seek employment in an urban environment; for people in a remote mountain community or in a distant fjord area, the city seemed far away and dangerous.

The lower social groups in the country, people from the cotter class and agricultural laborers, were better represented in the emigration beginning in the 1850s. But in the mountain community of Tinn the class of independent farmers continued to provide a majority of the

The mass exodus begins. This oil painting from 1861 shows emigrant ships from Bergen on their way across the Atlantic. In the foreground is the vessel Vikingen.

emigrants, whereas in a good agricultural district like Ringsaker in Hedmark the cotter class supplied more than half of the emigrants during the last quarter of the century.

The emigration protocols kept by the police from 1867, however, designate most men as laborers. By analyzing this group further, Elisabeth Koren showed in a recent Norwegian academic thesis that in Ullensaker, an agricultural community north of Oslo, the majority were young men from the class of independent farmers. For the mountain community of Dovre, a historian of emigration, Arnfinn Engen, found that even though there were more men from the cotter class than from the farmer class among the emigrants, the difference was not as great as previously assumed. These and other recent investigations have consequently elevated the social background and removed an unfortunate impression of poverty in regard to the composition of the emigrant body; the distribution between the two major rural classes was not as lopsided as was thought earlier. Research has also determined that the proletarian element became gradually stronger.

Struggle against want, poverty, and hardship, and a desire to escape political and religious constraints and class prejudice, were of course not the only reasons for leaving. At the moment when the decision was being made, the hope of advancement and a better future for oneself and one's children was of great importance. During the years after the Civil War the United States experienced undreamed-of economic growth. New regions were opened up to settlement, and the Homestead Act of 1862 made free land available; there was an enormous demand for labor and for settlers to develop the immense western land areas. Letters and prepaid tickets—some years as many as 40 percent of all emigrants received their tickets from America—encouraged people to emigrate and opened the way west to new social groups. Passage money from America contributed greatly to making the emigrant body more democratic, since it gave mobility to people without resources; a reduction in the price of tickets after the Civil War worked to the same end. The system of transportation was now well organized, and from several quarters there was an effort to persuade people to seek their fortunes

on the other side of the Atlantic. Mass emigration came to a halt in 1873, however, when an economic crisis broke out in America.

The Voyage to America

Most parties of emigrants after 1836 crossed the Atlantic on Norwegian brigs and barks. Some went to the New World via Gothenburg on Swedish or American ships that transported iron, and others left from Le Havre, which in these years became a center for the European emigrant traffic.

Norwegian shipowners were not immediately able to accommodate parties of emigrants aboard their vessels, but during the 1840s Norwegian emigrant shipping firms came into existence. The repeal of the British Navigation Acts in 1849 was an important stimulus; it permitted Norwegian ships to transport emigrants to Quebec and lumber from there back to Great Britain, guaranteeing cargo in both directions. Norwegian shipowners took advantage of this possibility. Almost all immigrants toward the end of the 1840s had landed in New York, but between 1850, when the first Norwegian emigrants came to Quebec, and 1865 most went by Norwegian sailing ships to Quebec and from there to the United States. Between 1854 and 1865 90 percent of all Norwegian emigrants took this route. The voyage across was long, lasting two months or more depending on weather and wind, and strenuous, with unsanitary conditions, illness, and often several deaths during the crossing.

The emigration season began in spring, and in coastal towns one might see peasants dressed in homespun clothes, with supplies of food and equipment, waiting to get passage to America. Shipowners advertised in newspapers, went themselves or sent agents through the valleys to offer their services, and were frequently accused of recruiting emigrants.

From Sail to Steam

From the middle of the 1860s there was a change in the emigration traffic as steamships

gradually replaced sailing ships. It was a revolution that made mass emigration possible. The steamships were much faster than the sailing ships, and the steamship lines offered regular departures and arrivals, and included meals in the price of the ticket. Norwegian companies were unable to make the transition to steam. British and North German firms competed for the Norwegian market, with British companies being dominant. Norwegian emigrants went to England and departed for America from Liverpool.

The different steamship lines, like the Allan Line, the most important in the early period, established a sales apparatus with a network of general agents and subagents. Through advertisements, handbooks, pamphlets, and posters they publicized their activity. In 1881 the Allan Line had 619 subagents, from Vardø in the north to Kristiansand in the south, and there were ten or more different general agencies in Oslo. According to an item in *Morgenbladet* in 1866, the steamship companies were sending "emissaries throughout the country to catch souls."

The steamship companies were active in Norwegian settlements in America as well, competing for the sale of prepaid tickets—tickets that were to be sent to Norway. They gave important information and assistance, and a fickle person might well be persuaded to leave. But it is not likely that the agitation either in Norway or in America caused many to emigrate who did not intend to do so for other reasons. In fact, the agents of the steamship lines were more like travel bureaus, which in the 1890s replaced the agent system.

There were, however, many interests that did try to influence the emigrants: the various states in the Middle West, railroad companies, and other commercial enterprises. They all published brochures in Norwegian and sent agents to Scandinavia and to the ports of arrival to attract emigrants to specific regions of the United States. The so-called Yankee system, in which Norwegian Americans functioned as agents for steamship lines and other economic interests, was perhaps the most effective propaganda apparatus. For a few years after 1870 there was also a Norwegian transatlantic steamship company, but not until 1913 was the Norwegian America Line started, enabling Norwegian emi-

Det Norske
Udvandrings-Selskab
i CHRISTIANIA.
Kontor: Prindsensgade No. 3.

Ovennævnte autoriserede Udvandrings-Selskab tilbyder Emigranter god og billig Befordring med Klipper-Seilskibe fra Christiania direkte til Kvebek og udstedet Gjennemgangsbilletter til alle Steder i Veststaterne.

Selskabets Forretningsfører er Herr L. Knoph, der som tidligere Medlem af Firmaet Blichfeldt, Knoph & Co. har mangeaarig Erfaring i Emigrationsforretningen.

Selskabets Skibe er alle af første Klasse, kobberforhudede, hurtigseilende og i enhver Henseende bekvemt indrettede for Emigranter. Det første Skib i 1870 vil

antagelig afgaa den 13. April; derefter expederer vi 2 Skibe til i April Maaned med ca. 8 Dages Mellemrum, et i første Halvdeel af Mai, et i Slutningen af samme Maaned og et i Midten af Juni.

Flere af vore Emigrantskibe vil i Løbet af Vinteren ligge tilstæde paa Christiania Havn.

Fragten fra Christiania til Kvebek er fortiden:

14 Spd. for Voxne.
8 „ „ Børn mellem 7 og 14 Aar.
6 „ „ do. „ 1 „ 7 „.

Børn under 1 Aar gaar frit. Desuden erlægger hvert Individ over 1 Aar 1 Spd. i Landgangspenge. I ovenanførte Fragt er indbefattet Ombordbringelse i Christiania, samt fornødent Brænde, Belysning og Medicin under Overreisen.

Fragten med Jernbanen fra Kvebek er fortiden for voxen Person:

			Spd.	ß
til Chicago,	Illinois,			
„ Milwaukee,	Wisconsin,		9	60
„ Madison,	do.			114
„ Monroe,	do.			90
„ La Crosse,	do.			
„ Lansing,	Iowa,			
„ Winona,	Minnesota,			60
„ Red Wing,	do.			102
„ St. Paul,	do.			96

o. s. v. Børn mellem 4 og 14 Aar betaler halv Fragt, hvorimod Børn under 4 Aar gaar frit paa de amerikanske Jernbaner.

Alt Passagergei medtages frit paa Skibet og; naar Gjennemgangsbillet kjøbes hos os, ligeledes, uden Hensyn til Vægten, frit paa Jernbanen i Amerika saalangt som Billetten lyder.

Tøiet bør være tydelig mærket med Eierens Navn og Bestemmelsessted i Amerika.

Proviant maa medbringes for 10 Uger og koster her i Byen indpakket og bragt ombord ca. 10 Spd. for voxen Person. Trykt Kostliste til Veiledning med Provianteringen tilstilles Dem efter Indskrivning.

Samtlige vore Emigranter ledsages enten af Kapteinerne selv eller i deres Sted af paalidelige Tolke paa Reisen indigjennem Landet fra Kvebek til Chicago eller Milwaukee.

Som Forskud paa Fragten betales ved Indskrivningen 5 Spd. for Voxne og det Halve for Børn mellem 1 og 14 Aar; Resten erlægges ved Afreisen. Naar hele Fragten er betalt, erholder Passagererne familievis en udførlig Passagerkontrakt, hvis Indhold er vedtaget af Politimesteren hersteds, og som der

efter forevises og paategnes paa Politikammeret. Vi skal i Forbindelse hermed bemærke, at ifølge Lov af 22. Mai f. A. Ingen er berettiget til at optræde som Emigrationsagent uden først at have stillet betryggende Sikkerhed for Opfyldelsen af indgaaede Forpligtelser og dernæst at have erholdt Autorisation af Stedets Politimester.

For Passagersei, som af de indskrevne Emigranter indsendes til os og ankommer til Christiania mindst 8 Dage før Indskibningen, skaffer vi frit Pakhusrum samt fri Transport fra Jernbanen til Pakhuset og derfra ombord. Fragten til Christiania maa være forudbetalt. Tøiet bør være tydeligt mærket med det Skibs Navn, paa hvilket man har indtegnet sig.

En i Kanada i Juni 1868 udkommen Lov forbyder herefter at ilandsætte Emigranter i Kvebek eller andetsteds i Kanada, medmindre de er forsynede med tilstrækkelige Midler til Reisens Fortsættelse indigjennem Landet til de Forenede Stater. Som Følge af denne Bestemmelse vil herefter ingen Emigrant tilstedes at indskibe sig, forinden han hos vedkommende Agent har deponeret enten Beløbet af Jernbanefragten fra Kvebek til Chicago eller Milwaukee eller løst Jernbanebillet, lydende paa Befordring derfra til et Sted i de Forenede Stater.

Pengeveksling besørges af os uden Godtgjørelse; Emigranterne kan efter Behag erholde amerikanske Gulddollars eller Vexler paa Amerika betalbare i Guld og trukne af vor Bankier, Herr Generalkonsul Sev. Chr. Andersen hersteds.

Forresten skal det være os kjært at bistaa de af os indtegnede Emigranter med Raad og Daad, f. Ex. ved paa Forlangende at anvise dem billigt Logis her i Byen, at være dem behjælpelig med Indkjøb af Proviant, at skrive Breve for dem til Slægtninge og Venner i Amerika eller forsyne egenhændig skrevne Breve med rigtige Adresser o. s. v. Al saadan Bistand ydes ligeledes uden Betaling.

Vi har altid Skibe, som er baade hurtigseilende og i andre Henseender tjenlige og vel skikkede for Emigrantfarten. Det tilstedes ikke andre end første Klasses Skibe (A 1 eller A 2) at gaa herfra i denne Fart; heri, saavelsom i den ombord i ethvert Emigrantskib før Indskibningen afholdt Søretsbesigtigelse, haves der hos al fornøden Garanti med Hensyn til Skibenes Godhed og hensigtsmæssige Udrustning.

Vi maa indstændig tilraade Enhver, som har bestemt sig til at reise over med Seilskib, at se til at komme afsted saa tidligt som muligt om Foraaret, baade fordi Overreisen paa Grund af Vindforholdene da sker hurtigst, og fordi det i flere Henseender er fordelagtigst at komme over til Amerika tidligt paa Sommeren.

Vor Forretningsfører gjorde Sommeren 1868 en Reise over til Amerika i den udelukkende Hensigt at gjøre sig nøie bekjendt med Alt, hvad der vedrører Emigranternes Befordring m. V. Han besøgte paa denne Reise blandt Andet de for den skandinaviske Emigration vigtigste Punkter i Veststaterne, saasom: Chicago, Milwaukee, Madison, La Crosse, Winona, Red Wing, St. Paul o. s. v., undersøgte de forskjellige Jernbanelinier og indledede Forbindelser til Bedste for fremtidige Emigranter. Vi vil saaledes bedre end de fleste andre Agenter være istand til at give de Emigranter, der henvender sig til os, Raad og Veiledning saavel betræffende selve Reisen over Søen og indigjennem Landet i Amerika som ved Reisen.

Vi holder til enhver Tid billigste Fragt, ligesom det stedse er vor Bestræbelse at skaffe vore Emigranter en god og sikker Befordring samt idethele en omhyggelig og samvittighedsfuld Behandling paa hele Reisen.

☞ Det bemærkes, at alle vore Skibe i Tilfælde af kontræ Vind vil blive bugserede ud fra Christiania ligesom ogsaa op Indseilingen til Kvebek.

Indskrivning kan naarsomhelst ske enten hos os selv eller hos vore befuldmægtigede udenbyes Agenter.

Christiania, i Januar 1870.

Det Norske Udvandrings-Selskab,
autoriseret for Emigrantbefordring.
Kontor: Prindsensgade No. 3.

Trykt hos H. J. Jensen.

Efternævnte Emigrantskibe er fortiden af os anlagte:
Concordia, 247 Læster, Kapt. Christiansen. Afgang: ank. 13. April 70.
Rodka, 325 „ „ Iversen „ „ 20. „
ank. Flere

For Emigranter

De der agter sig til Amerika til Vaaren, tilbydes herved en god Anledning og et godt Reisefølge. Undertegnede har boet i Amerika i 8 Aar og er her i Norge i Besøg i Vinter. De der ønske Oplysning om Amerika, og som vil gjøre sig Benyttelse af min Veiledning underrettes herved om, at jeg bliver at træffe hos Hr. L. Röhr, Staf i Ringsager Löverdag Eftermiddag den 12te Marts 1870

hvor Indskrivning til Nationalliniens Dampskibe foregaar.

Attester og Anbefalinger kan præsteres.

O. J. Berg
Commissionær.

Economic interests promoted emigration; these included states in the Middle West, railroads, and steamship companies. They established agencies and conducted a systematic recruitment of emigrants. Competition was stiff, and Norwegian shipping firms gradually lost out to North German and especially British steamship companies. The notices shown here are both from 1870. Above: A separate emigration society "authorized for the transportation of emigrants" has been formed. The public notice to the left reflects the so-called Yankee-system. A visiting Norwegian American offers "a good opportunity and company" for emigrants.

Boarding and farewell on an emigrant ship in 1871. For most emigrants there was no way back. The severing of ties with family and friends was permanent.

The illustrations to the left indicate a close social life during the voyage across, both on steamships (at the top) and on sailing vessels. Life on board might be festive in good weather, but crowded conditions prevailed, especially on the sailing ships.

Right: An emigration agent advertises "Emigration Conveyence" in the newspaper Christiania-Posten, *August 3, 1853.*

Right: The crossing by sailing ships might last more than 2 months. The list of provisions shows that the passengers themselves were required to take along kitchen utensils and provisions for 10 weeks. A grown person needed a supply of 70 pounds of bread, 8 pounds of butter, 24 pounds of meat, 10 pounds of pork, 1 keg of herring, 3/8 barrel of potatoes, 20 pounds of rye or barley flour, ½ skjeppe (ca. ¼ bushel) peas, ½ skjeppe pearled barley, 3 pounds of coffee, 3 pounds of sugar, 2½ pounds of syrup, and a little salt, pepper, vinegar, and onions. The skipper provided 3 potter, *about 3 quarts, of water for each passenger per day.*

Columbia.

Udvandrer-Befordring
til alle de væsentligste Havne i Amerika og Australien, hver 14de Dag regelmæssig, ved **Morris & Comp.** i Christiania.

Christiania, 1ste August 1853. **Morris & Comp.**

Proviantliste for 10 Uger
for en voxen Person:

70 Pd. haardt Brød, (mygt Brød eller Flabbrød i Forhold).

8 Pd. Smør,

24 Pd. Kjød,

10 Pd. Flæsk,

1 Dunk Sild,

⅜ Td. Poteter,

20 Pd. Rug= og Bygmeel,

½ Skjæppe Erter,

½ — Gryn,

3 Pd Kaffe,

3 Pd. Sukker,

2½ Pd. Sirup,

lidt Salt, Peber, Ediike og Løg.

Det er en Selvfølge, at Enhver kan medtage hvad Slags Proviant han behager, naar han kun har tilstrækkeligt for 10 Uger.

☛ Et Vandspand af Størrelse efter Familiens Behov (3 Potter daglig for hver Person) maa medtages; ligesaa Gryde, Kaffekjedel, Fade Tallerkener, Kaffekopper, Skeer, Knive og Gafler. Derimod leverer Skibet frit Brænde, Medicin og Belysning.

THINGVALLA-LINIEN.

Kahytspriser 1897.

BILLETTER

fra

Kjøbenhavn, Malmø, Helsingborg,

Frederikshavn, Gøteborg,

Christiania og **Christianssand**

til

NEW YORK

udstedes til følgende Priser for Afrejse

efter „Thingvalla"s Afgang

(den 16. Marts):

1ste Kahyt.

Med Dampskibene „Amerika" og „Hekla"	Kr. 225
Med Dampskibene „Thingvalla", „Island" og „Norge"	- 215

NB. I „Amerika": Køjeplads i Kamrene A, B og C samt i 2 Køjers Kamre koster **Kr. 50** extra pr. enkelt Tur.
I „Hekla": Køjeplads i Kamrene A og B koster **Kr. 25** extra pr. enkelt Tur.

Tur- og Returbilletter, gyldige til alle Skibene	- 420

2den Kahyt.

Med alle Skibene	Kr. 180
s/s „Island"s indvendige Kamre E & F (Familier med Børn maa ikke indskrives)	- 170
Tur- og Returbilletter, gyldige til alle Skibene	- 342

BØRN over 12 Aar betaler fuld Passagepris.
— under 12 men over 1 Aar betaler halv Pris.
— under 1 Aar befordres for Kr. 10.

Specielt henledes Publikums Opmærksomhed paa Dampskibet „AMERIKA", der afgaar fra Kjøbenhavn d. 11. Maj. Det har Plads til c. 150 Kahytspassagerer. Kahytterne ere beliggende midtskibs og paa Hoveddækket og ere udstyrede med al moderne Comfort og Luxus. Saavel Soveværelser som alle Salonerne ere forsynede med elektrisk Lys og Ringeapparater til Betjeningen. Særlig Damesalon, Læsesalon med Bibliothek, Rygesalon samt Badeværelser med kolde og varme Saltvandsbade. I den store Spisesalon i 1. Kahyt findes tilstrækkelig Plads til at samtlige Passagerer kunne spise paa én Gang. I anden Kahyt er der en Del Soverkahytter, hvori kun findes 2 Køjepladser.

Børnene erholde Køjeplads i Henhold til deres Alder og til den Pris, der er betalt for dem.
Naar Plads bestilles til 1ste Kahyt med S. S. „Amerika" og „Hekla" og 2den Kahyt i „Island", maa der bestemt opgives til hvilken Pris Pladsen ønskes.
Returbilletter skulle udstedes paa Hovedkontoret og ere gyldige i 1 Aar.
Indtegning til 1ste eller 2den Kahyt maa kun ske under udtrykkeligt Forbehold af, at Plads findes.
Telegrafiske Forespørgsler om Kahytspladser, hvori Kennet maa opgives, maa være ledsagede af Kvittering for forudbetalt Svar.
I den Tid af Sæsonen, Skibene ikke anløbe Frederikshavn, befordres de Kahytspassagerer, der ere indskrevne **fra Frederikshavn,** pr. Postdamper til Christianssand.

KJØBENHAVN, den 20. Februar 1897.

Thingvalla-Liniens Passager-Afdeling,

Larsens Plads.

Nærmere Oplysninger hos Liniens Agentur:

Fr. G. Knudtzons Bogtrykkeri, Kjøbenhavn.
Fr. G. Knudtzon & Søn? Linnoviten

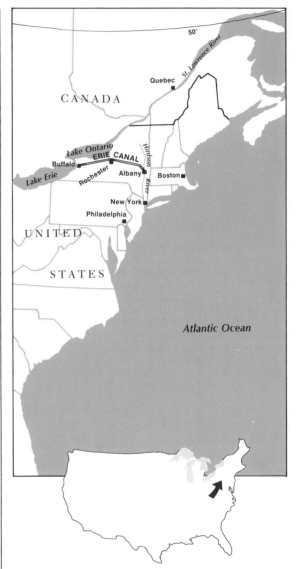

Above: The map shows the most important ports of entry for immigrants to Canada and the United States. The Erie Canal was opened in 1825, and it greatly improved communications westward.

Left: An advertising poster for the Danish Thingvalla Line, which in 1880 established the first direct passenger route by steamship between Scandinavia and the United States. Many Norwegian emigrants booked passage on this line.

grants to sail on Norwegian vessels. The fact that a nation with a strong tradition in shipping like Norway could not compete for the emigrant trade is telling evidence of the enormous capital that was required and which the established commercial transportation system had at its disposal.

The Second and Third Waves of the Great Exodus

Mass emigration occurred in the period between 1865 and 1915, and Thorvald Moe, a specialist in economic history, has claimed that 87 percent of this emigration may be explained by demographic conditions in Norway and the more favorable economic circumstances in America. Norway had a constant population pressure, and the emigration historian Ingrid Semmingsen has called attention to its periodic swelling and the effect this development had on the magnitude of the emigration. During the ten years between 1816 and 1825 the birthrate was unusually high, a circumstance that produced a large group of twenty-year-olds in the 1840s who were looking for work. In the 1850s this group became parents to another large generation, which reached maturity in the 1880s and made its way into the economic life of the country. It was this group primarily that made up the emigration wave of the 1880s.

In the course of these fifty years almost 677,000 Norwegians took part in the overseas crossing. But Norway's population, which in 1865 was 1,701,756, continued to increase in spite of this great drain, so that it passed two million around 1890, and by 1910, toward the end of the era of mass emigration, had reached 2,391,782. After the major exodus in the last half of the 1860s, there was a calmer period from 1873 on, but the year 1880 heralded the second and largest mass departure of Norwegians, lasting till the end of 1893, a period of fourteen years. On the average, 18,900 Norwegians left annually, or ten of every thousand

The emigrant vessel Geiser departing from Larsen's Place in Copenhagen in 1882. The man on the high stool is an official who supervises the ship's departure. By the gangway another official verifies that the emigrants have passenger contracts and medical certificates.

Right: Emigrants leaving Norway in 1903.

Above: The journey was not necessarily over when the immigrants landed in Quebec or New York. From Quebec many continued by steamboat through the Welland Canal and over the Great Lakes, or from 1856 they could go by rail to Detroit. From New York they traveled west by railroad, canal boat, and steamship. The above notice for the Pennsylvania Railroad Company promises transportation "without interruption from the landing place of the steamships to the distant western states and territories."

Above: Not until 1913 was the Norwegian America Line started. The photograph shows the steamship Kristianiafjord.

Left: The Statue of Liberty was frequently the first sight of the new land.

inhabitants. This gave Norway one of the highest rates of emigration in Europe, surpassed only by Ireland. It culminated in 1882 with 28,804 travelers to America, a number that exceeded the natural population increase.

Emigration was sensitive to market fluctuations in America. Most economists place the industrial take-off in America before the Civil War; from 1865 up to World War I there was an industrial expansion unmatched anywhere else in the world. The growth was interrupted by depressions, but the direction was clear. The

first crisis came in 1873, the "Panic of 1873," when a postwar boom ended, but the rate of growth picked up so that before 1880 there was great activity in all branches of the economy: in industrial production, in the extraction of raw materials, and in construction. Economic activity advanced until 1893, when the depression that then set in severely affected American economic life. The American economist Harry Jerome has shown in a study done in the 1920s that a recession results in lessened import of foreign labor after a lag of six months, and the sharp reduction in the number of Norwegian immigrants in 1894 is evidence of this.

From Family Emigration to Individual Emigration

The composition of the emigrant body changed greatly in the course of the emigration era. The early movement gave the impression of being a family emigration with the same percentage of children as in the Norwegian population in general. This situation lasted until the 1870s, when a shift toward individual departures became apparent. Toward the end of the period of mass exodus the movement had to a marked degree become a youth migration, and the men's share had consistently increased. Almost two-thirds of the emigrants in this later period were between the ages of fifteen and twenty-five.

The cities entered the picture in the 1860s, and even though the emigration from the countryside retained its lead in absolute numbers, from 1876 on the urban areas had a higher emigration frequency. It is interesting to note that family emigration continued longer in the cities than in the farming districts. This would suggest that many of the urban emigrants were country people who had stayed in the city for a time before coming to America.

Most emigrants were ordinary workers and had only their labor to offer. But in the urban exodus hundreds of engineers, technicians, intellectuals, artists, and other professionally trained people also participated. The composition of the emigrant body reflects the progress that Norwegian economic life was making and the changes that industrialization and urbanization had produced. From the 1840s the Nordic lands were pulled into the great European industrialization process, even though the development moved forward relatively modestly. Norway experienced a strong expansion in shipping and in the lumber trade; capital from abroad financed a modernization of industry.

In 1865 not quite 20 percent of the people of Norway lived in towns and cities, in 1900 more than 35 percent. Still, agriculture remained the most important branch of the economy until the end of mass emigration. Modernizations of the agricultural sector was a consequence of the crisis

that this branch of the economy experienced during the second half of the nineteenth century; the great masses of people who were liberated thereby sought employment in Norway's cities or went to America.

Those who emigrated can hardly be said to have been forced out; it was a voluntary emigration, resulting for the individual from an assessment of advantages and disadvantages. But in the 1880s prospects at home for the many young people were bleak, in Norway as in the rest of Europe. Throughout this decade crises and depressions befell the new age groups seeking employment. It was a period of economic stagnation. "Seldom has a generation of youths grown up under more difficult circum-

Ellis Island, a small island at the entrance to New York, in 1892 replaced Castle Garden as a receiving and control station for immigrants. It is difficult to imagine the tragedy of being rejected and sent home, here at the gateway to the promised land, for health or other reasons.

stances," writes Ingrid Semmingsen. The expansion in industry lagged far behind the growth in population. This, then, is the background for the peak in emigration from Norway and the other nations in northwestern Europe at that time, the largest wave from the old regions of emigration. Social ambition and a need for self-assertion in the rising generation quickened the emigration. Nor can one ignore wan-

27

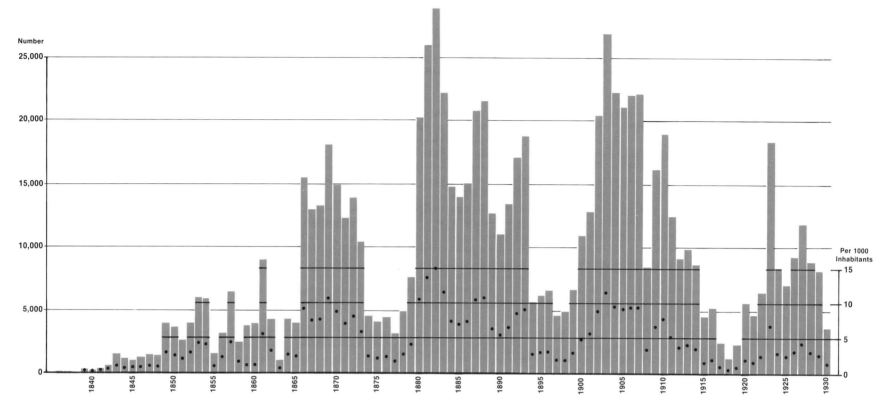

The diagram (above) shows Norwegian emigration through 1930. The number of emigrants per 1,000 Norwegian inhabitants is indicated by dots in the different columns, and the rate can be seen vertically to the right.

Right: Emigration, including immigration to Norway and net emigration, between censuses from 1845 to 1930.

	Births	Deaths	Births Minus Deaths	Emigration	Calculated Growth	Real Growth	Immigration	Net Emigration
1846-1855	445,378	253,260	192,118	32,270	159,848	161,576	1,728	30,542
1856-1865	520,550	283,135	237,415	39,350	198,065	211,709	13,644	25,706
1865-1875	525,870	305,460	220,410	119,545	100,865	105,144	4,279	115,266
1876-1890	896,040	489,665	406,375	226,932	179,443	194,017	14,574	212,358
1891-1900	633,575	343,190	290,385	94,854	195,531	239,115	43,584	51,270
1901-1910	635,900	328,980	306,920	190,858	116,062	151,750	35,688	155,170
1911-1920	621,760	346,780	274,980	61,521	213,459	257,993	44,534	16,987
1921-1930	551,770	309,070	242,700	86,612	156,088	164,419	8,331	78,281
1846-1900				512,951			77,809	435,142
1901-1930				338,891			88,553	250,338
1846-1930				851,842			166,362	685,480

Source: Arnfinn Engen, ed., *Utvandringa—det store oppbrotet* (Oslo: Det Norske Samlaget, 1978), p. 36

derlust and a desire for adventure, the hope of making a new beginning, the weight of authority and class prejudice, in short, almost any human motivation, as causes of emigration. America was, says the British historian Philip Taylor, like a distant magnet, and to try one's luck there was an ever-present possibility. Special local conditions might also affect emigration. In the two Agder counties, for instance, there is a clear connection between the strong flare-up of emigration during the two decades on either side of 1900 and a crisis in the shipping industry created by the difficult transition from sail to steam. Toward the end of the nineteenth century, there came to be an international Atlantic labor market, and Norwegian emigration was a part of this market. The improvements in communication and transportation provided easy mobility and created a common economic region.

The Final Wave of Mass Emigration

In 1905 the ninety-one-year-old union with Sweden was dissolved; a completely independent Norway made unusual strides in economic development, which continued until the depression following World War I. Because of this economic progress, the Norwegian historian Wilhelm Keilhau has called the first decade of this century the happiest in Norway's history, and he has claimed that there was greater economic and social growth during this decade than in several previous centuries. Nevertheless, during this period the third and final wave of mass emigration occurred; from 1900 through 1914, 214,985 Norwegians left the country. After 1905 Norwegian authorities asked the emigrants their reasons for leaving. Between 80 and 90 percent of the men and between 60 and 75 percent of the women said they left because they could not find profitable employment. Norwegian industry could not expand quickly enough to meet this need for jobs, and employment opportunities were greater across the ocean.

The American economy also prospered after 1900, and its great expansion pulled labor from all parts of Europe to America. It was the eastern and southern parts of the continent, Russia, Austria-Hungary, and Italy, that contributed most heavily to the prewar emigration. A brief economic crisis in 1907, however, caused a sudden fall in the number who crossed the Atlantic; only about half as many Norwegians went to America in 1908 as in 1907.

Emigration after World War I

There was a wave of emigration in the 1920s, when in the course of ten years, between 1920 and 1929, 88,520 Norwegians emigrated. But even though it peaked in 1923 with as many as 18,287 emigrants, the average annual number was only 8,852, as compared with 14,332 yearly in the period before the war. During World War I immigration had of course been minimal, although it had never ceased, and the wave of the 1920s represented a damming up of people who desired to emigrate. But the emigration may also be explained in terms of the unemployment that struck Norway in 1921, simultaneously with economic improvement in the United States after 1922. The large exodus in 1923 shows the interplay of such forces. Restriction on immigration to America through the quota laws of 1921 and 1924 greatly reduced the flow; in their final form, which became effective in 1929, Norway was awarded an annual quota of 2,377. Emigration from Norway would have been greater without these restrictions, for the country experienced bad times and unemployment toward the end of the 1920s. The serious depression during the 1930s, however, produced a radical decline in emigration, and during World War II there was no regular immigration to the United States.

Many Returned to Norway

The Great Depression prompted 32,000 Norwegians in America to return to their homeland; return migration was closely related to business cycles, to good or bad times, on both sides of the Atlantic. Official Norwegian statistics indicate that between 1891 and 1940 as many as a quarter of all emigrants to America after 1881 resettled in Norway. This figure may seem somewhat high, and existing statistics are unreliable.

Return migration was a function of labor migration; people sought employment as foreign or guest workers, intending to return when they had saved enough money. The early emigration had had a permanent character; people had fled from need and poverty to begin a new life somewhere else. The youth migration later in the nineteenth century was mobile, it was less permanent, consisting of people who might easily pull up stakes and move again. Most of those who moved back to Norway had stayed a relatively short time in America, and a large percentage of them resettled in their home districts.

Birds of passage, especially from the southwestern part of Norway, are an interesting manifestation of the labor migration. In the community of Skudesneshavn on the island of Karmøy, for instance, eighty fishermen took part in the fisheries on the east coast of America in 1904 and then returned to Norway for the next year's winter herring fishing—a singular example of seasonal migration.

Emigration Faded after 1945

The postwar development must be viewed as a continuation of the earlier exodus. Between 1946 and 1960, an average of 2,253 Norwegians moved to North America annually. This movement accelerated in the years immediately after World War II and peaked in 1952, when close to 3,000 emigrants departed. Then there was a noticeable decline from decade to decade: in the 1950s, 22,935 people took part in the transit to the United States; in the 1960s, 15,484; and in the 1970s only a few hundred left yearly, toward the end of the decade only slightly more than 200. A total of about 50,000 Norwegians have moved to the United States and around 10,000 to Canada since World War II.

A marked mobility has been evident, and a large return migration, which indicates that people can take advantage of opportunities wherever they exist. Family connections in America gave impetus to the first postwar emigration, as well as a damming up of people who wanted to leave, and a postwar shortage of consumer goods in Norway. As conditions at home improved, and as restrictions limited further access to the United States, emigration from Norway decreased. The impact of the Immigration and Nationality Act, which became effective July 1, 1968, was apparent in a dramatic drop from 1,574 emigrants in 1968 to only 434 the following year. It is also clear that America had lost some of its lure.

Most postwar emigrants belong in a broad sense to the laboring class; but there has been a major shift from an unskilled to a much more skilled labor supply. Norway has also been affected by the so-called brain drain, the transfer of highly trained personnel. Persons with professional training have continued to find greater opportunity in America's dynamic and expansive economy than has been possible in Norway. In the period from 1956 to 1961, American industry attracted annually an average of seventy-eight Norwegian scientists and engineers—a figure which in percentage of scientific and technical graduates in 1959 is surpassed in Europe only by Switzerland. In the health sector, a substantial number of nurses and a smaller number of doctors came to America in the 1950s and 1960s; in addition, many Norwegian students studied in American institutions and remained in America after completing their education.

For Norway as a whole, there was a near balance between men and women in the postwar emigration. From the 1930s on the percentage of married men increased, which indicated that the earlier labor movement of young people was over, and it is to a large extent possible to view the relatively small emigration during the years before and after World War II as a family phenomenon.

By 1980 the tradition of going to America had nearly ended, if not completely ceased. But the emigration left a legacy of common historical

A headstone on a grave in a churchyard at Syvds-botn in Sunnmøre carries an inscription relating that 6 of 7 children emigrated to America.
Emigrant ballads expressed the many emotions and experiences the emigration produced.

Farewell, Norway, and God bless thee.
Stern and severe wert thou always,
But as a mother I honor thee,
Even though thou skimped my bread.
All things vanish! Grief and care
Sink down upon the heart;
Still the memory of thee refreshes
The Soul like the deep sleep of a child.

memories and linked Norway to the multifarious and complex society that developed in America. Within the boundaries of America nearly every race and ethnic group, every nationality and linguistic minority, has sought economic security and social order. The topic of this book is the Norwegian element in this remarkable pluralistic society.

A Norwegian-American Society Comes Into Being

From the first Norwegian settlement in America in the state of New York, the Norwegian immigrant stream flowed westward. Pioneer leaders like Cleng Peerson showed the way. Life on the American frontier was hard, but the neighborhood gave strength and security.

32

Kendall Was the First Settlement

The first Norwegian settlement in America was founded by the Sloopers in the state of New York about thirty-five miles northeast of the city of Rochester. It was situated in the northeastern part of Murray township in Orleans county. This area had been separated from Murray township and named Kendall township shortly before the arrival of the Sloopers; consequently the colony that emerged between the newly opened Erie Canal and the shores of Lake Ontario became known as the Kendall settlement.

Together with a land agent, the Quaker Joseph Fellows, who represented the Pultney Estate, a company with large land holdings in the western part of the state, Cleng Peerson greeted the *Restauration* when the sloop docked in New York on October 9, 1825. It was through Fellows that Peerson had made arrangements to buy land. Each head of household would purchase five acres at a price of five dollars per acre and would pay for it over a period of ten years.

Two of the newcomers, the captain Lars Olsen Helland and the first mate Peder Eriksen Meland, remained in New York. The leader of the Sloopers, Lars Larsen Geilane, sent his wife and their child, born in transit, together with the rest of the company westward with Fellows as guide on October 21. The Sloopers arrived in their new home in early November. Quakers and other people in New York had supported the journey inland with money, food, and clothing.

Larsen stayed behind to sell the *Restauration*, and the $400 he got for the boat was far less than anticipated. In the meantime the Erie Canal had frozen over, and when Larsen set out westward, it is said that he skated from Albany to Holley, near Kendall. The following spring Larsen moved to Rochester and found employment as

Left: Mutual assistance was of vital importance in pioneer society, and Norwegian immigrants carried with them strong communal traditions from their rural Norwegian home communities. The photograph was taken by Andrew Dahl in the vicinity of Madison, Wisconsin, in the mid-1870s. It shows barn raising as a community project.

a carpenter; he established himself in time as a first-rate shipwright and thus was able to continue in the profession he had had in Stavanger. His and Martha's home in Rochester became a well-known way station for the Norwegian emigrants who in subsequent years streamed across the Atlantic and went to the Middle West by way of the Erie Canal and across the Great Lakes.

The Immigrants Go West

The Erie Canal was completed in 1825; it cut through the Appalachian mountain chain so that barges could be pulled from Albany on the Hudson River to Buffalo by Lake Erie. The canal, which was 363 miles long, opened up to settlement the enormous land areas in the upper part of the Mississippi River basin. Legions of Americans and Europeans took this route on their way west.

The Kendall settlers had undoubtedly heard about the opportunities in the West. With the good prices for land in western New York, a consequence of increased demand produced by improved communications, they could sell their small holdings at a profit. Cleng Peerson again showed the way, walking from western New York to Ohio, across southern Michigan, through northern Indiana, to Illinois and the small collection of log cabins that was Chicago. It was truly an epic journey.

Peerson made excursions to inspect the land, and he himself recorded, and embroidered upon, how he discovered the Fox River valley in La Salle county in Illinois, about seventy miles southwest of Chicago. In this region the second Norwegian settlement in America was founded; it was the first Norwegian colony in the Middle West and was known as the Fox River settlement.

It was the Promised Land that Cleng Peerson had found, the land of milk and honey. It is understandable that a religious people would draw a comparison between their own wanderings and the Jews'; the comparison was reiterated many times. But unlike Moses, Peerson not only

beheld this land, but reached it and guided his compatriots to it. He returned to Kendall and according to the amateur historian and farmer Hjalmar Rued Holand's account in *De norske settlementers historie* (The History of Norwegian Settlements) in 1908, Peerson explained that he had located a place for a Norwegian settlement "that in productivity, beauty, health, and favorable location was unrivaled in all of America."

During the following two years, 1834 and 1835, most of the colonists in Kendall moved to the Fox River region and bought property there. The Kendall settlement did not dissolve completely, but continued to have a Norwegian component. The land to be purchased along the Fox River had probably been selected as early as 1834, which is considered to mark the settlement's founding, but the actual sale of land did not commence before 1835. Speculators acquired much land, because it was assumed that its value would rise when a projected canal from Chicago to the Illinois River in La Salle county was finished. Such prospects had likely also influenced the Norwegian pioneers in their choice of land. In addition, the fertile and sparsely wooded prairie was easy to cultivate. New settlers flocked to the region after 1835, and there was heavy settlement in the entire valley of the Illinois River.

Many Came Directly from Norway

People in Norway received firsthand information about possibilities in the Mississippi River valley when Knud Andersen Slogvig made a trip to Norway in 1836. He had moved the previous year from Kendall to the Fox River region. The prolific letter writer Gjert Gregoriussen Hovland, who had settled there the same year, described the new region as "a Land of Canaan . . . which produces so richly without fertilizer that Norway can no more be compared to America than a desert to a garden of herbs in blossom."

Most of the 167 emigrants who crossed over from Stavanger in 1836 on the two ships *Norden* and *Den norske klippe* made their way to the Fox River settlement. In addition, a few more came to New York by way of Gothenburg. Thus about 200 Norwegians emigrated in 1836. Slogvig served as guide for the emigrants on *Norden*, and on the same vessel was also Bjørn Andersen Kvelve from Vikedal. Like Peerson, Kvelve was

The map shows Norwegian settlements in the states of Illinois, Wisconsin, Missouri, and southern Iowa. Cleng Peerson roved into this region in 1833; he thereby showed the way for a great Norwegian influx in the following decades.

tlement spread over several townships in La Salle county and on to Kendall county to the southeast, and had other branches. The expanded Fox River area had 221 families by 1850, with a combined population of 1,252 people, and during the next decade the number exceeded 3,200. And the settlement continued to grow.

The outflow of people to form settlements farther west began only a few years after the pioneer settlers had arrived in the Fox River district. As the best land was taken up, and news reached the settlement of better land farther west, many people moved on. But the Fox River settlement remained a significant mother colony and served as a way station for immigrants to the Middle West. It was for a long time the first goal for Norwegian emigrants.

Beaver Creek Was a Sad Chapter in Norwegian Immigration

The Beaver Creek settlement is of interest mainly because of Ole Rynning, who came to America in 1837 on the ship *Ægir* with eighty other emigrants, mostly from districts surrounding Bergen. Rynning was a pastor's son from Snåsa in North Trøndelag, twenty-eight years old, and his education and qualities of leadership made the emigrants view him as their spokesman.

The circumstances around his decision to emigrate are unclear. He did not belong to the social classes most prone to emigrate; when the *Ægir* left Bergen on April 7, there were only two passengers from outside the peasant class on board. Personal factors, such as his father's objection to his engagement to a young woman of inferior social class and Rynning's disagreement with his parents when he broke off his theological studies, may have had a bearing on his resolve to leave. It is also known that Rynning sympathized with the peasant class and harbored democratic and idealistic convictions. One reason for his departure may thus have been a desire to assist Norwegian peasants in getting land.

When the company came to Chicago intending

at odds with officialdom, and, as was the case with many early emigrants, he had connections with the Quakers in Stavanger and was influenced by their leader, Elias Tastad.

Two more emigrant ships, *Enigheden* from Stavanger and *Ægir* from Bergen, left for America the next year. Among the emigrant leaders that year were the brothers Ole and Ansten Nat-

testad from Numedal and the rationalist and spokesman for liberal reforms Hans Barlien, from Overhalla in North Trøndelag.

Not everyone on the two vessels or those who came later to America went to the Fox River settlement, but in the following years the first Norwegian colony in the Middle West received a constant flow of Norwegian newcomers. The set-to continue on to the Fox River settlement in La Salle county, the newcomers were advised not to proceed because of the unhealthy conditions there. According to the pioneer newspaperman Knud Langeland, it was the immigrants' ignorance about the frequency of malaria—or "climate fever" or "swamp fever," as it was often called at that time—in *all* river basins in the region which kept them away from the tracts by the Fox River. Instead they sent an expedition, with Rynning going along, to find an appropriate place. Unfortunately, under the influence of speculators, they selected a marshy area seventy miles south of Chicago known as Beaver Creek. The little settlement that emerged became one of the most unfortunate in Norwegian immigration history. Most of the settlers perished from malaria during the first two years, and the survivors fled.

Rynning had inspected the area in August and September, when the flat, marshy landscape was "dry and overgrown with thick grass that reached a man up under his arms," as Knud Langeland wrote in 1889. Not until the next spring, when it was too late, did the area reveal its true character, and the "swamp fever" ravaged the settlers.

Among the dead was Ole Rynning, whose "bones remained" by Beaver Creek. It was while he lay ill that he wrote his famous immigrant guide, *True Account of America*. This little book of thirty-nine pages was read widely, and it "circulated in the thousands throughout all Norwegian country communities" and greatly influenced later emigration.

Rynning's account shows an observant and matter-of-fact judgment. Its purpose was "to answer all questions, which I myself raised, to give information about every situation which I noticed people were ignorant of, and to refute false rumors that have reached my ears." *True Account of America* illustrates the importance to the emigration of the spread of information, and the book's wide distribution bears witness to the great need that existed for reliable reports after emigration had become a possibility.

A Norwegian Urban Colony in Chicago

The population of Chicago in 1832 included only half a dozen white families and a few Indians. The whole village consisted of five log cabins. In May, 1833, the settlers platted the city, and Chicago grew rapidly on the marshy ground at the mouth of the Chicago River. By 1836 there were almost 4,000 people in the city; in 1850 there were more than 29,000; and at the end of the next decade Chicago had become a large city with close to 110,000 inhabitants. Chicago's favorable location, which made it possible to take advantage of the trade between the agricultural west and the industrial east, explains its tremendous growth in population. A large percentage of the citizens of Chicago were immigrants, according to the census more than half both in 1850 and in 1860. A small Norwegian colony also came into being.

A sailor, David Johnson, who arrived in 1834, is considered to have been the earliest Norwegian in Chicago. However, a Norwegian settlement was not formed until 1836, when a few newcomers remained in the city that year rather than continue on to the Fox River valley. They settled on the north side of Chicago at a spot known as "The Sands," on Pine Street between Chicago Avenue and Superior Street. Every year a few more arrived, so that by 1850 the Norwegian colony had 562 members. The center of the colony was on the north side of the river, east of La Salle Street. One may assume that most Norwegians lived in primitive huts in a kind of immigrant slum. They were probably forced to move from this area because of construction of warehouses, factories, and railroad stations in the burgeoning city. As a result, in 1862, 62 percent of all Norwegian residents were to be found in the blocks around Kinzie and Milwaukee Streets on the west side. There were then a total of 1,573 Norwegians in the city.

Several of the newcomers, among them Johnson, got work as seamen on the Great Lakes, and a few became skippers. George Peterson, for example, in 1839 became captain on the schooner *St. Joseph*. Some were craftsmen who practiced their trade in America; others were construction

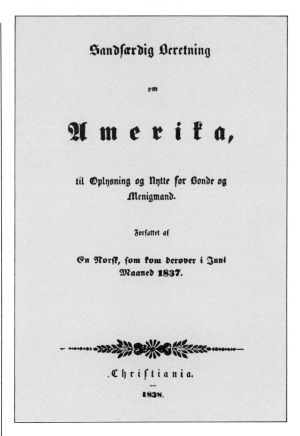

The title page of Ole Rynning's guide True Account of America.

workers, although the majority of Norwegians likely accepted whatever work they could get. There was a great demand for labor, and some people stayed in the city only long enough to save money for the purchase of land farther west. One early immigrant was Halstein Torison, originally Thorsteinson, who arrived in 1836. He built a house—not much better than a shack—where Chicago & Northwestern later built a railroad station. He worked as a gardener for Walter L. Newberry, the donor of the well-known Newberry Library in Chicago. Torison later moved to Calumet, south of Chicago.

The arrival in the city in 1836 of Niels Knutsen Røthe, his wife Torbjør, and their three children influenced the development of the Norwegian colony in Chicago. They are held to be the first emigrants from Voss, in western Norway. Other

Vossings followed them, and a colony—known as "the Voss Circle"—appeared in Chicago. The Vossings were to play an important role among Norwegian Americans in the city. As Chicago became the most important gateway to areas to the west, thousands of Norwegians passed through the city; some of these people, hailing from many parts of Norway, remained there and joined the Vossings' colony.

Among the Vossings there were several who sent letters home, and in a report from 1840 it is said of the Vossings that some had bought houses, others had acquired land, and several had moved from Chicago to the Fox River settlement or to Wisconsin, while still others worked on road and dock construction in summer and sawed wood in winter. The letter gives an impression of contentment and industry and of a close relationship among people who had emigrated from the same community. The letter writer observes that "none of us Vossings in Chicago now wishes to be back in Norway, and we are all well satisfied." There was hardly great wealth, even though some people had enough money to invest in homes, and a few did in time become well-to-do. By 1860 the Norwegian immigrants were well established in Chicago, and a foundation had been laid for a strong and influential colony.

Wisconsin Becomes a Center of Norwegian Settlement

In the 1840s Wisconsin became the main region of Norwegian settlement and remained the center of Norwegian-American activity until the Civil War. Norwegian pioneers were pulled along in the westward stream after the Indian threat was removed and new regions were opened to settlement. The Territory of Wisconsin was organized in 1836, and in 1848 it joined the union as the thirtieth state. Census figures show that Norwegian immigrants in 1850 made up 3 percent of the population, 9,467 persons, and in 1870 5.6 percent, or close to 60,000 people. By the 1870s the major areas of Norwegian settlement had

Ole Nattestad was the first Norwegian settler in Wisconsin.

been demarcated, and they have in the main persisted until the present time.

The First Norwegian Pioneers in the State

Ole Nattestad was the first Norwegian settler in Wisconsin. He and his brother Ansten had met Ole Rynning and his company in Detroit on their way to the Middle West and had gone with them to Beaver Creek. In the summer of 1838, while Ansten was in Norway, Ole left Illinois and went to the Wisconsin Territory, for he was convinced that the soil was better to the north and west. He reached what was later Clinton township in Rock county near Beloit on July 1.

There he bought land and founded a settlement that became known as Jefferson Prairie. He told Svein Nilsson in an interview printed in *Billed-Magazin* (Picture Magazine) that except for

Ansten Nattestad visited Norway in 1838. People traveled great distances to listen to him speak about America. The following year he returned accompanied by a large party of emigrants.

eight Americans who had taken up land in the same township, "for a whole year I did not see any countryman of mine but lived secluded, without friends, family, or companions." At night the howl of the prairie wolf became a constant reminder of his isolation. But he had made a fortunate choice of land, because, as Nattestad explained, "the soil was very fertile, and the dreariness of the prairie was broken by scattered groves of trees."

The settlement grew quickly when Ansten returned from Norway with a large group of people in the spring of 1839. Most of the company were from Numedal and northern Telemark. Group emigration played a large and important part in the early exodus, both by making the crossing less intimidating and by promoting later emigration, and it was also a main factor in the

The house "with three stories" that Gunnul Vindegg built in Christiana township in 1840. "Vindegg, who advised people to emigrate, has on occasion been blamed for letting his friends in Norway see the New World in altogether too rosy colors," Svein Nilsson wrote in Billed-Magazin, *November 6, 1869.*

growth of compact Norwegian settlements, often with a local flavor. People left together, and in America they acquired land close to each other; they became neighbors again and attracted others from their home community in Norway to the settlement. One may therefore talk about a local community phase of Norwegian-American history.

The group headed by Ansten Nattestad had sailed from Drammen on the ship *Emilie*, and a smaller contingent had gone by way of Gothenburg, the route most emigrants took in 1839. "In Chicago I was told," Ansten later wrote to Knud Langeland, "that my brother Ole had gone from Illinois to Jefferson Prairie, Rock county, Wis. Most of my company went there. Some of them went to Rock Prairie, west of Beloit, and took land there." The Rock Prairie settlement, which thus was founded in 1839, is often called the Luther Valley settlement, after the Lutheran congregation that was established in 1844.

Another emigrant leader from Upper Telemark was John Nelson Luraas, the eldest son on the Luraas farm, a property encumbered with a substantial debt. He had emigrated in 1839 because he saw no way of "buying out my sisters and brothers so that no injustice was done to them, and finally providing a pension for my father." Letters from earlier emigrants and Rynning's book had convinced him of the propriety of emigrating. In the company of about forty people—half of them from the four Luraas families that emigrated—was John Evenson Molee. In contrast to Luraas, he was a younger son, and the pioneer Norwegian-American scholar Rasmus B. Anderson has said that he emigrated because there were seven children at home on the farm and his eldest brother wished to inherit the ancestral farm unencumbered under the law of primogeniture (*odelsretten*). This law could lead to emigration whether one was an elder or a younger son.

To the left and next page: Prosperous farmers harvest their wheat on Koshkonong around 1875. Both photographs were taken by the Norwegian-American Andrew Dahl (1844-1923). He emigrated from Valdres, Norway, in 1869 and in America became an itinerant professional photographer, concentrating his activity in Norwegian settlements. The technical and artistic quality of his photographs is exceptionally good.

Settlements in the South and East of the State

Most of the emigrants in the Luraas company bought government land by Lake Muskego, south of Milwaukee in Waukesha county. It was the beginning of a settlement that has gained a unique place in Norwegian immigration history.

In Dane county, "close to the heartland of Wisconsin, on the prairies that surround the capital city of Madison," as John R. Reiersen wrote, there came into being a circle of Norwegian settlements. A settlement that became especially famous was founded in 1840 by settlers from Fox River and Jefferson Prairie. Gunnul Vindegg, who in his correspondence home tended to exaggerate his own success, is generally considered the first to clear land there. He named Christiana township, intending to give it the name of the Norwegian capital but misspelling it. The settlement grew large by beautiful Lake Koshkonong in eastern Dane and western Jefferson counties, and it received its name from the lake, Norwegianized to Kaskeland by the settlers. It prospered, so that in 1870 Svein Nilsson could write that "it seemed as if our countrymen first found here the America they had heard so many wonderful stories about in their homeland."

Newcomers streamed into Wisconsin, and the pioneer settlements were both receiving stations and points of departure for new settlements in other parts of the state. A family coming from Norway would usually stop for a while in an older settlement before setting out for regions farther west, and then frequently on the advice of pioneers who had left the older area.

The Distribution-Preemption Act of 1841 made it easier to acquire land; simultaneously the rapid tempo of railroad construction inspired settlers to look for more advantageous land purchases. The railroads, like the government, had land to offer and encouraged new settlement. The connection east to expanding markets at the same time made commercial agriculture feasible. The railroad between Milwaukee and Madison was opened in 1854 and reached Prairie du Chien on the Mississippi River in 1857. Still, most Norwegian settlers in the pioneer era—even in regions the railroad had entered—continued to use wagons pulled by oxen, the so-called prairie schooner.

Norwegian Pioneers Move to Western Wisconsin

Settlement in western Wisconsin began toward the end of the 1840s, after most good land in the southeastern part of the state had been claimed. The pioneer settlers were from the Koshkonong and Muskego settlements. The coulee country along the Mississippi River, from Crawford county to Barron county, was in time an almost solid strip of Norwegian settlements. The famous settlements of Coon Valley and Coon Prairie in Vernon county were established in 1848. Holand has called this district "America's Gudbrandsdal" because many emigrants from that valley in Norway made their home in this landscape which "resembled so comfortingly the hillsides in Gudbrandsdal." To the La Crosse area farther north Norwegian pioneers came in the 1850s; the town of La Crosse became a commercial and cultural center for the immigrants.

North of La Crosse, in the Trempealeau valley, another region of Norwegian settlement developed. The pioneers to this area came in 1852. In *Telesoga* in 1911 A. O. Houkom tells about the first Norwegian settlers in this uninhabited wilderness: "There was no trace of a path; they had to clear a way through the brush, make long detours because of rivers, and build bridges across creeks in order to get over with oxen and wagons. They saw no white person on this last part of the journey, and not for a long time after their arrival."

Every new settlement was a potential mother colony for those moving west. The historian Carlton C. Qualey has described the gradual westward movement. Newer and older settlements retained close relations. There were bonds of family and friendship between them, and on their way to new regions the settlers could stop and rest at the homes of Norwegian Americans along the route. In his study, *Norwegian Settlement in the United States*, in 1938, Qualey emphasized an important idea: "In place of thinking of Norwegian settlement as a part of the process of emigration from Norway to the American shore and thence inland, one may regard it as a separate process—an integral part of the westward movement of the American population." Norwegian settlers enthusiastically embraced the pioneer idea of always seeking better land to the

west; many sold their property at a profit and bought land cheaper on the frontier. Norwegians thus participated in the conquest of the enormous land areas in the Middle West.

Muskego, a Noteworthy Pioneer Settlement

Muskego is one of the most noteworthy of the Norwegian pioneer settlements in America. Its proximity to Milwaukee partly explains its significance. Milwaukee became an important gateway for immigrants to Wisconsin and areas farther west in the 1840s.

Those who acquired land by Lake Muskego did not, however, make a good choice. Conditions there were very similar to those in the unfortunate Beaver Creek settlement, a marshy landscape exposed to malaria epidemics. Reiersen visited the area in 1843, four years after the pioneer settlers had taken land there, and he described it as follows: "The entire stretch of land is flat, with many marshes; the arable higher land—rising only slightly above the level of the marshes—consists exclusively of glades between forests of white oak. The soil is composed of a thin layer of mold over clay. Immigrants from Voss, Telemark, Numedal, and elsewhere have settled there, close together. Although they have begun farming, their land does not yet provide them with sufficient foodstuffs." The malaria epidemic that broke out in 1843 and that "laid a great number of people in their graves" Reiersen thought was caused by "a flock of poor emigrants" who had come there, since Muskego "is the closest settlement to the city of Melwauki [sic]." These "lodged in the small pioneer huts," and there was "widespread disease" because many of the newcomers had become "ill during the ocean passage." He explains "the poor conditions in the colony" by "a large portion of laziness and apathy in many, and a lack of enterprise in most;" this in addition to the difficulty of clearing the area and the unfertile soil. He assumed that about half of all families had bought land, "mostly in small plots of forty acres."

Left: A settler's cabin in Wisconsin, reproduced in Billed-Magazin, *September 4, 1869.*

Below: The Muskego church, the first Norwegian Lutheran church in America.

One may wonder about the criteria Norwegian immigrants used in their selection of land. They likely measured according to Norwegian standards, a suitable mixture of wooded land, pastures, and arable land, and brooks and rivers to provide water. For a long time they showed a distaste for open prairie land and did not recognize its greater value for agriculture. Perhaps they were also more ready than Americans to pay the high prices speculators asked, that is, to buy land American settlers had passed up. Their lack of knowledge of English was also a severe handicap, as was their ignorance of American conditions, which made them easy prey to dishonest speculators. In addition, whereas American settlers took land on an individual basis, Norwegian pioneers often appointed two or three scouts to select land, and as a consequence a whole group might be placed in an unfavorable area. This was the case in Muskego, as it had been in Beaver Creek, where it is likely that speculators had led the Norwegian settlers astray on purpose.

The settlement by Lake Muskego gained importance because so many newcomers stopped there on their way west; the settlers shared their modest stores, showed the recent arrivals great hospitality, and gave advice. The name Muskego came to have a special ring in the ears of the newcomers. The fact that so many moved away from the settlement and its unprofitable land left it small. But it had a group of unusual leaders; many lines of development in the immigrant community go back to the early history of this settlement.

Even Heg arrived in 1840. He was the son of a prosperous farmer from Lier, and a Haugean, although not a follower of the more extreme practices of the movement. Heg became an energetic and pragmatic leader of the Norwegian Americans. Even Heg bought the property of John Nelson Luraas, the emigrant leader of 1839, and built a house and a large barn. The latter served as a receiving station for newcomers, with Norwegian immigrants filling it every summer.

The barn was also the social and religious center of the community, used for gatherings of all kinds and even as an infirmary. A unique document, a diary written by another immigrant, Søren Bache, gives insight into the life of the settlement. Bache was also a Haugean, and his father, Tollef Bache, had like Hauge himself a good head for business and had become a well-to-do lumber merchant in Drammen. The son Søren was, however, judging from his diary, an impractical dreamer. He was well supplied with money when he came to America in 1839 with a companion, Johannes Johansen. His father had insisted on sending along Johansen, "a shrewd and reliable old office clerk," as Hjalmar Rued Holand put it. After staying for a time in the Fox River area, the two men moved to Muskego during the summer of 1840. They got land in what was later Norway township by Wind Lake in Racine county, expanding the Muskego settlement farther to the south. Here they built a dwelling in an Indian burial mound and set up a country store with a limited offering of merchandise, consisting of sugar, coffee, salt, and some cloth. They were more affluent than most immigrants, and they helped their neighbors considerably with loans of money.

Bache's diary describes activities in the settlement until he returned to Norway in 1847. By then the first Norwegian Lutheran church in America, started in 1843, had been built there. The church historian J. Magnus Rohne writes that there existed a perhaps unconscious desire for church services by ordained Norwegian pastors. The Haugean lay preachers were unable to

Søren Bache's log cabin was built in the early 1840s. In Billed-Magazin *for November 14, 1868, Svein Nilsson tells about the Indian mound where Søren Bache and Johannes Johansen made their first dwelling: "Here was the seat of culture and learning, the center of pomp and luxury, the stronghold of finance."*

provide the systematic and thorough guidance that pioneer life demanded. The building of the church was supported financially by Tollef Bache in the amount of $400. Søren Bache recorded in his diary on March 12, 1845: "This forenoon Johansen, Even Heg, and I went over to the church to inspect it, since it is almost finished. It looks attractive inside. It has a lovely location, as it lies on a high hill about in the middle of the Norwegian colony." On March 13, the next day, the church was dedicated, and many participated in the ceremony.

In addition to the first church structure, the first Norwegian-American newspaper, *Nordlyset* (Northern Lights), made its appearance at Muskego in 1847, published by James D. Reymert, a lawyer from Farsund in Norway and a prominent man in the settlement. The lines of development are clear—the church and the press were to be the two most important institutions established and supported by Norwegian immigrants.

A Man from the Upper Classes Emigrates

Pioneer emigrant leaders, men like Peerson, Rynning, and Barlien, may seem to have been persons who to some extent placed themselves outside the society they left. They were individualists, people who defended their rights and who hoped through emigration to secure greater freedom and equality for their compatriots in the new land. The validity of such a generalization is of course difficult to determine, and especially its broader application to the many unknown men and women in the emigration drama. One is limited to judging from the writings of those who recorded their experiences and their options.

The generalization may at least in part apply to Hans Gasmann; he is described by a contemporary as "a liberal and sensible man with a noble spirit, and a great opponent of official arbitrariness." His decision to emigrate may have been hastened by his political stance; in any case, news of his plan to leave the fatherland attracted

attention. He was a very wealthy man—not from the classes that contributed most of the emigrants—a former member of parliament, and the owner of an estate. In November, 1842, the newspapers reported that he had sold his farm Foss in Gjerpen for the large sum of 7,500 *speciedaler* and was preparing to emigrate.

Gasmann and his company embarked on *Salvator*, owned by his brother Johan Gasmann, in May, 1843, and landed in New York on July 13. His contemporaries were puzzled by his action; it could hardly be thought that he was taken in by false prospects of quick profit in America. The reason for his departure is most likely to be found in his concern for his large family. He had thirteen children, and prospects in Norway seemed poor for the coming generation. Later Gasmann wrote that he had achieved what he had hoped for by emigrating: greater happiness for all his children.

Hans Gasmann at Pine Lake

Gasmann made his home by Pine Lake in northwestern Waukesha county, about thirty miles west of Milwaukee. A settlement had been founded there in 1841 by Gustaf Unonius, a thirty-one-year-old student from Uppsala, Sweden, and he and his companions had called it "Nya Uppsala." The outlook for success in this venture was poor, especially since the settlement received many emigrants who were not well equipped for pioneer life, adventurers and drifters of many kinds, "partly from noble families," as Gasmann wrote. All the same, Unonius described conditions there in enthusiastic articles in the influential Swedish *Aftonbladet* (Evening Paper), which were reprinted in Norwegian newspapers. It was the settlers' own wishes that sent Unonius to the modest Nashotah Episcopal Seminary close by, where he was trained as an Episcopal pastor, and Hans Gasmann and the other Norwegian settlers joined that church. In 1849 one finds Unonius in Chicago, where he assisted in organizing a Swedish-Norwegian Episcopal congregation.

After the arrival of Gasmann and his company at Pine Lake in 1843, Norwegians gradually came to outnumber Swedes. Reiersen tells about the cooperation between the two nationalities that extended beyond a common church organization, "a kind of Scandinavian union." But he relates that, strangely enough, "the Swedes had settled on the eastern side of a little lake—Pine Lake—whereas the Norwegians live on its western shores." Unity was preserved by "*Constitutionen* and *Unionen* . . . small boats in which the neighbors visit each other."

Gasmann purchased large stretches of land, one thousand acres, and divided all but 260 acres among his four grown sons. He lived simply on the acres he had retained, in a house that consisted of "only a living room, kitchen, and pantry, and on the second floor two small bedrooms and a little closet—this is the whole business." He built a "stable and cowbarn," which at the time was still unusual in the area. It was quite evident that he did not live in the same grand style as he had done in Norway.

Many back home anticipated Gasmann's reports from America; people postponed their own plans to emigrate in expectation of his advice. They counted on reliable information from a sensible man of the upper classes. The first letter from Pine Lake is dated October 18, 1843. In it Gasmann describes the settlement in detail, and assures everyone that conditions there "exceed . . . in many respects my expectations, so that I am very pleased with my decision to move here." He does not, however, counsel everyone to come, but praises the greater liberty, lack of class distinctions, and better future prospects for those who by their industry are able to take advantage of them. But people who want to buy land must have "something to live on the first year and a little for the second," in anticipation of a sufficient harvest. His letters contributed greatly to the spread of information about the new land.

Oleana, a Colonization Venture that Failed

Organized efforts at colonization have been of little consequence in Norwegian immigration history. But a few attempts were made to organize communal settlements, and many plans were formed but never tried, schemes with a religious base, as well as broader kinds of colonization

without communal ownership of land. The most commented-on venture, an experiment that ended in failure, was Ole Bull's colony—the New Norway—in Potter county, Pennsylvania. It was a brief episode in Norwegian immigration, and its impact on later developments is uncertain. The enterprise received luster and excitement from the founder's own fame and geniality, and among his contemporaries the colony created enthusiasm and great expectations, but it also produced criticism and ultimately profound disappointment.

Torstein Jahr, an authority on the project, believes that Ole Bull had such a plan in mind when he visited America a second time in 1852. Bull was a musical genius, a world-renowned violinist, who cut a romantic and appealing figure on stage. On a concert tour of the United States from 1843 to 1845 he had performed in many parts of the country and amassed a considerable fortune. He had also learned about conditions in the scattered Norwegian settlements in the Middle West.

Bull had left Norway a deeply disappointed man because of the lack of appreciation and support for the theater he had established in his hometown of Bergen in 1850. An expression of a rising Norwegian national consciousness, it was intended as a center where Norwegian drama and music would be cultivated. "Love of the fatherland was the creative force in his life," the Norwegian poet Bjørnstjerne Bjørnson said of him at his funeral in 1880, but he was in addition a democratic, freedom-loving man, inspired by the February Revolution of 1848 and its idealistic and socialistic message. He was probably also influenced by the ideas and activities associated with Marcus Thrane's socialistic movement in Norway.

America had witnessed many Utopian experiments, and these might have moved the easily inspired Bull to act, although little is known about his familiarity with them. Bull's intention was in any case to buy land in America for Norwegians and gather them in a colony, and he purchased a large area in the northwestern part of Pennsylvania. The first colonists arrived in September, 1852, and by the end of the year there were 250 people in the colony. On September 7 Ole Bull himself visited the place with an engineer, and that evening the colony was

The statue of Ole Bull in Loring Park in Minneapolis was executed by the Norwegian-American sculptor Jacob Fjelde.

In Oleana, that's where I'd like to be,
And not drag the chains of slavery in Norway.
 Ole—Ole—Ole—oh! Oleana!

Aye, go to Oleana, there you'll begin to live!
The poorest wretch in Norway is a count over there.
 Ole—Ole—Ole—oh! Oleana!

 Ditmar Meidell

consecrated with a solemn ceremony. Thirty-one hurrahs were shouted, one for each of the states in the union and three for Bull. The founder then spoke to the people in such moving terms that they lifted their hands toward heaven and vowed "that they would do their utmost to prove themselves worthy." Afterward Bull fascinated his audience with his masterful violin playing. The engineer and Bull laid out lots and founded the town of Oleana; they built a hotel for newcomers, and Oleana became, writes Jahr, the name of "the Northmen's new home."

Ole Bull had declared that he would "found a 'New Norway' dedicated to freedom, baptized in independence, and protected by the Union's mighty flag." But Oleana, the grandiose enterprise, with the great stretches of land Bull had bought and the hopes for a happy future that were placed in it, lasted only a year. In September, 1853, Bull sold the land to the original owners at a great loss. Most of the settlers had by then moved from the colony.

The reasons the Potter county colony failed lay, to be sure, partly in Bull's impracticality and lack of business acumen. His lofty and unrealistic plans could hardly have been carried out at any time. Because of several circumstances, the venture was in fact doomed to failure from the beginning. Bull had fallen into the hands of swindlers who sold him land to which they did not have clear title. This fraud cost Bull a considerable sum of money. Most colonists were besides very poor and dependent on Bull's generosity, and they relied perhaps more on him than on their own initiative. Bull would have had to support them for many years before they could have managed on their own, and this not even his fortune could have done. The soil was meager, and the hilly and wooded land was hard to clear.

There are still reminders of the brief experiment. In 1920 the Ole Bull State Park was established on 120 acres of the original purchase. Most people, however, remember the colony because of Ditmar Meidell's satirical ballad "Oleana"—for some, it illustrates the unrealistic expectations many had of America in general.

Pioneer Life in the Norwegian Settlements

One may well ask why Ole Bull did not found his colony in the Middle West, in the heart of the

Above: The Moravian church was started by Nils Otto Tank in Green Bay, Wisconsin, in 1851. Hjalmar Rued Holand describes Tank as "the most remarkable Norwegian emigrant to emigrate to America." He was the only son of Carsten Tank, the proprietor of the Rød estate near Fredrikstad. Nils Otto Tank joined the Moravian sect in Germany, and in 1850 he came to America. Here he assumed the responsibility for relocating a group of impoverished Norwegian Moravians from Milwaukee. That fall he guided these people, who in addition to children numbered 42 adults, to an area he had purchased south of the town of Green Bay. Here he established the Moravian community of Ephraim. It became another example of colonization efforts that failed; the colony soon dissolved.

Norwegian area of settlement. Most of the dissatisfied Oleana colonists went there eventually. It is possible that Bull avoided this region because he feared the poor health conditions that prevailed.

Below: A cholera graveyard on the farm of Dennis Houge near Norway in La Salle county, Illinois. "During the cholera epidemic in the Fox River settlement, Lars Brimsoe, being a carpenter, was employed in making coffins for the dead. In order that Lars himself should not be exposed to the terrible disease, the neighbors would run the boards through a window into his shop, where he made the coffins, which were returned through the same opening in the wall. For a time orders came in faster than he could fill them." (Rasmus B. Anderson, The First Chapter of Norwegian Immigration, Madison, 1895.)

A cholera epidemic ravaged the Norwegian settlements in 1849, and this disease, which could cause death in a few hours, flared up again in succeeding years. It disappeared, however, after 1854. Malaria was perhaps an even greater burden on the settlers than cholera. They were never rid of it, and year after year it could drain them of their strength and zest for life. Malaria went by many names, among them "climate fever" and "swamp fever," as well as "cold fever" and "ague." Claus L. Clausen tells in *Festskrift til Den norske synodes jubileum* (Anniversary Book for the Norwegian Synod), 1903, that the people of Muskego were so stricken by "the fever" in 1843 that "only in one single house was no one affected . . . almost daily someone died." Poverty in Muskego aggravated the misery. Malaria attacked settlers in all areas where marshes had to be cleared, and at times the consequences were catastrophic, as they had been in Beaver Creek. The infection was often spread by newcomers who had contracted it on the long journey, as was the case in Muskego. Typhoid fever, pneumonia, and especially tuberculosis also inflicted suffering upon the settlers.

One alarming aspect of pioneer life was an enormously high infant mortality rate. For Upper Coon Valley Lutheran Church, Holand has shown with the help of church records that in the pioneer period from 80 to 90 percent of all deaths were children below the ages of five—from 1861 to 1870, 114 of 133 deaths.

Unsanitary conditions and unhealthy storage of food must take most of the blame for the frequent illnesses. The pioneers lived in small and poorly ventilated log cabins, sod huts, and even dugouts in a hillside. Because there were ample woods in the Wisconsin settlements, log cabins and board shanties were probably the most common forms of dwelling. They were small, frequently with only one room and a loft, and crowded. From Koshkonong one hears of seven young couples for a time sharing such a cabin. The pioneer doctor J. W. Magelssen related from the same area that sick and well people often had to share a bed because of lack of space, and food and milk were placed uncovered on shelves not far from the beds of the patients. Medical attention was of course a rarity. Most people had to get by with home remedies or rely on people who had taught themselves medical skills or seek

the help of one of the many quacks who frequented the colonies offering miracle cures for all kinds of afflictions.

The Neighborhood Gave Strength and Solidarity

Poverty and illness might cause people to become despondent, and, as Søren Bache reported from Muskego, they "damned their journey here." But pioneer life also had its bright side. A settler from "Indielandet," a pioneer settlement in the north-central part of Wisconsin, recounted how "the whole neighborhood was like one big family. Everyone was equally rich or equally poor depending on how one views it. They stuck together in good weather and bad, under difficult circumstances, in work and in need, in other words, in everything." They transferred to America the old Norwegian custom of community projects and helped each other with barn raising and husking bees. Such solidarity gave them strength to endure the hardships of pioneer life.

In the Norwegian settlements as much of the old peasant culture as possible was preserved; in many respects the settlers continued to live much as they would have in the Norwegian home community. Norwegian language was in use, old customs and traditions lived on in the preparation of food and in clothing, and important ceremonies associated with baptisms, weddings, and funerals were carried out in the time-honored fashion. There were especially many traditions at Christmas, and these lived on in changed surroundings. Berge Hæve, a pioneer settler, tells of a Vossing settlement in Wisconsin in the 1850s where people came together during the holidays, and for weddings and baptisms, and "if they could get hold of a fiddler, they danced and had fun—much more than they have now."

In the more pietistic settlements, however, where Haugeans worked against worldly customs, less of the peasant culture survived. For the most part there was little surplus for festivities and luxuries; all their energy was absorbed in the daily struggle for subsistence. The pioneers were self-sufficient to a marked degree. During the pioneer period it was not uncommon for the women to card, spin, and weave the wool their

sheep gave, although store-bought cloth came into use very early in some settlements. A new settler would acquire a cow or two and many pigs. The latter were easy to feed. The historian J. S. Johnson described pork as "the firm foundation on which the settler [in Rock Prairie] based his nourishment." But hunting and fishing also contributed to the food supply.

The Land Had to be Cleared

The land had to be cleared before it could produce, and in a mixture of prairie land and forest this could be accomplished fairly simply, although the equipment was often primitive and generally made by the individual settler. Large plows for clearing the land had to be bought, however; it required four or five pairs of oxen to pull a heavy plow. Several settlers might invest in one together. But it was of course quite common for a settler to be alone with a small plow pulled by a single team of oxen when land was being cleared!

In forest regions the work was much heavier. Hans Gasmann wrote of his own property that "the trees stand at a suitable distance from each other, so that one can plow between them." The first year it might be necessary to plant among the trees. From the same district in Wisconsin Per Hagen described how the settlers worked together to clear each other's land: they felled the timber, gathered it in huge piles, and set fire to it. One left the roots, said Hagen, which rotted away in seven or eight years. But it was much more common to start "grubbing" the roots as soon as the forest was felled. Here the women participated: "It was not an uncommon sight in pioneer times to see women standing beside their husbands chopping and pulling at grub roots, so that the earth flew around them," a pioneer related.

In winter many men found employment as lumberjacks and earned much needed cash; opportunity for such income often brought settlers to a particular region. The lumber camps in the vicinity of Eau Claire in west-central Wisconsin consequently attracted many Norwegian pioneers in the 1850s. A decade or so thereafter Norwegians made their way to Michigan's forests and copper and iron mines for the same reason: quick income from work they were familiar with.

Norwegians in the Wiota area of Wisconsin had earlier found supplementary work in the lead mines there. Some Norwegians obtained work as day laborers with Yankee farmers or established Norwegian Americans. By working for a Norwegian-American farmer who had advanced him passage money to America a newcomer might repay his debt. The farmer could in this way get reliable and reasonable help from his Norwegian home community. The newcomer frequently moved into the pioneer cabin, and in a transitional period formed a kind of Norwegian-American cotter class. The relatively few Norwegians in Michigan—in 1870 only 1,254—rarely took up farming, however. The agricultural regions were farther west.

The move from a rural life in Norway to farming in America has been described as a conservative emigration, a move to preserve a traditional way of life. In this connection, though, it is im-

The women have taken out their carding combs and spinning wheels to be photographed by Andrew Dahl. This picture is from the 1870s.

portant to bear in mind that the immigrant who began to cultivate the land was the one who faced the greatest adjustment. American agriculture was very different from Norwegian. As soon as the settler had cleared a small piece of land, it was possible to grow corn and potatoes, important components in the pioneer diet. "Many were happy," writes Holand, "when they could set their table with salt and potatoes." The salt had to be bought, and it was expensive, three cents a pound. For some other items, they could find substitutes. They made a tea they called *bostathe* from a grass, and coffee beans might be stretched by adding a mixture of ground fried potatoes and barley.

Economic Growth and Progress

Wheat was the most important cash crop, and after a few years the settler could bring a small surplus to market. One of the most interesting rigs the settlers used was the *kubberulle*—a genuine Norwegian-American word. The wheels of the *kubberulle* were solid disks sawed from an oak log, or *kubbe,* and the simple vehicle was usually made entirely of wood. In such a wagon pulled by oxen the settler transported a load of wheat to the nearest market. The distance to market was frequently long, and the roads were poor; the settlers therefore joined forces and went together to town with their wheat.

In many districts, like the prosperous agricultural areas in Coon Prairie and Coon Valley and Koshkonong, Norwegian farmers took up dairying and delivered milk to a cheese factory and, after the turn of the century, to the dairies that were then starting.

Norwegians participated in the economic growth and rapid expansion of the Middle West. They soon learned about new agricultural products and new farming methods, perhaps as farm laborers with a Yankee farmer, and later adopted them themselves. For example, they began early to cultivate tobacco; in Wisconsin tobacco growing was in fact soon thought of as a Norwegian speciality. Better farming required better communications, and the railroad, when it came, provided easy access to markets. Small towns that were commercial centers also came into being. Many Norwegians made their homes in these towns, practiced their earlier trades or accepted whatever work was available. A small Norwegian business class also emerged and tried to provide their countrymen with needed goods and services. In the small town of Pigeon Falls in the Trempealeau valley of Wisconsin, with a

A load of logs being hauled to the World's Fair in Chicago in 1893. The load was transported to the Ontonogan River in Michigan by Thomas Nester. It was the largest load ever pulled by 2 horses; the height of the load was 33 feet and 3 inches, and it weighed 144 tons. 9 flat cars were required to convey the logs to Chicago.

large Norwegian element, Norwegian-American merchants in the post Civil War period were able to beat their Yankee competitors in attracting Norwegian business. An enterprising man like Peter Ekeren from Biri in Norway built a mill near the small town, invested in various business ventures, and operated a country store.

The pioneer period in this way gradually ended; a new period got under way, and the Norwegian settlements began to be important agricultural areas. A market economy replaced the self-sufficiency of the pioneer household. During the 1860s many people expressed an optimistic faith in the future, and pride at what had been achieved. There were new and larger houses, a better way of life, and a small surplus of energy and resources. In 1869 Svein Nilsson

Right: The farm of H. Hauge near Madison, Wisconsin. The fine herd of cattle gives evidence of prosperity. The picture was taken by Andrew Dahl around 1875.

wrote about the fortunate Koshkonong settlement: "Less than three times ten years ago poor toilers came to this region; now they are well-off, some of them even rich. They have changed a wilderness into flourishing meadows and fertile fields which give bread to thousands." The situation was hardly this favorable for all settlers or in every Norwegian settlement, but there was a common conviction that progress was being made and that prosperity would come. An irrepressible optimism and will to succeed characterized Norwegian settlers during the pioneer years.

The Relationship with the Homeland

"We have it good, *but America is not Norway.* There is always something strange and unfamiliar about everything here." In this way a newcomer in the 1850s expressed the dilemma of the immigrants, their position between the old and the new. Norwegians in America might suffer from homesickness and a sense of loss, become overwhelmed by memories of conditions and people they had left behind, and long for a life that belonged to the past. Such emotions were, however, mostly suppressed; they did not intrude into the daily toil, and the immigrants,

needing to justify their own decision to emigrate, rapidly developed a great loyalty toward their new surroundings. They therefore engaged with zeal in the debate over emigration and were on the watch for information about America that they deemed misleading.

The pioneer pastor J. W. C. Dietrichson warned in Norwegian newspapers in the 1840s against being tempted to emigrate, for "America is in truth neither the Paradise nor the Land of Canaan that people dream about." Another example of a negative view of America and emigration is the little book Peter Testman published in 1839 following an unsuccessful stay in America. He had written the book, he insisted, to show "if possible . . . that the North American States are far from able to offer their immigrants all the advantages that so many like to dream about after they have been taken in by several encouraging and appealing, but still false accounts, of the older emigrants' fate and present condition." Well known also are the reports by another dissatisfied emigrant, Sjur J. Haaeim from Granvin in Hardanger. In 1840 *Bergens Tidende* (Bergen Times) printed a letter from him, dated April 22, 1838, which had been sent to Bishop Jacob Neumann. The letter writer concluded that he longed to return to Norway "if the Almighty God would help him with that much capital." Haaeim was able to go back to Norway in 1841, and next year, probably with Bishop Neumann's assistance, he published his statement against emigration, *Oplysninger om forhol-*

dene i Nordamerika, især forsaavidt de derhen udvandrede norskes skjæbne angaaer (Information about Conditions in North America, especially as They Concern the Fate of Emigrated Norwegians).

An Official Report

During the years 1847 and 1848 an especially insightful description of conditions in America was

A kubberulle built by Lars Davidson Reque about 1840. Both the name and the vehicle are genuine Norwegian-American constructions. The wheels were made of disks sawed from an oak log, or kubbe.

written by Ole Munch Ræder, who had been sent to America with a stipend to study the jury system. His many letters were printed in *Den Norske Rigstidende* (The Norwegian National Times), and they present an objective and varied picture of the immigrants and their circumstances. Munch Ræder's traveling companion from New York to the Middle West was the Norwegian and Swedish consul general, Adam Løvenskjold. Løven-skjold had been assigned to give an official report about conditions among Norwegian settlers. His report to the Norwegian government is dated October 15, 1847; the following year it was published in Bergen as a book. Because the two men visited many of the same places, there are several similarities between the two descriptions; but Løvenskjold's official report sees the immigrants in a much more negative light: they lived in wretched houses, there was poverty and illness, Norwegians enjoyed little respect, they were slovenly and ignorant—circumstances that led Americans to call them "Norwegian Indians."

It was of course well that overly optimistic reports about opportunities in America should be modified—American streets were in fact not paved with gold. The authorities felt a certain responsibility to obtain reliable information, and

In America the milking chores were not performed exclusively by women, as was the custom in Norway. Here it is Eric Braarud who completes the morning chores in Town of Queen, Polk county, Minnesota, in July, 1903.

by also presenting the drawbacks, even if in a biased manner, they enabled potential emigrants to make up their minds more sensibly about the emigration alternative.

Those who were already at home in America turned to the Norwegian public to give their views. As expected, they objected immediately to the negative descriptions. Johan R. Reiersen attacked the claims Dietrichson made in his letters to Norwegian newspapers and characterized them as distorted and false. It is even more interesting that the immigrants acted together to counteract negative reports of America. In the fall of 1840, for example, Anders Flage had written on behalf of all Vossings in Chicago to his home community Voss in order to refute information that one Sjur Jørgensen Lokrheim, probably identical with Sjur Haaeim, had sent to Norway. "It is not true," wrote Flage, "that it is as bad in America as that Sjur Valdres has written. . . .

We have enough food and clothes." A second step was taken in the fall of 1848 when news of Løvenskjold's report created great bitterness among the immigrants. As a result, a group of Vossings in Chicago organized a "correspondence society" to systematically correct the erroneous information "concerning political as well as religious conditions in America, and in

The main street of the small town of Stoughton, Wisconsin, in 1869. "What especially has attracted my attention to Stoughton is the strongly marked Norwegian character of the town. A newcomer from Norway who arrives here will be surprised indeed to find in the heart of the country, more than a thousand miles from his landing place, a town where language and way of life so unmistakably remind him of his native land." (Svein Nilsson, Billed-Magazin, *May 14, 1870.)*

regard to Norwegians who have come here." This correspondence society sent eight letters to Voss in Norway. It is likely that these reports had a greater impact on Norwegian peasants than the official descriptions did.

The Muskego Manifesto

The most dramatic defense of the immigrants' new home and their move to America is perhaps a document that has become known as the Muskego Manifesto. It is in the form of an open letter signed by eighty men, dated January 6, 1845, and inserted in *Morgenbladet* on April 1 of that year. The manifesto is a noble and eloquent expression of the faith Norwegian pioneers had in their future in America; it indicated a self-assertion and an independence that have deep roots in the Norwegian peasant class. Johannes Johansen

Ingeborg Helgesdatter Naevra (1831-1916), born in Sigdal and married to Erick Olson, emigrated in 1867 and settled in Manitowoc county in Wisconsin.

wrote the document. The signers acknowledge difficulties, "caused by many kinds of illnesses and by lack of the most essential necessities of life." But these could be overcome, and future prospects were bright. "We harbor no hopes," the manifesto declares, "of acquiring wealth, but we live under a liberal government in a fertile land, where freedom and equality prevail in religious as well as civil affairs, and without any special permission we can enter almost any profession and make an honest living; this we consider to be more wonderful than riches, for by diligence and industry we can look forward to an adequate income, *and we thus have no reason to regret our decision to move here.*" These were people who knew what they were talking about and who had made a fateful resolution for themselves and for their children.

A warning against emigrating.
Ole: Where are you going?
Peer: I am going to America.
Ole: Go back home to your bowl of porridge, Peer. In America you will find hard work but little food, as you can see by looking at me. I come straight from there now.
Peer: Yes, it can't be easy to live there. When you left, you were about the same size as I am, and now you don't seem to me to be very bulky. I think I will turn back, Ole.
  (Illustrert Folkeblad, 1856)

Schoolhous and La de Farm p. Fosston Minn
This Country vos settlet 1886 all Timber
And only Skandinavien.

An Immigrant Community Develops

In a new and alien environment it was the church that became a focal point for many immigrants. Norwegian-American newspapers gave information about small and large issues that it was important to know about in America. In this manner the church and the press became fundamental social institutions in the Norwegian immigrant community.

A schoolhouse on Lade Farm near Fosston, Minnesota, in 1895. Norwegian Americans engaged in a lively debate about whether to send their children to separate Norwegian schools or to the American common school.

A Norwegian Colony on American Soil

In 1860 there were in the states of the Upper Midwest—Illinois, Wisconsin, Iowa, and Minnesota—about fifty-five thousand people of Norwegian birth or ancestry. About 68 percent of them had been born in Norway. In other regions of the United States there were perhaps a thousand Norwegians. The Norwegians in the Middle West consisted mostly of families, there were few single adults, and a large percentage of the children had been born in America. The statistics give the impression of a firmly rooted and growing Norwegian-American community. Norwegian settlers lived in compact colonies scattered over an enormous area. There were lines of communication between them, an increasing sense of solidarity was visible, and a Norwegian-American identity was emerging. "Our people in America . . . already act in unity and are thereby protected against foreign influence, since the internal relationship among them is stronger than between them and other people who live here," Ole Munch Ræder wrote in 1847. The new Norwegian-American identity may partly be seen as the self-assertion of an immigrant people toward the motherland. In this respect Norwegians acted like most colonists. But an even more important determinant of strengthened group solidarity was confrontation with other nationalities in America. Rivalry among the many ethnic groups stimulated Norwegians, as it did other nationalities, to attach greater importance to their own ethnic merits. In America they came to feel like one people with a unique Norwegian national heritage.

The homeland never took the initiative to attend to the immigrants' spiritual and physical needs. Norwegian authorities did not consider this to be their responsibility. Among Norwegians abroad, in the scattered colonies in America, there was an urgent need for men with university training, for doctors and pastors, who would find a wide field for activity there. Before 1860, however, very few, hardly half a hundred, Norwegians with university education emigrated. Among these were a handful with medical training. Conditions and earnings did not seem attractive to those who thought about making a living in the immigrant settlements. Hans Christian Brandt came to Illinois in 1840 to practice medicine among Norwegians. He was the first Norwegian doctor among them, but he soon sought a better income from American patients in Indiana, where, according to Svein Nilsson in *Billed-Magazin*, "he is said to have made a fortune of no mean proportions."

The best known of the pioneer doctors was Johan Christian Brotkorb Dundas (Dass), a descendant of a brother of the poet-pastor Petter Dass, and a distinctive personality. He emigrated in 1847 and became a doctor in Cambridge, Wisconsin, where he served Norwegians in their neighborhoods on Koshkonong. Dundas was, writes Nilsson, considered both by his compatriots and by Americans "as one of the ablest doctors in the Northwest." Another Norwegian-educated doctor was Gerhard S. C. H. Paoli, who emigrated in 1846 and who in the 1850s practiced medicine among Norwegians in Chicago. Both Dundas and Paoli were politically liberal. Freethinking men of their stature introduced a new dimension and new impulses into immigrant life. They were a counterweight to the strong pietistic influence.

The clergy was represented in greater numbers. Still, only one instance is known in which the emigrants themselves made an effort to recruit a religious leader from the Norwegian Lutheran State Church. In 1839 the emigrants on *Emilie* had requested of the department of ecclesiastical affairs that a theological student, Peter Valeur, should be ordained so that he could accept a pastoral call in America. The attempt did not succeed, even though the matter was thoroughly considered by the bureaucracy.

Because the hierarchy in the Church of Norway showed little concern for the emigrants, the university-trained pastors who wanted to work in the Norwegian colonies acted on their own. And later, when organized religious life was established, they went to the Middle West at the request and calling of Norwegian-American congregations. Motives might of course vary, but there is no doubt that many felt a strong mission call. Others perhaps hoped for greater influence in the new situation, since official positions in Norway were becoming less certain. The families of the official class were larger than in the other social classes, and there was an ever greater demand for positions. Still, most clergymen preferred to await an appointment in Norway rather than seek an insecure future among their compatriots in America, a fact that Norwegian-American churchmen frequently complained about. But some did choose to go, and the official families—with names like Koren, Brandt, Munch, Preus, and Dietrichson—were well represented in the Norwegian-American clergy.

Lay Preachers Served the Immigrants

It was, however, opponents of the orthodox clergy and of the practices of the state church who cared for the religious needs of the immigrants in the early period, lay preachers who held devotional meetings in the immigrant huts in the Norwegian settlements. "During these years," writes J. A. Bergh in his pious account *Den norsk lutherske kirkes historie i Amerika* (The History of the Norwegian Lutheran Church in America) in 1914, "when no ordained servant of God called the scattered sheep together around the Word and the Sacraments, these lay people in innocence broke the Bread of Life for hungry souls. And the Lord recognized their work." Even Heg, for instance, and other leaders in Muskego, conducted prayer meetings in a Haugean spirit in Heg's barn and baptized the children; other preachers in addition took it upon themselves to distribute the sacraments. In Norway lay preachers had worked in the shadow of the state church, where ordained ministers administered the sacraments and provided other religious services. This was a situation the lay preachers could not replace, and a widespread desire for a formal church organization therefore arose.

The lay preachers differed both in social background and in spiritual training from the pastors educated at the university. They had their roots in peasant society, and their formal education was limited to the normal school, the only educational opportunity for most gifted rural boys

Mikkel Berg at his evening devotion in Mount Horeb, Wisconsin, ca. 1900. "We were not actually persecuted," says Gullik Gravdal, "but the 'Readers' were the subject of much hostile gossip and we had to endure ridicule and scorn on the part of those who did not share our views. I do not mean to say that this intolerance was the cause of our leaving, but it undoubtedly helped ripen our decision to leave a land where we were exposed to so many insults because our religious teachings did not agree entirely with the beliefs of the majority." (Svein Nilsson, Billed-Magazin, *April 24, 1869.)*

in the nineteenth century. Almost all the lay preachers were Haugeans. Ole Olsen Hetletvedt, one of the Sloopers of 1825, was thus both a schoolteacher and a Haugean. In his book, *First Chapter of Norwegian Immigration,* 1906, Rasmus B. Anderson says of Hetletvedt that he was the first person to gather the Fox River settlers "to hear God's word in the Haugean tradition." He also visited other Norwegian settlements, and in a meek and pious manner preached repentance and conversion. He simultaneously sold Bibles for the American Bible Society. Anderson mentions the names of seventeen lay preachers, among them Bjørn Hatlestad, who came in 1836, and Ole Heier the following year. Heier's vacillation in his faith illustrates the prevailing religious complexity: in his youth in Tinn he was a Haugean; he was converted to Mormonism; and he ended his days as a Baptist pastor.

A new religious revival had swept across the frontier areas of the West from around 1800. It was carried forward by emotional camp meetings, large religious gatherings where many thousand people for days on end sang and prayed and were incited to religious ecstasy by itinerant preachers. At the same time the various American church bodies were prompted by the prevalence of religious indifference and skepticism to organize mission societies. They evangelized through an intense home mission activity; the American Bible Society had as its goal to bring a Bible "to every home and every immigrant." The most successful religious groups were the Baptists, and to an even greater degree the Methodists. The deep emotional and spiritual nourishment these gave, the little importance they accorded to intellectual exegesis of Holy Writ, their democratic and popular character, and their anti-authoritarian attitude suited the society on the western frontier. It was in this fluid religious environment that Norwegian lay preachers worked.

Elling Eielsen Founded a Lay Church

When Elling Eielsen (Sundve) arrived in the Fox River settlement in the fall of 1839, after having emigrated the same year, it was immediately apparent that he towered far above the other revivalists. He was a zealous preacher and had even preached the Gospel to a group of immigrants when he passed through Chicago on September 22. The settlement by the Fox River had an abundance of religious instructors before Eielsen's arrival; almost every sect and religious conviction sought followers. Ingrid Semmingsen maintains that the people there were especially receptive to revivalists who preached conversion and repentance because of the form the Haugean movement had taken among people from Rogaland, a dominant group in this settlement.

Eielsen was from the farm Sundve at Voss. Like his predecessor and great model, Hans Nielsen Hauge, he had crisscrossed his homeland and in addition visited the other Nordic countries. Eielsen proclaimed the spiritual life, a complete surrender to God, and a rigidly moral conduct, renouncing all worldly pleasures. He shared with Hauge a Biblical interpretation that was within the framework of Lutheran orthodoxy. Eielsen emphasized a strict message of penance. Bergh says about him that it made an impact "when this tall, strong man . . . with thundering voice exhorted people to convert and admonished that if they did not do so, they would all perish." The historian Theodore C. Blegen has stressed that Eielsen's activity marked in a special way the transfer to America of tradi-

Elling Eielsen (1804-83) in his later years. "As a child he had read 'Pontoppidan's Catechism Explanation,' and it and nothing else did he want the children to learn. In it he had discovered a way to peace with God, and this he wanted to impart to the little ones. And when he found out that there were no books to be had, he borrowed a book from Lars Skavlem, Rock county, Wisconsin, and went all the way to New York—mostly on foot—in order to have it printed. . . . This was in 1842. That year the first book in the Norwegian language was printed in America." (J. A. Bergh, Den norsk-lutherske kirkes historie i Amerika, *Minneapolis, 1914.)*

tional Haugeanism: the freedom and independence of lay preaching, a congregation of the awakened, a pietistic life, the necessity of conversion, and an emphasis on the confession of the Lutheran church.

Eielsen's great accomplishment was to establish a low-church organization within the Lu-

theran free-church movement among Norwegian immigrants. His initial goal was to bring the Norwegian settlers back into the Lutheran fold and to counteract the acceptance other denominations had gained. In 1842 he built a combined dwelling and meeting house two miles southwest of the little town of Norway in La Salle county. In keeping with Norwegian low-church custom, he did not call it a church, but a *forsamlingshus*, an assembly house. Eielsen became convinced of the importance of an organized church life, and he recognized the immigrants' attachment to Lutheran sacraments and traditions. In 1843, at the wish of his followers, he let himself be ordained by a German Lutheran pastor, F. A. Hoffman. His position now became, writes the church historian E. Kr. Johnson, instead of that of a lay preacher, "the position of a traveling missionary pastor." He continued to spread his message, and "in almost every older, larger settlement there were a few who flocked around him," Bergh recounts.

Eielsen, however, lacked both skill and interest in organizing. It was his younger followers who made him see that he had to unite his scattered "little flock" in a church body. Besides, he feared the organizational endeavors of the high-church adherents, and finally, the firm structure of American religious life influenced his thinking. At a meeting on Jefferson Prairie, April 14 and 15, 1846, "a number of the widely scattered believers" formulated a constitution: the "Old Constitution," as it came to be known in the later church controversy. The new church body was to be called The Evangelical Lutheran Church in America, but is better known as Elling Eielsen's Synod, or just Eielsen's Synod, and the members as Ellingians. The synod was to be "in harmony with the true Lutheran faith and teaching," and completely low-church, so that "the ordinary ecclesiastical garments we want nothing of." Their constitution had more the appearance of being a testimony and a confession of faith than a practical arrangement for a church organization. Eielsen clung to it until his death.

Cooperation with Other Synods Foundered

Dissension soon appeared within this synod, which to such a high degree was marked by Eielsen's leadership and by his "striking obstinacy"

and orthodoxy. Several of the young leaders left the new synod in 1848, among them Paul Andersen and Ole Andrewson, both dynamic and capable men. Andersen had emigrated from Valdres in 1843, at age twenty-two. He studied at Beloit College in Wisconsin, at that time an ordinary high school, and was thereby brought under the influence of the more liberal American theology in his association with Presbyterians and Congregationalists. The very year he left Eielsen's Synod he organized the first Norwegian and Scandinavian church in Chicago with economic support from the American Home Mission Society.

This mission society, which was operated by Presbyterian and Congregational churches, supported Ole Andrewson as well. He also served as a missionary in Wisconsin and complained about religious "indifference, formalism, and superstition" as the greatest obstructions to his mission there. He was simultaneously in conflict with American revivalism, represented by Mormons, Baptists, Methodists, and other creeds.

These two, with Ole J. Hatlestad, a schoolteacher and lay preacher who had come to America in 1846, chose after the breach with the Ellingians to join the Franckean Synod, a decision that moved them closer to liberal American Lutheranism. The Franckeans were considered to be the most liberal of all the Lutherans in America. They were evangelistic and indifferent about doctrine. This first attempt to come to terms with American Lutheranism foundered. Three years later, in 1851, the dissenters from Eielsen's Synod withdrew, and joined English, Norwegian, and Swedish Lutherans to form the Northern Illinois Synod. This association lasted until 1860, when the Scandinavians withdrew and organized the Scandinavian Augustana Synod, with seventeen ministers serving thirty-six congregations. They justified their action by claiming that the English members of the Northern Illinois Synod were not faithful to the "unaltered Augsburg Confession." The very name of the new synod is evidence of high confessionalism and obedience to orthodox Lutheran dogma and teachings, the ground on which all cooperative efforts with established Lutheran church bodies stranded.

The High-Church Arrangement

The task Lutheran church leaders of every persuasion faced in America was to transform and adapt a state-church tradition to a viable free church based on voluntary organization and direct financial support from the members. The pastor Herman Amberg Preus, who emigrated in 1851, thought that there was "great ignorance and spiritual indifference" in the average immigrant from the common people. He thought that the typical immigrant practiced an uninspired, naive, and perfunctory Christianity, but that at the same time there was "an apparent veneration for sacred things, a reverence and lasting attachment to the faith and teachings that had been passed down from his forefathers." Preus believed that "the Norwegian immigrant therefore as a rule wishes his home in the west of America to be arranged in the familiar fashion with church, pastor, and school." The problem was that "he will find none of this when he settles and forms a community." In a society where state and church were separated, the Norwegian immigrants, "in order to preserve the faith of their fathers for themselves and their descendants, would have to organize congregations, procure ministers, and build churches on their own." It was a responsibility they had to be educated to accept, frequently by authoritative and strong-willed church leaders. The process would inevitably strengthen religious life.

The First Lutheran Congregation

The first Norwegian Lutheran congregation that came out of the state-church tradition was organized in Muskego, December 14, 1843, by Claus Lauritz Clausen, who was born on the island of Ærø in Denmark in 1820, the son of a merchant. He became the first shepherd for the two hundred souls in the congregation. Clausen was a sensitive and humane person who assumed a multitude of duties, as pastor and missionary, publisher and settlement organizer.

J. Magnus Rohne, a student of early Norwegian-American religious life, points out that the

Claus L. Clausen (1820-92) was influenced by Grundtvigian thought. He ministered to the first Lutheran congregation in Muskego, and he displayed understanding for the Haugeans.

Haugeans in Muskego and their sensible leaders —Heg, Bache, and Johansen—dissociated themselves from Eielsen's form of lay activity. His derisive attacks on the Lutheran clergy produced only disgust in Muskego, whereas they were a source of strength and influence in the Fox River settlement. The people from Rogaland at Fox River had come from districts in Norway that had experienced religious persecution, Rohne argues, but this was not true of those who had come from Numedal and Telemark and who had settled in the Muskego area. The latter therefore preferred a more positive church arrangement. But they rejected what they interpreted as high church practices.

In his beliefs Clausen placed himself between the two Lutheran extremes; he was therefore well qualified for his work in Muskego. In addition, he had been influenced by the emotional content and optimistic view of humankind in Grundtvigian doctrine. In a remarkable manner he combined this with a strong sympathy for Haugean pietism, which no doubt worked to his benefit in the strongly Haugean Muskego settlement.

Clausen had spent time in Norway investigating the possibility of working as a missionary in South Africa. There he had become acquainted with the Haugean Tollef Bache, who encouraged him to go instead to Muskego as a teacher of the children there; Bache was familiar with the need for teachers because of his connection with the settlers. Clausen took his advice and arrived in Muskego in August, 1843. He soon realized that there was a greater need for a pastor, and he therefore let himself be ordained by a German minister, L. F. E. Krause, on October 18 of that year, shortly after Eielsen's ordination. He remained in Muskego until 1845. Before the unfinished Muskego church could be used in the fall of 1844, Clausen officiated in Even Heg's barn. At Easter 1844 the first Norwegian Lutheran confirmation in America was conducted there.

A Pastor Ministers to the Immigrants

The first representative in America of the university-trained Norwegian pastors was J. W. C. Dietrichson, who came to the colonies in the Middle West in 1844, because "the holy Word we have in the Bible drove him to visit his countrymen in the distant West in order to preserve among them the Lutheran faith they brought with them from home," as Søren Bache noted in his diary. The nearly thirty-year-old Dietrichson was conservative and authoritarian, and Bache described him as "a giant from the old rocky Norwegian mountains." The idea of coming to America was, as with Clausen, first awakened by an interest in missionary work among non-Christian peoples, which gained ground in Norway in the 1840s. To minister to emigrated countrymen was not quite the same, but there was a great need for religious guidance, and Dietrichson was well equipped to test his strength among Norwegians on America's frontier.

He headed first for Muskego, and here he heard from Clausen about conditions among the immigrants. In his brief publication, *Reise blandt*

Left: J. W. C.
Dietrichson (1815-83)
was the first
university-trained
pastor among the
Norwegian im-
migrants. The pastor
Ulrik Vilhelm Koren
writes about him in
Symra, 1905: "In
Christian III's church
ordinance there is a
provision that states:
'Pastors shall always
be dressed in the
right garments.' This
he carefully observed,
and it is told how he
standing in his
wagon had trans-
ported firewood or
water, and occasion-
ally 'other substance'
dressed in his long
ministerial garments
and with a ruffed col-
lar around his neck
which had lost its
starch, so that it
hung as best it
could."

*Right: Under these
oak trees on Knud
Aslaksen Juve's farm
Dietrichson conducted
a service with com-
munion on September
2, 1844.*

de norske emigranter (Journey among Norwegian Emigrants), Dietrichson characterized Clausen as "an attractive servant of the Lord with a sound Christian and churchly understanding," and found nothing irregular about his ordination. Clausen had initiated cooperation with Elling Eielsen, and they had even conducted joint religious services in Heg's barn, but already in the fall of 1843, the very year Clausen came to Muskego, there developed a definite break between them. Dietrichson also came to regard Eielsen as an adversary and his anticlericalism as a personal insult. He accused Eielsen of "having assumed uncalled the holy office of pastor." They hurled bitter accusations at each other—their conflicting views could not be reconciled. Lay activity was anarchy in Dietrichson's eyes. He was besides influenced by Grundtvigianism, perhaps in a more intellectual manner than Clausen, and he therefore had little sympathy for the pietism he found in the Ellingians. He regarded Eielsen as a dangerous visionary. Eielsen on his side reproved

Dietrichson for being more concerned with form than substance; he discovered in him everything he disliked in the Norwegian state-church priests. Eielsen viewed him as a man insensitive to genuine religious feelings.

The split in Norwegian-American Lutheranism became thereby a fact. Both parties had their adherents, and mutual denunciations strengthened and clarified the dividing lines between them. Lay activity was far removed from the prevailing principles of the state church in Norway. It was therefore inconceivable that the two persuasions should be able to coexist in one church organization.

Dietrichson pursued his mission with unusual zeal and energy. After having preached to a large audience in Muskego, where his "letter of ordination and vita" were read, he set out westward. He arrived in Koshkonong on August 30, 1844; here he made his headquarters. He also visited

Norwegians in Mineral Point, Wiota, and Jefferson Prairie. During his first stay at Koshkonong he conducted three services. "The first two times a barn was our church, and the third time a lovely meadow under a large oak tree served as our gathering place," Dietrichson relates. The communion service under the oak trees on the farm of Knud Aslaksen Juve on September 2 was remembered; the spot became a memorial to the pioneer church.

By October Dietrichson had gathered two congregations, consisting of forty families in the eastern part of Koshkonong and thirty in the western. The influential and productive letter writer Ole Trovatten, who had arrived in 1840, was the sexton and precentor for both congregations, which became known as East and West Koshkonong. Church construction began almost at once, and at New Year's, 1844-1845, two new edifices were consecrated. Membership in the congregations required a pledge to acquiesce in "the churchly organization that our fatherland Norway's church ritual determines"; to call or accept as a pastor only one who "according to the Norwegian Lutheran Church's order is a properly called and correctly ordained minister," and to show him, "as your ecclesiastical authority, the respect and obedience a church member is obliged to show his pastor." The expanding group of people who wanted an organized church, who were familiar with a mild church administration in Norway, had no way of knowing about Dietrichson's extreme tendencies in church discipline, and they enthusiastically agreed to his demands. Using Dietrichson's guidelines, more congregations were soon founded, at first set up as annexes to either Muskego or Koshkonong and later raised to independent status.

An organized religious life was instituted under difficult circumstances. The pioneer pastors shared the hardships and privations of life on the frontier with the flock they gathered. Dietrichson's existence as a bachelor in the tiny one-room cabin that served as parsonage called forth a longing for a more refined life and a companion of his own class. He felt, in addition, that his mission in America had been completed. In June, 1845, he went to Norway, and the following year he married Charlotte Josine Omsen Müller. Before he had left Koshkonong, however, he had received a letter of call from the congregations there—and in September, 1846, he returned to fill the call. During his stay in Norway he had tried in vain to create interest in the religious needs of the emigrants and to persuade theological students to work among Norwegians in America.

After a number of individual congregations had been formed, the next stop would naturally be to organize them into a church body. But when Dietrichson returned to Norway permanently in 1850, he had not succeeded in accomplishing this goal. In 1849 he had called a meeting at Koshkonong of delegates elected by the congregations and presented a constitution. This meeting did not, however, produce a church association.

A Synod Comes into Being

C. L. Clausen, then serving congregations in southern Wisconsin, and Hans Andreas Stub, who had come from Norway in 1848 to become a pastor in Muskego, cooperated with Dietrichson in 1849, but neither had been able to attend the Koshkonong meeting.

Work was resumed in January, 1851, at a conference in Rock Prairie, and an organizational form and a constitution were actually adopted. But a year later a new meeting in Muskego declared this action to be temporary, as H. A. Preus had detected Grundtvigian fallacies in the constitution, which had been based on the one prepared by Dietrichson in 1849. From that time on, Preus, who for forty years served as pastor in Spring Prairie, Wisconsin, appeared as a leader in the establishment of a synod. The lay church and the university-trained ministers were both anti-Grundtvigian; it is therefore interesting to note the influence of this orientation, which affected both Clausen and J. W. C. Dietrichson. It was first and foremost the primacy of the church in Grundtvigian doctrine that was incompatible with Lutheran orthodox emphasis on the Bible as the only basis for doctrine. The Grundtvigians held that the basis for doctrine was also to be found in the Apostles' Creed and in the living word when the congregation proclaimed Christ. N. F. S. Grundtvig's "matchless discovery" was that Christ was present in his word in the congregation when it gathered around the baptismal font or the communion table. The orthodox clergy preached that the Old and New Testaments were the only source and norm for Christian faith and life.

The Grundtvigian stumbling block in the constitution was a sentence stating that the church's doctrine was "what is revealed through the Word of God in our baptismal pact and in the Old and New Testament's canonical books." After the objectionable words about "our baptismal pact" had been removed, a new conference at East Koshkonong church on February 5, 1853, consisting of six ministers and forty-five lay delegates from thirty-eight congregations, adopted an acceptable church constitution. It was submitted to the congregations, and in early October of the same year a meeting at Rock Prairie approved this document as applicable within the church. The group adopted as its name the Synod of the Norwegian-Evangelical Lutheran Church in America; it was commonly referred to as the Norwegian Synod, or merely the Synod.

The immigrant church on the prairies and in the wooded groves in the Middle West, with its high-church ritual and its ceremony, gave the settlers a sense of solemnity and security. The accustomed and time-honored forms were a comfort and a firm point of orientation in the new environment. Within a free-church framework the Norwegian Synod retained as many of the state-church principles as possible. It adopted the ritual of the Church of Norway and its ecclesiastical garments, defended the Augsburg Confession's ban against lay preaching, was dogmatic in its teachings, and asserted churchly authority in all questions of doctrine. The Synod was to an unusual extent preoccupied with doctrine, with determining what were the Bible's true teachings. It considered the congregation to be a geographic unit, a Norwegian *sogn*, or parish. The name of the congregation was often applied to the entire settlement.

The Norwegian Synod was now the largest gathering of Norwegian Lutherans in America; around 1860 it consisted of twenty-nine ministers and one hundred congregations. From the 1850s

on it can with some justification be deemed the Norwegian church in America. The Scandinavian Augustana Synod, which represented a broad-church position, and the low-church Eielsen's Synod gathered fewer Norwegians. Some congregations remained outside all church organizations. The Muskego church, for instance, refrained from joining the Synod in spite of the fact that H. A. Stub, a Synod pastor, continued to serve there, and the congregation did not send delegates to the church conference in 1853. The situation indicated the Haugean strength among the immigrants. Haugeanism had a greater impact and following than statistics show. It was splintered and poorly organized,

Above: A second West Koshkonong church was built in 1852 as an octagonal structure that could seat 800 people. It was rebuilt in 1893.

Right: This picture was taken by Andrew Dahl at the dedication of East Blue Mound's church in Wisconsin in the 1870s. A long table is set up outside for the festive banquet. The scene is a reminder of the importance of the social aspects of church life.

but there were adherents of lay activity and of Haugean pietism and religious intensity everywhere in the Norwegian colonies.

The Funkelien Case

Church discipline, enforcement of high-church authority, met opposition both from churchly people and from Haugeans. Still, powerful pastors were to a certain degree able to maintain high-church Lutheran authority. It was necessary to establish discipline within the congregation. An especially well-known episode may illuminate to what extent this was possible. Halvor Christian Pedersen Funkelien, assumed to be the first immigrant from the town of Kongsberg, came to Koshkonong in 1842 and joined J. W. C. Dietrichson's congregation when it was organized in 1844. He soon got into a quarrel with the strict parson because of his "drinking, brawling, and blaspheming the most holy things," to quote Dietrichson himself. Hjalmar Rued Holand, who claimed to know the story as it was told by "most of the old pioneers," characterized Funkelien as "a drunkard and a quibbling troublemaker of the worst kind."

Dietrichson had him excommunicated from the congregation by the rules of the church ritual, and Funkelien could now attend services only if he sat in a special pew at the back of the church. Funkelien threatened to do harm to the pastor and to set fire to the church. The first Sunday after Easter, March 30, 1845, he showed up in church and occupied a seat in the front pew. Holand, who frequently preferred the most colorful and probably somewhat embroidered version of existing alternatives, relates that Funkelien regularly produced a bottle during the sermon and took "a little swig." When Dietrichson could no longer stand to watch this insult, he shouted: "I cannot preach any longer with this sinful, abominable brute drinking liquor in church! Throw him out!" What is certain is that Funkelien was removed from the church by force. He brought legal action against the pastor, the sexton, and two other men who had evicted him, and accused them of assault and battery. The reformer and Quaker Bjørn Andersen Kvelve, embittered by the Norwegian state church and officialdom, spoke for him, and the sympathetic jury, consisting of men with a feeling for frontier democracy and justice, agreed and sentenced Dietrichson to pay a fine. During the court proceedings Dietrichson had been accused of setting himself up as a "Pope." His authority must therefore be restricted. This time he had only ordered a man to be thrown out of the church, but, as Dietrichson himself relates, "who could guarantee that, if I had ordered the man's head to be taken off, this also would not have occurred."

Funkelien's legal victory may of course be interpreted as evidence of freedom and lack of class considerations in the dispensation of justice; in America officials could not treat commoners as they pleased. The judgment does not seem, however, to have concerned Dietrichson greatly. His defense had been based on the principle of nonintervention by the state in religious affairs. But what was important for Dietrichson was that within his own congregation he had preserved another principle—namely the minister's right to exercise church discipline. In the congregation authority had triumphed over freedom.

The Strength of Religion

The Funkelien affair was, according to Holand, an occasion for people on Koshkonong "to talk about something other than the price of wheat." What place the church had in people's minds, compared for instance to a desire for material success, is difficult to say. Rohne suggests, as H. A. Preus had done earlier, that the immigrants should be seen as being spiritually immature, and that a deeper religious consciousness was a product of the hardships of pioneer life. Rohne also thinks that there existed a certain distaste for religion, an aversion to submitting to conditions they had left, and that the pastor might become a symbol of such past conditions. Even those who joined the church might want only an occasional visit in order to show respectability through church attendance. It took time to change such an attitude.

The church increased its hold as the century progressed. All Lutheran congregations, from the high-church tradition to the low, were puritanical in the sense that they consistently assailed frivolity and worldly pleasures, drinking, dancing, wearing of frivolous clothes, and breaches of the Sabbath. The Norwegian Synod had perhaps a greater appreciation than the other Lutheran synods of the popular aspects of peasant culture, in legend, folktales, and music. But the puritan impulse grew stronger as a result of increased ecclesiastical authority, the expectations of American neighbors, and certain puritanical reform movements among the immigrants themselves. All American churches were congregations of believers, which the members had joined voluntarily; a state-church arrangement with automatic membership was in American eyes no church at all. Norwegian congregations were influenced in their religious life by the attitudes of American worshipers, and in the judgment of Marcus Lee Hansen the function of puritanism was to make Norwegian Lutheran congregations acceptable to Protestant churches in America.

The Influence of the Church outside the Congregations

The Lutheran Church was the largest and mightiest of the immigrant institutions; Lutheran and Norwegian were associated with one another inside as well as outside the Norwegian-American community. As an institution, the church enjoyed a central position. W. A. Passavant, a well-known Lutheran leader, told, following a visit in 1850 to Paul Andersen's church in Chicago, of a lively coming and going in the congregation. The exact number of members at any given time could not be determined, because the church "gave a helping hand in brotherly love and Christian charity" to the many Norwegian newcomers. The pastor O. Paulson wrote of the many visitors to his church in the 1870s who wanted him to perform ecclesiastical functions, giving him "occasional income from baptisms and weddings." The church was thus an active force outside the congregational fold. For many who never formally joined, it stood in "the mind of the peasant on a high place," to use Bjørnson's words. It was a part of their lives, and it played a significant role in Norwegian-American neighborhoods. Earlier, Ole Munch Ræder had written about Norwegians who lived among other Norwegians; they attended church, but never became members, perhaps from stinginess or lack of en-

terprise. Voluntary church membership was something new and an obligation many hesitated to accept.

There was of course considerable "lethargic indifference," as Knut Takla laments in his *Det norske folk i de forenede Stater* (The Norwegian People in the United States), in 1913. Many immigrants were also previously repressed opponents of the church, who, according to J. A. Bergh, "rejoice at having escaped the state church." Rasmus B. Anderson describes many of the early im-

migrants as agnostics without any deep religious conviction.

Support of the church therefore varied from place to place. In 1869 Svein Nilsson recorded about the Luther Valley congregation at Rock Prairie: "The congregation . . . was until recently a member of the Norwegian Synod. There probably are a few families that belong to the Augustana Synod, as well as five families that have not joined any congregation." The five families without church affiliation are singled out. Church at-

Norwegian-American wedding outside the old Norway Grove church in DeForest, Wisconsin, ca. 1875. The bridal couple and guests are dressed according to American custom. Church weddings were common even for those who did not formally belong to the congregation.

tendance in this settlement must, if Nilsson's assessment is correct, have been very good. It was hardly this good in most instances, and Norwegians who lived isolated from their compatriots

"A Halling from the West." Wedding photo of Timar Levorsen Quarra and Sigrid Halvarsdatter, née Haraldseth, in Fessenden, North Dakota. This photograph suggests that it was customary for immigrants to wear traditional Norwegian peasant dress on festive occasions. Wearing such clothes created a sense of closeness to the old homeland.

were more frequently cut off from all organized religious life. The institutional growth was, however, impressive; but it is still important to bear in mind that it was always a minority of Norwegian Americans who sought church membership. In 1909 Takla found that scarcely one-third belonged to a Lutheran church. The percentage was perhaps higher in the country and lower in the cities, where secular forces were stronger. The pastor O. Gulseth regretted in 1916 that "the great multitude . . . has been lost in the struggle for material gain."

Other Faiths

The Lutheran faith was only one of several religious options. Religious pluralism has on occasion been portrayed as "religious confusion," by church historians and contemporary witnesses alike. It was especially pronounced among the immigrants at Fox River—"a spiritual hornets' nest," Bergh called it. When J. W. C. Dietrichson visited the area in April of 1845, he did not even attempt to organize a congregation, for "the religious confusion among the Norwegians was great." To him it was evidence of "how it goes with the poor emigrants in religious matters when no pastoral help comes to them from the church of the fatherland."

Church historians have generally regarded Elling Eielsen's role in the Fox River settlement as an effort to create order out of the confusion, to rescue the pioneers for the Lutheran faith, and to diminish the sectarian influence. When Eielsen arrived, Rasmus Anderson recounts, some Norwegians were Quakers, some Baptists, others Presbyterians, Methodists, Lutherans, Mormons, or even agnostics. "Everything was in chaos and confusion," he writes. Eielsen undoubtedly strengthened the Lutheran strain; it nevertheless remained but one religious alternative. At a time when the immigrants had no religious leadership, they had proved to be receptive to aggressive recruiting by large and successful American church bodies. From the mid-1830s these forces had worked on the immigrants without any protests from Norwegian state-church pastors. It was natural for the immigrants to be responsive to friendly American missionaries who invited them to join their flock.

The Quaker Societies

But even within the different creeds there were choices; there were conservative and liberal traditions in most of them. Lars Larsen, the leader of 1825, held on to orthodox Quakerism in America, whereas others sought "the inner light" in one of several factions among the Friends. As a rule Norwegian Quakers became members of American Quaker societies because they belonged to an international organization. By 1873 seventy-two of the 230 members of the Quaker Society in Stavanger had emigrated. In the Middle West there were also independent Norwegian societies of Friends. The Iowa historian H. F. Swansen tells that the largest colony of Norwegian Quakers developed beginning in the late 1850s in a settlement called Stavanger in Marshall county, Iowa. The state of Iowa received many Quakers from Norway. As early as 1842 a Quaker, Ommund Olson, built a meetinghouse in the Sugar Creek settlement in Lee county.

The Methodist church on Washington Prairie. A congregation was organized here in 1852, and Norwegian Methodism derived from it. "This, the first Northwest Norwegian-Danish annual conference was held in Racine, Wisconsin, from September 9th to the 13th (1880). Following an appropriate devotional opening, the bishop read the names of all the members in full union who were seated at this our first autonomous conference." (A. Haagensen, Den norsk-danske methodismens historie, *Chicago, 1894.)*

Mormonism

Mormonism, or the Church of Jesus Christ of Latter-Day Saints, was viewed by Dietrichson and others as the greatest religious fallacy. In his *Journey among Norwegian Emigrants* Dietrichson explains carefully what "this sect" represents and estimates that in 1845 there were about 150 Norwegians who had joined it; most of them "live in this Norwegian settlement by Fox River." A Mormon congregation had been organized there by Gudmund Haugaas, a well-known Haugean preacher who after his conversion to the Mormons rose quickly in rank, became a high priest, and "possesses the gift of grace to speak in tongues." Other lay preachers had also become Mormons, and they had "the office of going about preaching and baptizing." One of the young evangelists was Knud Pedersen, who between 1852 and 1856 served as a Mormon missionary in Norway. In spite of intense counteragitation, the missionary activity of the Latter-Day Saints in Scandinavia caused considerable emigration to the Mormon religious colony in Utah, with Salt Lake City as the new Jerusalem. The Mormons made the most progress in Denmark; the headquarters of the Scandinavian mission was located in Copenhagen. By 1905 nearly 13,000 Danes had sought "a complete sanctification" in the earthly millennium in Utah. The corresponding number of Norwegians was an estimated three thousand. In this emigration there were more women than men, a circumstance which fortified popular prejudice against Mormon polygamy. In the Norwegian colonies in the Middle West this religious group made only modest advances after the great Mormon trek westward in 1846.

The Methodists Captured the West

Methodism had a much more enthusiastic reception; it was spread by evangelism and revival meetings. Its emphasis on conduct rather than doctrine and its free form of worship encouraged pietistic behavior and provided an emotional religious experience. Norwegians were attracted to Methodism, the Methodist historian A. Haagensen claims, because of its "earnestness . . . practical evangelical message, and . . . democratic form and appearance." The Methodist mission among Scandinavians began in New York in 1845. On board the Bethel ship *John Wesley,* a floating chapel which was anchored in the port, the Swede Olof G. Hedström preached to Scandinavian seamen. Swedish Methodism in America is dated from that year, but, as Haagensen puts it, Hedström's activity also opened "the door to the heavenly fold for many a Norwegian and Danish sailor." A Danish missionary, Christian B. Willerup, first preached the word to Norwegian pioneers in the West. In 1851, the year after he came to the Middle West, Willerup founded a congregation in Cambridge in Dane county, Wisconsin. Ole P. Petersen, a Norwegian sailor who had been converted to Methodism in an American port city and a close associate of Hedström, began missionary efforts west of the Mississippi River in the fall of 1851. In a conservative Lutheran area of northeastern Iowa near Decorah, known as Washington Prairie, he founded a Methodist church the following year. A viable Danish-Norwegian cooperation thereby came about. After 1880 this joint effort was given the name the Norwegian-Danish Conference and became a national conference within the Methodist Church. Its main activity was in Chicago, and a separate theological seminary was established in Evanston a few years later. In 1900 there were 4,640 members in "full union."

The Norwegian Dissenter Law of 1845 guaranteed full religious liberty; democratic and low-church American religious groups soon gained many adherents there. Norway became religiously pluralistic, an Americanization of Norwegian religious life. Ole P. Petersen officially carried Methodism to Norwegian soil in 1853, and his activity produced two small Methodist congregations, one in his hometown of Fredrikstad and the second in the Skien fjord district. Conversion to other faiths put barriers between Norwegians, in the homeland as in America. This may explain why there were not more immigrants who became Methodists, in spite of the great acceptance Methodism had in regions where Norwegians settled. Defections were likely also prevented by the organizational might of the Lutheran Church. Besides, Methodism's marked American character, its almost nativistic attitude, may have kept Norwegian settlers away. Still, Methodism became a significant spiritual force in the Norwegian-American community.

The Baptists Also Gained Entrance

The number of Norwegian Baptists in America has always been low; but as with other faiths its impact was much greater than statistics indicate. The Baptists had a message of conversion that was carried forward by zealous missionary work and the sale of religious tracts. A separate Norwegian conference was formed in 1910, following years of close cooperation with Danish and Swedish Baptists.

The Baptist church among Norwegians had its beginning in the unstable conditions in the Fox River settlement. Here a powerful personality, Hans Valder from Ryfylke, arrived in 1837. He had been a Haugean, a lay preacher, and a schoolteacher before he emigrated, and he was converted to the Baptist faith in 1842. Two years later he became a pastor in the church, probably the first Norwegian Baptist pastor in the world. Valder gathered a few believers who had been baptized by immersion in his home, and a few years later a Baptist congregation was organized at Indian Creek in the Fox River valley. Because the salary was too small to live on, according to Holand, Valder left his pastoral calling and went to Minnesota. There he did not serve as a preacher but had success as a farmer and hotel proprietor in the small town of Newburg, which he platted on his property. For a time he sat in Minnesota's state legislature.

A Norwegian Episcopal Pastor

There are no statistics on the number of Norwegians who joined American churches in regions where a separate Norwegian religious life was not sustained. There were, however, probably very few who became members of the Protestant Episcopal Church, which represented Anglicanism in America. The two Episcopalian congregations Gustaf Unonius had organized among Scandinavian settlers at Pine Lake returned to the Lutheran faith. His efforts to gain the approbation of the Church of Sweden for his work as an Episcopal pastor only brought him into conflict with Swedish Lutheran pastors in America, especially after he went to Chicago and in 1849 founded the Episcopal St. Ansgarius Church with Swedish and Norwegian members. After Unonius went back to Sweden in 1858, the Episcopal Church made little headway among Scandinavians. Unonius had stressed its similarity to the Swedish state church. Erik L. Petersen, who in 1873 was made an Episcopal pastor in Faribault, Minnesota, went one step further. He hoped that a union between the Lutheran and the Episcopal churches might be brought about in the West. Petersen retained his relationship with his compatriots; he was a frequent and respected contributor to Norwegian-American newspapers, especially on historical and literary subjects. Norwegian immigrants were, however, less dissatisfied with their churches than he had thought; others perhaps turned away from the Episcopal Church precisely because in organization and practice it reminded them too much of Norwegian conditions. After Petersen's death in 1887, at age forty-three, no lines of communication remained between the Episcopalians and Norwegian immigrants.

The contours of the immigrants' religious life—a strong Lutheran affiliation, though with marked inroads by other creeds—were thus established by 1860.

A Young Minister's Wife, Elisabeth Koren

On Christmas Eve, 1853, a young minister's wife was sitting in a small log cabin, fourteen by sixteen feet, on Washington Prairie, southeast of the little town of Decorah. She was Else Elisabeth Hysing Koren. She was twenty-one years old, and, with her six-years-older husband, the pastor Ulrik Vilhelm Koren, she had left a protected and cultivated existence in Norway to set out for the Norwegian pioneer settlements in the Middle West. The first Norwegians in this region of Iowa had come in 1849, and in the following years their numbers grew so rapidly that the missionary pastor Nils O. Brandt was able to organize three congregations there in 1852. A call letter, signed by 105 members of these congregations, had brought the young couple to America.

No parsonage was ready. From December 24, 1853, to March 10, 1854, they shared the tiny cabin, as house guests, with Erik and Helene Egge and their two small children. It was "divided by curtains of calico into two rooms, one of which affords the space for two beds."

While her husband looked after his far-flung parish and held religious services, as he himself relates, "in the settlers' small houses, where many a time the rose-painted emigrant chest had to serve both as altar and pulpit," Elisabeth, who did not have to do "any housekeeping," was busy with "correspondence and her diaries." Her diary from this period gives a vivid impression of the crude conditions she and Ulrik Vilhelm Koren shared with the settlers. It is an honest and unromanticized depiction of pioneer life, with touches here and there of an upper-class attitude, written by an intelligent young woman from a Norwegian aristocratic background.

Elisabeth learned to know "Norwegian peasants whom I earlier knew so little." It amused her when with great respect they came over to her and said, "Well, we wish you welcome to America." After their arrival at the Egges' house, they had been served "beer and *fattigmandsbakkels*." The next day, which was Christmas Day, Koren preached his first sermon "in the largest cabin they could find." She makes note of Vilhelm's endless journeys, and finds it strange that "he does not become seriously ill." One time he had preached in a place "so intolerably hot" that he "got a terrible cold."

A modest social life was conducted in the crowded cabins, and during the holidays the tables "were loaded down with fried pork, ribs, sausages, bread, butter, and excellent coffee." It was, however, "the everlasting pork" that was daily fare. The temporary parsonage at the Egges' home received many visitors. Occasionally Elisabeth complains about "many interruptions," even though the visitors were welcome since they had news from the outside. Worst were those days when she "read the entire day . . . without saying a word from morning until night." Among the many who came to the cabin there were some who requested churchly services, and marriage vows might be said while they were all congregated. On January 13, 1854, Elisabeth writes about an instance when it was such "awful weather" that the groom, quite drunk, arrived with a friend to be married by proxy to a woman who "waited in a house nearby." The wedding was postponed until the bride could be present the next day.

That they had to wait so long before they could move into the parsonage was a heavy strain. When after many delays and promises they were finally going to move in and discovered that the house lacked doors, Koren tells that he saw "tears in my wife's eyes for the first time." There was good reason, he explains, since it was "far into October, and in the beginning of December our eldest daughter was born." The parsonage on Washington Prairie was through the years a social and cultural center, open to everyone, and in life-style and reputation it gives evidence of an attempt to re-create a Norwegian parsonage in American surroundings.

The Norwegian Synod and the "Common School"

Norwegians placed themselves in a singular position among Scandinavians in America by being the only ones to question the American common school. The school was generally considered to be the cornerstone of American democracy. Still, many accused it of being godless and ineffective. In the pioneer period it was also a humble and primitive institution, and many of the teachers were poorly qualified. In general, however, Norwegian immigrants accepted the public schools, lauded the opportunity they afforded to learn English, and sent their children there. Wisconsin had voluntary school attendance until 1879, when it was made compulsory. In 1870 in Trempealeau county there were, to be sure, relatively fewer Norwegian children attending school than children whose mother tongue was English. But among families above a certain level of income, 76 percent sent their children to the public schools, the same percentage as English-speaking settlers with similar incomes.

As early as 1838 Ole Rynning had praised the arrangement whereby "the sixteenth section in every township is set off as school land," and in regard to the Fox River settlement Rynning predicted that the Norwegian language "would die with the parents," as the children learned English

at school. Elling Eielsen encouraged people to support the common school, in the spirit of enlightenment, and in 1844 J. W. C. Dietrichson helped to provide a more satisfactory school in Muskego, because the school was "a little, simple log cabin" with "a young American female" as teacher and "few Norwegian children" attended.

But Dietrichson realized that the district school was not sufficient, because "religion cannot be addressed there." The alternative to the secular American school was the congregational school, or religious school. The next year Dietrichson hired the sexton Ole Trovatten for three months at a salary of ten dollars per month, paid from his own means, to conduct a school on Koshkonong "where the children of the congregation can be taught our church's pure doctrine." As new congregations were organized, similar schools were established in the settlements. They were intended to operate alongside the common school, not replace it. Ole Munch Ræder relates that C. L. Clausen had started a congregational school in 1847 in Rock Prairie, where he was pastor. It was in session for six months, twice as long as the American school. Some schools were operated on an itinerant basis, in each house "as many days . . . as the owner was willing to pay," wrote A. L. Lien from Blue Mounds, a well-known settlement west of Madison. The salary was usually "50 cents a day and board."

The settlers continued in the 1850s to support the American school, or Yankee school, as it was also called. It was, however, at that time, when the Norwegian Synod showed strong organizational growth and received new ministers from Norway, that a controversy over the children's education developed. Initially a greater concern for the education of the young encouraged a strengthening of the congregational school, and added emphasis was given to preserving the Norwegian language. The orthodox clergy in this way worked against rapid Americanization. The "mother tongue is the language of the heart," it was said by the ministers, and the children ought therefore to be taught religion in "the family's daily and natural language." The Lutheran ministers wanted to safeguard the influence of the church, the Lutheran faith, and a Norwegian-American group identity.

There was, however, no objection to the children learning English. Quite the contrary, the

Erik and Helene Egge's cabin (above, and interior to the right), where the Korens were guests. Their endurance was tested before they could move into the parsonage on Washington Prairie (below). The oil painting of the parsonage is by the Norwegian-born artist Herbjørn Gausta and dates from the 1880s. The Koren family is seen in the garden.

church held that it was "every Norwegian-born American's duty as far as possible to acquire this knowledge." But the congregational school could also give instruction in English, and this possibility was the basis for the great school debate that began late in the 1850s. At that time the Norwegian Synod initiated cooperation with the German Missouri Synod, and this connection convinced the leading men in the Synod that it might be possible to substitute separate Lutheran schools for the common school as the Germans had done. By adopting this position the Synod pastors isolated themselves from the majority of Norwegian immigrants, and their stand produced heated objections. The other Norwegian Lutheran groups at first gave little attention to this issue but after a time sided with the opponents of the Synod's view. In October, 1858, a meeting of eleven Synod pastors and seventeen congregational teachers at Rock Prairie accepted a proposal concerning separate schools for the children.

A School Debate in the Norwegian-American Community

The public debate was introduced by a violent attack on the Lutheran clergy by Rasmus Sørensen, a Danish-born schoolteacher and lay preacher, who had worked together with Eielsen when he visited Denmark in 1838. In rather clumsy terms Sørensen criticized the pastors: "After this pastoral Norwegianization has come here to the Norwegian settlements, the Norwegian school is preferred by the people . . . instead of the American district school," he claimed. For Sørensen and others the district school was a means for melting different ethnic groups together and teaching them "Americanization." This attack was printed in the immigrant newspaper *Emigranten*, and in the same journal the clergy replied in a joint declaration "Concerning the Condition of our Schools and Language," in which they maintained a conciliatory tone. This fact, in addition to the nation's preoccupation with the Civil War in the following years, postponed further discussion of the issue.

After 1865, however, the debate was resumed with renewed zeal and much broader participation. An official proposal, adopted at a church conference in Manitowoc, Wisconsin, in June of 1866, encouraged the congregations to establish their own schools; "the English common schools are thus made superfluous," and "the children are [not] corrupted" by them. The Manitowoc resolution represented the Synod's firm commitment. Knud Langeland, then editor of the newly started newspaper *Skandinaven* in Chicago, retorted immediately. He rather venomously accused the clergy of wanting to make salvation a reward for ignorance and superstition. The defense of the common school as an institution that gave a broad education and secured full participation for Norwegians in American society was carried on with ardor in the columns of *Skandinaven*. Langeland had the strong support of John A. Johnson, a well-known manufacturer of farm machinery in Madison.

The position of the Synod leaders gradually became indefensible. They had promoted the idea of a separate school system because they feared they would lose their hold on the coming generation. At the same time, the pastors understood that they had engaged themselves in an uneven battle that the secular American schools would inevitably win. A separate system would cost too much, and the problem of providing teachers was too great. But the main obstruction was the fact that the immigrants continued to patronize the Yankee school, and many were besides convinced that American citizenship exacted loyalty to the common school. The debate quieted down toward the end of the 1870s; but distrust of a school that was not "Christian" lasted much longer.

A Pioneer Press Is Established

An ethnic subculture generally possesses an inner life, a unique development, that marks its boundaries with other nationalities. The various religious and secular publications of the Norwegian Americans are a vivid expression of this state of affairs. In America the written word gained increased significance; only through it could one stay in touch with one's far-flung compatriots. But to an equal degree the publication of all kinds of writing satisfied a need for information about America and was a part of the process of adjustment to the new surroundings. Internally the press created ethnic solidarity, albeit characterized by disagreement and conflict. In addition, it entertained its readers with suitable literature, thereby making their life in America easier and more pleasant; only by means of the press could a Norwegian-American community exist and function. The publications of the immigrants made possible as well an important exchange of points of view.

The pioneer press had a difficult birth: Norwegian peasants were not accustomed to reading newspapers; their schooling was deficient; and in the pioneer period their economic resources were limited. The idea of a separate Norwegian newspaper arose among "the more enlightened emigrated Norwegian peasants," writes Langeland. The newspaper *Nordlyset* (Northern Lights) was issued July 29, 1847, in Muskego, printed in Even Heg's log cabin, but with Norway Post Office, Racine county, Wisconsin, as a mailing address. With the exception of the joint Scandinavian organ, *Skandinavia,* which had come out in New York in January of the same year, *Nordlyset* is considered to be the first Norwegian newspaper in America, even though as the name indicates it took aim at a Scandinavian circle of readers. The list of 200 subscribers which this journal at last attained shows its distribution in the pioneer settlements. It was the young James D. Reymert who edited *Nordlyset* in the beginning. Not all later editors had Reymert's education and skill; many immigrant publications were therefore "less attractive" because of "the poor Norwegian in which they were edited," it was maintained by a contemporary newspaper contributor. For Reymert personally, his work for *Nordlyset* was a successful springboard into American politics. The press was thus from the very start a political tool for the immigrants.

Through *Nordlyset* Reymert championed the "free soil" movement, the political party that appeared in 1847-1848 and that gained a following from the opponents of the spread of slavery to the western territories. The newspaper had a distinctly American emphasis: an important purpose was to inform Norwegians who could not read English about the country's history and political institutions. The paper also contained brief articles about life in the Norwegian settlements. In the fall of 1849 Langeland committed, according to his own statement, "the folly of buying the printing press from Heg and Reymert." He issued the last ten numbers of *Nordlyset* in the town of Racine, the final one dated May 18, 1850. When the next issue of the newspaper came out on June 8, the name had been altered to *Democraten*. Langeland, whose son-in-law, Ole J. Hatlestad, served as his partner, "was quite conversant with political conditions," a contemporary witness writes. He understood the attachment of the immigrants to democratic principles and traditions. Politically the newspaper moved toward the Democratic party, and Reymert himself had also changed political course and found a philosophical kinship with this party. It was as a Democratic candidate that he was elected to the Wisconsin state legislature, the first Norwegian who achieved such an honor.

Norwegian settlers had not been receptive to Republican ideas as these had been presented in *Nordlyset*, even though they opposed the spread

Gilbertson school in Big Spring Valley in Arendahl township, Fillmore county, Minnesota. "The first Norwegian schools here were held in the small log cabins built by the settlers and were what one in Norway called ambulatory school (omgangsskole). The teacher went from place to place, and held school for about one week in each farmhouse, where he received board and a little pay." (O. S. Johnson, Nybyggerhistorie fra Spring Grove og omegn, *Minneapolis, 1920.)*

of slavery. Their political interest was perhaps not well developed at that time. But the Democratic party had without doubt a strong appeal for the common people; it was the party of Jefferson and Jackson, and the latter especially was living proof of the democratic principle of equality. Besides, the Democrats had consistently expressed a friendly attitude toward the immigrants. On the other side, the Republicans were suspected by some of being infested with the hatred of foreigners found in the nativistic Know-Nothing movement.

Before the Republican party grew strong, it was the Whig party, with its strong upper-class support, that was the Democrats' major political opponent. The Whig party found its electorate in the East among wealthy industrial and commercial groups and in the West among prosperous farmers. This party also had a Norwegian-language organ in the newspaper *De Norskes Ven* (Friend of the Norwegians). It was in conflict with *Democraten*, but without gaining "a single proselyte," the same witness says. The Whigs during this period were in rapid decline, and *De Norskes Ven* was discontinued after a few months. In October, 1851, Langeland also had to stop publication, and some thought this was because Langeland showed "lack of tact in the paper's editing . . . and kept poor control of his paper's columns."

The Norwegian Synod had its own journal *Kirkelig Maanedstidende* (Church Monthly), launched in 1851, two years before the official founding of the Synod. Under changing names and mergers with other periodicals (*Evangelisk Luthersk Kirketidende; Lutheraneren*) it continued until 1956. Only a few weeks after its founding Ole J. Hatlestad began to present the low-church lay view in the journal *Kirketidende* (Church Times).

Emigranten— the Major Pioneer Newspaper

The immigrant press was a fighting press, and the polemical tone at times became somewhat strident. This may have frightened away some readers. Enough paying subscribers and income from advertising were always difficult to procure. Many promising ventures therefore failed. By 1860 at least nine publications had seen the light of day. Except for the monthly church papers,

Three examples of the pioneer press.

Top: Nordlyset *was the first Norwegian newspaper in America. Its first edition appeared on July 29, 1847, in Muskego. The issue for June 8, 1848, is reproduced here.*

Middle: Emigranten, *February 30, 1862. This was the most important pioneer newspaper. In its initial issue on January 23, 1852, it carried a greeting in English to "OUR AMERICAN FRIENDS," and the ethnic inferiority feeling is obvious: "We look to You for help and assistance in our endeavors to emancipate ourselves from the degrading bondage of ignorance, regarding Your institutions and customs, regarding the privileges and duties devolving upon us with the rights of citizenship extended to us." The newspaper had a clear Americanization mission from the start.*

Bottom: Kirkelig Maanedstidende *was launched by the Norwegian Synod in 1851 and again in 1855, as is seen here.*

they were all weeklies; of all these, aside from the Synod's *Kirkelig Maanedstidende*, there was only one that survived the Civil War. This was *Emigranten*, the most important of the pioneer newspapers, which presented its first issue on January 23, 1852. The mailing address was Inmansville, Wisconsin, but the paper was actually printed in a simple log cabin in Newark in the Rock Prairie area. The background for this enterprise was that the Synod, on the initiative of C. L. Clausen, wished to publish a political newspaper in addition to its church periodical. Clausen became *Emigranten*'s first editor. At that time there was no secular paper in Norwegian. The Scandinavian Press Association was founded for the purpose of putting out such a newspaper. Even though lay people owned most of the shares, the Synod pastors had great influence over this modest undertaking. The difference between a secular and a religious newspaper was therefore not very important. *Emigranten* declared itself an independent Democratic organ, and it continued in this political track during the tenure of Clausen's successor, the Danish-American Carl M. Riise (Charles M. Reese).

After 1857 the newspaper changed its political course, when Carl Fredrik Solberg became editor and three years later also owner. Clearly *Emi-*

granten's most capable editor, Solberg moved the newspaper over into the Republican camp. He depicted the Republicans as champions of the distribution of free government land—a homestead act—a popular cause in the West in the 1850s. The newspaper wanted to have "no slavery for either blacks or whites." The number of subscribers rose to four thousand in 1860. This increase showed that the Republicans' leading issues and the question of slavery were to attract support from the immigrants. *Emigranten* worked for and was a part of this swing from a Democratic to a Republican direction.

The effort to stop the change in political course produced new Norwegian newspapers. The best known was *Den Norske Amerikaner* (The Norwegian American), published in Madison beginning in December, 1854, by Elias Stangeland. *Emigranten* had offered much space to accusations against Stangeland of irregularities while he was serving as an immigration agent in New York, and with personal bitterness he now attacked *Emigranten* and charged it with being aristocratic and opposed to the principle of equality stated in the American Constitution. The newly established Scandinavian Democratic Press Association bought *Den Norske Amerikaner* in 1857 and changed the name to *Nordstjernen* (The North Star)—"one of the comets in the Democratic heavenly firmament," *Emigranten* wrote. Even before the election campaign prior to the epoch-making vote in 1860, *Nordstjernen* had, however, ceased publication, absorbed by *Emigranten*. This was a sign of the weakened position of the Democratic party among Norwegian voters in the Northwest. Thousands of immigrant voters, the largest contingent German, gave their vote in 1860 to the Republicans and Lincoln and thereby participated in moving the Union toward an inescapable breach between South and North. "Without the votes of the immigrants Lincoln could not have won the Northwest, and without the Northwest, or with its vote different, he would have lost," concludes historian Donnal V. Smith in an article published in 1971. The immigrant press had played a significant part in the election victory.

All in all the pioneer press had an educational impact; it made the immigrants aware of their political power. It helped to develop and explain a Norwegian America and in this way became a fundamental social and cultural institution in the Norwegian-American community. In addition, the pioneer press laid the foundation for the later flourishing of journalism among Norwegian immigrants.

The Immense Land

Expectations of acquiring inexpensive or free land and thus securing a better future attracted settlers to new regions. During the first period of mass exodus from Norway, in the 1860s and 1870s, Norwegian settlement spread across enormous areas, from Texas in the south to Iowa, Minnesota, and the Dakotas in the north.

Norwegian Americans and The American Civil War

The Civil War between North and South from 1861 to 1865 was the great test of power that would determine whether the American nation would remain a firm federation or be dissolved at the wishes of the individual states. It also marked a decisive phase in the immigrants' process of adjustment. The enormous conflict created a new patriotism, a sense of having earned a legitimate place in America, for Norwegian blood had been spilled in the defense of the nation. From every settlement Norwegian immigrants went to war, willing to make the greatest sacrifice that could be asked of a citizen. For them, as for other people in the northern states, the war was a crusade against slavery and an affirmation of the American ideals of freedom and equality. Norwegian immigrants, and other Scandinavians, answered the call and stood behind Lincoln and the Republican party, which they had begun to identify themselves with in the years before hostilities broke out.

Historians disagree on the number, but it is estimated that at least 800 Norwegians from Minnesota, more than 400 from Iowa, and about 3,000 from Wisconsin, in addition to several hundred from the older settlements in Illinois, fought for the North. Another estimate assumes that one-sixth of the Norwegian immigrants let themselves be recruited, whereas only one-eighth of all Americans signed up. No one could doubt, says the historian Kendric Babcock, in *The Scandinavian Element in the United States*, 1914, that "many hundreds of them gave their strength and their lives for the unity and safety of their adopted country no less bravely and no less cheerfully than did the native-born Americans." It is a heroic and dramatic period in the history of the Norwegians in America, idealized by later generations and given great symbolic value.

Gunder Hanson's wheat field in Grant county, Minnesota.

The war created heroes. The most famous is undoubtedly Colonel Hans Christian Heg, son of the pioneer leader Even Heg. Hans Heg had emigrated from Lier at the age of eleven, and he became the commander of the Fifteenth Wisconsin Regiment, called the Norwegian regiment. With a few exceptions it was composed entirely of Norwegians. "Newcomers with insufficient knowledge of English" and men from the Norwegian settlements volunteered, and, with a banner that had the Stars and Stripes on one side and "For God and Our Country" with a lion, the Norwegian national emblem, on the other, the regiment marched in the campaign in the South and took part in "twenty-six battles and skirmishes," Waldemar Ager relates in *Oberst Heg og hans gutter* (Colonel Heg and His Boys), 1916. Its feats of courage have been celebrated on many occasions. In the Norwegian settlements veterans from the war were listened to and honored: Heg himself represented for posterity "the best and noblest in a citizen." He fell in the bloody battle at Chickamauga in northern Georgia in September, 1863, barely thirty-four years old when he led his men into combat on the smoke-filled battlefield. Before the war had ended, 299 men in all, one-third of the original regiment, had died in the fighting. At Chickamauga the state of Wisconsin has raised a monument in honor of the Fifteenth Wisconsin.

Norwegian Settlers in the South

The Civil War played an important role also for those Norwegians who had settled in the southern states. The state of Texas had a small contingent of Norwegians in 1860, all together 321 people. By 1870 this number had increased to 552, and in 1880 there were 941 Norwegians in Texas. Most of them resided in Bosque county, which was the third Norwegian settlement in Texas. Norwegian men joined the Confederate forces, fought for the cause of the South, and defended the right of each state to self-determination. Among Norwegians in the South, however, the war never became a crusade, a conflict that

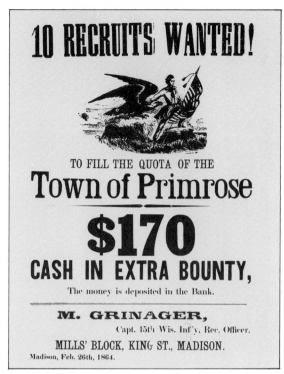

A recruiting poster for the Fifteenth Wisconsin Regiment, called the Norwegian Regiment. The poster promises a bounty of $170 to every man who enlists.

created heroes and fired the imagination. Statements that have been preserved, both by Norwegian volunteers and by conscripts, lack expressions of patriotism. The war objectives never became a noble cause for them; what is most evident is a fervent desire to have the war come to an end.

All the same, Norwegians identified themselves with their region of the country. They showed considerable loyalty to Texas. It is also important to bear in mind that the people of Texas were not especially strongly committed to the war and the Confederate cause. There were divided opinions about it both among immigrants and among older American groups in the state.

Most historians have maintained not only that Norwegians in Texas were lukewarm in their will to fight, but that a large percentage of them sided with the North and felt a loyalty to the Union.

The peak in the early Norwegian emigration coincided with the first phase of the Civil War in 1861. Norwegian immigrants responded actively and with enthusiasm to President Lincoln's appeal to volunteer for service in the armed conflict.

Very many also had a deep aversion to slavery. The last circumstance is frequently cited to explain why so few Norwegians moved to the southern states.

Attempts at Colonization in Texas

The two first colonization ventures in Texas are both linked to Johan R. Reiersen, who was convinced of the advantages of organized colonization. His *Pathfinder* was published in 1844, the year after he had toured the Norwegian settlements in Illinois and Wisconsin. The same year he visited the independent Republic of Texas. During his stay there he had talked to President Sam Houston. It was especially the opportunities for Norwegian immigrants to Texas that he emphasized in his *Pathfinder*, and he recommended the central highlands in the republic as "the most suitable place to establish a European colony."

Reiersen's role was, like Peerson's, to be an agent and guide—essential functions in the pioneer emigration. He returned to Norway, and in the late spring of 1845 he led a small group of peasants from Agder to land he had selected in Texas. He dreamed of founding a colony of solid peasants and capable workers. What position he had intended for himself is uncertain. In his newspaper *Christianssandsposten* (Christiansand Post), which he had established in 1839, he had opposed officialdom and worked for reform and general enlightenment. Before he left Norway he had begun to publish the monthly *Norge og Amerika* (Norway and America). Reiersen hoped to use the journal's columns to inform his readers about America, and to continue his participation in Norwegian social debate.

Christian Grøgaard, who like Reiersen was from the upper classes, came along with him to serve as teacher and pastor for the colonists. The immigrants waited in New Orleans for assurance that Texas would join the Union; when this had been received they continued on to their destination in northeastern Texas. It was there that Reiersen had arranged for the purchase of land, in Henderson county, and they formed a colony with the resounding historical name Normandy. Shortly afterward it was altered to the more prosaic Brownsboro. The colony did not attract newcomers. Reiersen's second colony, which he founded in 1848 in Prairieville in the two counties of Kaufman and Van Zandt southeast of the city of Dallas, also failed in spite of strong publicity.

Attention Is Directed toward Texas

Capable writers like Reiersen advertised the Texas settlements widely in Norway and in America. They have therefore attracted more attention than their size would justify. One of the most remarkable people to write about Texas was born Elise Tvede, a pastor's daughter. After her arrival in Texas she married a fellow emigrant, Wilhelm Wærenskjold. They took land on Four Mile Prairie, a few miles from Prairieville. Elise Wærenskjold knew Reiersen, and like him she worked for popular enlightenment and the temperance cause. She had edited the second and also the last volume of *Norge og Amerika*. As a diligent correspondent and contributor to newspapers both in Norway and in America, she parried critical reports about Texas and set forth the advantages the state had as a home for Norwegian immigrants. She became a leading personality in the Texas settlements.

Cleng Peerson himself made an effort to direct his compatriots to the splendors of the South. There, he thought, both the climate and the agricultural possibilities were far better than in the states farther north. The restless Peerson had visited his homeland in 1842, and on his return had stopped at Erik Jansson's communistic religious colony, Bishop Hill, in Illinois. He had stayed for a while in the Fox River settlement before his tireless wanderings took him to Texas in 1849. According to Rasmus B. Anderson, Peerson had been asked to investigate conditions

Colonel Hans Christian Heg at Chickamauga. Painting by Herbjørn Gausta ca. 1915. "After nightfall I walked to the hospital three miles away to see how our wounded men were faring. Here I found out that Colonel Heg's wounds were fatal and that he would not live. He was very weak and I spoke only briefly to him. He was prepared and calm concerning his own death. . . . Colonel Heg had by his kindness and valiant spirit wherever danger threatened become almost an idol among us, and his memory will always be highly regarded by every single one in the regiment." (Account from a letter written in the Libby prison in Richmond, Virginia, November 3, 1863, by Lieutenant Colonel Ole C. Johnson to his brother John A. Johnson.)

there by the pioneer emigrant from Ringebu, Johannes Nordboe. Nordboe had emigrated in 1832, at the advanced age of sixty-four, with his wife and four children. He had been an outsider in Norwegian society, in political opposition, and he did not adapt to the pioneer Norwegian settlements in America either. In 1838 he consequently went to Texas and was allotted a large area of government land south of Dallas, "as far from his countrymen as possible."

Peerson visited Johannes Nordboe and then roved about in Texas. In 1850 he was again in the Fox River settlement, "completely filled with Texas fever," and "advised everyone to move to Texas." A few took Peerson's advice. Ole Canuteson, who in 1850 had emigrated from Karmøy at the age of eighteen, led a company to Bosque county in 1853. Still another offspring of the mother colony along the Fox River thus was born. This settlement attracted people from the two other colonies in Texas, as well as from Norway. The little town of Clifton became a center. Peerson joined the move to Texas. In 1894 Canuteson wrote to Rasmus Anderson that Peerson had been "too old to be a forerunner and guide;" in December, 1865, Canuteson had closed Peerson's "eyes in the long sleep of death." Peerson was then eighty-three years old. He was buried in the Lutheran cemetery near Norse in Bosque county. A marker on his grave commends him as "the first Norwegian immigrant in America."

A Norwegian family posing for the photographer in front of their home near Madison, Wisconsin. Note the man in a uniform from the Civil War. The picture was taken by Andrew Dahl in the mid-1870s.

Elise Tvede Wærenskjold (1815-95), "The lady with the pen," who spoke warmly for Texas as a home for her compatriots in America: "Texas is a paradise for poor people; anyone who wants to work will have a good income at all times, and children are not a burden, but a great help for their parents. In the fall the children can make good earnings by picking cotton. . . ." (Elise Wærenskjold in Billed-Magazin, *February 19, 1869.)*

The Church and Slavery

Most Norwegians retained a distaste for slavery, whether they settled in the North or in the South. Elise Wærenskjold called slavery an abomination, because "all people as the children of God are equal in His eyes." But the settlers adjusted to the society in which they lived; and not all Norwegians in Texas had the same conviction as Elise Wærenskjold. Or at least they did not live in accordance with it, for it is quite certain that some Norwegian settlers were slaveholders.

In 1860 Ole Canuteson wrote that in this regard Norwegian settlers conformed to the ways of society. George and Helene Grøgaard Reiersen owned as many as nine slaves.

In 1860 the active Elling Eielsen carried his work of evangelism all the way to Texas. There was a need for religious guidance, and Elise Wærenskjold notes that he preached every day with great energy. The settlers wanted Eielsen to remain as their pastor, but he had a larger field among Norwegians in the North. The Four Mile Prairie settlers had, however, formed a congregation as early as 1853 and called a minister from Norway. This congregation was dissolved in 1857, and a new one within the Norwegian Synod was established in 1868. The Synod experienced an intense debate about the nature of slavery, but this had no relation to its mission among

Norwegians in the southern states. It was again the Synod's relationship with the Missouri Synod and its "pure doctrine" theology that produced a conflict. Eielsen's Synod, for instance, had already in 1846 declared slavery to be a sin, not merely a social evil. The Norwegian-American press, which had been launched under the influence of the "free soil" movement and which was inspired by American freedom and equality, supported and encouraged those who took a negative position on slavery.

The Missouri Synod had its base in a slave state in the South. Strongly antagonistic points of view became evident in 1861 when the question of the Norwegian Synod's relationship to this church group was raised by editor C. F. Solberg of *Emigranten*. It developed into a bitter debate over the Synod's teachings on slavery. The

Above: The first Norwegian settlers in Bosque county, Texas.

MR. & MRS. HENDRICK DAHL · MR. & MRS. OLE CANUTESON · MR. & MRS. JENS JENSON

MRS. JENS RINGNESS · MR. OLE WEEN · MR. & MRS. KNUT CANUTESON

MR. & MRS. KARL QUESTAD · MR. & MRS. BERGE ROGSTAD · MR. & MRS. PIERSON

The earliest settlement was located in southwestern Bosque county and appropriately called Norse. Here is the Norse post office, where Ole Canuteson served as the first postmaster.

Synod pastors, with their Biblical interpretation of all questions of doctrine, involved themselves in an abstract theological discussion; they finally arrived at the meaningless conclusion that according to the Word of God slavery was not "a sin in and of itself." This statement was intended as a compromise. The full text of their declaration shows clearly that the ministers expressed themselves against slavery. But the clergy's compulsion to find a strict Biblical basis for doctrine hindered them from taking a clear and unequivocal position against slavery as an institution. To their great annoyance, the theological faculty in Oslo did not agree with their interpretation. The Synod leaders held to their conviction and accused the Norwegian theology professors of placing reason above the Scriptures.

This was the second time the Synod pastors had isolated themselves from their flock; the first time was in the controversy kindled by their attitude to the "common school." It was unreasonable to expect lay people to appreciate the fine theological distinctions in the slavery debate, or the intellectual exercise the issue was for the theologians. Intense attacks came from several quarters. Other Lutheran church groups reproached the Synod "for losing itself in literal interpretations and human limitations." The Synod now got the reputation of defending slavery. In 1868 C. L. Clausen broke with the Synod because of it, at least twelve congregations followed suit, others were divided, and scores of individuals left. The Synod had, to be sure, evinced a certain will to find agreement, but it adopted a firm position for Lutheran principles. Its lack of flexibility in time had great and agonizing consequences.

"A Glorious New Scandinavia"

In 1850 the celebrated Swedish author Fredrika Bremer undertook a strenuous journey to the Middle West. From Chicago she traveled westward, visited Swedish and Norwegian settlements, among them Koshkonong, and from there proceeded to Madison and on to Galena on the Mississippi River. She continued by riverboat to the small city of St. Paul, capital of the Territory of Minnesota. Hardly had the boat docked before Governor Alexander Ramsey and "his pretty young wife" came on board and invited her to be their guest in the governor's mansion.

Few of Fredrika Bremer's compatriots who in subsequent years made Minnesota their home were accorded the same cordial welcome. But in her vision of the possibilities of the territory for Scandinavian immigrants she was prophetic. "What a glorious new Scandinavia might not Minnesota become!" Fredrika Bremer wrote after her arrival. "Here the Swede would find again his clear, romantic lakes, the plains of Skåne rich in corn, and the valleys of Norrland; here the Norwegian would find his rapid rivers, his lofty mountains, for I include the Rocky Mountains and Oregon in the new kingdom; and both na-

tions, their hunting-fields and their fisheries. The Danes might here pasture their flocks and herds, and lay out their farms on richer and less misty coasts than those of Denmark."

The landscape might in part be reminiscent of Scandinavia. In 1850, however, very few Scandinavians had discovered the wonders of the area; only twelve were officially registered that year. They were soon to arrive in force, however: the census of 1870 would indicate that in the course of twenty years the Scandinavians had overtaken the Germans to become the largest foreign-born element in Minnesota's population. Within the Scandinavian group Norwegians were definitely the most numerous in 1870, but toward the end of the century the Swedes took the lead in numbers. During the decade dominated by the Civil War Norwegians had spread themselves over a large area; the figures for their military participation in the Northern forces show where they had settled and in what strength.

Shelbyville—A Short-lived Settlement

Cleng Peerson had led his people west of the Mississippi River as early as 1837, when some dissatisfied families at Fox River wanted to look for land farther west. Peerson guided them to Shelby county in Missouri, and there the short-lived Shelbyville settlement was founded (See map on page 34). After a few years most of the pioneers deserted the area, in spite of the fact that Peerson had traveled all the way to New York to persuade newcomers to go with him to Missouri. This settlement ultimately failed because general poverty hindered the settlers from taking advantage of preemption rights to buy the land they had begun to cultivate. In addition, there were the ordinary hardships and difficulties that pioneer life entailed. It is striking that the two best-known negativists in the spread of information about America, Peter Testman and Sjur Haaeim, had both been a part of this unsuccessful attempt at settlement before they returned to Norway.

Large Contingents of Norwegians Move to Iowa

Most of the settlers left Missouri in 1839 and followed Peerson a few miles farther north to Lee

long. The men acquired teams of oxen and made their wagons ready."

Those who had brought back the tidings from Story county were scouts that the colonists themselves had sent. Before the company set out from the Fox River district, the colonists organized themselves as "Lutheran church people" into a congregation, elected a pastor, sexton, and teacher, and gave the congregation the promising name Palestine. They left Lisbon on May 16, 1855, and arrived at their new base on June 7. There were a total of 106 people who traveled west in ox-drawn covered wagons—twenty-one families, five bachelors, and one widow. The colonists formed the so-called southern settlement in Story county. A party of Haugeans in the farm communities by the Fox River also sent agents to central Iowa and formed a colony farther north. Religious conviction gave internal strength, but simultaneously separated the two colonies from each other, even though they had the same local origin in Norway. Both Story county projects are examples of carefully planned colonization ventures.

Economic and other motives worked together to push Norwegian pioneers westward. In 1846 Ole Valle had come to northeastern Iowa from Koshkonong, and the letters he sent back to Wisconsin opened the way to what became the main area for Norwegian settlement in the state. It was especially Winneshiek county that was to form a Norwegian center. Here in 1850 twelve families founded the famous Washington Prairie settlement. According to George Flom, an early Norwegian-American scholar, most of the pioneers were from Voss, Telemark, Sogn, and Valdres, and had first stayed some years in Wisconsin. The first group directly from Norway arrived in 1853. That year *Emigranten* was able to report that the number of Norwegians in the little town of Decorah was growing rapidly.

county in the Territory of Iowa. Even though Peerson served as guide, it was the aging peasant leader, inventor, and spokesman for enlightenment, Hans Barlien, who was the real leader and founder of the Sugar Creek settlement northwest of Keokuk (See map page 34). He had great plans for the colonization of this settlement, but few pioneers made their way to it. Peerson left the settlement after a short while to continue his wanderings, and Barlien died in 1842, at the age of seventy. Several of the Sugar Creek settlers joined the large Mormon colony at Nauvoo in Illinois, not far away, and trekked with the Mormons to Utah in 1846. The main stream of Norwegian migration, however, took place farther to the north, as a part of the great westward flow.

In 1846 Iowa became a state, and in the following years it received large contingents of Norwegians. Directly from Norway the immigrants could reach the state by boat up the Mississippi from New Orleans, or take the land route from

A paddle wheel steamer at the levee in Galena, Illinois, ca. 1852. The boat traffic on the rivers was efficient and inexpensive, and it was very important to the development of the Middle West.

Wisconsin and Illinois, joining the exodus from the older settlements. Some of the larger colonies were founded in Story and adjoining counties in the center of the state, with Story City as a focal point. Behind the earliest settlement stood a group of immigrants from Sunnhordland in 1855. The group had come to Lisbon in the Fox River area, but all the land had been taken there, and news of government land—"prairie and forest land in large stretches"—west of the Mississippi generated, as a local historian tells, "a magnetic current throughout the settlement. There was joy and exultation in the whole camp. The women wove, sang, and spun the whole day

Norwegians Flock to Minnesota

The main thrust of Norwegian settlement was into Minnesota. Pioneers followed close upon the Indians and fur traders. Treaties with the Indian tribes Traverse des Sioux and Mendota in 1851 opened up most of Minnesota for settlement. There were great and justified hopes for expansion. In 1858 the territory was made a state, and before 1870 there were more than 400,000 inhabitants in the state, as compared with a little more than 6,000 twenty years before. From the 1860s on, population growth was strongly marked by migration into the state of people born outside America. Most Norwegians at that time came to Minnesota via Quebec, and because the war arena lay far from the main region of Norwegian settlement and public opinion in Norway was on the side of the Union, there was a continual immigration also during the Civil War period.

The attention of both newcomers and older immigrants was directed toward the agricultural districts in Iowa and Minnesota because most of the good land in the Norwegian farm communities in Wisconsin and Illinois had been taken. The pioneer communities displayed great geographic mobility. It was a restless society, and people came and went, both older and younger settlers. Those who were poor in resources might move because they had lost their property, but more often it was rumors of better opportunities farther west or the possibility of getting a good price for their land that prompted the departure.

Norwegians were as a rule not the first to take land in pioneer areas; this distinction was usually reserved for Yankee farmers, speculators, and settlement promoters of different kinds. But Norwegians had perhaps a greater tendency than other Scandinavians to seek land on the farthest edge of settlement. They were welcomed by older American groups; settlement was a desired development, associated with progress, and the immigrants therefore represented a positive element. There are few examples of direct discrimination, and even though there might be a distance between Yankees and immigrants, there were on the frontier less marked social divisions and a more democratic spirit than elsewhere. In the local journals Norwegian settlers are most often characterized as hardworking, thrifty, and law-abiding.

Western expansion was given a powerful boost when the Homestead Act was finally passed in 1862. It gave every American citizen, or anyone who intended to become a citizen, 160 acres of surveyed government land, providing the settler stayed on his property for five years and made certain improvements on it. The many weaknesses in the law and its possibilities for abuse and

fraud by speculators resulted in the loss of enormous land areas for legitimate settlers. Still, the system helped to populate new regions where there was available land. The "free land" did not fall to everyone's lot, and not everyone who acquired a farm obtained the promised 160 acres, but sufficient numbers of pioneers achieved it that others were prompted to come after.

Norwegian settlement in Minnesota preceded the Homestead Act. After the settlers from the East reached the Mississippi River, they could either take the steamboat to St. Paul or cross the river and continue on foot or by ox-drawn wagons which could be arranged for at one of the small commercial centers along the river. The very first Norwegian pioneers arrived in 1851, and from then on "many different parties of Norwegians" moved to western Houston and eastern Fillmore counties, but independently of each other, Hjalmar Holand says. From this core, settlement expanded west along the Iowa border. But Norwegians generally avoided the open prairies. Like other immigrant people, they feared the windswept grassland and preferred forested parts. In the magnificent landscape of southeastern Minnesota one could after a time see "one ridge after the other . . . densely populated by Norwegians." They lived in compact Norwegian-speaking neighborhoods. In southern Houston county the completely Norwegian Spring Grove township came into being.

The second early core area lay farther north, in the southwestern part of the large county of Goodhue. This region Holand characterized as "a farmer's dream of Paradise." Here Norwegian pioneers began to settle in 1854. The "billowing plains . . . broken by lovely wooded groves" held strong promise of future prosperity. But those who subdued the land experienced the trials and privations of pioneer life for a second or even a third time. "The age of the ox and the *kubberulle*," Holand calls the pioneer period, with its material poverty and its crudity.

Pioneer pastors who visited the settlers could tell about the need for spiritual sustenance and ministerial services. The pastor U. V. Koren visited Spring Grove early in the pioneer period. He conducted religious meetings under the open sky and baptized eighteen children, a few of them old enough to walk up to the baptismal font. Laur. Larsen in 1857 came to Goodhue county,

and it is said that he "preached six days at a stretch for large gatherings, and many followed him from place to place." During the same time he baptized one hundred children. The formation of a congregation and the building of a church were the next steps. The church in Spring Grove was completed in 1868, but a congregation had already been gathered in 1855. In Goodhue county, the pastor Bernt J. Muus served the Holden congregation for forty years from 1859 and became, says Holand, "the dominant man in Goodhue county."

The names of congregations and settlements indicate that attachment to a particular community in Norway continued to affect patterns of settlement. Bonds of kinship to older colonies and to Norway promoted this development. Newcomers as a rule moved in with relatives and previous neighbors, and then got land or employment in the area. The congregations were therefore formed by people from specific districts in Norway, as for example the Valdres settlement Vang in Goodhue county. In this county there are also such Norwegian place-names as Toten, Eidsvold, Dovre, Sogn, and Aspelund. The church became the social and religious center in the settlement—white church steeples proudly point toward the sky in many Norwegian districts.

The Homestead Act influenced the direction of subsequent settlement. Even though a few Norwegian pioneers had made their way to the Minnesota River valley earlier, it was only after 1865 that Norwegians in search of land streamed into districts to the north and northwest, many of them from older farm communities in southern Minnesota. From southwestern Kandiyohi county up toward the Red River valley, bounded to the west by prairie and the northeast by forest, there appeared a belt of Norwegian settlements. The attractive area the Norwegians had come to was known as the Lake Park region, northwest of the so-called Big Woods, an impenetrable wooded area. They settled in a "landscape," says Holand, that "consists of a series of elevated, billowing meadows covered by deep, extremely fertile mold," and "the plains are divided and separated from each other by several thousand lakes in all shapes and sizes." In 1869 the first pioneers reached the Minnesota side of the Red River valley.

As many as 83,856 people of Norwegian descent lived in Minnesota in 1875. About 61 percent of them had emigrated from Norway. Of those born in America, 84 percent had been born in Minnesota, 11 percent in Wisconsin, and 4 percent in Iowa. These figures provide some idea of the internal migration patterns of Norwegians in America. Thousands of Norwegian pioneers who set out to the western frontier had never viewed the mountains and valleys of Norway. The second generation had arrived, and their ability to adjust was greater than their parents'.

The Homestead Act of 1862 was a great incentive for settlers to go west. Many Norwegian pioneers sought government land in regions newly opened to settlement.

The Great Plains to the West

Government land in regions with forest had become difficult to find, and later Norwegian pioneers had to adjust to the prairie landscape—the great plains to the West waited. In his classic im-

migrant novel *Giants in the Earth*, Ole E. Rølvaag depicts "Per Hansa, who with his family and all his earthly possessions was moving west from Fillmore county, Minnesota, to Dakota Territory. There he intended to take up land and build himself a home; he was going to do something remarkable out there, which should become known far and wide." This was in 1873. Per Hansa and his company came to the area by the Big Sioux River in Minnehaha county in the southern part of Dakota Territory. In 1889 the Territory became the two states of South Dakota and

Norwegian settlements in the states of Minnesota, Iowa, and the two Dakotas are indicated on the map.

across the plains, gathered strength, and in winter caused "terrifying blizzards, when sky and earth appeared to be a single whirling spume of snow." In the great snow winter of 1880-81 people ran out of both food and firewood. Rølvaag has given artistic treatment to this winter in his famous novel: Per Hansa became a victim of the great storm.

After the winter was over the scorching heat came, and the settlers might be exposed to the feared prairie fire, or *fairen*, as the Norwegians called it, which spread with tremendous speed and consumed everything in its path. Along the rivers, where many Norwegians settled, there were trees that could be used as material for log cabins, but because of lack of other resources the building material on the prairie was often sod. The settlers put up sod huts as a protection against the elements. They were small and dark, and when it rained the roof leaked, but they provided shelter and were snug against wind and cold weather. Trees could be planted around the sod huts as added protection against weather and wind. In time the huts were replaced with frame houses.

When the prairie sod had been turned and the land cultivated, it might with sufficient moisture give large harvests of corn and wheat. Thus did the prairie blossom and give rich crops. After a while the Red River valley claimed to be the breadbasket of the world, and the golden wheat fields lured many new Norwegian farmers.

As earlier, it was newcomers who provided cheap labor; they were numerous in the 1880s. The ticket to America generally cost a year's work with board. By 1900 there were 51,000 Norwegians in South Dakota, 12.8 percent of the state's population. A few Norwegians had moved south of the Missouri River to Nebraska, but it was northeast of the river, in the valleys formed by the Big Sioux River and its tributaries, that Norwegians established larger colonies. Many Norwegians came to the counties of Minnehaha and Brookings; in the latter county in 1873 a large group of Trønders settled by Lake Hendricks. The two towns of Sioux Falls, in Minnehaha county, and Canton, in Lincoln county farther south, became important centers of Norwegian-American life.

North Dakota became the most Norwegian of all states. In 1869 Norwegian pioneers had

North Dakota. A few Norwegian pioneers had ventured out on the prairie already in the late 1850s, but the actual conquest of the broad grasslands did not commence until the end of the following decade. The prairie seemed overwhelming and threatening. Adjustment became a new challenge, and some succumbed to the prairie's oppressive monotony and might. The struggle between nature and human beings grew ever more direct. A constant wind soughed

along the Mouse River (now the Souris), and finally they reached all the way to western North Dakota. Minot became the settlers' little metropolis. Olav Redal, himself a resident of the area, describes a district in northern Bottineau county by the Souris River as a Norwegian *bygd*, or community. He says that most of those who came were "young people who went west to make a home for themselves." "At that time it was no disgrace," he continues, "for a hefty girl from the dales of Norway or a Trønder maiden to accompany her strong husband out on the unknown plains and move into a house that perhaps did not cost over $20."

Around 1900, Norwegian pioneers moved into

Left: Vang Church in Goodhue county. Construction began in 1863, and the church was dedicated in 1868. It was named after the settlers' home community in Norway. The strength of the regional attachment became evident in patterns of settlement as Norwegians moved westward.

Below: Eric Braarud is clearing land in Polk county, Minnesota, in 1903. The enormous roots had to be removed before the land could be cultivated.

moved across to the North Dakota side of the Red River and taken land. That year marks the beginning of permanent Norwegian settlement in the state. It was in the valley, in reality a slightly sloping plain created by the Red River and its tributaries, that Norwegians settled in large numbers. In 1900 Norwegians made up 23 percent of all the people in North Dakota—nearly 75,000. Ten years later there were an additional 50,000 Norwegians. All the way up to 1920 Norwegians were the largest ethnic group in the state. In 1914 Norwegian farmers could boast of owning 7,868,140 acres of North Dakota's fertile land.

In 1879 they were, however, only 8,000 strong. But in that year the great Dakota land boom began. It affected the entire territory and produced a migration that can best be described as a large-scale folk wandering. Traill county in North Dakota in 1880 was 74 percent Norwegian. In Griggs county, Norwegians constituted half of the population. Along the valley they became numerous in many areas, and towns came into being. Fargo, Grand Forks, and smaller towns like Hatton, Mayville, and Hillsboro, in what became a new Norway, took on a Norwegian flavor that has been preserved until today.

Settlement moved westward. Straight across the immense, undulating plains there occurred a race between the railroads and Norwegian pioneers, Holand says. Early in the 1880s Norwegian settlers reached the Devils Lake area. A few years later they began to take land farther west,

eastern Montana. Others took part in the excavation of mineral riches in western Montana, Idaho, and eastern Colorado. Agriculture had, however, a greater appeal than work in the "mineral kingdom" in the Far West.

The Sioux Uprising

One treaty after another had transferred enormous land areas from different Indian tribes to land-hungry settlers, but the Indians often remained on their previous domain for several years after the treaties had been signed. It took time to move them to the reservations. Holand says that "they roamed about among the settlers meekly begging." They might frighten a settler by pressing a curious face against a windowpane, but they usually did no one any harm. From his association with the peaceful tribes in Wisconsin the pastor Olaus Fredrik Duus wrote home to Norway and related that on a cold New Year's Day he had found shelter in an Indian tent. When their first daughter was born, his wife Sophie received assistance from an Indian midwife.

The more belligerent Sioux Indians in Minne-

Norwegian immigrants had to learn new agricultural methods and get used to larger equipment and machines, larger farms and cultivated acreage, and a different topography than most of them had been accustomed to in Norway. The illustrations show this development.

Above left: Andrew Anderson Tofte clears new land with a team of oxen on the prairie near Madison, Minnesota, ca. 1880. The prairie sod was hard to break.

Below left: Plowing with machines on a large scale.

Above right: Haying in North Dakota around 1905. Several farmers help each other.

Below right: To the left, horses are pulling a self-binder; to the right, steam power is used in the threshing operations. Both photos from Pope county, Minnesota.

Sunday at Butte View

The great Dakota land boom began in 1879 and resulted in a movement into this region that can best be compared to a large-scale folk migration. There were especially many Norwegians among the pioneers, and until 1920 Norwegians formed the largest ethnic group in North Dakota.

Above left: Norwegians in Dakota transport wheat to market. Above right: Women as well as men might homestead alone, as indicated by this postcard from Carrie Einarson, Inland, South Dakota, dated May 11, 1911: Dear Clara, I am sending a photograph of myself in front of my hut. I ought to have sent you a letter, but I have too much to do at present. Greet your family. Your friend, Carrie." The name Kari had been Americanized to Carrie. Middle: Mrs. Endre Olson sitting in her horse cart in front of her home in Freeborn county, Minnesota. Below right: Ingeborg Folkedahl Johnson (standing) is serving Sunday afternoon coffee outside her home on the prairie, Landa, North Dakota, ca. 1902. "Belle" Johnson had moved there from Wisconsin. Below left: Mr. and Mrs. Henry Halvorsen, Zahl, North Dakota, pose proudly in front of their barn.

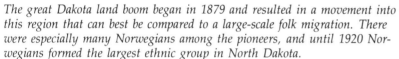

sota suddenly and unexpectedly revolted on August 18, 1862. They went on the warpath against white settlers with plunder, fire, and destruction. They thereby confirmed the worst fears people in the West harbored. Before the hostilities had been suppressed, late the same fall, nearly 500 white people had been killed. The immediate causes were a poor harvest and constant delays in the payment of government annuities. The larger reasons behind the uprising were the Indians' feeling of being pushed out by the explosive western expansion and their dissatisfaction with the gradual impoverishment life on the reservations brought about. Not all Sioux Indians vented their frustrations in warfare, but especially the younger braves were incited to use the only recourse they had. They were ably led by their chief, Little Crow.

Panic gripped people in all of Minnesota and neighboring areas. People sought shelter and built barricades far from the affected regions. They fled in terror from "the red skins" on the warpath. Bernt J. Muus and his family took refuge in Red Wing, even though they were far removed from the uprising. Many of the settlers in the most exposed areas went to small towns like St. Peter and New Ulm. The latter town was twice attacked.

The situation was more serious for those who were surprised on their isolated farms without any defense. The literature about the Indian War is filled with stories of heroism and courage; among these is the account of Guri Endresen Rosseland from Vikør in Hardanger. With her husband, Lars, and their children, she had settled by Lake Solomon, north of the town of Willmar in Kandiyohi county in 1857. The following year the so-called Norway Lake settlement farther north was established. It was the only large Norwegian colony in the Lake Park region before the uprising, and in 1860 about a hundred Norwegian settlers lived there. On August 20—a beautiful summer day—the Indians ravaged the settlement by Norway Lake. In the afternoon of the following day they assaulted the Rosseland farm. The Indians killed Lars and the oldest son and his wife, and wounded a younger son. The farm buildings were burned down. Before they left with two of the daughters as hostages, they butchered an ox, roasted and ate it. What saved "old Guri," as Holand calls the forty-nine-year-

Otto A. Jacobson, a pioneer in Adams county, North Dakota. Living conditions were extremely simple in the early days of settlement.

Family and guests at the home of Peter Danielson in Providence township in western Minnesota. The picture was taken around the turn of the century.

Above: Norwegian hotel—"Norsk Hotel"—close to Decorah, Iowa.

Left: The sod church near Hemmingford in Box Butte county, Nebraska, in 1903. The children in the congregational school are gathered outside the church.

Right: Railroad workers near the small town of Peterson, Minnesota, in 1896. Many Norwegian immigrants found employment on the large railroad construction projects. The town of Peterson was platted by Peter Peterson Haslerud from Numedal on his own property.

old heroine, was that she had remained with her youngest daughter in a cellar some distance from the house. Guri fled with the daughter, hid, and returned the next day to discover that the wounded son, whom she had thought to be dead, was alive. In a wagon pulled by oxen she transported them and two other wounded men from a nearby farm a distance of about thirty miles farther east, to safety in Forest City. The trip had been through regions controlled by Indians and took two and a half days. Among the refugees in Forest City, she found her two daughters, who had managed to escape from the captors. Guri was not bitter; "God allowed it to happen thus," she wrote to her mother in Norway.

By this uprising the Indians strengthened the impression that they were bloodthirsty savages. A public hanging of thirty-eight Indians in Mankato in December of 1862 was intended to put an end to the tragedy, but occasional attacks and raids by Indians continued for three more years, and fear of the Indians much longer. Many regions became deserted. Property losses through fire and the slaughtering of animals had been great, and some settlers left the state for good. The Indian uprising slowed the increase in population and the economic growth of the Northwest. News of the atrocities in the pioneer areas spread quickly to Norway. The terrifying accounts were included in newspapers and used to frighten people away from emigrating. A short-term decline in emigration resulted, but it soon subsided, and new hosts of emigrants headed west.

Many Interests Promoted Settlement

Scandinavians came to Minnesota, and later to the Dakotas, in large numbers after the Civil War. The region was strategically placed during a period that coincided with the first mass emigration from Scandinavia. Here was an abundance of good inexpensive, or even free, land. The two main hindrances to further settlement were now removed: the Civil War was over and

The Sioux Indians did not "own" the land that the immigrants bought or were given title to by the government, because the Indians had no concept of "land possession." But they were the original inhabitants. The picture shows 2 Blackfoot Indians.

the Indian danger was lessened. The westward folk migration advanced, and Norwegians and other Scandinavians were carried along.

The factors of time and geographic location thus explain the region's attractiveness for Scandinavians. But it was necessary to reach the settlers with news of the opportunities the area had to offer, and information and propaganda activity in the promotion of settlement therefore played a decisive role in the growth of new colonies. Depending on which interests were to be served, either older settlers or railroad companies spread information. Both those railroads that wished to transport settlers to the Middle West and the so-called land-grant railroads that had acreage to sell conducted publicity cam-

paigns. There was also agitation by certain industrial and commercial enterprises, by large private land companies, and by state and federal agencies.

Letters to the Homeland and to Older Settlements

Letters from early pioneers went both to the homeland and to older settlements. The Norwegian-American newspapers, like the Norwegian ones, willingly accepted accounts of the new land. Thousands of letters, of course, never appeared in any newspaper, but still made an impact. Ole Halvorsen Næss from Hallingdal settled in the Lake Park area in 1856; the following year he wrote letters to *Emigranten* about this region "which attracted much attention." His newspaper contributions were the direct cause of the settlement of Norway Lake. Through the press people might be encouraged to write about specific settlements, and those who had moved happily complied with such requests. From Fari-

Guri Endresen Rosseland (1813-81), who survived a bloody attack and managed to escape from the Indians. "I will now describe everything to you as thoroughly as I am able, and as far as my heart, which is trembling with fear, will allow me. That which I suspected and wrote about in my last letter has come about. The Indians have begun attacking the farmers. They have already killed a great many people, and many are mutilated in the cruelest manner. Tomahawks and knives have already claimed many victims. . . . I believe that even if I described the horror in the strongest possible language, my description would fall short of the reality." (Letter from E. O. in St. Peter, Minnesota, to his brother-in-law in Norway, dated September 9, 1862. It was printed in several Norwegian newspapers.)

bault, Minnesota, an immigrant wrote a letter to Norway in 1866, which was printed in *Aftenposten*, about "the multiplicity of Norwegian and Swedish settlements" in that area, and he predicted that Minnesota "before this century passes, will . . . probably be one of the most prosperous and powerful states in the whole Union."

Agents Enticed the Immigrants

The individual states and territories competed for settlers and immigrants. In the early 1850s Wisconsin had appointed an official whose assignment was to lure people to the state. Following a period of inactivity, a separate Wisconsin board of immigration was established in 1867. In the early 1870s the office was ably administered by the Norwegian Ole C. Johnson as commissioner. He was a hero from the Fifteenth Wisconsin Regiment and its commander after Heg's death. In 1870 the state of Iowa established its board of immigration. In Minnesota, state colonization work had begun in a small way in 1858. Printed propaganda about Minnesota's wonders was disseminated in newspaper and magazine articles. The most important form in which information was spread was, however, pamphlets. Those printed in Minnesota in 1865 were also available in Norwegian translation, and the demand was greater than the supply. State propaganda activity reached a high point in 1867 when Minnesota also created a board of immigration. With economic support from the railroad companies, Minnesota had placed a Norwegian immigrant, K. Hasberg, in Milwaukee and a well-known Swedish immigration agent, Hans Mattson, in Chicago. Each was charged with getting Scandinavian newcomers to move to Minnesota. The territorial assembly had previously supported an immigration commissioner in New York with an identical assignment, but he had only sporadically worked among Scandinavians. There were in addition agents at Quebec and Montreal. The immigration boards that were established after the Civil War also directed their attention to the delivering countries and aimed at reaching the emigrants with their propaganda before they left the homeland.

Hans Mattson, born in Skåne in Sweden, was both a pioneer and a soldier. He was a colonel in the Civil War, and was active in Swedish-American journalism and in the political life of Minnesota. In 1867 he was appointed to head the board of immigration. Later he was rewarded with the position of secretary of state. Mattson circulated information among all Scandinavians. The Norwegian journalist Paul Hjelm Hansen, who became an agent for Minnesota in 1869, was, however, more concerned with promoting Norwegian settlement. His name has to a special degree become associated with the Red River valley, and he is regarded as the one who opened up this area, in both North Dakota and Minnesota, to Norwegian settlement. He had emigrated from Norway at age fifty-seven, in 1867. In the summer of 1869 Hjelm Hansen went by ox-drawn wagon from Alexandria in Douglas county all the way to the Red River district. When he returned to Alexandria after three weeks, he wrote his travel accounts, sixteen in all. These were printed in the newspapers *Nordisk Folkeblad* (Nordic People's Paper) and *Fædrelandet og Emigranten* (The Fatherland and the Emigrant). Hjelm Hansen underscores how advantageous the new regions would be for "Scandinavian farmers" and how healthy "the clean air" is. For potential farmers, it was perhaps more important to know that the land was "to the highest degree fertile and extraordinarily easy to cultivate, for there was not as much as a stone or a stump to block the plow." Another noteworthy agent was the Norwegian journalist Johan Schrøder, who was secretary for the Minnesota board of immigration and the author of a survey of Norwegian settlements.

The Railroad Companies Sell Land

Even though a considerable number of agents were active, in 1872 state propaganda activity in Minnesota declined as other interest groups expanded their work. The railroad companies were especially active, in Minnesota as elsewhere, since they had to sell the land they owned along their lines. Where a projected line was to be built, the federal government had given them every other section of land in the public domain to an agreed-upon distance from the line. Along both sides of the tracks there was thus a checkerboard of government and railroad land; in order to amass capital and create traffic for the railroad, the land had to be sold and settled.

Not until 1862 was the first railroad built in Minnesota, and only five years later did construction on a large scale begin. The company that was most active in the spread of information was the Northern Pacific. It had completed a line in the northern part of the state in 1872, between Duluth and Moorhead. Agents worked in Europe and pamphlets were sent to persuade immigrants to make their homes along the line. Hans Mattson stayed awhile in Sweden as this company's agent. The Swedish historian Lars Ljungmark has shown that the Northern Pacific made little progress in its efforts to populate the land it owned, in spite of its intense exertions. The St. Paul & Pacific Company, which also employed Mattson as its agent, had greater success. In 1871 this railroad had completed a line northwestward from St. Paul to Breckenridge on the Red River. The tracks were laid through a region where Mattson, in his capacity as immigration agent, had placed Scandinavian settlers on government land. When cheap railroad land was offered, the earlier settlers acted as magnets to draw newcomers.

In the effort to promote settlement there was close cooperation between state and private interests. Newspaper publishers provided support through convincing editorials; far and wide the advantages of a specific region were proclaimed. All attempts stranded, however, on an economic crisis. Newcomers had been able to get work on railroad construction and thereby supplement their income. But suddenly, in 1873, a severe economic depression set in and for a while put a stop to further railroad building; it also radically limited emigration from the Scandinavian countries. In the Northwest the crash had an even greater impact because of a new curse that struck the settlers. This was the annual swarms of grasshoppers. The first came in 1873 and severely ravaged Norwegian districts. The grasshoppers destroyed the harvests year after year until 1877. A good crop that year rescued the farmers who had not already been ruined. It is said that there were in these years an unusual number of lay preachers "traveling around, who thundered sermons of damnation over the suffering people." The swarms of grasshoppers were supposed to be punishment for their sins, it was claimed.

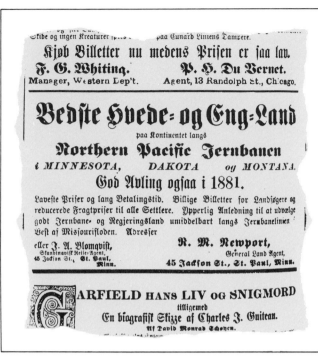

The Northern Pacific Railroad Company actively promoted settlement. In this notice, printed in the Chicago newspaper Verdens Gang on July 28, 1881, the company offers "the best wheat and farmland" along its railroad line. June 2 of the same year the following appeared in the Valley City Times in North Dakota, indicating how fierce the competition was for new settlers: "It is a most excellent arrangement that the principal passenger run on the Northern Pacific railway is by night through Minnesota, and by day from Fargo to Bismarck. To ride through the poverty-stricken prairies of Minnesota by daylight is enough to discourage anybody as to the Northwest in general, while the rich soil and manifest agricultural prosperity of North Dakota attract the attention of the passenger, and astonish and delight him."

Word of the destruction caused by this plague soon reached Norway. Combined with the difficult economic situation, the news had, of course, the opposite effect than the one the propagandists had worked for. At the end of the decade, however, the great conquest of the West began.

The "Dakota fever" of the 1880s was evoked by an enormous expansion in the railroad system to Dakota Territory, a series of years with sufficient precipitation, and an active publicity apparatus. The territorial assembly sent agents both to older settlements and to the ports of debarkation on the East Coast, and distributed pamphlets in several languages. Most of the settlers took the train as far as they could. But some continued in a traditional manner to use oxen and wagons. It was in this later settling of the Great Plains that the railroad became a real force. Expectation that a railroad would be built encouraged people to flock to specific areas. In 1880 the Northern Pacific crossed the border into Montana from the southern part of North Dakota. Ten years later the Great Northern, the company that the railroad king James J. Hill had reorganized, built a line across the northern part of the state. Norwegian settlers took land on both sides of the tracks.

Beginning in the late 1880s drought and the subsequent depression diminished movement; but after 1900 there was again heavy migration of Norwegians to North Dakota, where there was still free land for the settler.

Taking Land

Surveying of public land in Minnesota did not begin until 1853; the sale of land began two years later when land offices were opened. The major division in the survey was the township. Each township consisted of thirty-six sections, each section being one square mile, or 640 acres. The Preemption Act of 1841 permitted a settler to occupy as much as 160 acres, or a quarter section, by registering a claim at a federal land office. To *klæme* land, the Norwegian pioneers called filing a land claim. At the next land auction the property could be bought. Norwegian pioneers, as well as other settlers, preferred to buy public or government land, rather than land that was privately owned. Before the Homestead Act of 1862, government land was sold at a minimum price of $1.25 per acre.

Klæmeren, the one who claimed land, had to settle on the land and make certain improvements. The dwelling of those who took land was frequently a simple claim shanty. They might of course lose everything if they were unable to pay for the land they had claimed, and this happened many times before the Homestead Act made land free, as for example with the unfortunate settlers in Shelbyville, Missouri. The property would then go to the highest bidder, but, as J. R. Reiersen noted in 1844 in his America guide, "the purchaser risks inconvenience or even danger if he drives the man who has claimed the land from house and home without compensation." In these early communities there was a sense of justice that supported the settlers. They represented a pioneer spirit that was respected. If anyone wanted to buy a claim, it was therefore prudent to have talked to the owner in advance and to make compensation by purchasing the right to the claim.

People who settled on public land without taking out a claim, or who moved in before the land had been surveyed, became squatters without legal rights to the land they resided on. There were many of these in Minnesota, and it took time to survey all government land. The pioneers as a rule cared little about legal questions. They occupied land that had not been surveyed, laid out farms, selected town sites, and sent work gangs into the forests, all contrary to the law. But they maintained their right; they joined forces to defend the land they had taken possession of and to keep away speculators. They formed societies with laws and rules and elected officials, with a club as their symbol. If necessary, they used force to protect their possessions. This was called the "club law." It was quickly adopted also by Norwegian settlers.

The "Club Law" Is Used

Such a club society had been formed in pioneer times at Koshkonong. It was made up of Norwegian and American settlers, and it had set rules for its procedures. Holand writes that Primrose in the Blue Mounds settlement in Wisconsin "was one of the first places where the 'club law,' later so common, was organized."

The cover of a pamphlet printed in Norwegian by South Dakota's immigration office. The publication is dated 1913, and on the second page it proclaims that "Corn is King in South Dakota."

Among early Norwegians in Goodhue county, Minnesota, there was also a club society to protect the settlers' claims and the land they had taken in addition to the 160 acres the law permitted. A story about it is linked to the names of two notorious brothers, Tøge and Henrik Nilsen Talla, from Luster in Sogn. They came to Goodhue county in the summer of 1854. According to Torkel Oftelie's account in *Telesoga*, 1917, the two brothers wanted to own all the land they saw, and "in a circle of many miles they went around and wrote their name on all section markers and quarter-section sticks they found. When anyone looking for land arrived, they found the names

'Nilsen' or 'Talla' on the markers and had to go on." It was these two who, when they realized they could not alone defend all the wonders they had demanded, persuaded the other settlers in the area to join with them in a club society. Nils Kolkin, a pioneer, likely provides the most reliable account. According to him, all agreed that each farmer "should take 80 acres in addition to his own quarter section, and that every undesirable person should be kept away." They all therefore acted in self-interest. A club society was formed and a written club law adopted. When everyone had signed it, Oftelie relates, Tøge took up "an oak club, and by it they all took an oath to enforce the law and use the club on anyone who dared enter their domain."

The club law was resorted to the following summer when a party of Telemarkings from Dane county, Wisconsin, forced their way into the area. Their leader was Svein Norgarden, called Storesvein (Big Svein) because of his large size. The Telemarkings ignored all the stakes with "Talla" on them. When they began to fell trees to build a hut, some of the club society's members, led by the Talla brothers, went after the newcomers with stakes and poles and told them to get out. As the Telemarking Oftelie has it, Storesvein first gave the settlers "a salvo in Telemarking vernacular that startled them," and then he went "berserk, so that they were strewn about him in all directions," while "the women and children hollered and shouted." It was a definitive fight and a complete victory for Storesvein and his men. It was also the end of the club law. The Talla brothers lost the lawsuit they brought before the county judge in Red Wing to retain their land. They had to abandon their dream of becoming local squires in America.

Gro Svendsen, a Pioneer Woman in Iowa

Women participated fully in the conquest of the western lands. The pioneer's wife might make the difference between progress and ruin; a man could hardly put land under the plow alone. Through a collection of letters sent home to her

family in Norway, it is possible to follow one woman, Gro Svendsen, out on the frontier in Emmet county in northern Iowa. The letters provide a vivid picture of frontier conditions. The account is especially important because it illustrates a typical experience for women in the western environment.

Norwegians had discovered Emmet county at an early date, although in 1860, according to the census, they numbered only twenty-one. By 1870 their numbers had increased to 463. Norwegians then represented one-third of the inhabitants of Emmet county. Fear of Indian uprisings, following the fearful bloodbath at Spirit Lake a little farther west in 1857, had put an end to Norwegian settlement for a while.

In the summer of 1862 Gro Svendsen and her husband, Ole, came to western Iowa. The next spring they took land near Estherville to make a home for themselves in America. Gro, at the age of twenty-one, had married twenty-two-year-old Ole before departing from secure and solid peasant circumstances in Ål in Hallingdal. The transfer to uninhabited territories in the interior of America therefore was a hardship and a great change for the young woman.

Gro gave birth to her first child, a son, not long after her arrival in America. Proudly she sent a daguerreotype of herself, Ole, and the boy to her parents to find out what they thought about their grandchild. The family grew to include ten children, one of whom died of the measles. Son number two was born just before Ole was drafted to serve in the Civil War in 1864. A third son was born while the father was gone. Gro feared that she would never see Ole again, but he returned in good condition in August, 1865, with an honorable discharge.

The American school provided an opportunity for her to learn the language. In her zeal, Gro attended classes with her smallest child on her arm. Not long afterward she herself became a teacher in the Norwegian religion school, as an itinerant schoolteacher in the settlement. In 1862 C. L. Clausen had come over from the St. Ansgar settlement farther east, a colonization project he had headed in 1853, and organized a congregation. Gro and Ole joined it the following year.

Gro was greatly concerned about the education of her children. She informs her parents that the four oldest attended the Norwegian school but

Gro Svendsen's birthplace in Ål in Hallingdal. She came from secure and solid peasant circumstances.

were far behind in their schoolwork. "It is slow work to try to teach the boys at home," she complains. Housework and farm chores demanded most of her time and energy. Her own reading was often limited to her periods of confinement. Her letter writing suffered especially during the busy harvest season. Like other pioneer women, she toiled hard in miserable and primitive conditions, whether they lived in a sod hut or a log cabin. There were endless pressing duties associated with child rearing and the preparation of food. There were also the many births, assisted only by a neighbor woman, and illnesses without a doctor. Even worse was the deep loneliness. Women were often left alone with responsibility for the children while their husbands went to market or were away at work for weeks at a time. When settlers gave up and left the pioneer communities, as many did, it was often at the instigation of a wife who could not adjust. Both emotionally and physically pioneer life exacted the greatest toll on women.

"It's a fine piece of land," Gro wrote about their claim, which they called Skrattegaard after Ole's birthplace in Norway. Even though the land was easy to cultivate, Gro missed trees on the open prairie, and she longed to be back in Norway. But she reconciled herself to the conditions. She assured her parents they would not return. Gro therefore selected names for the children, such as Albert and Carl, that would not sound too strange to Americans. This tendency toward Americanization is also in evidence when she tells that they named a pony "Greeley." At the same time they subscribed to the newspaper *Emigranten*. It kept them informed about world events.

Adversity came. There were blizzards and freezing temperatures in winter, animals were lost, and human beings perished. The terrifying prairie fire might rage in both fall and spring, consume everything in its way, and "race faster than the speediest horse," Gro explains. In their neighborhood it raged several times, destroying crops, animals, and houses, but miraculously their property was spared. Grasshoppers attacked their fields in 1873 and 1876; they came again in 1877, but without laying eggs. The next year Gro died in childbirth, at age thirty-seven. Ole sent a lock of her hair to her parents in Norway. About her grave, Ole wrote that "it has a white marble stone, on which are engraved her name and the date and place of her birth, the date and place of her death, and the names of those she left behind."

Gro Svendsen (1841-78). May 30, 1877, she wrote to her parents: "We are now well housed, both man and beast. This means a great deal to a pioneer because during the first years he is deprived of many comforts previously enjoyed. Nobody must doubt that we are living comfortably. We have whatever we need. As long as God gives life and strength, we shall not fear the future."

The Spirit and the Mind

Between 1846 and 1900 Norwegian immigrants founded fourteen Lutheran synods. In spite of the dissension and strife that characterized the immigrants' religious life, the congregation was central to their existence in America. The several church bodies assumed responsibility for bringing up children and young people in the Lutheran faith by establishing institutions of learning.

Midtoe Forest River Church, Dahlen, North Dakota, 1904. The morning service served an important social function, and people traveled great distances to attend. For some, the Sunday visit to church took up the entire day.

Norwegian Lutheranism in America: A Tradition of Disharmony

"Dissension was of course . . . the order of the day," a church historian says of the situation within organized Norwegian-American Lutheranism. There were disputes over doctrine, personal clashes, conflicts between high-church, broad-church, and low-church views, and factions within each of these. Scandinavian cooperation foundered on national dissimilarities. Time after time there were splits and new formations—civil war among fellow believers. J. A. Bergh laments what he called "the curse of dissension." In many places one could see "two or three church steeples point toward the sky, where one would suffice," and within the same family it sometimes happened that one saw "husband and wife take separate ways to church or mother and daughter . . . meet on the street when they went to their respective houses of worship."

In the many conflicts that arose, the Norwegian Synod was as a rule one of the main participants. The Synod considered itself a daughter church of the Church of Norway. Still, it drew away from the mother church, to some extent because that church showed a lack of interest in immigrant religious life, but even more because the Synod found the homeland's church to be unstable in doctrine, and because the Synod could not reconcile itself to the new theological currents. With support from the Missouri Synod's great theologian and leader, Carl Wilhelm Walther, a man who believed that theological development had been completed with the dogmatists in the seventeenth century, the Synod could confidently challenge and criticize the Norwegian mother church. The prevailing view in the Synod was that theologians who did not follow the old dogma were heretics. Attacks on other immigrant churches were in many instances also indictments of theological developments in Norway. In the 1850s the Synod clashed with Eielsen's Synod; in the 1860s the conflict was "between Augustana and the Synod, and in the seventies between the Conference and the Syn-

Headstone in the cemetery by East Koshkonong church in Dane county. The inscription reads: "Gunsteen Rolfson Aandall, born year 1798 in Norway, died December 7, 1873, came to America year 1844." In a letter to Pastor Jacob Aall Ottesen in Manitowoc dated August 27, 1859, Carl Wilhelm Walther wrote: "Consider what a glorious work is entrusted to us here; here our weak voice is not a voice in the wilderness; here there is no fruitless speculation and theologizing while everything remains nicely as it was, but here all public speaking becomes action and takes shape and is changed into practice! Unsullied souls will bless us when we are slumbering in the grave if through our faithful warfare we bequeath them the treasure of pure doctrine and of practice based on and in accord with its principles."

od, and in the eighties between the Anti-Missourians and the Synod." And of the last controversy, the student of Norwegian-American life, O. M. Norlie, noted that it was so heated that "the other synods nearly forgot their own disputes and stood as observers."

The boundaries between the church of the laity and the cleric's church—the low-church and the high-church persuasions—were drawn early and firmly. The difficult transition from a state-church structure to a free-church system was therefore fraught with deep disharmony from the beginning. Incompatible views were defended by uncompromising men, and the dissension was intensified by an almost undisciplined sense of freedom and opposition among the immigrants. Impulses from American religious life, sectarian groups, and contact with Norwegian theological debate led to new controversies. It was, however, the Synod's long involvement with the stagnant Missouri Synod theology that created the most bitter disputes over doctrine. Out in the congregations, at synodical meetings and intersynodical conferences, at proceedings on doctrine, in newspapers and church journals, lay and learned were pulled into the conflict. The controversy itself contained an unexpressed conviction that only one Lutheran point of view could exist; Norwegian Americans were not numerous enough to accommodate more. But it would require time to digest the many ideas and theological persuasions, and to reach a consensus.

Regardless of theological position, Norwegian-American Lutheranism displayed a strict adherence to the traditional confessional writings. This was the case in the dogmatic high-church persuasion as well as in the pietistic low-church view. It was important for both to set boundaries against and to emphasize differences from non-Lutheran churches; Lutheran symbols and Lutheran beliefs were in this manner strengthened. The common confessionalism of Norwegian-American Lutheranism put a distance between it and non-Lutheran denominations and distinguished it from American Lutheranism, a religious development with roots in the German immigration during the Colonial period. The latter had come to terms with American Protestantism and attached less importance to Lutheran principles. The Lutheran church that grew strong among Norwegians in America was to a marked degree an immigrant church.

This altarpiece was made by the woodcarver Lars Christenson (1839-1910). Christenson emigrated from Sogndal in 1864. The altarpiece is now in the collection of the Norwegian-American Museum Vesterheim in Decorah, Iowa.

A detail from the altarpiece is shown to the right.

The Lutheran Advance

The Norwegian Synod

In 1873 the Norwegian Synod ministered to nearly 80,000 souls, served by seventy-four pastors in 335 congregations. The historian Laurence M. Larson maintains that the Synod's major architects were H. A. Preus, Jakob Aall Ottesen, U. V. Koren, Bernt J. Muus, and Laur. Larsen. All had emigrated in the 1850s. These five men dominated the Synod and were its faithful guides for more than a generation. They belonged to the aristocratic classes and had been trained at the national university of Norway. In America they were brought together by a common background, became good friends, thought alike, and appreciated each other's company. As opposition, attacks, and dissension arose in the church, they showed a remarkable unity and accord.

The need for Lutheran pastors could not be satisfied by appeals to Norwegian theological students. Norwegian settlements were growing and spreading so rapidly that the church leaders became convinced that they had to find a temporary arrangement to train ministers until the Synod could establish its own theological seminary. In 1857 they came to an understanding with the Missouri Synod so that pastors could be educated at its Concordia Seminary in St. Louis. This was the beginning of what many have called a fateful relationship. The alliance strengthened conservative attitudes and made the Synod less effective within the Norwegian-American community.

The slavery issue is an example. The question had been raised in earnest at a synodical meeting in June, 1861, at Luther Valley Church on Rock Prairie. Greatly disturbed by the slavery debate, the lay delegates pushed through a resolution to open a separate school to train pastors immediately, so that the Missouri connection could be broken. Already that fall Luther College had opened, patterned by the clergy after the traditional Norwegian Latin school and limited to male students. Laur. Larsen, who from 1859 had served as professor and adviser for the Norwegian students at Concordia Seminary, was appointed to administer the small school. The first winter the school occupied the parsonage at Half Creek, near La Crosse. It was moved to Decorah, Iowa, in the fall of 1862. As head of the school, Larsen gained considerable influence. But Luther College never trained pastors, as it was originally intended. What it offered was a preparatory course for theological training at the schools of the Missouri Synod, Concordia and Fort Wayne, the latter in Indiana. A beginning of a separate theological seminary, with instruction in some disciplines, was made in 1876 in Madison, Wisconsin, but not until two years later was the Synod able to establish a complete training institution.

An Intermediate Church Position

A broad-church direction became evident for the first time in the formation of the Scandinavian Augustana Synod in 1860. The emergence of this church body was an expression of dissatisfaction with what was seen as clericalism and dogmatism in the Synod. But this intermediate position also rejected the extremes of the Ellingians, even though the Augustanians regarded themselves as heirs of Haugeanism. They simultaneously dissociated themselves from the American Lutherans, who were less bound to Lutheran tradition.

This Lutheran persuasion received impulses

Augsburg Seminary, now Augsburg College, in Minneapolis. The pastor O. Paulson deserves much of the credit for moving the seminary to Minneapolis in 1872. Paulson's memoirs suggest the strength of the Lutheran traditions: "I was much against many of the common customs in the Norwegian congregations, especially the ministerial vestment . . . and I fought . . . long and manfully against 'the long frock.' I thought that it was so inhumanly old-fashioned, homely, and ugly that I could not comprehend why sensible people would demand that their pastor should be burdened by such a monstrosity. I had the entire congregation against me, however, and succumbed to its wishes." (Erindringer af pastor O. Paulson, Minneapolis, 1907.)

from the new spiritual orientation that was associated with the name of the Norwegian professor of theology Gisle Johnson. The Johnsonian revival got its first spokesman in America when August Wenaas emigrated in 1868. Wenaas represented a pietistic lay conviction in its freer and more evangelistic West Norwegian form. He joined the Scandinavian Augustana Synod. In 1869 he was able to separate the Norwegian division from this synod's theological seminary in Paxton, Illinois, and established an independent Norwegian institution in Marshall, Wisconsin. He gave it the name Augsburg Seminary; by his choice of the German form of Augustana, he stressed the body's loyalty to Lutheran confessionalism. Wenaas headed the school and also taught. It was now only a question of time before the Norwegian Augustanians would part company with their Swedish brethren. This hap-

pened in 1870, when the Norwegian congregations after amicable agreement left and formed a Norwegian Augustana. A middle ground thus appeared in a Norwegian dress.

A couple of months later, however, the Norwegian Augustanians experienced a second split. This dispute concerned the form of the new church body. A minority objected to a movement toward a nationalistic, Norwegian-Danish church tradition. The majority then organized a new synod and called it the Conference of the Norwegian-Danish Evangelical Lutheran Church in America, generally referred to as the Conference. The energetic and versatile C. L. Clausen became its president. The Conference was oriented toward tradition; it supported the use of ministerial garments and Danish-Norwegian church ritual. But at the same time it functioned in the low-church tradition as a loose federation of independent congregations.

The Conference, and the congregations that continued as the Norwegian Augustana, constituted the broad, intermediate position in Norwegian-American Lutheranism. Whereas the Augustana remained small and stunted, the more nationalistic Conference grew rapidly, in spite of losing the Danish congregations in 1884. The Conference became the major Lutheran church body alongside the Synod.

The Conference's center was Augsburg Seminary, which it took over and in 1872 moved from Marshall to Minneapolis. It was the teachers at this seminary who provided leadership and gave content to the Conference. Fresh forces came from Norway: Sven Oftedal in 1873, Georg Sverdrup and Sven R. Gunnersen in 1874. Like Wenaas, they had studied under Gisle Johnson's tutelage at the theological faculty and had become inspired by his message. They had a common conviction of a living Christianity within a free-church framework, with unrestrained independent congregations. It was an attitude that reflected the democratic spirit in Norway, associated with both the emergence of the Liberal party and the religious awakenings that these men were associated with. In America they challenged the position of the Synod. For the first time the capable leaders in the Synod had opponents who were their equals, and this to a degree that made the Synod refer to the Conference as its greatest and worst enemy.

A Conference Leader Attacks the Synod

It was the Synod's Missouri connection that caused animosity. In January, 1874, Sven Oftedal took the offensive in a vehement "Open Declaration" printed in the newspaper *Skandinaven*. In somewhat ill-considered terms he accused the Synod of being "anti-Christian" and "papistic," because it limited itself to "scholastic and intellectual orthodoxy" that "disintegrated faith in dead knowledge" and created "a distinct contempt for all awakenings." Oftedal threw in for good measure the old controversial issues—from lay preaching to the Synod's "teaching about slavery's divine justification."

This ill-advised document was later to create dissent within the Conference itself. The Synod first expressed surprise, but then took up the gauntlet. U. V. Koren charged the Conference with using empty phrases, "sophisms and bombastic platitudes." He claimed that this was evidence of confusion in doctrine within the Conference and that the only thing holding it together was a common enmity to the Synod.

The Unitarian minister Kristofer Janson used the example of a Synod church and a Conference church that stood side by side on a hilltop in Winchester, Wisconsin, as strong symbols of the dissension in Norwegian-American Lutheranism. There it had allegedly happened that "corpses were dug up and thrown over the board fence to the other church's graveyard," because "it would be so unpleasant and detestable in the resurrection that the righteous and the ungodly should rise together." There is little to support the truth of this account, but the bitterness of the conflict gives it a certain credibility. The story was used to criticize sterile religious bickering and the intolerance it spread.

"The Holy" Organize

Many newcomers in the 1870s and 1880s found a religious home in the Conference. The adherents of the Conference and the Synod might be called "the churchly," and those who belonged to the lay movement "the holy." The latter were extremely ascetic and condemned all worldliness and frivolity. Immigrant memoirs tell of a joyless pietism in many houses: no festivity, no worldly songs or needless talk. Church atten-

dance, prayers, and the singing of hymns marked their lives, even on festive holidays like Christmas. This religious persuasion eventually became more firmly organized, but it remained the smallest of the three major Lutheran developments—"the churchly" parties gathered most Norwegians.

Eielsen and his flock cared little about church organization, on either the local or the synod level. The church body he led was united rather through personal loyalty to himself than by any firm organization. There was therefore ample opportunity for conflict and the formation of factions. In the 1860s a group of men in Eielsen's Synod began to work for a stronger organization. These new forces gained strength; the example of other churches had an effect; and the Ellingians of "the old school," headed by Eielsen, became a minority. In June, 1876, at a meeting in Chicago, a new organization was completed. This church body became known as Hauge's Synod. The old Ellingians did not join.

The revised constitution that applied in Hauge's Synod established an organizational structure similar to the Synod's. It did not require, as the old constitution did, "a true conversion" to be admitted to the congregation, but replaced this requirement with "a Christian conduct." It was still, however, a church of believers, since the constitution considered as rightful members only those "who are converted and born again." Hauge's Synod encouraged an emotional form of Christianity. It had about 7,500 members, distributed among fifty-nine congregations served by twenty-four pastors. By comparison, the Conference then had three times as many members and the Synod nearly twelve times as many. After a number of unsuccessful attempts, the new synod managed in 1879 to open its own training institution for ministers in Red Wing, Minnesota. The constant and urgent problem of providing enough pastors was thereby solved.

The Norwegian Synod Is Split

It was nearly inescapable that in time there would develop within the Synod itself a reaction against the dominance of the Missouri Synod. As preoccupied as both church bodies were with theological unity, it was equally inevitable that the reaction would express itself in new strife over doctrine. At its annual synodical conferences toward the end of the 1870s, the Missouri Synod took up predestination as a topic. These doctrinal discussions were the immediate cause of the split.

Antagonism against the Missouri Synod was clearly evident at the Synod's annual meeting in 1880. It recognized that two different interpretations existed in the Synod about the doctrine of Election. The learned German dialectician F. A. Schmidt, teacher at the Synod's seminary in Madison, led the opposition to the Missouri position. The Missourians had an able leader in U.

The pastor Lars Markhus of Norway Lake in Minnesota had the humiliating experience of being carried out of his church by the anti-Missourian party. ". . . in his time the fateful Election controversy arose; it raged like a storm through most the congregations, destroying old friendships and neighborly relationships." (Hjalmar Rued Holand, De norske settlementers historie, Chicago, 1912.)

V. Koren. The Election controversy became unusually bitter, almost alarming in its intensity, and efforts to keep it within the church leadership failed. The clergy placed itself in two camps and debated the issue publicly.

Younger ministers revolted against the aging leaders' blind obedience to the Missouri Synod; new pastors from Norway in the 1870s and after were generally anti-Missourian. Both the temperance cause and the question of building colleges in addition to Luther College were mixed into the conflict. There was an abundance of explosive issues, the pastor S. Sondresen claimed following a stay in America from 1890 to 1894. Even though the clergymen displayed an external brotherly unity, clashes of interest smoldered below the surface. Sources of tensions included differences in educational background – some ordained pastors had only completed the Latin school – and in social origins. Sons of farmers were beginning to fill the ranks of the clerics, and the old elite's position was being challenged. Many had, for instance, a suspicion that the sons of the elite were favored in appointments to leading posts in the church. The church fathers were "shrouded in a cloud of blind adoration," Sondresen says, and they held on to their power.

A certain amount of national pride was also in evidence with the so-called Anti-Missourians, since they considered the Missourian interpretation of the Election to be a disavowal of their religious training in childhood as this had been formulated in 1737 by Erik Pontoppidan in *Sandhed til Gudfrytighed* (Truth unto Godliness). This explanation of Luther's Catechism was a major textbook in Norwegian primary schools for nearly 150 years, and by usage was virtually elevated to confessional status.

Evidently the Synod could not accommodate two views; it soon moved toward a breach. No departure from what either side held to be pure doctrine could be tolerated. The Anti-Missourians accused their opponents of crypto-Calvinism, and were in return derided for synergism, the heretical doctrine that in salvation there is cooperation of divine grace and human activity. No one who was pulled into the complicated controversy, either lay or learned, managed to limit the debate to an exchange of theological interpretations. The strife had its own momentum. Previous confrontations had sharp-ened the understanding of confessional issues in the congregations. Those who found faults in their pastor were here given an opportunity to form a party against him. H. A. Preus and J. A. Ottesen, both known for practicing strict church discipline, had the embarrassing experience of being removed from one of the congregations they served. Dissension intruded into all relationships, made enemies of friends, split congregations, and produced many legal suits about the right to church property. The internal bickering of the clergy wasted energy and weakened the church it was set to serve.

The strife culminated in 1887 at a joint meeting of the Synod in Stoughton, Wisconsin. The previous year the Anti-Missourian party had established its own seminary at St. Olaf's School in Northfield, Minnesota. This action was designated as churchly revolt at the meeting in Stoughton, and a total schism was thereby unavoidable. A withdrawal from the Synod began immediately, and by 1888 the Norwegian Synod had lost one-third of its ministers and congregations.

The United Norwegian Lutheran Church

The Anti-Missourian forces resisted, however, the idea of forming a synod; there were too many synods already. Instead they worked for a merger of all Norwegian-American Lutherans, with the exception of the Missourians, in the Synod. The congregations that had departed from the Synod were gathered in a temporary association called the Anti-Missourian Brotherhood (*Det antimissouriske broderskap*).

Peter A. Rasmussen, a Norwegian schoolteacher and an eloquent preacher who in 1856 had broken with the Ellingians, became a force in the union movement. It succeeded beyond all expectations. On June 18, 1890, the Anti-Missourians celebrated a union in a grand service of thanksgiving in Minneapolis together with the Norwegian Augustana and the Conference. More than 5,000 people attended. The new synod became known as the United Church (*Den forenede kirke*); Gjermund Hoyme of the Conference, a prominent man in Norwegian-American Lutheranism, was elected president. Augsburg Seminary, headed by Georg Sverdrup, was the common theological school. At the time of its organization, the United Church had about 152,000 members and was by far the largest Lutheran synod among the immigrants.

The Fight against Drunkenness

When J. W. C. Dietrichson visited the little Norwegian colony in Chicago in 1844, he deplored the fact that "many of the Norwegians . . . [are] intemperate and have by their disorder and brawling given the Norwegians a bad reputation among Americans." There are numerous similar reports. Few issues were given more attention than drunkenness: in the immigrant press, in short stories and novels, and in tracts that agitated for the temperance cause. These statements have left an unnecessarily harsh and exaggerated impression of widespread drinking, fights, and moral decay. Undoubtedly, however, there were excesses. The saloon had become a permanent institution in small and large urban environments, and it was frequented by church people. According to Hans A. Foss, a zealous temperance speaker, even predestination and other questions of doctrine were sometimes loudly debated in the saloon by Norwegian farmers who had come to town to sell their wheat.

In the homeland the consumption of alcohol was common, and it had increased enormously after 1814. It has been estimated that by 1833 consumption had risen to nearly seventeen quarts annually per inhabitant; the abuse of alcohol was one of the great social evils of that time. Many people who lost both home and farm from addiction to alcohol sought emigration as the only way out. The county governor in Sogn og Fjordane in 1845 consequently pointed out that in Sogn emigration was heaviest from those districts where local stills were most widespread, and he thought that the connection was obvious.

Pietistic groups in Norway worked against the abuse of alcohol and took this attitude with them to America. But they frequently lost out to cheap liquor and good company. For the Norwegian immigrants, the use of alcohol was culturally

Above left: A saloon in Kathryn, North Dakota, ca. 1908. "In the month of February 1890 the great battle in Hatton took place when about fourteen women, armed with small axes, entered the saloons and destroyed everything they could get hold of." (Hans A. Foss, Trediveaarskrigen mod drikkeondet, *Minot, 1922.)*

Above: A liquor license from Chicago. Saloonkeepers were the main targets of attack for the temperance movement; all Lutheran synods denied them the sacraments.

conditioned, associated with solemn occasions like baptisms, confirmations, weddings, and funerals, and at Christmas people both baked and brewed. Liquor penetrated the busy work seasons, "especially the harvest season," writes J. L. Nydahl in his history of the temperance movement in 1896, when "the whiskey jug and the beer keg had to be along in the field." American neighbors frequently regarded Scandinavians as intemperate, but this might, as Nydahl admits, be due to the fact that "Americans drink more on the sly and seek to conceal themselves when they get drunk; but when a Norwegian gets drunk, he staggers out into the middle of the street so that everyone can see him."

The evil of drinking was harshly condemned by the Lutheran clergy, and all synods denied the sacraments to saloonkeepers. But in wide circles the custom of drinking was accepted. People from the upper classes who belonged to the Synod continued to consume moderate amounts of wine, beer, and hard liquor. A glass of wine was generally served at synodical meetings. Andrew A. Veblen, who taught at Luther Col-

lege from 1877 to 1881, claimed to be the first temperance man at the school. In her diary from the 1850s, Elisabeth Koren reveals how wine and beer were served as a matter of course. At that time, however, the first temperance societies were starting to appear; but they were directed only against hard liquor. The Synod was suspicious of these societies, for the congregation, according to its view, formed "a completely sufficient temperance society." The promise given to God in baptism and confirmation "of refraining from all sin" made all other vows superfluous. The clergy feared influence from other denominations and Lutheran groups and from secular societies.

In their isolated settlements the immigrants were for a long time untouched by the American temperance movement, which indicted the evil of drinking as a social vice with great destructive consequences. Toward the end of the 1870s the immigrants were, however, swept along in the movement. This can partly be understood as a reaction against the abuse that obviously existed; drunkenness was probably greater among Nor-

wegians in America than in Norway, since there were fewer restrictions on personal conduct here. Religious considerations do not, however, appear to have been of great importance in the fight against abuse of alcohol. To the contrary, the Lutheran clergy was on occasion quite skeptical of the large organizational apparatus that was set up. Still, the various Lutheran synods adopted resolutions about work for temperance. Opposition to organized temperance work was most visible among pastors and lay people in the Synod. Congregations and clergymen in the Conference, in the Lutheran Free Church, with Augsburg Seminary as its center, and in Hauge's Synod gave early support to the temperance cause. Georg Sverdrup spoke eagerly on its behalf. The Methodists made personal abstention from alcohol an article of their moral code.

The most significant impulses to a vigorous temperance movement among Norwegian Americans came from an exploding American total-abstinence movement, but there was also close cooperation with the Norwegian movement. In 1884, for instance, the secretary of the Norwegian total-abstinence society, Lars Øwre, worked for this cause among Scandinavians in the Middle West. Many, like the schoolteacher and pastor Jens T. Lønne, educated at Augsburg Seminary and a champion of the cause of temperance in North Dakota, had made their vows of abstinence in a Norwegian temperance hall before emigrating. A growing pietism and an increasing focus on reform issues made people receptive to agitation for temperance. Lay people promoted the cause. The demand for total abstinence thus came from the common people. In 1896 Nydahl ascertained that a large percentage of the Lutheran pastors had become temperance men by then, so that "almost no one takes a strong position against" the temperance cause.

In 1876 Lauritz Carlson organized a temperance society in Chicago, built a lodge hall, and published *Afholds-Bladet* (The Temperance Newspaper). This example was contagious, and other Norwegian settlements followed suit. The first society in Minnesota was formed the following year, with the purpose "of working against the widespread destructive and debasing vice of drunkenness among us and our countrymen."

The great breakthrough for the temperance cause among Norwegian immigrants came in the 1880s. Newspapers and countless temperance tracts agitated for the cause; traveling temperance speakers crisscrossed Norwegian settlements. Augsburg Seminary sent a student quartet that could "sing as well as speak the cause." Temperance societies and Good Templar lodges were founded, and these were organized into statewide and national total-abstinence societies. The meetings in the lodge halls were social events. There was an impressive organizational

growth. In 1914 the international temperance order I.O.G.T. had more than fifty Norwegian lodges in America. The Minnesota Total Abstinence Society (Minnesota Totalavholdsselskab), formed in 1885, comprised as many as 125 local units by 1914. Statewide total-abstinence societies united the local lodges in the Upper Midwest and on the Pacific coast. A national total abstinence society was established in 1905. In *Avholdsfolkets Festskrift* (The Temperance People's Festschrift) in 1914 Waldemar Ager claims that in relation to their numbers Norwegians had made a greater contribution to the temperance cause than any other nationality within the boundaries of America. No single cause concerned them more.

The War on Orthodoxy

Opposition to and criticism of narrow intellectual and theological orthodoxy was a product of the political liberalism and the positive view of humanity that prevailed in the nineteenth century. The attack occurred on a broad front. Spokesmen for the new orientation visited the immigrants from Norway and strengthened the liberal opposition among them.

In September, 1879, the Norwegian author and folk high school teacher Kristofer Janson embarked on a six-month-long lecture tour among his compatriots in the Middle West. Janson admired the American form of government, with its tolerance and broad vision. In America he was fortified in his faith in the "ability of democratic institutions to mature, educate, and ennoble a people," as he wrote in his book *Amerikanske forholde* (American Conditions). He soon discovered, though, that the Norwegian immigrants, instead of breathing in the pure air of freedom and democracy, were kept in ignorance by the Lutheran clergy. He was merciless in his criticism of the orthodox clergy in the Synod, who he thought wanted "to close the Norwegians off as much as possible from American influence, . . . put them into a hermetic box filled with the air of pure doctrine, and then seal a lid on so that no other puff of air can reach them."

In *Hvad jeg har oplevet* (What I Have Experi-

enced), Janson describes his lecture tour as a triumph. He wisely waited until his last lecture, given in Chicago, to publicly assail the clerics for what he called "rote learning and intolerance." Janson himself considered this lecture the beginning of his later ministry as a Unitarian pastor in America.

Bjørnstjerne Bjørnson Meets the Norwegian Americans

In the meantime, new shock waves struck the Norwegian-American community when Janson's friend and mentor, Bjørnstjerne Bjørnson, came raging into the Middle West during the terrible winter of 1880-81. His widely trumpeted proclamation that he had lost his childhood faith and his intense attacks on "the old prophets" invited opposition. On his lecture tour Bjørnson also interfered in the scandalous court case between B. J. Muus and his wife, Oline. She had finally rebelled against her tyrannical husband and taken legal action against him because he appropriated an inheritance she had received from Norway and had tried to enforce church discipline to make her "submit unto her husband." The court ruled in Oline's favor, and she was later granted a divorce. The case was an embarrassment for the Synod, and in the immigrant press it provided the impetus for discussions of women's rights. "Norwegian laws concerning the relationship between husband and wife we could easily do without in this country," a contributor wrote in *Skandinaven*. Bjørnson's crusade in the Middle West, according to Einar Haugen, who has conducted a detailed study of his tour, made conspicuous the many splits that existed among Norwegians.

It was now possible for a small radical intellectual elite to be heard. Marcus Thrane, the Norwegian socialist who had emigrated in 1863, was one of those who now came to the fore. In 1866 the Synod had felt sufficiently threatened to issue "A Warning to all Christians," which condemned his socialistic ideas, but the writings he put out in Chicago actually reached only a small number of fellow socialists. Inspired by Bjørnson's visit, and not free of malice toward the master himself, he published a satirical depiction of the visit which he called *Den gamle Wisconsin-bibelen* (The Old Wisconsin Bible). It was mainly directed

they could believe in it as long as "it was truth for them."

Janson contributed to newspapers receptive to his free humanistic message and liberal views. He discussed both feminism and Christian Socialism. From 1887 to 1894 he published the monthly *Saamanden* (The Sower), for which his wife, Drude Krog Janson, also wrote.

The internal Lutheran church controversy might, of course, be considered a family feud in comparison with the threat Janson's activity posed, and the Lutheran synods joined forces in condemning his preaching. Janson found the most fault with the Synod. His bitterest and most uncompromising antagonist, however, was Sven Oftedal, professor at Augsburg Seminary and editor of the Conference's news organ, *Folkebladet* (The People's Newspaper). The Lutherans had less to fear than they thought; the number of Norwegian Unitarians was small when Janson returned to Norway. But at a time when American orthodoxy was being challenged, as Janson's biographer Nina Draxten concludes, he gave Norwegian Americans a real taste of liberal orientation. A layman once wrote to Janson and asked: "Pastor! Are you the Antichrist who is to come, or should we expect another?" To this Janson replied: "It is best to wait for another."

against the church leaders in the Synod; the book's wit and striking satire assured it a wide distribution. In the circle of liberal spokesmen and hosts for Bjørnson were Luth. Jæger, editor of *Budstikken* (The Messenger), and Judge Andreas Ueland, both in Minneapolis. His host in Willmar was the lawyer John Wilhelm Arctander. These men were to be found in the many secular organizations that were formed toward the end of the century; they were a counterweight to the conservative influence of the church.

The Unitarian Minister Kristofer Janson

In the fall of 1881 Kristofer Janson returned to the United States. He was in touch with the American Unitarian Association in Boston, and as an ordained Unitarian minister he came to Minneapolis in November to work among Scandinavians. The liberal elite welcomed him. He stayed in the city until 1893, for twelve years, be-

fore moving back to Norway. During this period he was a distinctive figure in the Norwegian colony. The Minneapolis newspaper editor Carl G. O. Hansen says that people planned their trips to Minneapolis so that they could hear one of Janson's lectures and enjoy his great eloquence. His home became a cultural center, and it was here, as Janson's secretary, that the Norwegian author Knut Hamsun got his impressions of American cultural life, which he later censured with such force.

Of the five Unitarian congregations Janson organized, only Nora congregation in Hanska in Brown county, Minnesota, is still active. Janson relates with enthusiasm how he convinced the small group of Norwegian farmers who formed the congregation to depart from "the contradictory belief in the Trinity, the bloody doctrine of atonement, and eternal damnation." The most difficult part to give up was the divinity of Christ, but Janson states that he assured everyone that

The Norwegian-American Congregation

"No one can imagine the confusion, enmity, grief, and misery all this eternal church strife has caused in the Norwegian people in America, unless he has been there," wrote Knut Takla in his history of 1913. The dissension resulted in "more than enough" pastors and churches. In small towns and in rural areas the various synods erected their own edifices and gathered competing congregations. Takla gives as an example the little Iowa town of Roland, where the Synod, Hauge's Synod, and the United Church all had separate church structures.

The church performed a social as well as a religious function. From pioneer days in Wisconsin, Aaste Wilson tells of people walking to church:

"They left early and might stand outside the church to wait for each other. They were so happy to meet and find out if everything was all right, and then they were eager to find out if anyone had received a letter from Norway, because almost all of them longed to hear news from the home community." This was the time to exchange news about people and events, about prices of grain and agricultural machinery, perhaps even to conduct a little business and look for help on the farm for the busy seasons.

The pastor frequently became the undisputed leader in the immigrant community; his advice might be sought in worldly as well as religious matters. The congregation became a tightly knit unit. In an investigation of rural communities in Minnesota between 1885 and 1905, Jon Gjerde showed how the church became an all-encompassing institution for the members. The service on Sunday morning was followed by social gatherings in the afternoon. Youth societies, choirs, and ladies aid groups brought people together. The women were responsible for preparing what became the traditional church supper, consisting of *lutefisk* and *lefse*. The whole congregation sometimes assembled under the open sky at Sunday school picnics and on other occasions. Many found a spouse in the congregation. The members had in addition financial obligations to the church. Some farmers, for instance, pledged a part of their crops to assist in the building and operation of a church. When farmers needed help on the farm, they looked for a hired man or woman in the congregation. When purchasing or selling property, it was also most convenient to do business with people who belonged to the same church. During hard times the members provided mutual assistance. Social and economic bonds thus strengthened congregational life.

Under such circumstances it is clear that church membership would segregate Norwegians from other church groups and from other nationalities, and thereby promote an ethnic identity. In a 1949 sociological study of Norwegians in a community

Left: The congregation strengthened a sense of community through different kinds of social gatherings. Here is a Sunday school picnic in the vicinity of Madison, Wisconsin, photographed by Andrew Dahl in the 1870s.

in Illinois he calls "Jonesville," W. Lloyd Warner finds that their pietistic conduct and strict moral code prevented Norwegians from being fully accepted by the larger society. The earliest Norwegians had had a reputation of behaving in an uncouth and wild manner. Pietism thus had moved the Norwegians from "disreputable" to "respectable" behavior. But during the years after World War II they were still viewed as being different from other Protestants. In his 1949 investigation of young people in the same community, A. B. Hollingshead relates that the Norwegian pastor in the low-church Lutheran congregation had banned, among other things, dancing, use of cosmetics, permanent waves, movies, alcohol, bowling, cardplaying, and parties at the high school. The minister did, however, permit visits to the roller-skating rink, as long as the young people kept to the one owned by a Norwegian. Hollingshead thinks that the many social taboos prevented young people from more prosperous Norwegian homes from being accepted by Americans with a similar economic background. Norwegian families with greater social ambitions therefore often chose to join a more liberal church, or they remained outside all organized religious life. Hollingshead and Warner have been faulted for generalizing too much. Regarding the Norwegian "Jonesville" citizens, there is, however, less cause to doubt their findings. The strong attachment to Norwegian Lutheran ideology and the limitation of socializing to the congregation made Norwegians retain national cultural characteristics longer than, for example, Danes or Swedes.

The Church and Secondary Education

In 1881 Kristofer Janson called the Lutheran isolationism, and even more the Synod's educational policy, "a box policy." But by then the Synod leaders had capitulated to the "common school" and a compromise was worked out. Already in the Manitowoc declaration of 1866 a hope was expressed "to bring the English school as much as possible under the control of the congrega-

tion" by "appointing Norwegian teachers, who are good Lutheran Christians." The district school might thereby be conquered from within. In certain regions of strong Norwegian settlement, the Synod in addition established Lutheran high schools, or academies, to a great extent patterned after secondary schools in Norway.

The increasing interest in education beyond the elementary level originated at a meeting in Madison, Wisconsin, on March 4, 1869. The young Rasmus B. Anderson, Knud Langeland, and C. L. Clausen had arranged this meeting to form a Scandinavian Lutheran educational association. One of its purposes, which already had been adopted, was to work for the creation of a Scandinavian professorship at an American institution. H. A. Preus objected to the idea, and for that reason he left the meeting, together with most of the 300 participants. Later that spring this latter group reconvened in West Koshkonong. Here a program for academies was formulated which in the main applied during the rest of the century. In a contemporary newspaper article in *Emigranten* the American secondary school was denounced as "atheistic and blasphemous." Separate Lutheran high schools were to be established, with Luther College as the goal for young men who wanted a higher education. Few at the time, however, believed that the program was financially feasible.

Distrust of the American public school system was far less pronounced outside the Synod's leadership. To the contrary, men like Georg Sverdrup and Sven Oftedal in the Conference thought that public education was praiseworthy. Like Janson, they maintained that the American schools opened the way to full participation in American society, preserved the democratic principle of equality, gave the individual self-esteem, and built a nation of enlightened citizens. In 1874 Oftedal had, for example, accused the Synod leaders of having "clear animosity toward any instruction, the common school as well as national Norwegian schools, not controlled by the Synod."

The Academy—a Flourishing Type of School

The major critic of the "common school" in the Synod was B. J. Muus, even though, like his fel-

Above left: The congregation and pastor in Gausdal Lutheran Church, New London, Minnesota, 1897. In keeping with Norwegian custom, men and women are seated separately. The church was organized February 14, 1891, by pioneers from Gudbrandsdalen who settled on the Ringville prairie. In the congregation people had a feeling of unity based on common origin and common religious conviction.

Below left: Ladies aid groups were organized as a part of the congregational life. There were also young people's societies and choirs.

Right: The funeral of Ole Bjornlie in Madison, Minnesota, 1909.

low pastors, he devoted himself to the academy program. An academy in this context is any school that goes beyond the elementary level. As the man of action he was, he had already in 1869 started Holden Academy at the parsonage in Holden in Goodhue county. This school did not, however, solve the problem of providing the youth in the congregation with secondary education. Muus therefore was instrumental in getting St. Olaf's School incorporated on November 6, 1874. It opened its doors for instruction in January, 1875, in the nearby town of Northfield. The school accepted both men and women and was a typical representative of the academies. These institutions came into being at a time when American high schools were making their entrance into the Middle West and to a degree filled a void where high schools had not been established. Town promoters encouraged new schools; they were good publicity for the town. The Norwegian academies could in addition adjust their curricula to the needs of newcomers from Norway. During the first year St. Olaf's School had two teachers and about fifty students. Instruction was given in mathematics, English, geography, penmanship, music, history, religion, and Norwegian—the following year Latin, German, and algebra were added.

In a survey of Norwegian-American academies in 1944 B. H. Narveson lists as many as seventy-five schools in the United States and Canada. The overview begins with the short-lived Moravian school Nils Otto Tank founded in Green

Bay, Wisconsin, in 1851, and continues up to World War II. Almost all of the academies were very small; there were generally from two to five teachers, and the number of students varied from fewer than ten to close to a hundred in a few academies. Most academies lasted only a few years.

Higher education in America is greatly indebted to religion. The various creeds were concerned with preserving their teachings and their influence, and from their concern many institutions of higher learning came into being. All the way from the Colonial period American denominations had played a dominant role in the building of academies, colleges, and universities.

All Norwegian-American church bodies felt responsibility for the education of their young people. They could follow the example set by Catholics, Methodists, Congregationalists, and other creeds that had established schools. The competition between the Norwegian Lutheran synods stimulated the creation of schools. Most academies were linked to a particular Lutheran synod. Religious instruction was important, and the rules for the students' conduct were strict: no use of tobacco or alcohol, no cardplaying or frivolous behavior. It was important to reach the young at an impressionable age and keep them in the Lutheran faith. For many, the academy became the first step in a theological education.

The academies naturally assisted the immigrants in adjusting to American society. Inevitably they also strengthened a national Norwegian self-assertion. "The schools are—together with the Norwegian-American press—the living bond between Norway and its people and the Norwegian-American community," wrote D. G. Ristad in 1906. Even though practice varied, most instruction was given in Norwegian until the latter part of the century. One of the larger academies was established by a private corporation in Willmar, Minnesota, in 1883. This was Willmar Seminary, which sought students from all Lutheran and Protestant groups. When the school closed its doors in 1919, more than seven thousand students had been enrolled there. The academy movement flourished until the first decade of the new century, when it gradually lost out to the free, tax-supported, and secular American high schools. A wind blew over them, says Norlie, and they were gone.

The College Movement Created Permanent Institutions

Some of the academies survived by being transformed into colleges. This expansion occurred at a time when people in the West were showing evidence of self-assertion in regard to the prestigious eastern schools. The educational institutions that were founded by church bodies, both the Norwegian-American ones and the American, sought to keep the young people at home and give them higher education in a specifically Christian spirit. The Norwegian-American college movement belongs in such a context. Concordia College had been established as an academy at Moorhead, Minnesota, in 1891, by men from the United Church. Augustana College, which had its roots in the Scandinavian Augustana Synod, was located in Canton, South Dakota, from 1884. These two academies eventually developed into complete colleges after the model of the American church schools in New England. In 1918 Augustana College was moved farther north to Sioux Falls and merged with Lutheran Normal School, which the Synod had built there in 1889.

Missionary concern, in the service of the Synod, for the growing Norwegian population in the Far West took the pastor Bjug Harstad, born in Valle in Setesdal, to the state of Washington where an academy began instruction in Parkland near Tacoma in 1894. In 1905 the United Church opened an academy in Everett. In 1920 these two schools were merged into Pacific Lutheran College—since 1960 Pacific Lutheran University. The new school was located in Parkland, and as early as 1920 had a college division in addition to training teachers. This division was gradually expanded into an American four-year liberal arts institution—a private college.

The college movement had been inaugurated with the establishment of Luther College in 1861. Its founding was a part of the Synod's effort to train pastors, but little by little Luther College moved toward the American system. Its longtime president, Laur. Larsen, was receptive to such a change. In 1881 the preparatory theological department was separated out, and a college division was created. From then on there occurred a slow transition to English as the language of instruction and an Americanization of the cur-

riculum. Not until the 1930s, though, when women students were admitted, did Luther College depart from its classical ideal and move completely into an American educational mode. But people continued to refer to it as the "minister's school" (presteskolen) in Decorah. Until the 1920s close to half of all its graduates entered the ministry.

St. Olaf's School was able to move into its own building on Manitou Heights in Northfield in 1878. The school's growth into a college is connected with the bitter strife in the Synod in the 1880s. B. J. Muus, himself of a pietistic background and conviction, had dreamed of making the school the second college of the Synod. He sided with the Anti-Missourians, and in 1886, when the school housed the Brotherhood's seminary, Muus was able with a promise of their support to establish a college department. In 1889 the name was therefore altered to St. Olaf College, and the year after, it became the official school of the United Church when that synod was formed. Between 1893 and 1899, however, this relationship was severed by the so-called Augsburg Conflict.

St. Olaf College was less influenced by classical educational ideals than Luther College, and it emphasized what it termed a broad Christian education. The goal was to make the students good and useful citizens. From the beginning much of its instruction employed the English language. The school was accused, by Georg Sverdrup among others, of being "humanistic" and "worldly."

Augsburg Seminary, where Sverdrup was president, had begun as a training institution for pastors. In 1874 a college division, called the Greek department to distinguish it from the Latin classical curriculum, was created there. It was the forerunner of Augsburg College, but during the next forty years instruction was limited to the needs of future ministers. In 1879 five young men completed the four-year program as the first graduating class and were given the bachelor of arts degree. The curriculum showed innovation. Less weight was placed on classical languages, even though Greek, as the original idiom of the New Testament, was emphasized. The most important subjects were those that concerned "truth in and of itself—and humanity's struggle to acquire it and practice it." Sverdrup and Sven Of-

Above left: Luther College dedicated its new building in 1864. It had been raised at great sacrifice through collection of funds and voluntary work involving many people.

Above right: St. Olaf College moved into its own building, "Old Main," in 1878. This is how the building appears today. When the school was dedicated on January 8, 1875, the founder, Bernt J. Muus, gave a speech to his "Dear brothers and sisters in the faith! Norwegian men and women! Teachers and students at this future institution of learning!" He said, among other things, that "if we could succeed in conveying an abundance of knowledge about God's Word and the power of God's Word, if we could succeed in making them [students] able instruments in God's hands to promote His honor and the temporal and eternal welfare of their fellow man, then we would very much like to do so—and to this end this school has been established."

Left: The baseball team at Luther College in 1887.

tedal feared that this program might be threatened. There was no guarantee that within the United Church the college department would not be eliminated for the benefit of St. Olaf College.

For the schools that were laboriously developed into four-year liberal arts colleges, it took time to establish academic standards, win approval by the respective states and by academic accrediting associations, find qualified instructors, and create a reputation that both attracted students and gained recognition by graduate institutions. They were for a long time small, marked by an ethnic inferiority complex, and limited in their budgets. In 1915 both Luther College and St. Olaf College were accredited by the important North Central Association of Colleges. From the years prior to World War I up to 1922 the college department at Augsburg Seminary was transformed into Augsburg College. The institution adopted a complete program patterned after private American colleges. In the years between the two world wars the Norwegian-American colleges entered on a broad front into the mainstream of American higher education. The really great and impressive expansion, along with strengthened self-respect, came, however, in the postwar period and was a part of the large general growth of higher education in America. In 1920 Augsburg, Augustana, Concordia, Luther, St. Olaf, and Pacific Lutheran colleges had a combined student body of 1,980, including the academy departments at some of the schools. Pacific Lutheran and Augustana had only that year introduced college-level courses. The number of students at the six colleges in 1980 was a little under fifteen thousand. They all have large and well-kept campuses with modern dormitories and instructional facilities. In spite of the many changes, they have managed to retain their own distinctive features and traditions. These institutions must be considered one of the great and permanent structures that Norwegian immigrants erected in America.

Dissension and Reconciliation

The last great church controversy, the so-called Augsburg Conflict, occurred within the United Church. That synod was composed of Lutheran groups that had traditionally been at odds with one another. The Augsburg Conflict had many historical roots, but it was not a disagreement about doctrine. It concerned the control of Augsburg Seminary. Sverdrup's view that church schools existed mainly to educate ministers contrasted sharply with the opinion at St. Olaf College that these schools should also stress general education. This disagreement developed into a question of transferring ownership of Augsburg Seminary to the United Church, which both Sverdrup and Oftedal opposed. In 1893, the United Church therefore removed its theological training from Augsburg. Simultaneously, to avoid further strife, it withdrew its support of St. Olaf College, though that was renewed in 1899.

Some ministers from one of the two factions in the Conference—the so-called New School (*nye retning*)—"some forty or fifty ministers and a few congregations," says Bergh, formed a circle around Augsburg and called themselves the Friends of Augsburg. But the majority of the old Conference remained in the United Church. In 1897 the Friends of Augsburg formed the Lutheran Free Church and adopted an extreme free-church arrangement, formulated by Sverdrup in *Principer og Regler* (Principles and Rules). Augsburg Seminary, and later the College, remained under the control of the Lutheran Free Church.

Norwegian immigrants participated in founding no less than fourteen synods between 1846 and 1900. They all bore the Lutheran name. Agreeing with other church historians, E. Kr. Johnson finds in this situation an explanation of why non-Lutheran societies gained relatively little support among Norwegians. "No matter what orientation they had belonged to in Norway, they could all find a [Lutheran] church home in America." In comparison, there was only one Lutheran synod, the Swedish Augustana, among the Swedes. And Swedish-American Lutheranism never attained the strength of the Norwegian.

The Desire for One Norwegian Lutheran Church

The idea of union among Norwegian Lutherans was an old one. Proceedings on doctrine among the synods had strengthened this idea further. The Election controversy had, however, disrupted all attempts to find agreement, but toward the end of the 1890s negotiations were resumed. By 1912 the foundation was being laid for a merger. With the exception of men like H. A. Preus and U. V. Koren—they had even called the loss of the Anti-Missourians "a cleansing"—there was support for the union movement in the Synod. Also in Hauge's Synod the idea won sympathy. Meetings of delegates were able to settle the old doctrinal controversies over absolution, lay activity, the call, and conversion. The doctrine of Election continued to be an obstacle to merger. Not until 1912 at a meeting in Madison could the Synod and the United Church agree. A compromise was worked out in a document known as "Opgjør" (Settlement). It was now only a question of time before a merger would occur. The United Church had shown the greatest missionary activity in the cities. It was also this church that became the main force in the movement toward union.

In the work for merger, appeals were often made on ethnic grounds—it was desirable to have one Norwegian Lutheran Church in America. The idea of union probably had much greater support among ordinary churchgoers than it had among doctrinaire church leaders. New circumstances contributed to a decline in interest in fine theological distinctions. It was easier to find similarities than differences between the synods. They had a common heritage of hymns, a catechism explained by Pontoppidan, and a Lutheran tradition in a separate Norwegian formulation.

Norwegian Americans by the end of the century had achieved a certain amount of prosperity. Their horizon was expanded. They met compatriots in other connections than the church: in secular organizations, in temperance lodges and singing societies, and in political associations.

Right: An aerial photograph of the campus of St. Olaf College in Northfield, Minnesota (1980).

Central Lutheran Church in Minneapolis. The church was organized as an English-language congregation in 1919. The present church structure was dedicated Palm Sunday, 1928. In its time the church was considered to be the "cathedral" of the Norwegian Lutheran Church in America."Old men and women have prayed to God that they might experience this moment as the crowning event of everything life had given them. And for the great majority of us, who by human reckoning can anticipate many years of labor and struggle for God's church here on earth, it would appear that anything greater than that which we experienced June 9, 1917, we do not dare look forward to." (Lutheraneren, *June 13, 1917.)*

The rapid growth of urban colonies of Norwegians, where secularization had greater force than in the farming communities, worked to the same end. People who were less tied to doctrinal issues were brought into the church at this time. Besides, the merger occurred during the last great wave of immigration. Thousands of newcomers, better educated than those who came earlier, were unappreciative of a conflict that had its roots in an older immigrant tradition, and which they could not comprehend.

On Saturday, June 9, 1917, a merger was consummated at a grand celebration in St. Paul, Minnesota. The United Church, Hauge's Synod, and the Norwegian Synod formed a new society; it was given the name the Norwegian Lutheran Church in America (*Den norsk lutherske kirke i Amerika*), and in the name itself there was a pro-

gram: ethnic solidarity was important. Church bells chimed to announce that a new era had begun in Norwegian-American religious life. The new synod comprised 3,276 congregations, 1,054 pastors, and almost half a million members. Hans Gerhard Stub, son of H. A. Stub, was elected president. He preached at the new society's first service on June 10—the four-hundredth anniversary of the Reformation.

The great merger gave Norwegian-American Lutheranism increased resources. Within the framework of the Norwegian Lutheran Church, the college movement was coordinated and directed more firmly. The church historian E. Clifford Nelson has pointed out that the new church body combined three orientations: traditional pietism in its Norwegian form, the old Lutheran traditions transferred and modified in America, and the Lutheran orthodoxy of the seventeenth century. It was an unusual merger, though not without parallels in American church history.

The Press and Public Life

Norwegian-American newspaper publishing flourished to an unusual degree, responding to a great need for information about conditions in America. The newspapers also created contact and promoted solidarity within the immigrant community, and they educated the immigrants to become politically conscious. Many Norwegian Americans entered political life, joined reform movements, and championed individual causes, such as temperance and prohibition, which were especially important to Norwegian-American politicians.

America, "the Land of Newspapers"

Thus did the pioneer editor Knud Langeland describe America. Newspapers were a part of American life; the press made its way into the smallest villages. Local newspapers were regularly published in small towns and larger urban centers throughout the country. That the Norwegian immigrants helped make America "the land of newspapers" bears witness to the vital importance the press had in the new circumstances. Flourishing newspaper activity was one of the most visible aspects of immigrant life. Norwegian-American newspapers carried news about great and small events to thousands of immigrant homes.

In 1946 O. M. Norlie listed the names of 570 Norwegian immigrant publications, while claiming that there had been many more. In his survey, however, Norlie included both religious and secular writings and also annuals. If only newspapers—both those Norlie listed and others—are considered, it is still safe to assume that at least 400 were published from first to last. The immigrants obviously did not lack the ability to express themselves; many who had never subscribed to a newspaper in Norway became avid readers in America. The press filled more needs here, and there were therefore relatively more people who subscribed to a newspaper than in the homeland. The impressive number of newspapers is also evidence of the relative ease with which a newspaper could be started, but the enormous mortality rate in the immigrant press —one-third of the newspapers lasted less than one year—indicates how difficult it was to acquire enough subscribers and advertising to make a profit. The many publications also reveal a society consisting of numerous factions: there was great inner dissension in an ethnic group that

Norwegian-American newspapers and periodicals. "There is occasionally in some newspapers a bit much of the kind of filler that is given space only because one does not wish to offend a subscriber who has gotten writer's itch, as well as all these letters from small towns and Norwegian-American country districts which are only read by people from the place concerned. And it could not hurt for some editors to exercise a little more critical evaluation in regard to grandiloquent accounts from this or that club or society. . . ." (Juul Dieserud, 'Den norske presse i Amerika: En historisk oversikt," in Nordmands-Forbundet, *April, 1912.)*

John Anderson (1836-1910) was the founder and president of John Anderson Publishing Co., which among other things published the newspaper Skandinaven. *The editorial offices were located in Chicago.*

outwardly displayed solidarity. Petty quarrels, polemics, and disagreement filled some newspapers. An appeal was made to the like-minded, while opponents were attacked without mercy.

Pettiness and envy might at times be the prime reason for a newspaper's existence.

The press, like so much else in Norwegian-American life, was strongly influenced by the

Lutheran clergy. Many newspapers served as official organs for one or the other of the several synods and represented a particular viewpoint in the bitter church dissensions: the strife itself produced new publications. Some newspapers managed, however, to stay neutral on controversial issues. These frequently were the most successful and most widely circulated because they offended no one.

The majority of the newspapers expressed the prevailing political views among the immigrants and had their confidence. "You cannot believe what's in these Yankee papers," Clarence Anderson, a local historian, quotes a farmer in Traill county, North Dakota, as saying in 1915. Partisan political agitation was in general less pronounced in the most popular journals. Newspapers published to promote a specific cause or political candidate tended to be the least successful; and many of these publications were owned by people outside the immigrant community.

The newspapers had a distinctly democratic and popular appearance, and they were written for the common people. "We are not ashamed . . . of Ole Olsen, either the newspapers or their readers," wrote *Decorah-Posten* in 1913. There was an intimate relationship between newspapers and their public; every issue contained letters from the readers. Gustav Amlund made *Visergutten* (The Errand Boy), established in Story City, Iowa, in 1894, a "medium of correspondence for the circle of readers." In its columns the subscribers exchanged opinions and inserted letters to family and friends. The immigrant newspapers included news of occasions and events of every kind, told about ladies aid groups and "surprise parties," gave advice and hints for daily life, and in addition offered guidance on farming and information about new farm machinery. They took part in every aspect of the immigrants' lives. The newspapers wrote with pride about Norwegians who were a credit to their nationality. Today "we also have the pleasure of showing our readers the photograph of a new and worthy member of the Norwegian colony," *Washington-Posten* reported in 1900, and the newspaper steadily presented "well-known countrymen."

The newspapers ran advertisements for foodstuffs, "such as Norwegian matjes herring, rosefish, mackerel, fish balls, cloudberries, and goat

cheese," and for Norwegian drugstores that sold "cod-liver oil, naphtha, and Hoffmann's drops." But like American newspapers, they carried advertising for patent medicines, such as the one claiming that "healthy, happy children and adults are found in homes where Dr. Peter's Kuriko is used." Norwegians advertised professional services, and there were notices about meetings of all kinds.

The immigrant newspapers were characterized by the fact that they sought support in a population of common national origin and wide geographical spread. They carried local news from a large area. By binding the individual groups of Norwegians, the Norwegian-American newspapers gave meaning to the concept of a Norwegian America.

Norwegians in American Politics

Norwegian immigrants probably cultivated their common identity more eagerly than did their Scandinavian brethren in America. George Stephenson, a well-known Swedish-American historian, has pointed out that Norwegians left their fatherland in a period of rising nationalism, whereas Swedish nationalism at the same time had reached a low ebb. The isolationist tendency among Norwegian immigrants exposed them on occasion to prejudicial treatment. At the constitu-

A drugstore advertises Norwegian merchandise and a Norwegian pharmacist in a text that mixes Norwegian and English words. In keeping with the practice in Norway, the drugstore has been given an animal name.

These advertisements suggest something about life in Norwegian-American communities. Several of the notices announce social functions of various kinds. Verdens Gang in Chicago, July 28, 1881, contains notices of church picnics.

tional assembly meeting in Wisconsin in 1846, for example, a politician expressed the view that "the Negroes here are more intelligent, more civilized, and better acquainted with our institutions than the Norwegians."

Praise and flattery were, however, more common than criticism, in any case as they appeared in American newspapers. The positive statements, though, were frequently attempts to recruit votes. The critical comments might therefore appear more honest. Still, as Stephenson says, "one searches in vain in America letters for any kind of denunciation of the American political system." To the contrary, the Norwegians had, claims Kendric Babcock, a certain passion for the political arena. Laurence M. Larson thinks that "the Norseman is by nature a politician" and therefore demands "a full share in the management of local concerns." Familiarity with democratic reforms and local self-government in Norway, a dislike of officialdom, and a heightened assertiveness stimulated them to participate in local government in America. All male immigrants could vote by declaring that they intended to become citizens. Almost from the start they constituted a potential political force in their compact settlements. American politicians, and in time also politicians of their own nationality, competed for the votes of the immigrants.

Politics in the Local Community

The immigrants first learned about the American democratic form of government in the smallest political unit, the township. Where they formed a majority, they had no choice but to assume responsibility for local administration. It therefore happened that they managed both district and town meetings before they learned English. In the two townships of Arendahl and Norway in Fillmore county, Minnesota, organized in 1860, Norwegians occupied all positions at the first election, and they dominated the administration of the townships for twenty years. Their assumption of the responsibility for administering the two townships, arranging political elections, levying and collecting taxes, planning and building roads, illustrates how Norwegian settlers might be brought into American politics. Elsewhere, even if Norwegians were the largest group, language barriers and feelings of ethnic

Following their active participation in the Civil War, Norwegians became more acceptable to their Yankee neighbors as political candidates. The position of sheriff of a county was a greatly coveted elected office. Pictured here is Otto K. Olson (1874-1933), who served as sheriff in Laona, Wisconsin.

inferiority might keep them from actively taking part in local political life. Politically conscious Norwegians complained in the early period that their compatriots were most concerned with farming and religious controversy and had little interest in public issues. If they voted, it was generally for established Yankee candidates. Only after the Civil War did they discover their might and enter fully into civic life.

The following example of self-assertion, in fact revolt, among the immigrants reveals much about a maturing political consciousness. In Pigeon township in Trempealeau county, Wisconsin, Norwegian voters at the election in 1877 rejected all Yankees, with one exception, and chose Norwegians instead. The exception was J. D. Olds, who afterward was called a "Norwegian Yankee." But he had learned his lesson; thereafter he was careful to flatter the Norwegian voters and even learned to speak Norwegian.

The Convention Riot at Benson Grove

In the 1870s a greater political consciousness became evident among Norwegian Americans. Efforts were made to form a Norwegian caucus within the American political parties. The well-known riot at the 1876 convention of the Republican party at Benson Grove in Winnebago county, Iowa, is vividly described in *The Changing West* (1937), by Laurence Larson. During the nomination of county officials, a gang of Yankees tried to disrupt the meeting because they feared that the Norwegians were in the process of getting a majority of the candidates. Among those who spoke loudest for the Norwegian side was one Hans Petersen, commonly called "Kjæftehans" (Big-mouth Hans). A rotten apple was thrown in his face, and this became the signal for a bloody riot with fence rails and neck yokes as weapons. The casualties were many, but only a few were serious, and no one was killed. At the election in November, a couple of weeks later, Norwegian voters went to the polls determined to cast their votes for compatriots who were candidates. They completely took over the county administration and retained their hold at least until World War I – or, as Larson wrote in 1937, "kept this control to the present."

From Township via County to State Offices

From township administration to county the distance was short. Quite early there were Norwegians in some county offices. The positions they preferred, Babcock suggests, were sheriff, treasurer, auditor, and registrar of deeds. Offices requiring more special expertise, such as coroner, surveyor, and superintendent of schools, they generally left to Americans.

The Civil War had created some Norwegian-American heroes, and Norwegian candidates became more acceptable to their Yankee neighbors. Simultaneously their contribution to the war effort encouraged greater self-reliance among the Norwegians themselves. An even more important development was the emergence of an American-born generation among the immigrants; it could participate with more confidence in civic life. Men of this generation became political leaders, and they could educate their compatriots. Political issues could be discussed with leaders who spoke Norwegian. This created interest and trust.

Those who entered into the political life of the individual states, or who moved into the national arena, had first worked in county politics; they were a grass-roots product. Before the Civil War Norwegians had played an insignificant role at the state level. Still, James D. Reymert had, as indicated earlier, sat in the state legislature in Wisconsin in the 1840s. An example from Minnesota is Lars K. Aaker, who between 1859 and 1869 was elected to the state legislature from the Norwegian Goodhue county. After his appointment to the government land office in Alexandria, he sat in the state senate. Also the Swede Hans Mattson prepared himself at the county level for a larger political career. His candidacy for the office of secretary of state in 1869, to be sure, aroused a spirit of rivalry between Swedes and Norwegians, who had wanted a Norwegian candidate.

Even though tensions existed just under the surface between the two nationalities, they marched in many instances under a common Scandinavian banner. They met in several Scandinavian clubs. In Minneapolis the Republican Viking League was organized in 1896; in addition to contending for political influence, the League advised immigrants on how to become American

citizens. Within the Republican party there were Scandinavian leagues formed in the Seattle area in 1900 and in North Dakota in 1904. The political parties were beginning strenuously to court the allegiance of the various ethnic groups. The Scandinavian population element in Minnesota was dominant, and after 1890 it became nearly a rule that at least one of the two major parties nominated a candidate for governor of Scandinavian origin.

Ethnic loyalty, however, was not sufficient to unite the Norwegians politically. In Minnesota one cannot really claim that the issue of nationality was a decisive factor in many elections; an appeal for support was rarely made on ethnic grounds. Other considerations were more important when Norwegian voters took a political stance. These might be regional or economic concerns, political convictions that went from socialism to moderate Republicanism, or simply the popularity of a specific candidate. And immigrant politicians learned about both political horse trading and manipulation of the vote from their Yankee colleagues. They made their way in the political power structure. Through the patronage system there were offices to be had for faithful party members or rewards to bestow on political supporters.

Participation in political life accelerated the Americanization process; new loyalties were created, and the immigrants were more firmly tied to American society. A rather high percentage of the Norwegian-American electorate owned land. The Norwegian-born journalist N. A. Grevstad saw this as a contributing cause of increased political activity. Landowners had a stake in the country. Economic considerations might easily offset ethnic solidarity. But discrimination against an immigrant people might make tempers flare and call forth joint action. Many Scandinavians, for instance, joined forces with the Germans in Wisconsin to have the nativistic Bennett Law of 1889 repealed. It required, among other things, that certain common subjects should be taught only in English in all schools, private as well as public.

It took time before Scandinavians were represented in county and state political institutions in proportion to their share of the population. With a certain complacency, however, the Minnesota newspaper *Nordisk Folkeblad* boasted in

1870 "that we will have five members in the legislature, a number that fully shows how significantly the Scandinavians' political power has increased in recent years." Toward the end of the century Scandinavians had caught up with and passed other groups in regard to relative representation. Sten Carlsson, a Swedish historian of the immigration, has shown that during the early decades of the present century Norwegians and Swedes in Minnesota were overrepresented in the state administration as well as in the legislative body, and also in Congress. The North Dakota historian P. V. Thorson's less systematic investigation in 1981 of the situation in North Dakota shows strong overrepresentation of Norwegians, both as political candidates and in public offices, from the time North Dakota was admitted to the Union in 1889.

The Norwegian-American Press after the Civil War

The Norwegian-American press had from its beginning been politically oriented. Both Norwegian and American politicians realized the power of the press in the competition for the voters' favor. In political life the newspapers were obviously a strong force in spreading information and creating interest.

In 1864 *Emigranten*, then the only secular Norwegian-American newspaper, got a competitor in *Fædrelandet* (The Fatherland), which that year began publication in La Crosse, Wisconsin. La Crosse gradually became a significant center of Norwegian cultural and social activity. Frederick Fleischer, a pastor's son from Våler with a Norwegian law degree, was the major figure in this enterprise. His newspaper was a great asset in pursuing his personal political ambitions and gave him considerable influence in the Republican party in Wisconsin. In 1868 he bought *Emigranten* and merged the two newspapers as *Fædrelandet og Emigranten*. *Fædrelandet og Emigranten* was eagerly perused and commented on by Norwegian settlers. The journal's coeditor,

and from 1878 owner, the Danish-American F. A. Husher, gained special popularity with his good-natured travel letters from Norwegian settlements. As *Emigranten* had done, the newspaper supported the Synod on church issues; this connection, however, had no noticeable impact on the journal's political stance.

It is without doubt correct, as a historian of the press, Arlow W. Andersen, has stated, that the press both encouraged and reflected a growing

Luth. Jæger (1851-1925) was a pioneer newspaperman and a prominent citizen of Minneapolis.
Jæger became a spokesman for the rapid Americanization of Norwegians, and he had high expectations that this could occur with Norwegian-American youth. He wrote in 1913 in Symra *that the "result of work for Norsedom . . . is disunion and confusion, ambiguity and uncertainty between the old and the new, a generation that nearly does not know whether it is Norwegian or American." In choosing between Norwegian and American, the young people must choose the latter, "they cannot split themselves."*

Norwegian-American patriotism for the new homeland in the years following the Civil War. At the same time the press formed a part of and guided the immigrants into the Republican party. The Norwegian-American newspaperman N. A. Grevstad believed that the transition to this party, prompted by the immigrants' loyalty to the ideals of human liberty and equality that Lincoln represented, was so complete that "for a generation or more after the Civil War the Norwegians remained massively Republican in both national and local politics." It is more reasonable to see the situation as Theodore C. Blegen does: Norwegians for a time after the war were in the main kept within this party because it was by far the largest, in fact almost the only political organization in the Upper Midwest at that time. Newcomers were in general supportive of the party the older settlers belonged to. The Republican party represented for Norwegian voters Protestantism, high moral ideals, and prohibition; whereas the Democratic party might be associated with Catholicism, the saloon, and corrupt machine politics among the immigrants in America's great cities. New issues and interests, however, weakened their loyalty to the Republicans, and Norwegian voices in opposition were not completely silenced. It was an attempt to hinder the move to the Republican party that in 1857 had been behind the publication of *Folkets Røst* (The Voice of the People) in Minnesota. The newspaper was actually a Democratic campaign sheet. At that time the Republican and Democratic forces had been more or less equally strong.

The first real representative of the immigrant press in Minnesota was *Nordisk Folkeblad* (Nordic People's Newspaper), founded in Rochester in 1868 and the same year moved to the dawning urban center of Minneapolis. It clearly affiliated itself with the Republican party and had a Norwegian-Danish character and circulation. F. Sneedorff Christensen, later the Danish vice-consul, edited the journal and encouraged joint Scandinavian political action. He was probably the first person in the state who agitated for greater participation in civic life by "Nordic people."

Nordisk Folkeblad folded in 1875, but already in 1873 *Budstikken* (The Messenger), the primary press organ in Minnesota during this period, had

Smuler

Af O. S. Hervin.

No. 120. :: August :: 1916.

Sandhed blot i Ord og Virke
River Taarn af Løgnens Kirke.

Udkommer af og til, helst hver Maaned.
Pris $1.00 for 8 Maaneder (eller Numre).

Enkelt No. koster 15 Cents.
Samme Pris til alle Lande, hvor Post gaar.

Office: 643 Thomas Street, St. Paul, Minn.

Above: Smuler *(Crumbs) was the name of a magazine published by Ole S. Hervin. Hervin was an excellent humorist and satirical writer. Under the heading "Smaasmuler" (Small Crumbs), he printed the following piece in* Smuler *in August, 1901. "After having pondered carefully about this matter for forty-five years, I have come to the conclusion that Hell must be a treeless field where the temperature at all times is 97 degrees in the shade and the wind stands or glides from south-south-west. The devils that torment the doomed are presumably like the smiling beings, who when the temperature is this high, come toddling up to you to inform you that 'it is warm today,' as if this is supposed to be news to you."*

started publication. Paul Hjelm Hansen edited this newspaper for a time. Luth. Jæger was, however, the most influential man associated with *Budstikken*. He was from the Arendal area of Norway and had studied at the university before emigrating to America in the early 1870s. Jæger was editor-in-chief of *Budstikken* from 1877 to 1885. His liberalism marked the journal, which he turned into an opposition organ, independent in church matters, and for most of the period Democratic. Jæger gained favor in the Democratic party; he is a good example of how strongly a desire to build a political career influenced immigrant editors. There were many newspapers serving the political ambitions of individual men. Jæger, however, kept the journal's columns open for free discussion, and the issues debated at that time were discussed in *Budstikken* in contributions by a number of prominent individuals.

In addition to serving as political organs and platforms for individual interests, the journals functioned of course also as local newspapers in their own districts. In 1900 there were no fewer than eight secular Norwegian publications—newspapers and periodicals—in Illinois, six in Wisconsin, seven in Iowa, two in South Dakota, eleven in North Dakota, and seventeen in Minnesota. A network of newspapers thus served the immigrants. The political winds that had swept over the Middle West at the end of the century had ruined some newspapers, made others change political course, and given birth to new ones.

The Three Largest Newspapers in the Middle West

Three newspapers were popularly known as "the Big Three." They were *Skandinaven* in Chicago (1866-1941), *Decorah-Posten* in Iowa (1874-1972), and *Minneapolis Tidende* (1887-1935). These three became the leading journals in the Middle West, with a large circulation throughout the region. The steady improvement of communication through the expanding rail service brought the newspapers to the most distant regions of Norwegian settlement. The newspapers also had subscribers in other parts of America than the Middle West, and they therefore to a certain extent functioned as national Norwegian journals.

Skandinaven

Skandinaven, the oldest of the three, was sold by newsboys at the railroad station in Chicago, and it was therefore frequently the newcomers' first contact with immigrant newspapers. It was given free of charge to newly arrived immigrants. This was an unexpected welcome and was especially appreciated since the immigrants had been warned against all kinds of salesmen. "*Skandinaven*'s history," writes Johannes B. Wist, "is in its general outline the history of the successful Norwegian pioneer in this country." The newspaper made progress, grew large, and changed with the times. In 1912 it reached a high point with almost 54,000 subscribers to its semiweekly edition. A daily edition had a circulation of 25,000.

Skandinaven was consistently Republican, and political candidates eagerly sought its support. The newspaper was popular in tone, spoke for the common citizen, and was strongly critical of aristocratic tendencies. The publishers had themselves come from modest circumstances and easily identified with the position of the immigrant. Consequently, *Skandinaven* became low-church and sympathetic to the lay movement, and an opponent of the Synod's high-church practices. Long after *Skandinaven* had discontinued giving space to the issue, the Haugeans considered the newspaper to be an organ for their orientation.

The basic tenet of *Skandinaven*, the newspaper's popular attitude and democratic spirit, explains much of its large circulation. But also the fact that it came out in an urban center and that it, like the two others, was owned and published by an experienced printing firm and had capable editors contributed to the newspaper's unusual success. In addition, it satisfied the needs of the immigrants. After examining the newspaper's editorial position in several volumes, Agnes Larson concluded that *Skandinaven* undoubtedly played an important role in making the transition to American ways easier for the immigrants, politically as well as socially.

The dominant person in the history of *Skandinaven* was John Anderson. As a nine-year-old he had emigrated from Voss, Norway, with his parents in 1845. He was an experienced typographer when he and Knud Langeland launched *Skandinaven* on June 1, 1866. One of the co-owners was Ivar Larson Boe from Voss, who had emigrated in 1844. He Americanized his name to Lawson and became a force both in the Norwegian colony and in the political life of Chicago. Langeland was the first editor of *Skandinaven*, while Anderson administered the business. In 1890 the firm was incorporated as the John Anderson Publishing Company.

Langeland himself thought that *Skandinaven*'s defense of the "common school," its attacks on the Synod clergy, and the debate over slavery "attracted general attention and served greatly to spread the paper everywhere where Norwegians lived." In 1872 Langeland was succeeded in the editorial post by Svein Nilsson, a reformer and champion of enlightenment from Namdalen in Norway. Nilsson had been a co-worker of the editor Chr. Friele on the influential Norwegian newspaper *Morgenbladet*. He edited the first illustrated periodical in Norwegian in America, *Billed-Magazin*, published by the printer B. W. Suckow in Madison from 1868 to 1870. Here Nilsson printed his observant accounts of Norwegian settlements. Between 1892 and 1911 N. A. Grevstad from Sykkylven in Sunnmøre occupied the chief editorial position; he assumed this responsibility after having gained experience as editor of *Dagbladet* (The Daily Paper) in Oslo. Grevstad mastered English to an unusual degree and had a knack for making political contacts. His later career therefore was pursued outside the narrow bounds of Norwegian-American journalism.

Decorah-Posten

Decorah-Posten was a high-quality newspaper that achieved great fame. It first appeared in Decorah, Iowa, in 1874. Like so many immigrant journals, it had an extremely modest beginning. It can be traced back to La Crosse, where the twenty-two-year-old B. Anundsen made an attempt to publish a literary monthly *Ved Arnen* (By the Hearth) in 1866. In 1869, after having moved to Decorah to take over the printing of the publications of the Norwegian Synod, he tried in addition to publish a newspaper, *Fra Fjærnt og Nær* (From Far and Near). But he gave up both these ventures in 1870. They led, however, to his launching *Decorah-Posten* as a local news and advertising paper four years later. The newspaper grew and achieved a wide distribution, a fact that obviously was owing to Anundsen's own enterprise and business acumen. But it took time. In 1877 the newspaper lost money because subscribers did

not pay. "So little money comes in on subscriptions these days that it makes us quite confused," Anundsen complained in the newspaper. Its eventual success may also be attributed to the fact that, as George Strandvold, who for many years was a staff member, wrote, "Anundsen kept a great distance from . . . political and religious controversies." Involvement in these had caused the demise of many a newspaper. "*Decorah-Posten,*" says Johannes B. Wist, editor from 1901 to 1923, "took a strict position of merely reporting any public issue." Through changing editors *Decorah-Posten* managed to steer clear of devastating conflicts. Alongside Wist, Kristian Prestgard, associated with the newspaper from 1898, was the best-known editor. He succeeded Wist and held the position until his death in 1946.

The newspaper's major appeal was perhaps its firmness in form and content and its traditional and familiar style that never surprised the readers with disturbing headlines or discordant editorial opinions. To read *Decorah-Posten* was like an encounter with an old friend. It was in harmony with and reflected through its long life an older immigrant tradition: the newspaper entertained, gave advice, and reported news from the old land and the new. *Decorah-Posten* secured a circle of faithful readers from coast to coast in America, and also in Norway. In the 1920s the newspaper reached about 45,000 subscribers. It was the only immigrant newspaper to have a cartoon series, "Han Ola og han Per," created by the Spring Grove, Minnesota, farmer Peter J. Rosendahl. From 1918 to 1943 he entertained the readers in more than 700 contributions. His characters are genuine Norwegian-American types who amuse by poking fun at the immigrants' own peculiarities.

*Billed-Magazin ap-
peared from 1868
until 1870, and it
was the first il-
lustrated Norwe-
gian-American
magazine. The issue
shown here presents
one of Svein Nils-
son's articles, enti-
tled, "The Scandi-
navian Settlements
in America."*

*Far right: Svein
Nilsson (1826-1908)
edited Billed-
Magazin and the
newspaper Skandi-
naven. The early
articles about Nor-
wegian immigration
that he printed in
Billed-Magazin
made him "the
father of Norwegian-
American historical
writing."*

Billed-Magazin.

No. 6.]   Madison, Wisconsin den 5te Februar.   **[1870.**

Gartnerboligen i Christiania.

Christiania Slotspark hører nu til de smukkeste Anlæg i Christiania, medens denne Del af Byen en Menneskealder tilbage i Tiden var en Udkant, en slet opdyrket Mark og kun undtagelsesvis en Del af en Lotte. Kunst og Natur have i Forening omdannet det Hele, og især er Haven paa Syd- og Vestsiden af Slottet det vakreste offentlige Anlæg, der staar aabent for Almen-heden. Vort Billede viser Gartnerboligen med nærlig-gende Drivhus; rundt omkring ere mange Blomsterpar-tier, der fremvise ligesaa sjeldne som vakre Planter, me-dens et almindeligt velordnet Haveanlæg giver det Hele et venligt, hyggeligt Præg, saa at man med Glæde dvæ-ler under de høie, skyggefulde Træer. Baade Formiddag og Eftermiddag er denne Del af Slotsparken meget be-søgt; de mange Spadserende nyde her Synet og Vellug-ten fra de talrige Blomsterbed eller gjør sig en liden Tur

Gartnerboligen i Christiania.

rundtomkring og betragter Svanerne, der svømme om i Dammen, og som opfange de Hvedebrødsmuler, der til-kastes dem. Publikum paaskjønner ogsaa, hvad Park-anlægget yder dem af Hygge og som forfriskende Op-holdssted; thi neppe nogetsteds ser man i eller udenfor Anlæggene saa lidet Spor efter et uhindret Besøg af en hel Del forskjellige Mennesker: Publikum er her selv Politi og passer selv paa, at Blomster, Buske og Træer forblive uantastede og at ingen Uorden begaaes. Saa-ledes burde det være overalt; de offentlige Anlæg burde overlades Publikum, og dette burde overtage et almin-deligt Politiopsyn.

De skandinaviske Settlementer i Amerika.
(Fortsættelse fra No. 5).

Pleasant Spring.

Men saa fik jeg efter to Ugers Forløb Besøg af Ny-kommerens farligste Fiende, Klimatfeberen, der i hine Dage sjelden gik nogen forbi, og her, blandt lutter Fremmede og ubekjendt med Sproget, blev jeg for nogen Tid fængslet til Sygeleiet. Til Forladthedens Kvaler sluttede sig Længsler efter Venner og Hjemland, idet Minderne fra Ungdommens glade Dage i verlende Skikkelser fremmanedes for mit aandelige Blik og op-

Minneapolis Tidende

Decorah-Posten had a growing circulation at a time when other immigrant publications were experiencing a disturbing decline. The reason was in part that it inherited the subscribers of newspapers that were discontinued. Mergers and consolidations of newspapers were commonplace both in the immigrant press and in the American newspaper world in general. *Minneapolis Tidende*, the third major newspaper in the Middle West, began as *Grand Forks Tidende*, published as a local journal in Grand Forks, North Dakota, from 1880. A couple of years later Thorvald Gulbrandsen purchased the newspaper. Gulbrandsen had emigrated from Moss, Norway, in 1874, and like Anderson and Anundsen knew the printing business. Consequently the newspaper could be printed by its own printing shop. In January, 1887, Gulbrandsen moved to Minneapolis and began to publish a daily, following the lead of *Skandinaven,* which enjoyed great popularity in Minnesota. He called the newspaper *Minneapolis Daglig Tidende* (Minneapolis Daily Times). The following year he moved *Grand Forks Tidende* to the city and issued it as a weekly addition to *Daglig Tidende.* The name was altered to *Minneapolis Tidende.* In 1893 both *Budstikken and Fædrelandet og Emigranten* were merged with *Tidende.* By 1910 the newspaper had attained a circulation of nearly 33,000 for its weekly edition.

Tidende had outstanding men, such as the pioneer editors R. S. N. Sartz and Sigvart Sørensen, on its staff. Carl G. O. Hansen became especially

125

well known in the newspaper's later history. He possessed a great feeling for cultural matters, specifically in music and literature, and the newspaper gained recognition for its valuable reviews in these areas and for significant reports about Norwegian cultural and social life. In church affairs it was wisely neutral. *Tidende* did not profess any specific party loyalty. If in individual elections it threw its support to a certain candidate, that support was generally based on nationality. When *Tidende* was discontinued in 1935 and absorbed by *Decorah-Posten*, Prestgard wrote to Carl G. O. Hansen and characterized the event as "one of the greatest misfortunes which has befallen our people in this country." Many interpreted it as a sign that the Norwegian-American press was dying. But *Decorah-Posten* continued for a generation longer before it came to an end. An era was then over.

Knute Nelson, Norwegian-American Politician

"The greatest political talent which our race has produced in this country," Juul Dieserud wrote about Knute Nelson in 1914. During his long political career Nelson became to a special degree

The popular cartoon series 'Han Ola og han Per" appeared for many years in Decorah-Posten, *and the cartoons have since been reprinted in other Norwegian-American newspapers. The series was created by the Norwegian-American farmer P. J. Rosendahl in Spring Grove, Minnesota. The characters speak an authentic mixture of Norwegian and English, and they entertain by poking fun at the immigrants' own peculiarities.*

a dominant figure among Norwegian Americans —a source of ethnic pride and boasting. He retained a close relationship with his compatriots and spoke "his good Vossa tongue . . . purely." Nelson was in political philosophy a moderate to conservative Republican and therefore frequently out of step with the progressive wing of the Republican party that worked for reform —the wing of the party that his compatriots together with most Midwestern voters apparently preferred. It was also the orientation most of his Norwegian-American colleagues in state assemblies and in Congress represented.

To begin with, Nelson's political career was based on ethnic solidarity; he was carried forward on the shoulders of his fellow Norwegians. In a scholarly study Torgeir E. Fjærtoft has shown how Nelson moved toward political independence by expanding his power base and by interacting with the American political environment. The key to his success was his ability to take advantage of the opportunities the Ameri-

can political system gave, to bind groups and individuals to his cause, and in this way to establish a broad base for his position of power. A humble beginning as a poor newcomer might also be exploited to create and enhance an advantageous political image. Nelson personified the American dream. In the immigrant communities he was an alternative and a counterweight to the occupational model the ministry offered young men.

Knute Nelson had arrived in Chicago at the age of six in 1849, together with his mother, Ingeborg Johnson, from the Kvilekval farm in Evanger, west of Voss. Her marriage to Nels Nelson a few years later gave Nelson the short and sturdy Norwegian name Knute Nelson. He graduated from Albion Academy, a school started by Seventh-Day Baptists which attracted both students and teachers of Norwegian origin, and was a soldier in the Civil War. Afterward, Nelson found employment in a law office in Madison, and he began to practice law in 1867. This moved him into politics. In 1868 he was elected to Wisconsin's legislative assembly; Nelson's political career was, however, to be pursued in Minnesota. In 1871 he opened his own law office in the little town of Alexandria, in a district that steadily received new Norwegian settlers. He took a homestead near the town. Nelson's acquaintance with the Norwegian-American politician Lars K. Aaker assisted his entrance into the Republican political party structure.

126

Right: Knute Nelson and his family and friends at Alexandria, Minnesota, ca. 1910. "When it concerns conditions in the political area, our brothers the Norwegians have especially in earlier times been better represented than the Swedes in all respects. The national sentiment has played the greatest role and has contributed to their political advancement, because regardless of which party they have belonged to, they have supported the candidacy of their own countrymen." (Alfred Söderström, Minneapolis minnen, *Minneapolis, 1899.)*

Below: Knute Nelson was born in Voss, Norway, in 1843 and he came to America at the age of 6. He served for 3 years in the Union army during the Civil War. In 1867 he became a lawyer and entered political life, and in 1892 he became governor of Minnesota. From 1895 until his death he served as United States senator. Nelson was the first Norwegian-American politician to attain great prominence in American politics.

The historic election of 1882, in which Nelson beat the American Charles F. Kindred for the Republican nomination in Minnesota's fifth congressional district and was elected to the House of Representatives, launched him on his career of national leadership. The hard-fought election was later referred to as "the Bloody Fifth." Nelson won because he was able to unite the Scandinavian voters around his candidacy in a district with several Scandinavian politicians. In his appeal to the voters he exhibited great cunning. He made his nomination appear as if the position sought the man and not vice versa. By previous agreement, and partly as repayment for earlier favors, editor Luth. Jæger wrote an editorial in *Budstikken* earnestly encouraging Nelson to become a candidate. Although Democratically oriented, *Budstikken* persisted in its support throughout the campaign. Kindred also turned to the Norwegian voters in their mother tongue; he bought *Red River Posten*, established in Fargo in 1878 as the first Norwegian-language journal in North Dakota. But the ethnic factor was decisive for Nelson's victory.

In 1892, following two reelections to Congress, Nelson was elected governor of the state of Minnesota. Increasing agrarian opposition split his opponents and worked to his advantage in the election. In January, 1895, the state legislature chose him to become U.S. senator. This election was the beginning of a long period of service as senator, in all twenty-eight years, until his death in 1923. Knute Nelson attained a unique position. He became an institution, a living legend, re-

Political Reform Movements

In 1898-99 Knute Nelson visited his childhood home in Evanger. From there he had emigrated as a 6-year-old boy with his mother. When they arrived in America, poor and without anyone to turn to, Knute, according to his biographer Martin W. Odland, supposedly comforted his mother by saying: "Don't cry, mother! We are poor now, but when I get big I shall be next to the king."

spected by high and low, and reelected regardless of the political currents in the state. After the constitutional amendment of 1913, he had the satisfaction in 1918 of being directly elected by the state's citizens.

Ethnic leadership functions at two levels: in the local community with its special institutions such as church, saloon, singing groups, and various societies; and in the larger ethnic subculture, bound by newspapers, organizations, political leaders, and other well-known persons. The former belong in the realm of everyday life; the latter combine the scattered communities into an ethnic unity and represent it to the outside world. The relationship between leaders at the two levels has not been fully clarified. National leadership of Nelson's stature bestowed a certain prestige on all Norwegians. After his death, no Norwegian-American politician stepped forward to assume his role. This is an indication of the process of assimilation that was occurring and that was slowly eroding the conditions that had made Nelson's position possible in the Norwegian-American community.

Knute Nelson was himself a farmer and enjoyed great confidence among this group. Economic forces and special regional circumstances produced a strong agrarian movement toward the end of the century in western Minnesota—where Nelson himself came from—and in North and South Dakota, especially in the Red River valley. The farmers endeavored to gain control over the marketing of their own products, diminish the power of the railroad companies, and establish a better credit arrangement. The movement caused revolt and defections from the Republican party. Many had hoped that Nelson would ally himself with these forces, but he remained faithful to the party instead.

The cultivation of wheat moved westward with the spread of settlement. On the frontier wheat was the most important crop; diversification came later and was tied to growth in population and the increased profitability of other agricultural products which the larger population provided. Theodore C. Blegen has stressed the tendency of Norwegians to move out on the frontier. In 1890, for instance, more than half of all Norwegians in Minnesota lived in the western counties. Thus they became involved in political revolt movements that were brought on by the special problems faced by wheat farmers—their dependence on those who stored, transported, and distributed their product.

Norwegians Speak for Populism

The new directions in politics were led by a vocal immigrant press. *Normanden*, established in Grand Forks in 1887, was the largest Norwegian-American newspaper in North Dakota. It supported the Farmers' Alliance, an organizational uprising against the state's dependence on and exploitation by Eastern financial interests, and together with other Alliance newspapers *Normanden* was sent to its members.

This protest movement was strengthened by continual agricultural crisis, and in 1890 it culminated in the formation of the Populist party,

One of the American politicians who greatly influenced the political thinking of Norwegian Americans was Robert M. LaFollette (1855-1925). La Follette grew up in Primrose in Dane county, Wisconsin, in a Norwegian district, and during the early 1880s served as district attorney for the county. As a member of the United States House of Representatives, governor of the state of Wisconsin, and from 1906 to 1925 United States senator, he advocated reforms, among them direct primaries, equalizations of tax rates, and the regulation of railroads. In 1911 he helped organize the National Progressive Republican League, losing leadership to Theodore Roosevelt in 1912 when the movement LaFollette headed formed the Progressive party. He regained his leadership of the liberal forces after World War I and in 1924 ran as the Presidential candidate of the Progressive party, receiving nearly 5,000,000 votes. LaFollette's form of Progressivism inspired the reform movements in the Middle West, and his reform message was spread through such Norwegian-American newspapers as Skandinaven.

or the People's party. *Normanden*, edited by Hans A. Foss, was the party's official organ; in 1892 the Populists gained political control in North Dakota. *Normanden*, however, returned to the Republican party the following year—an indication of the Populist movement's fleeting character. P. O. Thorson administered and later owned *Normanden* and made it independent progressive Republican.

Conservative Republicanism had a Norwegian organ in *Statstidende* (State Times) in Hillsboro. It was a newspaper owned by politicians outside the Norwegian population. On the other side of the political spectrum, Foss himself in 1894 went to Moorhead, on the Minnesota side of the Red River valley, and began publication of a radical Populist journal he called *Nye Normanden* (The New Norseman).

Toward the end of the 1890s, when a new period of prosperity replaced depression, the Populist movement faded away. The majority of the defectors returned to the Republican fold. It was probable, as Blegen says, that the experience stimulated independent political thought—and that blind political loyalty had been weakened. Analyses of election results confirm that political instability was much greater after 1900. Within the Republican party Norwegian voters continued to give support to the progressive wing and joined forces with those who sought to assume the leadership of the party. Theodore Roosevelt became a favorite of Norwegian voters; in 1912 *Normanden*, for instance, spoke for the Progressive party and for Roosevelt's candidacy for President. Even the neutral *Decorah-Posten* supported the Progressive movement, which "has gained much ground in this country."

Robert M. La Follette and the Progressive Movement

In Wisconsin Norwegian voters followed the lead of Robert M. La Follette, who had grown up in a Norwegian neighborhood and reportedly spoke some Norwegian. His form of progressivism shaped the reform movement in the Middle West, which sought to enact laws—both laws to protect the poor, ignorant, and defenseless, and those to hinder the accumulation and abuse of power and wealth by a few. *Skandinaven* was the major Norwegian organ for La Follette. Nils P. Haugen, a prominent Norwegian-born politician and in the 1890s a congressman, championed the Progressive movement and had "an excellent pen both in Norwegian and English." Norwegian voters closed ranks around the Progressive candidates, who gradually consolidated their hold on the Republican party.

Jon Wefald, a student of the reform movement, finds that communalism was a major factor in the strong reform conviction that Norwegian-American voters had. In a Norwegian rural community there was considerable feeling of mutual responsibility. This spirit of community the immigrants had brought with them from Norway. Perhaps there also was an element of distrust of the power of wealth and the sinfulness and corruption rural folk associated with city life. Wefald mapped the congressional voting of a number of prominent Norwegian members of the United States Senate and the House of Representatives between 1905 and 1916—during the Progressive era. Except for Senator Knute Nelson, they all as one cast their ballot for the great reform measures of that time. To some legislative reform issues, like the direct election of senators and the adoption of a lower tariff, which would benefit the farmers, Nelson also gave his support.

The Nonpartisan League

The Republican Nonpartisan League was formed in North Dakota in 1915 as a radical offspring of the Progressive movement, and it led thousands of Norwegian voters toward the left. The League advocated socialistic reforms such as state control and operation of grain silos and of the sale of wheat. The Nonpartisan League was a new expression of agrarian unrest and yet another attempt to lead the Republican party. Elwyn B. Robinson, a North Dakota historian, thinks that Norwegians brought radicalism into the state. Norwegian immigrants were not unfamiliar with public control and ownership in the transportation and production sectors of the economy. This ethnic political legacy, in addition to economic self-interest and local conditions where they settled, made Norwegian wheat farmers receptive to radical solutions to the problems that confronted them.

But the League's form of radicalism alarmed many progressive men from the middle classes; they feared what they perceived as self-appointed leaders. A tumultuous campaign was mobilized against the League; *Normanden* became a virulent opponent of its program. It is difficult to determine what portion of the Norwegians in North Dakota *Normanden* represented on this issue, but it is certain that many opposed *Normanden*. Perhaps as many as half of the subscribers cancelled their subscriptions, and enraged farmers demonstrated by publicly burning copies of the newspaper. The newspaper *Fram* (Forward) served from 1916 as the voice of the Norwegians in the Nonpartisan League. In spite of opposition, the movement gained ground, and in 1918 the Nonpartisan League held political control of North Dakota.

Private capitalistic interests were fearful that the Nonpartisan League would spread to other states, but two attempts at setting up separate candidates in Minnesota failed. The time was not propitious. World War I caused all radical movements to be suspected of disloyalty. In addition, in South Dakota the governor Peter Norbeck, who was also of Norwegian origin, had preempted much of the League's program by legislation favorable to the wheat farmers. Norwegian wheat growers praised his actions and gave him their votes.

Work for Socialism

Outside the Red River valley, Minneapolis and St. Paul were the main stages for Norwegian political radicalism. In a study from 1965 Michael Barone has shown that the Populists won support among Scandinavian workers in the Twin Cities. Ethnocentric as well as economic and class considerations were at the base of their radicalism. Still, the purely Socialistic newspapers made rather modest progress. Around 1900 *Fram* in North Dakota, with Laurits Stavnheim from Sandnes, Norway, as editor, took on a Socialistic coloring. Emil Lauritz Mengshoel from Gjøvik was responsible for the most successful Socialistic newspaper, *Gaa Paa* (Forward), which appeared in Minneapolis from 1903 until some time

after World War I. *Gaa Paa* exerted considerable influence in the Norwegian working-class wards of Minneapolis.

The socially radical publications that Marcus Thrane had issued in Chicago from the mid-1860s, however, reached only "a little flock" of Scandinavian Socialists, who formed a small radical society in Chicago.

Reform Groups and the Democrats

Mengshoel's stepson and collaborator, Andrew Devold, represented the Socialists in the Minnesota legislative assembly. In the 1920s Devold became active in the Farmer-Labor party, founded in 1922. In this party, which had the most impact in Minnesota, many protest groups found each other in a radical third-party movement. Its economic base lay in a dawning labor union movement in the Twin Cities and in cooperative undertakings among the farmers in the old protest areas in northwestern Minnesota. The Scandinavian-American connection to the party was close and intimate. Under the banner of the Farmer-Labor party Floyd B. Olson—who was of Swedish and Norwegian origin—won the governorship in 1931. In 1944 the Farmer-Labor party merged with the Democratic party.

During the politically stormy 1890s the Democratic party had embarked upon a historic change. In alliance with the Populists the party had mobilized small farmers and laborers in the cities, left its laissez-faire conservatism, and promoted economic radicalism. Woodrow Wilson's "New Freedom" was a revival of the liberal principles of equality expressed by Jefferson and Jackson, transplanted and adapted to an industrial society that was characterized by large corporations and concentration of wealth. There was a close relationship between progressive reforms and the social gospel—a Protestant movement that arose in America toward the end of the nineteenth century with the purpose of creating a social order that conformed to the teachings of Christ. During the presidency of Woodrow Wilson many legislative reforms were enacted that were of great importance to groups of workers and farmers. On the other hand, the Republican party came to represent the conservative voices of business and the middle class.

Progressive men in both the Democratic and

the Republican parties had cooperated to enact the reform program. The Republican *Normanden*, for instance, cast its support in 1906 to the Democrats in North Dakota in order to defeat conservative candidates. Scandinavian voters therefore came to associate the Democratic party with reform.

Historians cannot agree whether Franklin D. Roosevelt's "New Deal," called forth by the Great Depression of the 1930s, was a continuation of the Progressive movement, or whether in its makeup it was conservative or radical. The Farmer-Labor party viewed the "New Deal" program with favor. In the presidential election of 1932, a revitalized Nonpartisan League in North Dakota endorsed Roosevelt. In 1939 the Norwegian-born John Moses was elected governor of that state on the Democratic ticket. The turn toward the Democratic party this indicates applied also to Minnesota. In 1932 Roosevelt had won the state, the first Democratic presidential candidate to do so. Even N. A. Grevstad, who had come back to edit the Republican *Skandinaven* a second time, received a personal thank you from Roosevelt for his support during the campaign. By the 1930s, however, the immigrant press had lost much of its political clout.

Work for Prohibition by Norwegian Voters and Politicians

Progressive forces had been concerned with eradicating "the sins of the city," and many thought that alcohol and the saloon owners were at the root of the evils they saw. The fight against drinking became a leading issue that pulled many Norwegians into the Progressive movement. The drive for total abstinence, with its network of temperance newspapers and lodges and with enthusiastic support by Norwegian voters, gave Norwegian-American politicians an edge in the political game. They gained experience in democratic procedure in the temperance lodge, entered local politics to prohibit the sale of alcohol under local option ordinances, and moved from there to the state and national political arena. In Norway the temperance movement was associated with the increasing political consciousness and increased sympathy for the growing labor movement. Norwegian-American Populist newspapers like *Vesterheimen* (The

Home in the West) in Crookston, Minnesota, and *Dakota* and *Den fjerde juli* (The Fourth of July) in North Dakota worked for the cause of temperance. The task temperance people had assumed was "to get the man away from the glass." The next step was "to remove the saloons," and it was this goal that moved the struggle into the political sphere. The great goal was to pass legislation forbidding the sale of all intoxicating beverages. Many powerful interests were thereby challenged. In the work for prohibition many Norwegian-American politicians found a mission.

Prohibition was in addition a reform cause that might cut across all political divisions. *Normanden* had actually been established as a temperance journal, and *Fram* was for a time the official organ of the temperance movement in North Dakota. In that state there were also newspapers with pompous declarations of their purpose incorporated into their name, like the Hillsboro newspaper *Afholds-Basunen* (The Temperance Trumpet), founded in 1887. During the first two years *Afholds-Basunen* spoke officially for the Prohibition party, which linked prohibition of the sale of alcohol to social justice.

Reform, in Eau Claire, Wisconsin, was undoubtedly the most interesting of the weeklies that made agitation for temperance and prohibition major causes. The newspaper was published under this name from 1890, but its origin was earlier. Waldemar Ager became the leading personality in *Reform* and in time its owner. He issued the newspaper as a highly personal organ until his death in 1941. Through *Reform* Ager championed his two leading causes: preservation of Norwegian culture in America and *temperance*.

The work for prohibition bore fruit in 1889, when temperance people with support from Scandinavian voters got a prohibition clause into the constitutions of both North Dakota and South Dakota. Duane R. Lindberg, himself a Lutheran pastor and historian, has shown that the efforts made by Lutheran pastors and lay people in agitating for the reform and in organizing temperance societies were decisive in securing wide support for the measure among Norwegian voters. Only one of the eight Norwegian-American newspapers published in North Dakota in the 1890s argued against the prohibition clause. Opponents of prohibition considered it to be a "Norwegian" law; outside the Norwegian districts, the law was pointedly ignored in North Dakota. It is quite appropriate that the name of a Norwegian politician be associated with the national prohibition legislation passed in 1920. Prohibition was adopted in the Volstead Act, named for Andrew J. Volstead, congressman from Minnesota.

How Reform-Minded Were Norwegian Americans?

Scandinavian politicians and voters in the Middle West were clearly reform-minded. But this is not the whole picture. The Scandinavian politicians' careers were not unique—many politicians who were not Scandinavian followed a similar political course. And it is important to stress that many Norwegians and other Scandinavians were to be found in conservative and traditional Republican camps. In Minnesota, for instance, the more affluent Norwegian districts in the southeastern part of the state rejected the reform message of the Farmer-Labor party. Knute Nelson was not the only Norwegian-American politician in Minnesota to the right of the political center. Two governors, Jacob A. O. Preus and Theodore Christianson, both third-generation Norwegian Americans, were spokesmen in the 1920s for the prevailing conservative business philosophy. It may appear as if Norwegians in the Middle West had a predominantly progressive political orientation. But the historian Carl H. Chrislock has demonstrated that this tendency was counterbalanced by other influential strains, as for instance the Knute Nelson tradition. Norwegians therefore played a part in the formulation of several aspects of the political culture.

Newspapers and Political Participation outside the Middle West

Norwegians in the East

"In the Middle West the Norwegian element has had an impact also on political life," wrote Karsten Roedder, who in the 1960s edited the Brooklyn newspaper *Nordisk Tidende* (Nordic Times). "In this regard," he continued, "Norwegians on the East Coast have accomplished nothing." Describing the situation in 1920, Roedder relates that the large Norwegian colony in Bay Ridge in Brooklyn lay in a strongly Republican district and that this suited "the leaders in the Norwegian Brooklyn colony as well as the clergy and the leaders in the congregations." But there was no united Norwegian Republican front. Except for those who belonged to labor unions, most church people were Republicans; outside the church, there were a small group of Republicans and a larger group of Democrats, but most Brooklyn Norwegians were politically indifferent.

A newspaper publisher in a Norwegian colony was a businessman, and he associated with and became a friend of the leaders of the community. He must also of course be sensitive to the interests of the subscribers in general. Especially for the immigrant newspapers, every subscriber was important; they could ill afford to lose any. In 1920 *Nordisk Tidende* chose to become more active politically. A Republican election committee was appointed. No Norwegian candidate was elected, but the newspaper was able to report "an emerging political consciousness and sense of duty." It was difficult for Norwegians to make their presence felt politically where they constituted a small percentage of the population. The newspapers, however, had the same function in the East as in the West; they were a prerequisite to a separate ethnic group existence. At least twenty Norwegian-language newspapers were published in the East. The earliest were joint Scandinavian journals. Norwegians, Swedes, and Danes were more prone to view themselves as one group when they were numerically few.

Nordisk Tidende was established in 1891 by the printer Emil Nielsen from Horten, Norway. On occasion Nielsen turned the newspaper into a scandal sheet. The love of reading was thereby increased considerably in the Norwegian colony, it was claimed. The newspaper's growth followed on the crest of the new wave of immigration after 1900. In 1910 its circulation was seven or eight thousand, and as an urban medium half of it was distributed by single-copy sale. Sigurd J. Arnesen, who had emigrated with his family in 1904 at the age of seventeen, was a major force in the business side of this newspaper enterprise between 1911 and 1958. A. N. Rygg edited *Nordisk Tidende* from 1912 to 1929. He had a great interest in the immigrant experience and wrote a history of the Brooklyn colony. Carl Søyland was probably *Nordisk Tidende*'s most distinctive and prominent figure, both as staff member and as editor.

Norwegians on the Pacific Coast

On the opposite coast, in the states along the Pacific Ocean, newspapers also appeared as immigration made itself felt there. As early as 1876 *California-Posten* came out in San Francisco, as the first Danish-Norwegian newspaper on the West Coast. The most attractive regions for newspaper activity were the two cities of Seattle and Tacoma in the state of Washington. In both cities the number of Norwegians was increasing rapidly; they were natural centers for immigration to the Pacific Northwest. Several short-lived attempts were made to issue newspapers; in his survey of Norwegian publications, Johannes B. Wist includes twenty-three newspapers on the Pacific coast. For the large contingents of Norwegians who arrived on the coast, from the Middle West as well as directly from Norway, *Washington-Posten* was the most important one. It was launched in Seattle on May 17, 1889, by Frank Oleson from Trondheim. *Tacoma-Tidende* printed its first issue on July 4, 1890; this newspaper existed at least until the years around World War I. For a long time *Washington-Posten* had a miserable existence; it faced economic hardship, and in the fall of 1905 it was put up for sale. Gunnar Lund from Stavanger then purchased the newspaper

Nordisk Tidende is published in Brooklyn, New York. It is the largest of the remaining Norwegian-American newspapers, and as the facsimile indicates, it still functions as a news organ. Its greatest circulation is in the East, although the newspaper seeks a national subscription list.

and turned it into a profitable business venture, operating it as both owner and editor until his death in 1940.

Norwegians on the West Coast had close ties to the Upper Midwest, and they were therefore characterized by the same political party spirit as their compatriots there. They took less part in politics, however, since the circumstances were different. In few places had they been pioneer settlers, as Norwegians farther east had, and in very few areas did they constitute a dominant population group. Nor were they pulled into politics by such compelling economic concerns as the ones that had enraged the wheat farmers in the Red River valley. For such reasons they were, as the historian Kenneth O. Bjork has indicated, likely to be less dogmatic in their political convictions regardless of party color. The major groups of workers and small farmers in the 1890s were generally Democratic or Populist, and these made up the majority of Norwegian settlers on the West Coast.

During its first years *Washington-Posten* was edited by the liberal Democrat Peter Røthe. Later the newspaper declared that its editorial stance was independent Republican, but it was also sensitive to political convictions to the left. In 1897, when *Washington-Posten* absorbed a short-lived Populist newspaper, *Fram*, the editor assured readers that the Populists would get "all the latitude they wished" if they only steered clear of "religious controversies."

The Norwegian newspaperman Thoralv Klaveness has accused Norwegian Americans of lacking the political solidarity and courage needed to bring compatriots "to a position of public influence." But this is not quite true even for Norwegians on the West Coast. Small groups of politically interested people worked consistently to have Scandinavian candidates placed in nomination. An example is the Scandinavian Republican League that was organized in Seattle in 1900. In 1911 there were twelve Norwegian Americans in Washington's legislative assembly. It is worth noting that many of the Norwegian-American politicians in the Far West had their roots in the Middle West. O. B. Iverson, the pioneer settler in Stanwood who sat in the territorial legislature, had moved to Washington from North Dakota. Ole Hanson, who was elected mayor of Seattle in 1918, had grown up in Wisconsin. Governor Arthur B. Langlie, governor of Washington during and after World War II, was born in a Norwegian district in Minnesota.

Relations with Norway

It was said that people in Norway subscribed to *Decorah-Posten* in order to keep informed about what was going on in their own country. In 1924, for instance, this newspaper had twenty-five correspondents in Norway. They wrote of great and small things from town and country, births and deaths, weather and wind, old ways of livelihood and new enterprises, in other words everything that occurred in the old home districts. Kristian Prestgard described the immigrant newspapers "as a large, clear window that faces toward the home community and the immigrants' youth with all its precious memories." No purely Norwegian or American newspaper could do the same.

Liberal Societies

Certain issues in Norway had a special impact in America; they reveal the strong ties the immigrants had to the homeland. The constant stream of immigrants carried with it impressions and impulses from political movements and social reforms in Norway. In addition, the Norwegian-American journals kept their readers well informed. The political battles between liberals and conservatives in Norway in the 1880s over constitutional principles aroused a nearly passionate interest and caused the formation of Norwegian-American liberal societies (*venstreforeninger*). In Minneapolis Luth. Jæger in *Budstikken* and Andreas Ueland—son of the Norwegian peasant leader Ole Gabriel Ueland—were among the prime movers. People rallied to the cause. Carl G. O. Hansen relates that it seemed as if all Norwegians in Minneapolis "were ardent Liberalists as far as Norwegian politics were concerned." In 1883 *Budstikken* printed suggestions that money should be collected to assist rifle clubs in Norway in case the political conflict should lead to an appeals to arms. At a mass meeting in January of the next year Den norsk-amerikanske Venstreforening (The Norwegian-American Liberal Society) was formed, and Andreas Ueland became its president. A letter in *Budstikken* from the society's directors contained "an urgent appeal to join this Society," as "our old fatherland's independence and freedom are at stake." Several other liberal societies came into being in the Middle West, and a fund drive was conducted. In 1884 the society in Minneapolis sent 4,000 *kroner* to the Liberal (Venstre) party in Norway. When Johan Sverdrup that year was able to appoint his government, the first parliamentary ministry in Norway, the society extended congratulations for "the victory won by the people in Norway through the recently adopted constitutional reforms."

The Norwegian-American actions had little impact in Norway, and the liberal societies were soon dissolved. Still, the inspiration from what had happened to create a strengthened democracy in the homeland must have had an influence on the immigrants' political thinking in America. Liberal groups in Norway were in addition made aware of their compatriots in America and could learn about the progress they had made. The Norwegian public, however, was quite ignorant about the Norwegian-American community. Even though there were, of course, close relations on an individual level, Norwegian organizations and societies, church groups and associations, as well as official Norway, were slow in trying to create a closer and more systematic contact with the immigrants. The interest and connection were for a long time cultivated rather one-sidedly by the Norwegian Americans themselves.

Cultural Growth

Norwegian immigrants brought with them as cultural baggage a twofold linguistic heritage: their local Norwegian dialect and a Dano-Norwegian literary language. The immigrants continued to speak the local vernacular, although English made inroads into their speech as they adjusted it to a new environment. The written Dano-Norwegian linguistic tradition was for a long time preserved in a conservative form. In time a separate Norwegian-American literature describing immigrant life was created; its foremost exponent was Ole E. Rølvaag, who produced masterly literary treatments of his compatriots in America.

Even though many of the early immigrants could not read or write when they arrived in America, newspapers and books soon gained entry into the immigrant community. Here is a Norwegian-American family reading together.

A Norwegian-American Intellectual Elite

In the service of the press, as teachers at congregational schools, academies, and colleges, as theologians at the several synods' seminaries, as pastors, and as agitators for temperance, in short, in a series of intellectual pursuits among the immigrants, one finds the names of many gifted men and women who possessed cultural tastes above the usual. Many had strong literary interests; some wrote sensitive poems, short stories, and even novels. Frequently people moved from one position to another, worked as teachers for a while, then moved into publishing newspapers, or found a political cause to champion. They were often known only to Norwegian Americans, but within this group they might enjoy much greater respect than if they had tried to pursue a career in the larger society. Lack of facility in English locked others into the ethnic subculture; as cultural leaders they could only function within its narrow bounds. Those who rose in esteem outside the group might still retain close ties to their compatriots and contribute greatly to an ethnic cultural growth.

A high percentage of the cultural leaders were associated with the church. The American-born Peer Strømme, who claimed to know more Norwegian Americans than anyone else, had a theological degree, served as a parish minister in Minnesota and elsewhere, was a teacher at St. Olaf College, edited *Norden* (The North) in Chicago and later other immigrant newspapers, was for a time director of the Norwegian academy in Mount Horeb, Wisconsin, and then returned to journalism. Strømme was for a while a very widely traveled correspondent for *Normanden*. He was also a popular public speaker and became noted as an author of novels. His novel *Hvorledes Halvor blev prest* (How Halvor Became a Minister), published in 1893, is strongly autobiographical. Bernt Askevold, the first editor of *Decorah-Posten*, was later a minister in the Norwegian Synod, and he also wrote fiction. In 1876 Askevold published *Hun Ragnhild, eller billeder fra Søndfjord* (Ragnhild, or Pictures from Søndfjord). Askevold had been a schoolteacher in Bergen before he emigrated.

Like Askevold, some of the church leaders and cultural figures had been trained as teachers in Norway. They had begun as students in a normal school, entered a folk high school, graduated from a Latin school, and possibly studied for a while at the university. During the 1800s the normal school, or *seminar*, was often the only educational opportunity for gifted rural youth. A few who had completed a Norwegian academic education found their lifework among compatriots in America. The background of those who through the years served as editors of *Skandinaven* indicates something about the recruitment to such positions. Knud Langeland had been an "itinerant schoolmaster" in Norway. Svein Nilsson was a *seminarist*, that is, a graduate of a normal school. The newspaper's third editor, David Monrad Schøyen, had been a lawyer in Oslo. Peter Henrickson, who succeeded him, had emigrated at the age of three and was trained as a philologist in America. N. A. Grevstad, the fourth editor, was the son of poor cotter folk and had attended a normal school, and John Benson, editor from 1911 to 1930, had worked on several newspapers and published a fine collection of poems, *Ved gry og kveld* (At Dawn and in the Evening). No one could, of course, expect to make a living from writing books. An artistic calling was pursued alongside another profession, not infrequently a meager livelihood on an immigrant newspaper.

Norwegian Americans — a Literate People

Conditions existed for a separate immigrant literature, but there was some doubt about how this literature would be received. "The large and rich Norwegian-American family had only two children," wrote Waldemar Ager in 1914, "and they were both well nourished. The two were the church and politics. When prophecies were heard about a Norwegian-American literature, Sarah laughed in her tent. This was nonsense. Sensible people knew that they had the church and politics—what would one do with books?"

A writer like Ager, who dreamed of creating a permanent and independent Norwegian-

Peer Strømme (1856-1921) was a minister, a teacher, a journalist, a translator, a speaker, a novelist, a politician, and a worldwide traveler. He was confident that a worthy Norwegian-American literature would develop; he claimed to know more Norwegian Americans than anyone else. In Symra, 1907, Peer Strømme wrote: "It has been a kind of article of faith among us that the art of literary creation, just as little as any of the other fine arts, can thrive in Norwegian America. Suttung's mead cannot be had for money; therefore it has not been given to us. We can assuredly cultivate wheat and tobacco, but not flowers. And for the time being we will have to accept this fact and be comforted by the idea that if no one among us has been given the divine gift of poetry by the gods, then some one must have it coming. It cannot fail that some time among the sons of the saga land in the New World there will appear men who can see great visions and dream beautiful dreams."

American subculture, manifested mainly through literary art, might with some justification feel ignored and discouraged. He and other immigrant writers were often victims of their compatriots' indifference. But there is, all the same, much evidence of the great importance reading had in the lives of the immigrants, even though the modest products of immigrant authors were not sufficiently noted or appreciated.

The ability to read and write was common among Norwegian immigrants, but not as widespread as people have assumed. Many immigrants no doubt took out the important "first papers"—a declaration of intent to become a citizen—by signing with an "X." A study of Milwaukee shows that up to 1860, 37.6 percent of all Norwegians who sought American citizenship could not write their names. The school authorities in Trempealeau county, Wisconsin, found in 1870 that 48 percent of the parents of Norwegian children could neither read nor write. In comparison, 55 percent of Polish parents were illiterate. Immigrants later in the century had, of course, a better education. The literacy rate among the peasants in Norway increased rapidly with the

Waldemar Ager (1869-1941) eagerly and enthusiastically promoted cultural values, and he wished to realize a Norwegian-American literature.

Top: Decorah-Posten's *literary supplement* Ved Arnen *spread knowledge of Norwegian and Norwegian-American literature, and it presented novels and stories in translation.*

Middle: Vor Tid *was published in Minneapolis between 1904 and 1908 "with educational and entertaining reading."*

Bottom: Kvinden og Hjemmet *also carried entertaining reading matter. The women's cause was the magazine's chief serious concern. In the issue for April, 1903, reproduced here, the first page presents an article entitled "Who Shall Govern the Home, the Husband or the Wife?" Many received impulses from the American feminist movement through this magazine.*

adoption in 1860 of a law that established public schools in rural communities.

Norwegian-American Publishers

Religious literature, Bibles, and books of sermons were common in many immigrant homes; in addition, the newspapers provided entertaining reading, frequently serialized and thereby creating anticipation of the next installment. Delays in the printing of *Decorah-Posten*'s literary supplement *Ved Arnen* when a new printing press was being installed produced loud cries from disappointed readers. *Skandinaven* began in 1873 to publish a similar literary supplement which it called *Husbibliothek* (House Library). Three years later *Skandinaven*'s bookstore (*Skandinavens* Boghandel) was opened in Chicago; it became a leading seller of Norwegian books. Several newspaper firms, like John Anderson Publishing Company, publisher of *Skandinaven*, B. Anundsen Publishing Company, which put out *Decorah-Posten*, and Fremad Publishing Company, publisher of *Reform*, functioned as book publishers. The books they sold—Norwegian volumes, works translated from English, and accounts written by Norwegian-American authors—had likely first appeared serially in the newspapers.

There were, in addition, purely literary periodicals. The best known and most original was *Symra* (The Anemone), issued by Kristian Prestgard and Johannes B. Wist in Decorah from 1905 to 1914. The publishers set themselves the praise-worthy goal of uniting a fractured Norwegian America "on a national basis." A whole generation of immigrant writers made *Symra* their own organ.

Eidsvold was another example; it came out in Grand Forks and Fargo for a few years before World War I. Even a New Norse (*nynorsk*) magazine, *Norrøna* (The Norse), appeared for about two years, 1914-15. It was difficult to gain support for literature written in this language, a medium formed from Norwegian rural dialects and popularized by some prominent writers.

Still, the widely distributed periodical *Vor Tid* (Our Time) in Minneapolis printed Arne Garborg's story "Den burtkomne Faderen" (The Lost Father), written by the author in New Norse, but only with a long explanation to the readers.

A special purpose was served by the monthly magazine *Kvinden og hjemmet* (The Woman and the Home), which began publication in 1888 in Cedar Rapids, Iowa, with Ida Hansen from Ringsaker, Norway, as editor. In 1924 the magazine had 34,000 subscribers. It was not a literary periodical, but engaged itself strongly in the feminist movement. In a supplement, however, it provided reading material, novels and short stories, for a "thousand homes in America." It continued to be published until the post-World War II years.

Reading Clubs and Literary Societies

Literary taste varied, of course. Some immigrant homes had libraries with the best of Norwegian literature; parsonages might become cultural as well as religious centers. The pastor Samson Madsen Krogness, for example, assembled 8,000 books and encouraged greater interest in Norwegian-American history.

In the spirit of enlightenment of the time, reading clubs and literary societies were formed in a number of Norwegian settlements and urban colonies. These groups collected money to purchase books. Examples are Fremad Læseselskab (Forward Reading Society) in Moscow, Wisconsin, and Holmes City Læseforening (Holmes City Reading Association) in Minnesota, both from the 1870s. On the West Coast there later emerged a Skandinavisk Bibliotek (Scandinavian Library) in Stanwood, in "the heart of the Scandinavian population . . . by Puget Sound." More exclusive were such prominent literary societies as Ygdrasil in Madison, established in 1896. Membership was limited to men with academic training. A similar society is Symra in Decorah, formed with the purpose of securing financial support for the magazine of the same name. Both of the latter groups are still in existence.

What Did They Read?

A systematic examination of a literary supplement like *Ved Arnen* reveals much about the popular taste in light literature. *Ved Arnen* presented through the years a whole library of verse and imaginative prose, mainly translated novels and short stories. It also offered the literature of the homeland. The newspaper printed numerous sentimental tales, and on occasion even detective stories. Names like Charles Dickens and Anatole France were also represented. Of Norwegian fiction, the supplement had a preference for Bjørnson's peasant stories, regional writers like Jacob Breda Bull and Hans Aanrud, Trygve Gulbranssen's hero-filled novels, Bernt Lie's simple and straightforward works, and "Gjest Baardsen Sogndalsfjæren's Life with Addendum," the story of a master thief. Especially well liked were the tales and poems by the Telemark writer John Lie. But there was no doubt that Norwegian-American writers could also gain the public's favor. Hans A. Foss achieved enormous popularity with his novel *Husmands-Gutten* (The Cotter Boy), a male Cinderella story of one who made good in America. It was first serialized in *Decorah-Posten* and reportedly attracted 6,000 new subscribers to the newspaper. In 1885 it was printed in book form. It was reprinted many times and was received equally well in Norway and in America.

The Norwegian-American Language

"One does not understand what a mighty cultural effort Norwegian-American literature is before one has sat on the western plains and felt the imperceptible withering of the language under new cultural conditions and in new surroundings, under the pressure of a foreign culture and language environment, and deprived of a constant cultural exchange with Norway."

Fremad Läseselskab, a reading society, on an outing in Moscow, Wisconsin, October 9, 1875. This society was an early example of literary interest among the immigrants, and men, women, and children participated. The photograph was taken by Andrew Dahl.

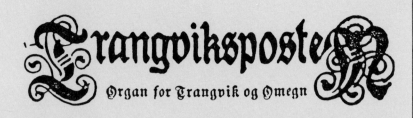

Mr. Jens Træby.

Interview.

Forleden Dag da vi intet anede havde vi pludselig Besøg paa vort Kontor af en meget flot udseende Herre, som raskt bankede paa vor Dor og kom ind. Det viste sig da, at være ovenstaaende Mr. Træby, som vi tidligere har omtalt her i Bladet og ønsket velkommen hjem efterat han i nogle Tage havde vakt adskillig Opsigt i vor Bys Gader ifort sin flotte amerikanske Pels og i det heletaget, som en Herre der maatte tiltrække sig Opmerksomhed.

Theodor Kittelsen's and Trangvikposten's caricature of the "typical" Norwegian American who has returned to the homeland, popularly perceived as a person with expensive habits but without culture. The satirical newspaper Trangvikposten, referring to an imaginary town Trangvik, was the creation of the Norwegian author Jacob Hilditch, and it appeared in three volumes between 1900 and 1907.

In this way Sigurd Folkestad expressed himself in the magazine *Nordmands-Forbundet* in 1925. As author, pastor, and newspaper editor, Folkestad was concerned with the language—a "little flower garden of Norwegian words that one has laboriously preserved . . . during the transit to a foreign land, where the soil is tropically rich in weeds."

In contrast, when Kristofer Janson first came to the Middle West in 1879, it struck him with surprise "how the Norwegians have managed to isolate and bunch themselves together in colonies and maintain their Norwegian memories and customs." He had to ask himself if he really was in America. Of a settlement in Wisconsin, "which to boot was called 'Scandinavia,'" Janson wrote: "The landscape was exactly like that in eastern Norway, with ridges, slopes, hills, and valleys, and wholly resembled Ringsaker. The farm women strolled on the road with their knitting and conversed in their peasant vernacular." The Norwegian immigrants brought with them as a heritage their urban or rural speech, the local dialect, and in settlements of fellow Norwegians they proceeded to use it in their daily associations. Under special conditions, wrote the linguist George T. Flom in 1912, the local Norwegian country speech could prevail and be "as pure and unadulterated as in Norway." In the large Koshkonong settlement there were gatherings of different local groups of rural folk side by side. The Telemarkings were most numerous in Pleasant Spring township, the Sognings in Christiana township east of the Telemarkings, and still farther east the Numedøls. After a period of seventy years Flom insisted that they spoke "their own dialects authentically." Because of the sharp linguistic divisions between these three rural vernaculars, there was no mixing of dialects.

A Formal Language with a West-Norwegian Flavor

In the American cities where Norwegians settled, the pressure to speak English was stronger, and less of the Norwegian language was preserved. In the Norwegian neighborhoods of Chicago and Minneapolis, and in smaller towns in the Middle West with concentrations of Norwegians, there were, however, conditions for preserving Norwegian speech beyond the immigrant generation.

In addition to the daily speech, there developed in America what Flom calls a "high Norwegian" pronunciation. It was first in the church, and then in colleges and seminaries, that this language was given its form. Because those who filled the ranks of the pastors for a long time came from West Norway, the "formal speech" among Norwegian Americans developed strong West-Norwegian characteristics. It represented a Dano-Norwegian linguistic tradition with a

West-Norwegian flavor. Because the teachers at the Norwegian-American schools "for the most part were of West-Norwegian origin," the young people who were educated there acquired this pronunciation. Many of these students were children of farmers and felt closely attached to West-Norwegian speech, for the majority had "at least parents who spoke [this] dialect."

The Effects of Bilingualism

But the influence of English soon made itself felt. This circumstance can most easily be seen in the Norwegian-American vocabulary. In a large scholarly work Einar Haugen analyzed the changes and adjustments the Norwegian language experienced in America. Linguistic development was dictated by the impact of new conditions and surroundings, in addition to the need to make oneself intelligible in English. It was therefore to a certain degree necessary to become bilingual. As a consequence, Norwegian-American became a mixed language, for the most part in speech, but also to some extent in writing. Newcomers to established settlements naively expected that people would talk as they themselves did, and they were shocked at the Norwegian they heard. Haugen gives as an example an immigrant who in 1911 came to Madison and over the telephone was given the following instructions by his brother: "You must take *stritkarsen* [the streetcar] to Schenk's Street." What kind of vehicle that was, the newcomer could not figure out, and so he decided to walk. Visitors from Norway found the speech of the immigrants confusing and barbaric; Norwegian Americans were made fun of when they visited the homeland; and even they felt their language was inferior and might describe it as Iowa-Norwegian or Minnesota-Norwegian. But the development was natural and far from chaotic. The changes followed a fixed pattern. The language adjusted and made it possible to describe and talk about new conditions.

Of Norwegian-American authors, Johannes B. Wist has probably best reproduced natural Norwegian-American speech. How the characters should express themselves often presented a dilemma to immigrant writers: Were they to speak Norwegian as in Norway or as in America? Newspapers and other publications had to accept

linguistic neologisms in order to write about life among their compatriots. Simultaneously there existed a strong conservatism in the language. Many old words and expressions were preserved orally, even when they had been lost in Norway. In the literary language the immigrants were slow to accept orthographic reforms adopted in Norway. There was always something old-fashioned about the Norwegian-American language, as seen from a Norwegian point of view. This impression was strengthened by the fact that Gothic script was used long after it had been discontinued in Norway. *Decorah-Posten* continued to be printed in Gothic type until 1952. Kristian Prestgard explained in 1926 that *Decorah-Posten*'s "linguistic form in 1926 was almost exactly the same as in 1874." In other words, the language reforms in Norway of 1907 and 1917 had been ignored.

Such linguistic reforms, motivated by cultural and social forces within Norway, had of course little importance for an immigrant people. The confusion they created made it, to the contrary, more difficult to preserve a written Norwegian language at all. Neither efforts to create a new Norwegian language — New Norse — nor the Norwegianization of the Dano-Norwegian literary language gained much support or sympathy among Norwegians in America.

A Norwegian-American Literature Is Created

Nearly fifty years passed after Norwegians began going to America before anyone among the immigrants started to write short stories and novels. The reason, writes Laurence M. Larson, was that "the energies of the pioneers were engaged first with the conquest of the soil and next with the building of a new social order." The literary historian Gerald H. Thorson has pointed out a connection between the emergence of a regional American literature and interest in a special Norwegian-American literature in the years during and just after the Civil War. Examples of such literature are "The Luck of Roaring Camp" and other stories by Bret Harte, and the masterful

Rasmus B. Anderson (1846-1936) was professor of Scandinavian languages at the University of Wisconsin in Madison from 1869 until 1883. He was a dominating figure in the Norwegian-American community. In his newspaper Amerika, *which he published from 1898 until 1922, he abandoned his earlier liberalism and allied himself with Norwegian-American pastors and lay people in their condemnation of modern Norwegian literature. It was accused of being godless and of giving an impression of the homeland that might damage the immigrants' reputation in America. January 23, 1903, Anderson wrote in* Amerika: *"Give us back the old Romanticists! It was Romanticism that awakened in us a sense for history, in Norway for the saga literature, and gave impetus to the national sentiment. . . . But during the last quarter century we have had Realism, Pessimism, Decadence. We have had winter instead of spring and summer."*

tales of Mark Twain. The immigrant literature was, however, different, even though it followed the main pattern of other literature that was created in the West.

In the 1870s Scandinavian authors found an American audience. Two men, Hjalmar Hjorth Boyesen and Rasmus B. Anderson, exploited the popularity of Scandinavian literature for their own benefit, but in doing so they also released creative forces in their own compatriots in America. Boyesen, who in 1881 became professor of Germanic languages at Columbia University, had in 1874 published a peasant idyll under the title *Gunnar*, written for an American audience. The same year Anderson published two books, *America Not Discovered by Columbus* and *Den norske maalsag* (The Norwegian Language Issue). Both men worked to make Norwegian literature and mythology known among Americans and among their compatriots. This would of course help their own positions, but through their efforts they also provided important cultural impulses. Boyesen had, however, little contact with Norwegian Americans. Anderson, who was professor of Scandinavian languages at the state university in Madison, Wisconsin, had a more intimate relation to the Norwegian-American community. In the contributions he sent to *Skandinaven* in the 1870s, he encouraged the immigrants to write.

It may be asserted, as Laurence Larson maintains, that Boyesen and Anderson, both young men in 1874, introduced a new chapter in the artistic and intellectual life of the Norwegian colonies in America. Travel pieces, ballads, and informational literature of various kinds had appeared shortly after the beginning of emigration, and hundreds of poems and lyrics had been sent to the newspapers. They revolved mostly around "'the home we left' and only occasionally about the 'home we found,'" Ager says in his overview. Precious memories from the old country provided inspiration for occasional poetry. *Skandinaven*, for instance, printed lyrics by Dr. J. C. Dundas (Dass), the pioneer physician in Wisconsin. Rasmus O. Reine sent religious poetry to *Fædrelandet og Emigranten*. In 1871 Reine published a book of these poems, the first printed collection of verse by a Norwegian American. It reflected a strong pietistic tradition, and it was this tradition that produced the early writing. In the landmark year 1874 the first two immigrant

novels were published, in the same pietistic spirit. Nicolai Severin Hassel wrote two short novels for the magazine *For Hjemmet* (For the Home), "an entertaining and educational monthly in a Christian spirit," which came out in Decorah from 1870 to 1888. The two were *Alf Brage, eller skolelæreren i Minnesota* (Alf Brage, or The Schoolteacher in Minnesota), and *Rædselsdagene, et norsk billede fra indianerkrigen* (Days of Terror, A Norwegian Picture from the Indian War), both didactic and excessively moralizing religious tracts. In the second story, for instance, the observation is made that few Norwegians perished in the Indian wars in 1862 because they were faithful to God's word and Luther's teachings, while there was great destruction among the German agnostics in New Ulm.

In spite of their obvious weaknesses, Thorson has claimed that with these two novels Hassel was a pioneer. In addition to having written the first works in prose, the author found material worthy of literary treatment among the immigrants themselves. Besides, Hassel's novels contained ingredients that characterized later immigrant fiction: the setting was Midwestern, major interest was directed at the Norwegian settlers, the situations described were close to real life, there was an annoying amount of moralizing, and the author was concerned with the immigrants' own problems.

The Longing for Norway—an Enduring Motif

Interest in Norwegian literature sometimes led directly to imitative literary endeavors among the immigrants. Askevold, for example, who in 1876 published *Hun Ragnhild*, the first Norwegian-language novel printed as a book in America, placed three of the four novels he wrote in a Norwegian setting.

Nostalgia permeates the whole of Norwegian-American literature. The longing for Norway—the life the immigrants had left behind—runs like a red thread through most of this writing, in verse as in prose. Whether Norwegian society and history are directly mentioned or not, it is still this yearning that gives Norwegian-American literature its uniqueness and separates it from both American and Norwegian literature of the same period.

Askevold did not write for a cultured American audience, as Boyesen did, but for ordinary immigrants throughout the great Middle West. Tellef Grundysen did the same in his novel *Fra begge sider af havet* (From Both Sides of the Ocean), published in 1876. This work also takes the reader back to the Norwegian landscape, but in addition it treats life in a Norwegian settlement in Minnesota. Grundysen, who was of poor cotter stock, emigrated from Bygland in Setesdal in the early 1860s at age seven. He grew up in Fillmore county, Minnesota. A critic will discover little that is of interest about the novel as literary art. Its direct and simple narrative about the experiences of ordinary folk, centered on the solving of a crime, appealed, however, to the immigrants. The novel was a success and went through several editions.

The model for the immigrant writers was Bjørnstjerne Bjørnson's masterly peasant tales; *Synnøve Solbakken, Arne,* and *En glad gut* (A Happy Boy) were popular in the Norwegian-American community. Many attempted to imitate them. They thereby created what might be called a Norwegian-American National Romanticism. The heroes in this literature are the new Vikings, the men and women who settled in a new Normandy, and Viking symbolism is a prominent and cherished aspect. The writers were unaffected by contemporary European Naturalism. Instead they created romanticized depictions of folk life in the spirit of the Norwegian National Renaissance. They also found an audience in the homeland. In their novels they employed Bjørnson's proven formulas, but without possessing the master's talent. Boyesen's *Gunnar* is reminiscent of Bjørnson's early works in nearly every chapter, and attempts at imitation are even more visible in Askevold's books. They are also present, though less evident, in Grundysen's novel.

Hans A. Foss

The most successful use of Bjørnson's recipe is found in the novel *Husmands-Gutten* by Hans A. Foss. After having edited newspapers, among them *Normanden* in North Dakota, Foss became a grain inspector for the state of Minnesota. In *Husmands-Gutten* Foss tells about Ole Haugen,

Ulrikka Feldtman Bruun (1854-1940) was a temperance writer. She came to Chicago in 1874, established a mission house, a home for girls, and a temperance lodge, and published the temperance magazine Det Hvide Baand *(The White Ribbon). She wrote poetry, songbooks, and literary works to promote the temperance cause. Her novels have characteristic titles like* Menneskets største fiende *(Humanity's Greatest Enemy, 1879),* Lykkens nøgle *(The Key to Happiness, 1880), and* Fjendens faldgruber *(The Enemy's Pitfalls, 1884).*

a poor but intelligent cotter boy from Sigdal, Norway. In America Ole acquires wealth, and when he returns to Norway, everyone agrees that he "more resembled a big merchant from the capital than a cotter boy." Ole overcomes class prejudices in his home community, arrives in time to marry a farmer's daughter he had dreamed about in America, and the two live happily ever after in a large white house on a Norwegian hillside.

A Chicago publisher had returned the manuscript as "unacceptable." The fact that *Decorah-Posten* was willing to print it was therefore his last chance. As a piece of literary work the novel is weak. Foss continued to write "in about the same spirit of innocence," as he himself expressed it. His didactic style and awkward construction are evident weaknesses, but Foss does present an accurate and insightful depiction of the lives and attitudes of the immigrants. His later novels frequently become moralizing expressions of the author's two major causes: prohibition and the Populist party. *Livet i Vesterheimen* (Life in the West) in 1885 has both drunkenness and church controversy as themes, and takes up the problem of the saloons in Norwegian settlements in the Red River valley. In *Kristine*, published the year after, the setting is Norway, but here also work and sobriety are rewarded by wealth. In 1889 *Den amerikanske saloon* (The American Saloon, published in Norway in 1892 as *Fisker-Tobias*) appeared, which deals with the competition between the church and the saloon. Both were dependent on "the same people for their existence and their sustenance." *Hvide slaver* (White Slaves), with the subtitle *A Social Political Story* (1892), presents the saloon as the tool of "Plutocrats and Whiskey Barons" and contains sharp Populistic attacks on the Republican party, which liberated the "poor black slaves — and then put . . . white slaves in their place."

Kristofer Janson and Drude Krog Janson

No issue concerned the immigrant authors more than the temperance cause. Many of the best writers became advocates of it; the American saloon intrudes into almost every novel. Kristofer Janson was also preoccupied with drunkenness among Norwegians and treated the subject in his literary works after he came to Minneapolis as a Unitarian minister in 1881. In three novels, *Præriens saga* (The Saga of the Prairie) in 1885, *Et arbeidsdyr* (A Beast of Burden) in 1889, and *Fra begge sider havet* (From Both Sides of the Ocean) in 1890, Janson assails the immigrants' drunkenness and pettiness. It is the intolerant Lutheran clergy who are blamed for the intemperance and for the servile position he thinks immigrant women assume. The last theme is more fully developed in the novel *Sara* (1891). In it he does battle with exploitative American capitalism and with the prejudices in the immigrant community. His main protagonist, Sara, who finds meaning for her life through enlightenment, is greatly disappointed with her compatriots. This might reflect Janson's own disenchantment. He was, however, more positive in his depiction of the immigrants in the two books *Femtende Wisconsin* (Fifteenth Wisconsin) and *Vildrose* (Wild Rose), both appearing in 1887. The first novel was inspired by Norwegian-American heroes of the Civil War and the second by the situation of Norwegian immigrants during the Indian uprising in 1862.

Janson was an idealist and a humanist; both tendencies were at the heart of his authorship. His socially critical novels became organs for his liberal humanism and for his faith in the social gospel. He was a major critic of social conditions; many of the most significant works by other immigrant writers of the time belonged in this literary tradition. Janson's labor novel *Bag gardinet* (Behind the Curtain) from 1889 is a powerful attack on the American environment with its hypocrisy and cultural poverty. In it he indicts American society for its degrading treatment of workers, women, and immigrants. It is Minneapolis in the 1880s that is portrayed, and the title refers to the evils that "are concealed under the disguise of the parvenue millionaires." In his novels Janson preserved a deep feeling for the individual human being and revealed an intimate understanding of American life. In 1893 he left America for "a temporary stay in Norway," as he stated in his magazine *Saamanden*. He never returned.

Drude Krog Janson, his wife, was also an author, and in her books she too relied heavily on the life around her. In 1889 Drude Janson published the novel *En saloonkeepers datter* (A Saloonkeeper's Daughter, published in 1887 in Norway as *En ung pige*, A Young Girl). The novel became a strong contribution to the feminist cause. The main character, Astrid, escapes the degrading life in her father's saloon on Cedar Avenue in Minneapolis, and at a meeting with the great Bjørnson during his lecture tour of the Middle West in 1880-81 she is encouraged to speak for the liberal cause and become a Unitarian minister. In her novel *Tore*, in 1894, she describes the life of an immigrant woman in a rural district. Drude Janson did not create literature of great consequence, but her novels are interesting documents of a specific situation and

Drude Krog Janson (1846-1934), Kristofer Janson's wife, wrote literature about social issues, with women's special circumstances in society as a central theme. She was inspired by the great Norwegian writer Bjørnstjerne Bjørnson, and she in turn served as a model and inspiration both for Bjørnson and for Knut Hamsun, who stayed in the Janson home while serving as Kristofer Janson's secretary.

Ole and Anlaug Buslett in the post office portion of the grocery store they operated in Northland, Wisconsin. The photograph is from 1917. Ole Buslett (1855-1924) was proclaimed by Waldemar Ager to be "the first Norwegian-American writer."

historical period, and of a social debate as it affected the immigrants themselves.

Ole Amundsen Buslett

Ole Amundsen Buslett has been declared, by Waldemar Ager among others, to be "the first Norwegian-American writer." The literary scholar Lloyd Hustvedt maintains that he was the earliest Norwegian immigrant to make literary art a lifelong pursuit. Buslett created no school and had no special audience. With his writing he wanted to awaken the immigrants' appreciation for cultural values and free them from their inferiority complex, their *husmannsånd* (cotter spirit), in their attitude toward their own national heritage. But he was no great interpreter of Norwegian-American life.

Like his fellow writers, Buslett penned tales in the Bjørnson style. In 1882 he wrote a poor imitation he called *Fram* (Forward). His most interesting efforts are fables and visionary sagas, full of symbols and allegory. Buslett produced lengthy epic poems like *Skaars skjæbne* (Skaar's Fate) in 1882 and *Øistein og Nora* two years later;

the latter poem has numerous melodramatic episodes. Buslett also worked poems into his prose writing. His most significant literary works were completed after the turn of the century. The 1908 novel *Sagastolen* (The Saga Seat) includes a depiction of a socialistic colony. *Veien til Golden Gate* (The Road to the Golden Gate), which was finished in 1915, is an allegorical statement of Buslett's rejection of the "melting pot" ideology. His best work is perhaps the 1918 novel *Fra min ungdoms nabolag* (About the Neighborhood of my Youth). It is a straightforward account of Buslett's own family, youth, and local community.

In Poetic Form

Many gifted writers cherished and wrote verse as well as prose. Even more literary artists gave themselves exclusively to the poetic form.

In 1903 Ludvig Lima published a collection he called *Norsk-amerikanske digte i udvalg* (A Selection of Norwegian-American Poetry). In this anthology as many as forty-five poets were represented. Knut Martin Teigen, born on Koshkonong and a physician, here praises Koshkonong as "you precious, you wonderful land, the jewel among Norwegian settlements." Impressions from childhood in America could thus also be interpreted in lyrics. Norway was the creative inspiration for Wilhelm Pettersen and Theodore S. Reimestad, both immigrants and professors at Augsburg Seminary. Pettersen wrote sensitive lyrics about "Norges skjønhed" (Norway's Beauty) and "Til Norge" (To Norway). But it was also possible for an immigrant to develop new loyalties. Pettersen wrote in English, using terms commonly applied to Norway to describe Minnesota as "the fairest country, home of nations brave and strong."

D. G. Ristad created moving lyrical poetry; with pathos he lauded "the land we won under the Western sky, by Leif and his men discovered." In 1930 he published a small collection, *Kvad* (Poems). Talented also was Agnes Mathilde Wergeland, teacher at the state university in Laramie, Wyoming, although her poems in *Amerika og andre digte* (America and Other Poems), published in 1912, seem obscure and constricted. One of the finest Norwegian-American lyric poets is Julius B. Baumann. He came to America from Vadsø in 1891 and worked for a time as a

Agnes Mathilde Wergeland (1857-1914), professor of history at the state university in Laramie, Wyoming, from 1902 until 1914. The photograph is from 1913. Wergeland was the first Norwegian woman to earn a doctoral degree, and her appointment exemplifies how American society in many instances gave women greater opportunity than at that time existed in Norway. Wergeland had contact with such Norwegian feminists as Aasta Hansteen and Gina Krog. Aasta Hansteen, the great pioneer for the women's cause in Norway, had herself lived in America from 1880 until 1889.

lumberjack. In the two collections *Digte* (Poems) in 1909 and *Fra viddene* (From the Wide Open Places) in 1915 he presents intensely felt lyrical poetry, frequently with his own North Norway as his inspiration: "A land of memories with walls of mountains, with glaciers on fire, with the roar of waterfalls, with the sigh of forests, with the singing of birds, with the roar of waves, with flowers on the meadow." (Translated by Gerald Thorson)

Peer Strømme—a Sharp Observer of His Time

Of those who contributed to Norwegian-American belles lettres in the nineteenth century, Peer Strømme was the least polemic. In the 1906 novel *Unge Helgeson* (Young Helgeson) he continued the story begun in his first novel *Hvorledes Halvor blev prest*. The reader accompanies Halvor to the Red River valley, where he fills a pastorate among Norwegian immigrants. The novel is in several senses a transitional work; it moves away from a depiction of the Norwegian background toward a discussion of the inroads the American environment makes in a separate ethnic existence. Even Pastor Helgeson's visit to Norway underscores the author's interest in a Norwegian America and brings out the Norwegian ignorance about the immigrant community in the West. Helgeson explains to people who "found it difficult to believe" that there existed a Norway also in America with good Norwegian schools and Norwegian teachers, and that there were people who had been born in America who spoke only their parents' Norwegian dialect.

The setting of Strømme's final novel, *Den vonde ivold* (In the Clutches of the Devil) (1910), is Chicago. It belongs to a literature of decadence, written in the same spirit as *Fra Kristiania-bohemen* (About the Kristiania Bohemia) by the Norwegian novelist Hans Jæger. With striking psychological realism and sure knowledge of the many aspects of immigrant life in a large city, he depicts individuals who are at odds with society. Kristofer Janson's novel *Sara* also deals with the Norwegian colony in Chicago. Both Janson and Strømme view the immigrants' meeting with the urban environment as a dangerous, even destructive experience. Sara triumphs because she preserves her ideals and her intellectual strength; Strømme's decadent protagonists perish.

Lars A. Stenholt

The only Norwegian-American author who is purported to have made a living from his literary production, "even though the livelihood was extremely miserable," as Ager stated it, was the Minneapolis writer Lars A. Stenholt. He had emigrated from Ørskog in Sunnmøre in 1882. Between 1887 and 1909 he wrote an average of two books annually. Stenholt published sensational novels and journalistic exposés. In 1906 he based a novel on the true story of a Norwegian-American bank president and pillar of society in Chicago who had absconded with all the bank's funds: *Paul O. Steensland og hans hjælpere, eller milliontyvene i Chicago* (Paul O. Steensland and his Helpers, or The Millionaire Thieves in Chicago). The book makes a moral judgment and is an intense criticism of the author's adversaries. It projects a sense of rivalries and power struggles within the Norwegian-American community.

Stenholt was "to the liking of the reading public," Ager remarked disapprovingly in his survey of immigrant literature. In 1888 he had written *Chicago anarkistene* (The Chicago Anarchists), which treats the infamous Haymarket Massacre of 1886. In 1901 he found the topic for *Falk og jødinden* (Falk and the Jewess) in a scandal about a well-known pastor and fellow writer in Minneapolis. The same year he issued *Minnesota bibelen* (The Minnesota Bible), and in 1908 he lambasted Rasmus B. Anderson in *Paven i Madison, eller Rasmus Kvelves merkværdige liv og hændelser* (The Pope in Madison, or Rasmus Kvelve's Remarkable Life and Doings). Stenholt also harbored historical interests: in 1898 he published *Norge i Amerika* (Norway in America), which is an attempt at depicting the life and history of Norwegians in the new land.

A Literary Tradition Is Carried Forward

A new generation of writers appeared after 1900, although those who had begun to write earlier continued to produce. Several of the later authors display greater literary powers than the first generation, and they concern themselves with new aspects of the immigrant community. Gerald Thorson has called this chapter of Norwegian-American literary history "Defending the Heritage." During this period the children of the immigrants surpassed the Norwegian-born generation in numbers. The literature is therefore concerned with the question of preserving Norwegian culture and language in the coming gen-

erations. The picture of a large white house on a Norwegian hillside is gone; the longing and the sense of loss are no longer meaningful themes, nor is the dream of returning to Norway. Happiness and progress are to be found in America, but without renouncing the Norwegian cultural heritage. The privation and self-denial that characterized depictions of the immigrant experience disappear in the accounts of the immigrants' successful descendants.

In the novel *Harald Hegg* by M. Falk Gjertsen, published in 1914, the second generation finds success in the field of politics. In addition to the theme of success, the well-worn temperance question is injected into the narrative. What is new is that the protagonist makes progress because he has preserved such Norwegian qualities as honesty, sincerity, and reliability—and that he honors the country of his forebears.

Simon Johnson—"The Prairie Writer"

Simon Johnson began his first book, *Et geni* (A Genius), published in 1907, with a description of the wheat harvest on the North Dakota prairie. With his parents he had moved from Øyer in Gudbrandsdalen in 1882, when he was eight years old. He grew up in the wholly Norwegian Norway township in Traill county. Johnson's masterful depictions of pioneer life and of the prairie environment made him known as "the prairie writer." But he was also a temperance man and a champion of Norwegian cultural values, and in his books he agitates for the preservation of ethnic traditions and culture on the mighty plains of the West. *Et geni* moralizes about the abuse of alcohol and the main character succumbs to this vice, but the novel is well constructed and interesting. His second book, *Lonea* (1909), gives a realistic picture of immigrant life and underscores the need to retain historical memories.

In 1914 Johnson published *I et nyt rige* (In a New Kingdom, which appeared in English translation in 1916 as *From Fjord to Prairie*). This novel is perhaps the best portrayal of the prairie in Norwegian-American literature. The loneliness of the new surroundings makes the settlers in the colonies think about Norway; Johnson attributes to the pioneers a strength which disappears in later generations. In the two following novels, *Fallitten*

paa Braastad (The Bankruptcy at Braastad) in 1922, and *Frihetens hjem* (The Home of Freedom) in 1925, Johnson reveals his disappointment at the zeal for Americanization among his compatriots. *Fire fortællinger* (Four Stories), published in 1917, shows Simon Johnson as an able writer of short stories. Several authors wrote essays and sketches about Norwegian-American conditions. B. B. Haugan's "Et besøg hos presten" (A Visit to the Pastor) in 1895 should be mentioned. This story was described by Waldemar Ager as "a pure Norwegian-American tale."

Waldemar Ager

Waldemar Ager wrote a number of novels and short stories, among them *Fortællinger for Eyvind* (Stories for Eyvind) in 1906, *Hverdagsfolk* (Common Folk) in 1908, and *Fortællinger og skisser* (Stories and Sketches) in 1913. In the last collection is found the sentimental story "To tomme hænder" (Two Empty Hands), which was often read aloud at gatherings. The temperance message is a central concern for Ager, which is apparent in many of the titles themselves, for instance *Paa drikkeondets konto* (To Be Charged to the Evil of Drinking) (1894) and *Afholdssmuler fra bokhylden* (Temperance Crumbs from the Bookshelf) (1901).

Ager's younger years in his hometown of Fredrikstad had been full of difficulties, and his father had deserted the family and gone to America. With his mother and two siblings, Ager followed after in 1885, at the age of sixteen. Ager was gifted, perhaps the most original Norwegian-American novelist besides O. E. Rølvaag. His agitation for temperance, however, at times stood in the way of his creative powers and he became didactic and moralizing. Sentimental and wholehearted he might also be when he championed his second major cause: Norwegian-American cultural growth. His organs were the newspaper *Reform* and the magazine *Kvartalskrift* (Quarterly), which he edited for the Norwegian Society from 1905 to 1922. In addition, there were his novels and stories and his ubiquitous appearances as speaker at Norwegian-American events. Ager's breakthrough as a novelist was *Kristus for Pilatus* (Christ before Pilate) in 1910, published in Norway the following year as *Presten Conrad Walther Welde*. The novel contains unforgettable personal portraits, and its tension lies in the conflict between the idealist Welde and the coarse provincialism he encounters in a Norwegian-American congregation.

In 1917 Ager defied prevailing public sentiment by publishing the novel *Paa veien til smeltepotten* (On the Way to the Melting Pot) as a protest against the war hysteria with its demand for "100 percent Americanism." In *Gamlelandets sønner* (Sons of the Old Country), published in 1926, the reader meets another representative from the upper classes who is ill at ease in the society in which he finds himself. Even though *Gamlelandets sønner* does not achieve the excellence of *Kristus for Pilatus*, it draws with cautious realism a picture of life in the woods and lumber camps of northern Wisconsin. In 1929 Ager published his last novel, *Hundeøine* (Dog Eyes, translated into English as *I Sit Alone*). It is an account of an old man who sits alone in a shack on the North Dakota grassland and reflects on his life. He is poor and feels that he has wasted his life. This is the tragedy of the immigrant as Ager sees it; perhaps Ager's was a tragic vision of human existence. He realized, as a student of Ager's writings, Clarence Kilde, expresses it, that "those ideals he so gallantly had committed his life to could not be realized."

Johannes B. Wist—Humorist and Satirist

In the 1920s *Decorah-Posten*'s editor Johannes B. Wist, who generally used the pseudonym "Arnljot," wrote a humorous trilogy about Jonas Olsen, a newcomer who had moved from the working wards of Minneapolis to the western part of Minnesota, where he founded his own town. *Nykommerbilder* (Immigrant Scenes) appeared in 1920, *Hjemmet paa prærien* (The Home on the Prairie) in 1921, and *Jonasville* in 1922. In the final novel Wist satirizes the immigrants' efforts at Americanization, but he also touches upon the church strife of the 1880s and trivial local politics—among other things he gives a lively account of two communities' fight to gain the county seat.

Jon Norstog—"The Enigma on the Prairie"

Jon Norstog was the most inaccessible of the immigrant writers, partly because he wrote in a peculiar Telemark dialect and partly because his works had an obscure character and employed symbols and allegory. "The enigma on the prairie," he was called.

Norstog wrote a total of twenty volumes—lyrics, epics, and plays. Out on the North Dakota prairie he set, printed, and bound his own books and functioned as bookseller. Many of his works have biblical names as titles. *Moses* (1914) is a dramatic work in five acts and 531 pages. *Israel* (1917) is a twelve-act drama with an incredible 885 pages. With *Exodus* (1928) Norstog became a novelist. In much of what he wrote, Norstog treated universal themes relating to the immigrant experience; his works received obvious impulses from the neo-Romanticism of Norwegian literature in the 1890s.

The Last of the Immigrant Authors

A Norwegian immigrant writer is generally defined as a person of Norwegian birth or descent who writes books in the Norwegian language for a Norwegian-American audience. A few tried to write in English as well as Norwegian. Dorothea Dahl published in 1915 the simple depictions of *Hverdagslivet* (Everyday Life). In 1920 she wrote *Returning Home*, and then in 1925 went back to the Norwegian language with *Byen paa bjerget* (The City on the Hill). Martha Ostenso, who had emigrated from Bergen as a child, limited herself to English. Her best-known novel, *Wild Geese*, (1925), portrays a farm community in the Middle West. Kathryn Forbes achieved recognition in 1934 with her book *Mama's Bank Account*. These novels written in English also grew out of the immigrant experience.

Disregarding difficulties and disappointments, several writers persisted in addressing their readers in Norwegian. After the 1920s it was, however, nearly impossible to get works published in the Norwegian language in America; there was not a sufficient audience. This fact explains the urgency with which Norwegian-American authors worked. They wrote under the most distressing circumstances, with a constant feeling of the loss of cultural values and thus of the very basis of their literary activity.

Many of the later works appeared only in serialized form in Norwegian-American newspapers. Einar Lund, editor of *Decorah-Posten* after Prestgard, had his novel *Solveig Murphy* printed in *Ved Arnen* in 1931. Lund dealt with the problem of the second generation. "The old had memories and traditions from their fatherland and family. The young are without roots and searching," he contended. Those who wrote during this time designed their stories under the influence of this generation's escape from their Norwegian background. A few years later, in 1934, Lars Hellesnes attempted unsuccessfully to find a Norwegian-American audience for his novel *I onkel Sams land* (In Uncle Sam's Land). As late as 1938 J. A. Erikson published *Det forjættede land* (The Promised Land). In this novel one of the characters says of *Ved Arnen* that it was "the best magazine in the world. I would not be without it even if it cost a cow!" And it was through this literary supplement to *Decorah-Posten* that it was still possible to find interested readers. Erikson published his last six stories here, the final one, *Et forlis* (A Shipwreck), in 1946.

Ole E. Rølvaag: Immigrant Literature Comes of Age

The idea of preserving Norwegian culture in America, of protecting the ancestral heritage, is the collective force behind Norwegian-American literature in the twentieth century. But this literature attained its zenith only shortly before it faded away, in the 1920s. Perhaps this was natural; a tradition had first to be established. It then made possible the "lesser classics," as a Rølvaag biographer, Paul Reigstad, describes Ole E. Rølvaag's major literary works.

Rølvaag shared with his fellow authors an attachment to and a love of Norway's past and his people's cultural heritage. He was at the same time concerned about his compatriots' future in America and attributed great importance to the retention of a transplanted cultural form. A dominant idea in immigrant literature is that the immigrants can take part in building the American nation only by safeguarding their own traditions and cultivating their national charac-

Waldemar Ager (left) and Ole E. Rølvaag (1876-1931) outside Rølvaag's home in Northfield in 1929. Ager and Rølvaag cooperated for a number of years in the task of promoting the Norwegian language and cultural heritage in America. "We turn up our noses at the inheritance that has come down to us. We cast on the scrap heap the noblest traditions of our race. We set higher value on aping strange manners and customs than in guarding our God-given heritage. So wise have we become and so far-seeing! God's command to the Israelites means nothing to us. We are ashamed of the age-old speech of our fathers. And we find it embarrassing to admit our Norwegian ancestry. Such an attitude can never, I tell you, never build a nation." (O. E. Rølvaag, Their Fathers' God, *New York, 1931.)*

teristics. "A people without traditions is doomed," says the pastor in Rølvaag's novel *Den signede dag* (That Blessed Day, in English translation called *Their Fathers' God*). Rølvaag's vision of how it feels to be an immigrant is tragic, filled with deep rootlessness: "strangers we are to the people we left, and strangers we are to the people we came to," Rølvaag wrote in his first book, *Amerika-breve* (America-Letters), published in 1912 under the pen name Paal Mørck. The immigrant therefore became an outsider, without a firm foothold in either culture.

In 1896 Rølvaag bade farewell to his childhood home on the island of Dønna off the coast of Helgeland in North Norway to go to an uncle in South Dakota. He was then twenty years old. With a newcomer's courage he defied adversity and acquired an education, was called to teach Norwegian at St. Olaf College in 1906, and served in this position until his death in 1931. From there he defended his cultural philosophy,

dreamed of creating a center for Norwegian studies, and gave his strength and enthusiasm to the Norwegian Society, to the organization For Fædrearven (For the Ancestral Heritage), and to the establishment of the Norwegian-American Historical Association in 1925. In addition, Rølvaag was a productive author, wrote school textbooks, and conducted an extensive correspondence.

He used the pseudonym Paal Mørck also for his second book, *Paa glemte veie* (On Forgotten Paths), published in 1914. It was his first novel and anticipates in many ways his masterpieces, *I de dage* (In Those Days) in 1924 and *Riket grundlægges* (The Kingdom is Founded) in 1925, which were later to be combined in *Giants in the Earth*. In all these works he treats pioneer life and the loneliness of the wide open spaces. He published *To tullinger* (Two Fools, later in a somewhat reworked form issued as *Pure Gold*) in 1920, and the following year he secured his position as the most prominent Norwegian-American novelist with *Længselens baat* (The Boat of Longing). In the former novel the main figure is destroyed by a materialistic society. In the latter the reader meets Nils Vaag, an artistic personality who is true to his ideals. In the New World he is lost, crushed by the environment. Nils Vaag survives the dark side of society, the saloons with their filth and wretchedness, but he loses his soul and his identity and disappears in an indifferent and suspicious American society. The tragic pattern that Rølvaag follows in all his novels, the movement toward an inescapable, final catastrophe, is here given its "most personal, intimate, and moving treatment," writes Kristoffer Paulson in an analysis of this work.

In 1927 *I de dage* and *Riket grundlægges* came out in English as one volume with the title *Giants in the Earth*, masterfully translated by Lincoln Colcord. The Norwegian editions of both parts had already been published in Norway. *Giants in the Earth* was selected by the Book of the Month Club, and nearly 80,000 copies were sold before the end of the year. As in *Paa glemte veie*, the prairie is an enemy, but at the same time its beauty is apparent. It is natural for Rølvaag to compare the prairie in its endlessness with the ocean. As the caravan of immigrants moved westward through the tall grass, "the track that it left behind was like a wake of a boat—except

GIANTS IN THE EARTH
By O. E. RÖLVAAG

The fullest, finest and most powerful novel that has been written about pioneer life in America

BURT

POPULAR COPYRIGHT

FICTION

75¢

that instead of widening out astern it closed in again." Historians were the earliest reviewers to discover the novel's underlying themes; they saw it as a psychological, in contrast to an economic, interpretation of the westward movement. The price this transfer demanded in human happiness is represented by the two main figures, Per Hansa and his wife, Beret. Per, with his forward-looking invincible optimism, is the ideal pioneer as he builds his kingdom on the South Dakota frontier. Beret holds on to her old life and fears the unknown; her sensitive mind takes her into an unreal world where no one can follow. In spite of the struggle with the great plains, a permanent community comes into being. But Per himself becomes a victim of the prairie, and dies in a snowstorm. He loses in his fight with the forces of nature, but his death perhaps also expresses hope and courage; he is found dead behind a haystack with his face set toward the west.

Beret is the main figure in *Peder Seier* (Peder Victorious), published in 1928 as the third novel in the trilogy. The main theme is the son Peder's revolt against his mother's values. He abandons his cultural moorings and marries the Irish Catholic Susie. Rølvaag continues the narrative in *Den*

No Norwegian-American author has enjoyed the same success as Ole E. Rølvaag did with his classic novel of pioneer life, Giants in the Earth. *It contains the two novels* I de dage *(In Those Days) and* Riket grundlægges *(The Founding of the Kingdom), which were combined in the English translation that appeared in 1927. The poster above was designed by the American publisher for display in bookstores.*

signede dag (1931). This novel completes the picture of the second generation: the mixing of the many national groups and the conflicts between them. The plot revolves around how this difference breaks up Susie's and Peder's marriage. Peder enters local politics, but he never achieves "the blessed day" because he neglected his Norwegian heritage. The novel is an artistic formulation of Rølvaag's cultural view as he had stated it in the collection of articles *Omkring Fædrearven* (Concerning the Ancestral Heritage) in 1922. Here he encourages "the ancestral-heritage people" to save the heritage—"first for ourselves and thereafter for the country, for America."

Literary Works as Social Documents

Norwegian-American literature was local in character. It recorded and interpreted the immigrants' lives and experiences as the authors observed and understood them. During the seventy years it flourished, no less than two hundred novels were published. There were also collections of essays, anthologies of poetry, plays, and a great number of literary contributions that were printed only in newspapers and magazines. Outside the genre of fiction, there were travel sketches, temperance tracts, books of homilies, and other religious devotional literature. Nordahl Rolfsen was the first author of textbooks in Norway to recognize the existence of a Norwegian-American literature. In 1917 he included selections by Norwegian-American authors in his school readers. In 1920 Ole E. Rølvaag and P. J. Eikeland filled the second volume of their *Norsk læsebok for akademiene, høiskolen og hjemmet* (Norwegian Readers for the Academies, the High Schools, and the Home) exclusively with immigrant writings. For Rølvaag, this was evidence that the Norwegian-American community was no longer dependent on the old ancestral land for its culture.

Dorothy Burton Skårdal in her work *The Divided Heart* (1974) made use of the Scandinavian-American works of fiction as historical source material and claimed that the authors "to the last man . . . were amateurs as literary artists" and lacked sufficient imagination to free themselves from models. Therefore, their production became strongly realistic, dependent on recording factual events and circumstances. Skårdal discovered that, taking into account differences in time and place, the authors have surprisingly similar conceptions of the immigrant experience. She employed what she terms "these moody accounts" in an effort to trace certain themes: changes in the immigrants' attitudes, morals, and mores as they adjust to the American environment.

Like other imaginative literature, the Norwegian-American reflects the society and the circumstances in which it was created. But it must of necessity be correlated with more conventional sources to give an acceptable historical view of reality. It is obvious that issues and problems that are raised in fiction, such as the temperance cause, may be seen as a contribution to a larger social debate. Simultaneously the constant preoccupation with abuse of alcohol shows that the writers were convinced that drunkenness was the greatest obstacle to realizing the expectations the immigrants had had when they emigrated. In other areas the immigrant writers might diverge more from the point of view of their compatriots. In their agitation for the preservation of Norwegian culture, and in their opposition to assimilationist zeal, the authors did not always represent the immigrants' attitude. But here also literature is an expression of the dilemma the immigrants faced the day they set foot on American soil.

At times the authors were likely too concerned about the tragic aspects of immigrant existence: the longing, the nostalgia, the loss of cultural values, inner strife, toil, and poverty. In spite of some humorous accounts, happy events and bright vistas are often missing from this literature. A tragic theme may have innately greater appeal to a creative mind than tales of happiness and success.

A more positive picture emerges in a different kind of literature, the America letters. These documents as well may be misleading as sources. The Norwegian-American community was no idyll. Many who grew up in a Norwegian-American environment, however, look back on their childhood as especially happy, associated with festivities at which Norwegian food and Norwegian customs were honored. The immigrant experience was of course by no means only one of longing and renunciation. It was filled with all the human emotions, a mixture of sorrow and joy, of progress and failure, and varied depending on circumstances and individual differences. The Swedish-American historian H. Arnold Barton has maintained that the authors' own immigration experience, regarded as a tragic repudiation of the homeland, caused them in their writing to attribute their own sense of defeat and loss to the immigrants as a whole. Still, no student of society interested in the Norwegian-American community can overlook the body of writing that this literature constitutes. In 1900 Waldemar Ager wrote to his fellow author Ole Buslett that if the Norwegian people should in time disappear in the larger American society, the literature they had created would become the yardstick for Norwegian-American culture, "because it is art and history all in one."

New Conquests— Country and Town

Norwegian immigrants settled in all parts of the United States, from the Pacific coast to the eastern seaboard, and they formed colonies in both rural and urban environments. Excavation for gold, fishing, logging, and shipping employed many Norwegians. They also worked on railroad construction and in the building trade, and they toiled in the mills and factories. Life in the great cities of America was difficult, but it was mitigated by charitable institutions established by the immigrants themselves, and by a flourishing of Norwegian-American cultural activities.

The Distribution of Norwegians in the Cities

"'Minneapolis! Minneapolis!' the brakeman called through the train—'Minneapolis! Minneapolis!' " In this manner Nils Vaag in Rølvaag's novel *Længselens baat* came back to the city after a bout in the great forests farther north. The urban environment is treated by Norwegian-American authors in all its colorings: saloons, anarchistic rebels, decadent excesses, but also cultural contributions such as art, song, and theater, and an abundance of organizations and charitable undertakings.

The majority of Norwegian Americans persisted in living outside the larger cities. Of the 336,985 Norwegian-born persons in America in 1900, only a little over one-fourth resided in towns with more than 25,000 inhabitants, the lowest percentage of any European immigrant group. The Norwegian people in America clearly did not participate as enthusiastically as other nationalities in the process of urbanization. In 1910, for instance, following a new wave of newcomers who to a greater extent than earlier emigrants headed for the cities, the urban percentage for all Norwegian-born was still only 42.2 percent. And these U.S. census figures include inhabitants of towns with 2,500 or more citizens. The percentage of town dwellers among native-born Americans was 46.3 percent, and among all foreign-born an astounding 72.1 percent. An attachment to life in the countryside and in the small towns was retained and passed on to the children of Norwegian immigrants. "The emigrants came to stay on the land and their children remain on their lands after them," wrote T. A. Hoverstad in 1915. In 1940 over half of all Norwegian Americans in the Middle West were still living outside urban areas of more than 2,500 inhabitants.

The first generation of Norwegian Americans reached its peak in 1910 with 403,858 persons;

The lumber operations employed many Norwegians in America.

more than 80 percent of them were to be found in the states of the Upper Midwest. There were in addition 607,267 of the second generation, which attained its maximum size in 1930 with 752,236 members. In 1940, when the number of Norwegian-born Americans had fallen to 262,088, there were still 658,220 Americans who stated that the language of their childhood home was Norwegian. These statistics from the census indicate the size of the Norwegian-speaking group in America during the early decades of this century. It was from this group that different ethnic activities emanated and found support. The fact that Norwegians in such large numbers settled in rural districts promoted a segregated ethnic community. But Norwegians who came to the cities also separated themselves from other nationalities; they pursued a common life more vigorously than any other Nordic group, with the possible exception of the Finns. The emigration wave of the 1920s reinforced to a special degree the Norwegian urban colonies—America's cities received most of these emigrants.

On the eastern seaboard a solid urban colony developed in New York. In 1900 it could boast of 11,387 Norwegian-born citizens and 16,118 of the second generation. In the Middle West in 1900 Chicago still had the lead with 22,011 Norwegian immigrants and almost twice as many born in America. Concentrations of Norwegians were to be found in Milwaukee, Superior, and Madison, Wisconsin; in Duluth, Minnesota; in Grand Forks and Fargo, North Dakota; in Sioux City, Iowa; as well as in other smaller towns. From the 1890s Minneapolis gradually assumed the role of the new Norwegian-American capital. The city's location in the heart of Norwegian America made this development natural. Minneapolis was the commercial center for a large Norwegian-American population, and many Norwegian-American institutions and organizations established headquarters there. The city did not, however, have the largest urban concentration of Norwegians. Compared with Chicago, Minneapolis in 1900 had 11,532 Norwegian immigrants and its twin city St. Paul 3,000. The two cities had in addition a combined number of 26,000 of the second generation.

In the Far West, by Puget Sound in the state of Washington, Seattle in time became an important Norwegian-American center. At the turn of the century the city had, however, only 1,642 citizens born in Norway and another 2,577 with Norwegian parents. At that time Tacoma had a comparable Norwegian population. The older colony in San Francisco had a few hundred more of both generations.

Norwegian Immigrants in the West

The pioneer settlement of Norwegians on the Pacific coast was associated with the discovery of gold in the lower Sacramento valley of California in January, 1848. News of this discovery spread the gold fever—California fever—to the Norwegian colonies in the Middle West. In the fall of the same year fabulous accounts in Norwegian newspapers about an easy road to wealth roused the gold thirst also in Norway. One of those who tried his luck in the gold fields was Hans Christian Heg from Muskego settlement, later to be a Civil War hero. Christian Poulsen, who had emigrated from Arendal in 1841, carried the message back to Norway in 1849. Rumors of his enormous wealth in gold aroused considerable excitement. The exodus of gold diggers directly from Norway was different from the emigration in the period in general. It was no family movement; the gold seekers were mainly young men without ties, adventurous, with a desire to travel. Many were sailors who abandoned ship when they came to San Francisco. Accounts of the gold finds lived in people's imagination and colored their conceptions of America generally. The gold in California in itself, however, played only a small part in the history of Norwegian emigration.

San Francisco Bay

The small urban colony of Norwegians that emerged in the San Francisco Bay area in the 1850s was largely made up of sailors and craftsmen from Norway. In his book *West of the Great Divide* Kenneth O. Bjork has shown that several Norwegians who settled there, even before the gold fever had subsided, were businessmen and

men of finance who had been attracted to the city during a time of great speculation and easily amassed fortunes. In its early years the colony had an elitist character. Many prominent Norwegians settled there, like George C. Johnson from Bergen, who operated a large hardware com-

Before the railroad lines had been completed, stagecoach mail routes provided the only means of travel westward except for the lengthy route seaward around the southern point of South America. In addition to the "bold, grand and picturesque scenery" that the poster to the right promises, the overland route to the gold land involved considerable hardships and drama.

Below left: The Toftezen monument commemorating the first Norwegian settlers in the state of Washington near Stanwood. The monument was unveiled in 1939.

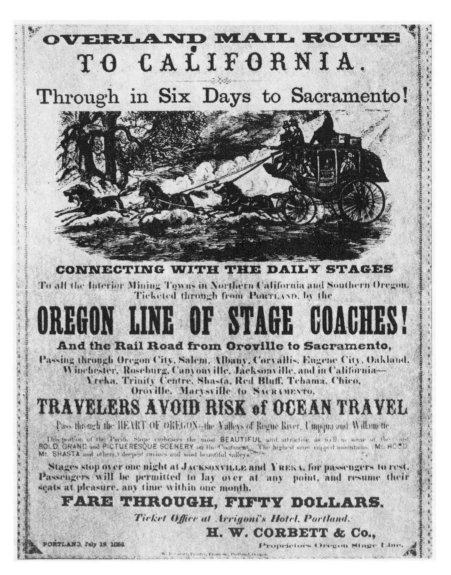

pany, and Knud Henry Lund from Moss, who founded a major import firm. Peder Sather from Trondheim came to the eastern United States in 1841. Nine years later he moved to California, where he became a prominent banker and leading personality among Scandinavians in San Francisco. Norwegians settled in towns on the east side of San Francisco Bay as well, especially in Oakland, where churches and organizational life were gradually established. Because of the small numbers in each of the three Scandinavian immigrant groups, they cooperated in the early

period for religious, social, and cultural purposes. This gave the colony in San Francisco Bay area a joint Scandinavian character.

The Attractions of the Pacific Northwest

Some people went farther north and found work in fishing and shipping, or as log drivers in Puget Sound, and some took land. Zakarias Martin Toftezen from Levanger, Norway, abandoned the gold fields in 1850 and shortly after Christmas of that year took land on Whidbey Island, where the city of Oak Harbor is now located. Toftezen is considered to be the first Norwegian pioneer in Washington. Another unsuccessful gold digger, Anthon Lassen, acquired land near Portland, Oregon, the same year. More Norwegians followed in the 1870s and 1880s.

Norwegian settlement of larger proportions in the Pacific Northwest is closely associated with the completion of the transcontinental railroads. In 1883 Northern Pacific had its line completed both to Puget Sound and to Portland; ten years later Great Northern had connections to Seattle; and a third line, built by Chicago, Milwaukee, and St. Paul, reached Tacoma in 1909. In the late 1880s the railroad companies intensified their advertising campaign in Norwegian-American newspapers, and land agents worked to influence the immigrants. In 1888 a considerable exodus from the Middle West to the Pacific coast commenced. There was both railroad and government land to be had. Reports emphasized the beneficial climate, without drought, swarms of grasshoppers, blizzards, or scorching heat. In the Norwegian settlements in North Dakota people talked about the Washington fever.

The scenery itself might induce people to move. "Being from Northern Norway I feel at times an intense desire to see the ocean and mountains and forests," Peder Nicolaisen wrote to *Washington-Posten* in 1900. He was one of the many from North Dakota who discovered that the West Coast was strongly reminiscent of home. The second stream came from Norway, but rarely by sea. Most Norwegian immigrants went overland from New York by rail. Many came from the coastal districts of western Norway, with large contingents from the two Agder counties, Rogaland, and Sunnmøre. Also from Trøndelag and Nordland people set out for the West Coast of America. Emigration from the coastal areas of Norway increased rapidly at the time.

Settlement in Oregon, Washington, and Puget Sound

Where Norwegians settled on the Pacific coast, in the states of Oregon and Washington, most of the land had been only partially cleared or not cleared at all. Those who had previously farmed in the Midwest took land in the northern part of the Willamette valley in Oregon and raised wheat and corn on smaller acreage than they had left. They also took up hop and fruit growing.

The largest concentration of Norwegians was in the Puget Sound region. Here, by the protected sea lanes and bays in the sound, they formed separate communites. The Stillaguamish flats near Stanwood in Snohomish county and the northern part of the Kitsap peninsula, with the town of Poulsbo in Kitsap county, became strong areas of Norwegian settlement. Poulsbo was founded by people who had first come to the Middle West from West Norway. The first Lutheran church was thus given the name Førdefjord. The later movement to Poulsbo directly from Norway included many from the Mosjøen district in Nordland. One of the early pioneers in the Stanwood area was the politician O. B. Iverson from Hardanger. He had left the great swarms of grasshoppers that ravaged North Dakota in 1874, and he moved into the new area the following year.

Before the land could produce, the virgin forest had to be cleared. This was an immense chore and there were "many Norwegian root diggers whose backs became crooked," writes C. M. Thuland, an early resident of the region, "before they got so much land cleared that they could feed a few cows." These farms required investment of money as well as toil, and some gave up and returned to the Middle West. Fish and shellfish frequently became the main food—one pioneer complained that "we ate so many clams that our stomachs regularly rose and fell with the tide."

In the 1870s Silvana, the second Norwegian settlement in the Stillaguamish valley, was also established. In this fertile agricultural region the farmers turned to cattle raising and dairy farming; a cooperative dairy was started by the farmers in Stanwood.

But during the early period agriculture was less important than work in logging, in the sawmills, and in the shingle mills. No capital investment was required in these occupations and they gave immediate income; besides, it was work Norwegians were familiar with. Prospects of higher wages attracted many people to the coastal districts; the rapid economic growth caused wages to rise. The Norwegian John I. Hals operated a shingle mill in the Silvana area near the village of Florence, but most Norwegians were of course

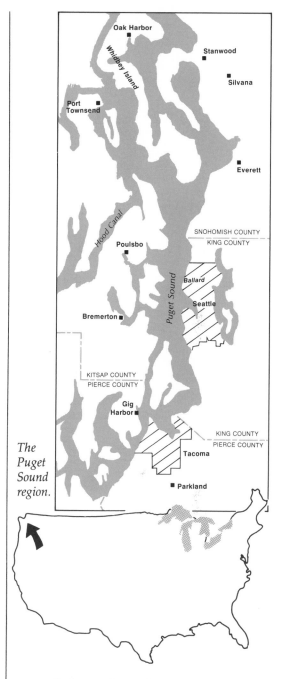

The Puget Sound region.

compelled to seek employment as common laborers. Gradually they might begin farming or go into some other occupation.

East of the Cascade mountains there came into being a small Norwegian colony in Spokane. In the Puget Sound country most Norwegians were in King and Pierce counties, where the cities of Seattle and Tacoma formed natural centers. By 1870 the small village of Seattle had grown to 1,107 inhabitants, and it is during this decade that the first Norwegian names appear. Twenty years later, in 1890, there were nearly 43,000 people in Seattle. In the ensuing decades the whole region experienced a phenomenal growth, and Seattle became an important metropolis by the Pacific Ocean.

Seattle took on a Scandinavian flavor. As in other pioneer settlements, young men dominated the early influx. In 1900 there were as a consequence 176.7 men for every 100 women in the city. Some nationalities had an even greater imbalance. As late as 1940, 60 percent of all Norwegian-born persons there were men, reflecting the labor migration from the turn of the century. In 1940 Norwegians were the largest ethnic group in Seattle; the Ballard section in the northwest part of the city had the largest concentration of Norwegians. In 1920 people of Norwegian birth and descent formed an urban colony in Seattle with 17,628 members. A little more than one-quarter of the Norwegian-American population in the state lived in this city.

Logging, Sawmills, and Construction Work

The forest, the mighty stretches of cedar and Douglas fir, formed the basis for pioneer settlement in the Kitsap area. Here the trees could be felled along the shore and floated to a sawmill nearby. Poulsbo's central location made it the most important town, and the entire region quickly established itself as "Little Norway." Ole Stubb from Sunnfjord came there in 1875 as the first Norwegian settler. One of the best known of the early inhabitants was John Storseth, who arrived in 1889. His autobiography provides insights into the development of the region.

The demand for lumber was increasing because of the rapid population growth in California. And when transportation improved greatly toward the end of the century, markets were opened also in the East, where large forest resources had already been depleted. The forests and the refining of forest products gave employment to many Scandinavians. The congressional Dillingham Commission found in 1900 that Scan-

dinavians constituted as many as 25 percent of all those who were employed in forestry in Washington. Everett, the administrative seat of Snohomish county, Tacoma, and Seattle were important mill towns. Its central location and excellent harbor by Elliott Bay made Seattle the commercial center of western Washington. The first steam-powered sawmill in the territory was started there by Henry L. Yesler as early as 1853.

In the cities many entered the building trade; people found employment as carpenters, paint-

Above: Floating logs in western Washington around 1910. Below: A team of oxen pulling logs to the river, ca. 1895. "The oxen used to pull the logs were huge beasts and they could pull large loads. But they were as a rule sadly abused. There are numerous legends about the ox drivers on the Pacific coast at that time. The slave drivers in the South were unadulterated saints compared to these 'bull punchers' in the forests of Washington." (John Storseth, "Fra gammel og ny tid," manuscript.)

Left: Even with a crew of 6 men, using saws and axes, it required 6 hours to fell such a giant. The photograph was taken in Washington, ca. 1907.

twenty-four-year-old from Finnmark, and two Swedes, Erik Lindblom and John Brynteson. "Despite all hardships and tribulations every vessel that has Alaska as its destination is completely packed with men and a good many women who want to try their luck up there." They came from all parts—which was not surprising, since the newspapers continually gave accounts of fantastic wealth. Both *Tacoma Tidende* and *Washington-Posten* kept Norwegians informed about "the rumors having become certainty." Among the lucky argonauts was John Eriksen, "Klondike Eriksen," who in one season alone amassed an enormous fortune of $350,000. In 1900 there were more than thirty prospectors from Stranda in Sunnmøre alone in the Klondike, Gerhard Kjølås relates, and "gold from the West built the first electricity works" in that Norwegian community. But even though many made good in the gold fields in Alaska and the Klondike, not all of them got "their gold bags filled," one who had visited Nome in 1906 wrote to *Washington-Posten*.

Those who were unable to go themselves sold equipment to their compatriots. One of them was Geo. B. Helgesen, who advertised: "Before going to the Klondike outfit yourself at . . . Alaska Outfitter." Many outfitters made a brisk profit in this business. Those who stayed at home could also buy shares in Scandia Alaska Company, established in 1898 for the purpose of securing "a part of the enormous profit that the transportation and gold excavation companies will earn."

ers, and construction workers, frequently on a seasonal basis. Many urban Scandinavians made a living in construction, whether they lived in New York, Chicago, Minneapolis, or Seattle, and they often dominated this branch of the economy. Some joined forces and established their own construction companies, often with a very modest starting capital. Peter D. Wick from Syvden in Sunnmøre emigrated in 1913, worked in sawmills and in fishing, and in the off-season built houses. As early as 1914 he was able to sell a house he and another man had built. Such activity might provide funds for larger enterprises. After 1932 Wick developed one of the large construction companies in Seattle, which now bears the name Wick Construction Company.

Discovery of Gold in the Klondike and Alaska

Discovery of gold in the Klondike at the end of 1896 and the subsequent trek to the gold fields in 1897-98 made many people go west with high hopes. As outfitting center and embarkation port, Seattle was transformed from a frontier town into a bustling city. People who came believed, according to *Washington-Posten*, that "the gold grows as large as pears on the trees." While the excitement about the Klondike raged, a new and almost equally large discovery of gold was made on Seward Peninsula in the Nome area of western Alaska. Responsible for the discovery there were the Norwegian Jafet Lindeberg, a

Norwegian Contributions to the Shipping and Fishing Industries

It was of course natural that Norwegians should work in shipping on the West Coast. From the 1870s on there are many Norwegian names among those who sailed on the coast, including quite a large number of skippers. To begin with, they were employed in the transportation of lumber in California; later they sailed on Puget Sound and to Alaska. In 1900 as many as 16 percent of all Norwegians in Seattle worked in shipping. Several of the Norwegian captains became famous along the whole coast. For instance, Gudmund "Midnight" Olsen sailed in the so-called Scandinavian Navy, which dominated the

lumber freight between San Francisco and the redwood forests farther north.

Besides shipping, the coastal areas provided rich opportunity for fishing. Sverre Arestad has corrected exaggerated notions about Norwegian pioneering in this industry. He has shown that in the 1880s Norwegians entered fishing operations that were already established; only after 1900 did they become the major participants in the fishing industry of the Pacific Northwest. For the sake of completeness it should, however, be mentioned that Norwegians who settled in Astoria, Oregon, and other places along the Columbia River took part in the salmon fisheries as early as the 1870s. From the beginning of the 1890s the salmon industry on Puget Sound developed rapidly. Important in this connection was the introduction of the fish trap. Norwegian fishermen led in this method of catching fish, whereas the Slovenians, the other large ethnic group in the salmon fishery, employed purse-seine fishing. In Alaska the industry developed along

Above right: The business district in Ballard around 1910. This section of Seattle received the most Norwegians.

Below right: The steamship Willamette *docked in Seattle ready to set sail for the goldfields in Alaska and the Klondike. "The folk wandering to Alaska, where everyone thinks that the gold grows as large as pears on trees, has begun in earnest. The streets of the city are filled with people day and night, and there is a barking of dogs, a bellowing of oxen, and a bleating of goats without stop. Down by the docks it is nearly impossible to hear what people are saying because of the racket these four-legged creatures are making. The 'Klondike fever' seems to have affected most severely people from the East, because from the eastern states there arrive regiments of crazed Klondike travelers, who do not realize the hardships that await them, and who will not let themselves be convinced that as far as one knows there are no new goldfields."* (Washington-Posten, *February 25, 1898.)*

Left: Inside one of the logging cabins by Puget Sound, ca. 1900. The men rest following a hard bout in the forest.

Left: Gold diggers on their way to the Klondike goldfields across the infamous Chilkoot Pass in British Columbia in 1898.

Above right: Excavating for gold on Gold Hill close to Dawson City in Yukon Territory in 1898.

Below right: Gold diggers paying with gold dust. Dawson City, Yukon Territory, 1899.

similar lines, and Norwegians became the principal trap fishermen, although they also were gill netters and salmon trollers, both there and on the Puget Sound. Already in the early 1890s Norwegians in Tacoma and Seattle had become interested in the fishing possibilities in Alaska; Norwegians made a great contribution to the cod fishing operations in the Bering Sea. Norwegians also made up a majority of the herring fishermen, and in Alaska the herring fleet was occasionally referred to as the "Norwegian Navy." Besides being fishermen, they were of course boat owners, fish buyers, and founders of shore stations.

Norwegians have been most prominent in the development of the halibut industry. The catching of halibut began in 1888, initiated by old-stock Americans from the eastern states. But Norwegian fishermen gradually became the major developers of this industry. A. K. Larssen, who has closely watched its growth, thinks that around 1920 95 percent of all halibut fishermen and an even higher percentage of the boat owners were of Norwegian birth or descent. The two-masted schooners, from 65 to 105 feet long, were frequently owned by several men. Nearly all boat owners had worked their way up and had gained the confidence and respect of outfitters who would extend credit for the purchase of a vessel. Relations among the crew in the halibut fleet were good. They were all of the same social background; they were comradely and democratic. Norwegians were accustomed to deep-sea fishing. In the spring the fleet sailed from the colorful Fisherman's Dock in Ballard to spend the season in Alaska. Smaller halibut schooners fished for shorter periods along the coast of Washington. Sivert E. Sagstad, who came from Norway in 1905, was a pioneer in shipbuilding in Ballard, and his shipyard could boast of having built at

Paying with Gold Dust. Fall 1899.

least 300 fishing vessels. In 1940 about 400 schooners were participating in the halibut fishery, mainly from Seattle, but a smaller fleet was also stationed in Alaska. Fishing was fourth among the major industries in Washington; forestry occupied first place.

Alaska in 1900 had a Norwegian-born population of 1,234. Twice as many lived in the coastal areas of British Columbia, which constituted a natural extension northward of the West Coast settlement. There were somewhat more than 2,000 Norwegian immigrants in Alaska in 1920. They were the largest immigrant group, even though they were numerically few. Petersburg in southeastern Alaska was the only Norwegian colony. In 1896 Peter Thams Buschmann, who emigrated from Trøndelag in 1891 with his wife and eight children, came to this region. He bought land and built a salmon cannery, warehouses, and dwellings, and got Norwegian workers, fishermen, and supervisors to settle there. During a celebration of the Fourth of July, it was decided to name the new town Petersburg after its founder, who had played such an important role in the development of the fishing industry in Alaska.

Social and Religious Conditions

Norwegians in the cities and in the country on the Pacific coast performed the same social and religious activities as Norwegians in the Middle West, from which so many of them had come. A rich organizational life was sustained, with temperance lodges and societies of many kinds. The church came along, even though it took time for the mother church in the Middle West to sacrifice a little of its strife and gather its modest resources for missionary work among compatriots in the Far West. Religious controversy was also transferred, to begin with through competition between the Synod and the Conference; later

Above: The halibut schooner Pioneer. *Nearly all halibut fishermen were Norwegian Americans who had first practiced deep-sea fishing off the coast of Norway.*

Left: Inside a salmon canning factory by Puget Sound around 1900. The photograph was taken by the well-known Norwegian photographer Anders Wilse, who around the turn of the century worked as a photographer in Seattle. He returned to Norway in 1901.

both the Lutheran Free Church and the United Church were added to the fray. The Methodists and the Baptists both had Scandinavian missionary divisions, and they recruited many on the West Coast. The Lutheran ministers complained about their inroads and the obstruction this was to their own activity.

Because of local conditions, the church in the West had several distinctive features. There was extensive Scandinavian cooperation. But the influence of the Lutheran faith was reduced. In the Far West some of the unity and intimacy which existed in the farming districts in the Middle

Above: A halibut fisherman in Alaska pulls in the catch with a line around 1910.

Right: Many Norwegian Americans and new-comers from Norway found employment in the profitable king crab fishery as halibut fishing gradually decreased. This fishery developed after World War II and occurred in the sub-Arctic areas off the coast of Alaska. In 1974 the king crab harvest in Alaska amounted to as much as 97 million tons. The ship West Point of Seattle is here seen heading for the king crab grounds. Note the large crab pots on deck.

West was missing. On the coast many more Norwegians settled in cities, and people who were occupied in professions outside farming frequently had less interest in organized religious life. The distance from the regions where the different synods enjoyed their major strength, which likely caused loss of ecclesiastical discipline, also seems to have produced religious indifference. The percentage of Lutheran church members therefore lagged far behind that in the Middle West. Christian Hvistendahl, who in 1870 was sent by the Synod to minister to Norwegians in San Francisco, lamented religious apathy.

The tendency toward secularization increased in the twentieth century. In 1906 only about 15 percent of all Norwegians in the state of Washington belonged to a Lutheran congregation. On the other hand, the freer conditions and the religious indifference might also call forth evangelistic revival movements. An example is the fanatic Brækhus movement, which emanated from Poulsbo in 1894. The young Edward Brækhus

spread his message through appearances where he engaged in self-hypnosis and ecstatic trances. He spoke to the gatherings in a loud voice and was received "as a messenger from on high."

Andrew Furuseth Champions the Cause of the Seamen

Already in the early 1890s a strong class solidarity was becoming evident among Norwegian laborers, as well as cooperation between country and town. Since it grew out of loyalty to principles, the solidarity might of course transcend ethnic boundaries and thus aid the Americanization process. For example, the anti-capitalistic and anti-Chinese Workingmen's party of California, headed by Dennis Kearney, had a separate Scan-

dinavian division. The halibut fishermen on the West Coast in 1912 founded the Deep Sea Fishermen's Union of the Pacific to protect their interests, and two years later the boat owners formed their own organization. Both in Seattle and in Tacoma Norwegian workingmen's associations came into being. These had a social purpose, and in addition they taught their members about the political process. Ordinary workers were thus being united.

Andrew Furuseth, who himself knew what hard physical labor was, became the spokesman for a segment of the oppressed laboring classes —the defenseless seamen who sailed on the oceans of the world. Furuseth was born in Romedal in Hedmark, Norway, in 1854. He went to sea at the age of nineteen and experienced the drudgery and toil that was a sailor's lot. Seamen were exposed to acts of cruelty and abuse on board ship and to the tyranny of crimps on land. Furuseth, like so many sailors, deserted from a British ship when it docked in San Francisco. He quickly discovered how difficult it was to get a berth again without going through the crimps and boardinghouse operators who procured crews for the ships that sailed from the city. Furuseth joined the labor union movement. In 1887 he became secretary of the Sailors Union of the Pacific Coast, gained experience in the movement, and fought for the rights of seamen in relation to the shipowners.

In his struggle against capitalist exploitation, Furuseth was to a high degree pragmatic in his approach. His greatest efforts were made in Washington, D.C., where he worked for legislative reforms to protect sailors the world over. In this endeavor he tempted strong financial interests, both American and foreign. He proposed legislation that would also protect foreign seamen when they were in American ports. The attacks on his proposals consequently also originated with foreign governments that were sensitive to protests by their own countries' shipping interests.

Of people who were outside the labor unions, hardly anyone was closer to Furuseth than the progressive senator from Wisconsin, Robert M. La Follette—a "landcrab" from the Middle West, as he himself said. He introduced Furuseth's bill in the Senate, and in 1915 it was enacted into law under the name the La Follette Seamen's Act.

Andrew Furuseth (1854-1938) was called the Abraham Lincoln of the sea. Through his efforts the working conditions of seamen were greatly improved. Furuseth's accomplishments exemplify the immigrants' significant contributions to the American union movement.

Furuseth became a well-known figure in the labor movement. He was viewed by many as the great liberator: an Abraham Lincoln of the sea, as the Yugoslavian-American writer Louis Adamic called him. He resisted all of the many attempts to repeal the law. This legislation protected working conditions for seamen and by its example influenced the situation in the merchant fleets of other nations. The strength of the movement spearheaded by Furuseth led to higher wages, but it also contributed to strengthening the unity and sense of brotherhood that has characterized seamen of all nations.

The Cities as a New Frontier

Immigrants in the Labor Movement

An organized American labor movement took shape during the years from 1870 until the end of the century. In its early development immigrants played an outstanding part; in 1886 a surprising 79 percent of the members of the trade unions in Illinois were ethnic, 12 percent of them Scandinavian. Immigrants as well as older-stock Americans, whether they worked at sea, in the forests, in the mines, on the great railroad projects, or in the labor force in the cities, had a need for solidarity. The idea of organizing for joint action and mutual support was close at hand. The unions took it upon themselves to provide sick

The Scandinavian-American workingmen's club Karl Marx in Chicago moved into its own Folkets Hus (People's House), or Workers Lyceum, in 1918. It was difficult for Socialistic organizations to find a place to meet: "In most cases they had to be satisfied with the saloons, which as a rule had a fair-sized back room for such purposes. . . . The club's members have unlimited access to the Lyceum's library and reading room; during the winter months study circles dealing with the English language, social economy, history, and similar topics are open to everyone." (From a printed program in 1928 for Folkets Hus Ten Year Anniversary Festival.)

pay and death benefits to survivors. The Independent Scandinavian Workingmen's Society (Den uavhengige skandinaviske arbeiderforening), which was founded in Eau Claire, Wisconsin, in 1893, functioned, for instance, as an insurance company and had local chapters in the states of the Upper Midwest.

Even though the union movement encouraged worker solidarity across national lines, many of the individual unions functioned as ethnic organizations. The Brooklyn Norwegian Workers' Federation (Brooklyn Norske Arbeiderforbund), the Norwegian Bricklayers Club (Norske Murerers Klub), and the Norwegian Painters' and Decorators' Union (Norske Maler- og Dekoratørforening) were all formed in New York. Similar labor societies were organized in Chicago and elsewhere. The Scandinavian printers, an elite among the working classes, founded their own union in Minneapolis in the late 1880s and published a magazine.

Minneapolis—the New Norwegian-American Capital

The milling town of Minneapolis was first settled at St. Anthony Falls on the Mississippi River. In 1870, 1,000 of the city's 12,000 inhabitants were Norwegians, who formed colonies in two districts of the city. On the north side of town where there was a concentration of people from Trøndelag, mostly from Selbu, an urban regional colony emerged. They worked in the forests in winter and in sawmills and other occupations in town the rest of the year. Also the large flour mills provided a livelihood for Norwegian Americans from all parts of Minneapolis. The largest and most active Norwegian ethnic community was located in the central district and on the south side of town. It was here that churches and organized activity flourished.

The first Scandinavian business establishments soon appeared on Washington Avenue. But it is the Scandinavian commercial district that developed from the early 1880s a few blocks farther south and east along the Mississippi River in the Cedar-Riverside area that has attracted most attention. Its growth was promoted by the establishment of the Scandia Bank there in 1883; Scandinavian merchants wished to operate their businesses close by. Cedar Avenue became the main

Garment and textile workers organized strong unions. Immigrants—especially Russian Jews, Italians, and Poles—frequently made up the majority of the members. Women as well as men joined the unions. The photograph shows members of the United Garment Workers Union in the Labor Day parade in Minneapolis in 1905.

thoroughfare for Norwegians and other Scandinavians in the city. One business after another was opened. Norwegian was the language of both store clerks and customers. Carl G. O. Hansen relates that as a newcomer in 1882 it had struck him how Norwegian the surroundings were. He had come to an uncle and aunt, and "my aunt," writes Hansen, "sent one of her children out to make some purchases. Some things were to be bought at Haugen's, some at Tharaldsen's, and some at Olsen & Bakke's." There were grocery stores, clothing establishments, furniture

The Scandinavian sections of Minneapolis.

165

merchants, bakeries, and even a Norwegian funeral home. In this district newspapers were printed and social and cultural activities pursued.

Dania Hall was finished in 1885 and became a much used meeting place and auditorium. Popular artists entertained in other public halls and in saloons. Their role is a little-studied chapter in Norwegian-American history. Ethnic humor had a common Scandinavian audience. "Slim Jim" Iverson appeared in saloons along Washington Avenue. Through personal appearances or recordings some of these artists became known from coast to coast, like "The Olson Sisters," Ethel and Eleanora, and the tremendously popular ballad singer and comedian Olle i Skratthult, whose version of the ballad "Nikolina" sold more than 100,000 phonograph records before 1930. Near Dania Hall a Norwegian gymnastic society, a rifle club, and a singing society had their meeting rooms. And there were plenty of Norwegian-owned saloons. These were popular gathering places. Dance halls were also a part of the environment. In the years around World War I Paul Paulson played at dances in the Viking Dance Hall. This was one of several dance halls, and Paulson relates that Scandinavian newcomers filled them several nights every week.

In a circle of a few blocks there were at least six Norwegian churches that competed with the saloons and other amusements in the Cedar-Riverside district. Not far away was Augsburg Seminary. Many of the patrolling policemen were Norwegian or Swedish. Hansen relates that public disturbances were rare, and there were therefore few occasions where they had to take action. But even though it is certain that criminality was in general low among Scandinavians, the police records for Minneapolis, St. Paul, and Chicago show clearly that Scandinavians were also among those most frequently arrested for public drunkenness and disorder.

The urban environment was hard. The immi-

Dania Hall (above) became from 1885 a separate assembly hall for Scandinavians in Minneapolis. People came here for entertainment and organizational activity. In this neighborhood there were also many Norwegian-owned saloons and dance halls, where Scandinavian artists performed. Several of these artists gained fame from coast to coast. Right: One of the bands, Thorstein Skarning & His Norwegian Hillbillies, in 1938.

Slim Jim & The Vagabond Kid, photographed in 1940. "Slim Jim" Iverson was one of the Norwegian-American artists who achieved fame in many parts of the United States through recordings and concert tours. In Minneapolis he performed in saloons along Washington Avenue. Norwegian churches in the same area competed with the saloons for people's allegiance.

grants frequently lived at a subsistence level and were especially vulnerable during periods of economic decline and unemployment. A modest livelihood that gave a slim margin of security became the fate for most. Near the Scandinavian business district in Minneapolis was a large and well-known tenement building referred to as Noah's Ark. Here ordinary workers and newcomers might find cheap shelter. Living conditions were nevertheless usually not as poor in Minneapolis as in the miserable tenement complexes in the working-class districts of Chicago and New York. Josefa Andersen recalls how her mother found the lack of trees and grass around their apartment house in a workingman's ward in Chicago depressing. The notes about suicides printed in Norwegian-American newspapers speak of the difficulty of immigrant life. Stress and emotional strain are also revealed in the statistics of patients in mental institutions. There were proportionately far more of the mentally ill among Norwegians in America than in Norway. Both in the cities and in the farming districts Scandinavians in America showed a greater inclination than other immigrant groups to develop emotional problems. No empirical evidence, however, can identify possible emotional and cultural causes that might be unique to the Scandinavian population.

Women had the fewest opportunities in the cities and were the most vulnerable. In 1890 as many as 80 percent of all Norwegian immigrant women who worked outside the home were listed in the census under "domestic and personal services." Otherwise they might be seamstresses, tailors, or charwomen. A small percentage worked in professional occupations or in business. Salaried employment as domestic servants was the most common occupation for women of the second generation as well.

A Seamy Side of the Immigrant Community

Women formed national organizations and did battle with a social vice that affected the cities — namely prostitution. The debate surrounding this social evil established a causal relationship between poor working conditions and recruitment to the brothels. There are examples of innocent young women being either enticed or forced into this activity. Immigrant women were especially susceptible because of ignorance and lack of means. In 1889 *Skandinaven* took the unusual step of making public the names of Norwegian women arrested during a police raid on one of the twenty brothels operated by the infamous Sadie Richards in Chicago. The newspaper maintained that they had been lured into prostitution by first having been employed as maids in Richards's own home. A report about how this was possible was published in *Scandia* in 1911.

The director of the employment agency run by the Norwegian National League (Det norske nasjonalforbund) in Chicago was arrested by the Chicago police and charged with "white slavery" in connection with Norwegian women who applied for domestic positions. Similar conditions were disclosed in other cities. In some places brothels flourished quite freely, as in the sawmill town of Everett in Washington. The numerous Norwegian workers in the mills along the seashore might visit Norway Tavern or one of the other combined saloons and brothels on Hewitt Avenue nearby. A second-generation Norwegian, Omar Lowell, who as a boy delivered newspapers to the prostitutes, has clear memories of red stairways and doors leading up to the brothel area. The extent of this traffic with respect to Norwegian immigrant women has never been determined, but it was quite obviously a reality. Prostitution was a social evil that could only be effectively curbed by providing more and better work opportunities for the many young women who came to the cities.

NOTICE
TO YOUNG WOMEN AND GIRLS

Do not go to the large cities for work unless you are compelled to. If you must go, write at least two weeks in advance to the Woman's Department, Bureau of Labor, St. Paul, or to the Young Women's Christian Association in the city where you want to work.

They will obtain for you such a position as you ask; tell you about wages, boarding places and whatever you want to know.

Two days before you leave home, write again and tell the day and hour when your train will arrive and a responsible woman will meet you at the station and take you safely to your destination.

Do not ask questions of strangers nor take advice from them.

Ask a uniformed railway official or a policeman.

This advice is issued by the State Bureau of Labor and posted through the courtesy of the Railway Officials of this road.

Mrs. Perry Starkweather,
Assistant Commissioner
Woman's Dept.

W. E. McEWEN,
Commissioner of Labor.
STATE CAPITOL, ST. PAUL

In the harsh city environment prostitution was common. It posed a threat to immigrant girls and young women, who might be lured into this activity through ignorance or lack of employment. The notice above is a warning to young women seeking work in a city. Numerous women's groups and organizations took it upon themselves to provide a place to stay and work for young women. Norwegian immigrants built and operated homes for young women.

Young unmarried women might declare their independence by going to America alone. Finding work there was one way of gaining economic independence. But they encountered discrimination based on both sex and nationality, and employment was not always readily found. Most Norwegian and Swedish immigrant women got hard and poorly paid work as maids. The photograph above shows Hilma Swenson Anderson at work in St. Paul, ca. 1915.

Class Differences in the Urban Environment

The many occupational opportunities and the greater economic diversification created sharper class differences in the cities than in the country. In Minneapolis Norwegian settlement moved south along the Mississippi River. It was in no way a question of solid Norwegian neighborhoods as one might find them in farming communities, but some did have a distinct Scandinavian composition. The movement can be followed by looking at when new churches were dedicated and older ones moved. Lake Minnetonka, which was located near the city,

became a popular recreational area for church picnics and other social activity. Scandinavians who desired to be exclusive in their social relations, writes the Swedish American Alfred Söderström, "built their own elegant summer dwellings" by the lake.

Social distinctions and the distance that might exist between people in the churches and those in the lodges, or between the church and secular associations, were more evident in Chicago than in Minneapolis. The solid Norwegian bankers, physicians, lawyers, and businessmen resided in the fashionable Wicker Park district of Chicago, cultivated their own social life, and built their separate churches. Wicker Park Church was ready for use in 1875. They called the district "Homansbyen," after an exclusive section of Oslo. Norwegian workers in 1900 were still concentrated around Milwaukee Avenue, referred to as the Norwegian street. But there was a gradual drift toward the Humboldt Park neighborhood. North Avenue and Kedzie, with Logan Square, the last station on the elevated railway, as a central point, became the main Norwegian area. Wicker Park was not far distant. In the 1920s North Avenue was the main street in the colony; it was here that the newcomers flocked. Along this street there were Norwegian businesses, restaurants, and saloons. Artists had their studios here and people in a variety of professions their offices.

In this building on Hewitt Avenue in Everett, Washington, there was a saloon and a brothel. Such establishments were frequently located in poor ethnic ghettos and gave Americans the impression that it was a problem created by the immigrants themselves.

The tenement here is typical for the years before the turn of the century in Chicago. It was located in a Norwegian neighborhood on Erie Street.

Cultural Life in the Norwegian Urban Colonies

The coffee houses (*kaffistover*) became cultural institutions in many urban colonies. They were meeting places that counteracted the influence of the saloons. The coffee houses could offer meeting rooms for debate groups, literary societies, lecturers, and musical entertainment. On North Avenue in Chicago there were in the 1920s both Den Norske Kafé (The Norwegian Cafe) and Kaffistova (The Coffee House). In Minneapolis J. J. Skørdalsvold, for a time editor of *Folkebladet* and an eager temperance man, had from the early 1880s operated a Scandinavian coffee house on Washington Avenue. Actors, painters, and intellectuals had a meeting place there.

The Artists

In some places there were colonies of painters and sculptors. In Chicago Rolf H. Erickson collected the names of 100 artists from the period 1890 to 1930, and he claims that more than a third of them must be considered to be better than amateurs. John Olsen Hammerstad, who emigrated from Kristiansund, Norway, to Chicago

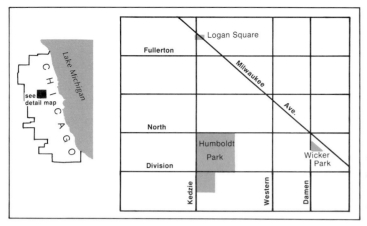

The map shows the areas around Milwaukee Avenue and Humboldt Park in Chicago.

This building was the home of the wealthy Norwegian American O. A. Thorp, who had emigrated from Eidsberg in Østfold. From 1880 on he operated a profitable import and export business in Chicago.

Wicker Park Church was dedicated in 1875. Here the more prosperous Norwegian immigrants assembled.

C. Blegen was concerned with cultural boundaries; he describes how the immigrants extended these boundaries in America, developed institutions, and contributed lasting cultural values. Cultural activities that in the homeland had for the most part been for the upper classes were in America shared by everyone, regardless of social or cultural background.

In Chicago Marcus Thrane tried to transfer the Norwegian literary culture to the new surroundings. Between 1866 and 1872 he worked with a small group of amateur actors to establish a Norwegian stage in the city. The troupe performed for a small audience Ivar Aasen's National Romantic ballad opera *Ervingen* (The Heir), *Til Sæters* (To the Mountains) by C. P. Riis, which was later to be very popular, and plays written by Thrane himself. One of them, *Syttende Mai* (May Seventeenth), is a satirical piece that among other things pokes fun at the Americanization of the immigrants. Such activity enhanced the cultural scene in the immigrant community and gave the immigrants a sense of achievement. Another early effort was The Norwegian Dramatic Society (Den Norske Dramatiske Forening), established in Chicago in 1868. Both in its philosophy and in its repertoire the Society displayed a distinct Norwegian national spirit. Napier Wilt and Henriette Naeseth compare it to the theater Ole Bull founded in Bergen, Norway. The company kept the theater going for four years. It represented the beginning of a Scandinavian theatrical tradition in America that flourished for a long time.

The theaters had a common Scandinavian identity while each of the three national groups was small. "As long as Minneapolis was a small town, 'Scandinavianism' was fashionable," writes Carl G. O. Hansen. Cooperation partly stranded on national sentiments, which were strengthened by the political changes in the homeland in the 1880s. An example is The Scandinavian Dramatic Society (Den Skandinaviske Dramatiske Forening). It was founded in Minneapolis in 1870 and shortly thereafter changed its name to Norden (The North)—"a union of the sons and daughters of the North." But soon the Danes pulled out, and a few years later the Norwegians. Norden continued as a Swedish theater.

The Forward Dramatic Society (Frams Drama-

in 1869, was a gifted landscape painter and likely the first professional artist of Norwegian birth in America. Between 1920 and 1930 there were annual Norwegian-American art exhibits in Chicago. In pictorial art, motifs from Norway were most popular; very seldom were the immigrants themselves portrayed.

In New York Jonas Lie achieved fame; he is best remembered for his paintings from the construction of the Panama Canal. The artist Herbjørn Gausta from Telemark, Norway, was an early practitioner among Norwegians in America. He emigrated when he was thirteen years old in 1867, and from 1888 on he lived in Minneapolis. In this city also Jacob Fjelde from Ålesund

worked. He was of a gifted family; his father had excelled in the traditional art of woodcarving, and Jacob himself became a sculptor. Among other works, he was responsible for the statue of Ole Bull that was erected in Minneapolis in 1897.

The Ethnic Theater Was Popular

Even though they were culturally and socially a part of the Norwegian milieu, painters and sculptors looked for a livelihood outside the Norwegian-American community. The Norwegian-American theater, on the other hand, was exclusively an ethnic institution. Theodore

Den norske Dramatiske Forening.

Præsident:—C. S. Howland...Regisseur:—C. Møvel.
Secretair:—J. Warneis......Kasserer:—N. Antersen.

Første Forestilling
gives i

☞ **GERMAN HALL** ☜
Lørdagen den 28de Marts, 1868.

Til Optørelse kommer:
En Hallingdøl, som Prolog,
uttierer ai................. ....Hr. C. Møvel.

Derefter:
Den graae Paletot,
Vaudeville i 1 Akt af Erik Bøgh.

Personerne:

Jægermeister v. Zentel...............Mr. Svereland
Holger hans Broterfien.......... ..." Warneis.
Wilhelm Valberg......................" Møvel.
Clara Helmgaart..... ....Miss Mjertsen.
Affeslor Sievert.....................Mr. Møller.
Peter, Holgers Opvartser. ...." Howland.
Melchior, en Jøte...................." Berg.
Strættermeister Jesperfien.............." Reis.
Anette, Claras Pige................Mrs. Warneis.

Til Slutning:
Soldaterløier,
Sangspil i 1 Akt af Cosrup.

Personerne:

Vange, Godseier............,........Mr. Howland.
Emilie hans Datter..........Mrs. Svereland.
Prokurator Barting ....Mr. Berg.
Magister Glob, h. Broterfien........." Reis.
Anter, Landstabsmaler ...." Møvel.
Leitnant Vilmer....................." Warneis.
Mats, Gaardskar........ ...." Møller.

Handlingen foregaar paa Vanges Gods.

The Norwegian Dramatic Society (Den norske Dramatiske Forening) was established in Chicago in 1868. It represented an early effort to retain national spirit through cultural activities. The program above is for the theater's first production,

tiske Selskab), organized in Minneapolis in 1900, was a Norwegian undertaking. It had begun as a young people's club and literary society in the 1880s. The company presented a number of dramatic works. Amateur actors might gain an audience and become well known; especially popular was Anton Sannes in the main role in Ludvig Holberg's comedy *Jeppe paa Bjerget* (Jeppe on the

Mountain). Several actors were more than amateurs and had had experience on the Norwegian stage before emigrating. The Norwegian-American actress Borgny Hammer, who worked in New York, had for instance performed on the stage in both Bergen and Oslo before she came to America. In 1925 she founded The Norwegian Theater (Det Norske Teater) in New York, went on tours, and established herself as an excellent interpreter of Ibsen.

Societies, clubs, and lodges had their dramatic groups. The Norwegian Club (Den Norske Klub) in Chicago played folk comedies, but also attempted more demanding productions. In the early 1930s an independent theater, The Chicago Norwegian Theater (Chicago Norske Teater), was again formed in Chicago. One of the instructors and stars in this institution, Bergljot Raaen, tells of enthusiastic audiences. The troupe on occasion bit off more than it could chew; it even performed Ibsen's *Peer Gynt* in its entirety, a performance that lasted far past midnight. In the fall of 1950 the theater closed its doors.

A Tradition of Song

Musical activity received its strength and inspiration from more than one source: congregational singing with its rich legacy of hymns, folk music in all its variations, and works by Norwegian composers. All Norwegian Americans could cultivate this heritage. The most typical musical form was the men's choir. Numerous societies were formed in order to promote male singing. The Swedes had their *sångarföreningar*, the Germans their *Gesangevereine*, and the Norwegians their *sangforeninger*. Choirs from these ethnic groups arranged large song festivals, and prizes were given for the best performances. Male choirs and song festivals were a common Ger-

This is a performance of C. P. Riis's popular play Til Sæters (To the Mountains) at the Academy of Music in Brooklyn in March, 1945. It played to a full house of 2,200 people. Carl Søyland served as stage director.

man-Scandinavian tradition, but in America the Germans and the Scandinavians cultivated the tradition separately. Carl G. O. Hansen wrote in 1916 that "hundreds of Norwegian men's choirs have in the course of the years been active in this country, and locally, as well as at regional and national festivals, have done much to make this amateur art popular."

Directors like F. Melius Christiansen at St. Olaf College, Carl G. O. Hansen himself, and August Werner at the University of Washington in Seattle lifted the musical performances to a high artistic level. The singing societies were, in Hansen's words, "one of the foremost factors in the service of work for Norsedom." The first society was Normanna Sangerkor (Normanna Singers' Choir), founded in La Crosse, Wisconsin, in 1869. In Chicago Det Norske Sangerforbund (The Norwegian Singers Association) was formed the next year. The numerous choirs that eventually were organized were given names like Bjørnson Mannskor (Bjørnson Men's Choir), Den Norske Glee Klub (The Norwegian Glee Club), Nordmændenes Sangforening (The Northmen's Singing Society), Grieg, Larken (The Lark), and Norrøna (The North), or only the name of the town, like Ballard Sangerforbund (Ballard Singer's Association). The song festivals, to begin with, had a common Scandinavian banner. In 1886 a federation of all Scandinavian singing societies was formed, and before the federation was dissolved a few years later it had conducted several festivals.

The Norwegian Singers Association (Det Norske Sangerforbund), originally organized in 1906, was the largest association of male choirs, with as many as fifty member choirs in 1914. For a number of years Emil Biorn functioned as chief director. Large, spectacular festivals were arranged every other year; both soloists and orchestras participated in the program. Since 1912 *Sanger-Hilsen* (Singers' Greetings) has carried news about the federation's activities. The singing societies on the West Coast had, however, formed The Pacific Coast Norwegian Singers Association (Pacifickystens Norske Sangerforbund) in 1902, and in 1912 a regional association came into being on the East Coast, under the energetic leadership of Ole Windingstad. The distance was too great for East and West to be able to perform together.

The Luther College Band in the 1880s. With directors like Carlo A. Sperati, this form of music attained a high artistic level. Here he himself is a student and sits as number three from the left. Carlo Sperati (1860-1945) served as director of music at Luther College for 38 years from 1905.

Norwegian-American composers, for instance Alfred Paulsen in Chicago with his extremely popular "Naar fjordene blaaner" (When the Fjords Are Blue), gave impulse to the movement. His composition was sung at almost every meeting of the singing societies. In addition, Grieg was an inspiration. His mighty music to works by Bjørnson, such as "Landkjenning" (Sight of Land) and "Sigurd Jorsalafar," as well as his folk melody to "Den store hvide flok" (The Great White Throng) could be heard at many song festivals.

The festivals were joyous occasions where thousands of Norwegians gathered in a holiday mood. The program could be enjoyed by everyone, even by those who did not know Norwegian. A person might even join a singing society without mastering the language; the words and melodies could be learned by rote. These are factors that explain the longevity of the choral tradition. It has been the easiest cultural heritage to preserve. The song festivals continue today, even if not in their earlier splendor.

Public Spirit in the Urban Environment

In 1921 the pastor C. O. Pedersen, although not without a certain complacency, could boast on behalf of his compatriots that "Americans in the Norwegian group take care of their own." Norwegian Americans were not a burden on society; there was no "alien problem." To the contrary, he claimed, "they share generously of their resources with others." As a part of the home mission of the Norwegian-Lutheran churches, he mentions nine hostels and seamen's homes, two homes for wayward girls, and eight organizations for finding homes for orphaned children. There were also nursing homes, deaconess homes, hospitals, and a number of other available social services. The exact number of such institutions is difficult to determine, and perhaps not so important, for many of them were short-lived. Others flourished and have become permanent institutions. In his history in 1925 O. M. Norlie lists the names of twenty homes for the elderly, twenty-eight hospitals, and fourteen orphanages that were then in existence. They had been founded by Norwegian-American religious groups and by independent organizations.

Many Immigrants Encountered Hardships

Circumstances among the immigrants themselves called forth the initiatives for assistance. It was natural to seek the company of Norwegian Americans and promise each other mutual help; only in this manner could they survive in the cold and impersonal urban environment. Many emigrants arrived in America without sufficient financial resources. Especially in the 1860s there appear to have been many poor Scandinavian newcomers. Scandinavian assistance societies were started to take care of immigrants in need; also the church collected money for this purpose. The pastor O. Juul, the earliest permanent Lutheran minister among Norwegians in Brooklyn, relates in 1867 that what caused a pastor in a city the greatest worry was "how he would be able to lend or give monetary help to everyone who comes and complains to him about their need."

Nordmændenes Sangforening, a male singing society in Seattle in 1889. Male choirs were a German and Scandinavian tradition. The magnificent song festivals assembled many choirs.

There were newcomers, people who were stranded in the big city without means, and Norwegian sailors who had lost their berths or deserted ship.

In 1873 Pastor Juul got an assistant, the normal-school graduate Peder B. Larsen. Larsen was the first Norwegian Lutheran missionary to be stationed at Castle Garden, the receiving station for immigrants who landed in New York, to work among arrivals from Norway. The city was filled with danger for the naive person. Newcomers and sailors were subjected to abuse from "runners," who were in the employ of transportation companies or boardinghouse keepers, or from swindlers. Not a small number of the latter were Norwegians who won the confidence of ignorant newcomers or seamen in order to victimize them. "Deceit and cheating of every kind might befall people," wrote J. R. Reiersen in the 1840s. He gives the names of persons who "have made a black living by exploiting their countrymen." Conditions were not much better in the other cities the immigrants passed through. Consequently there existed a great need for guidance and protection.

Charitable Institutions

As the Norwegian colony in Brooklyn grew larger, it became apparent that assistance to poor and ill immigrants and sailors had to be given a more permanent basis. In 1883 the Norwegian Lutheran Deaconess Home and Hospital of Brooklyn was established on a small scale; in time it grew into the major charitable institution among Norwegians in the East. In 1899 the Bethesda Society was founded; it was a missionary effort to bring young people under Christian influence. In addition, it practiced charitable work. In the early 1920s this society assumed major responsibility for giving assistance to the approximately one thousand unemployed Norwegian sailors who were in the city. In Brooklyn a home for elderly people was opened in 1902 and an orphanage in 1914. Organized help was the only

The Martin Luther orphanage in Stoughton, Wisconsin, in 1918. Need among the immigrants prompted the churches to respond with charitable acts: In 1866 "the Synod recommended that a collection should be taken at its closing service, and that everyone should work in his own area to collect money for this purpose." (Kirkelig Maanedstidende, September, 1866.)

The immigrants were exposed to swindle and trickery by so-called runners, who were in the employ of boarding-house keepers or other establishments or who acted independently to cheat the immigrants by taking advantage of their ignorance. The drawing is entitled "Runners of the Olden School" and appeared in Harper's Weekly, June 26, 1858.

spokesman for the social gospel, predicted an inescapable conflict between capital and labor. The Catholic Church had found its place in America among poor immigrants who lived in the cities. In contrast to the American Protestant churches, it was therefore not foreign to the laboring class. The Catholic Church was much closer to the new social problems than the Protestant middle- and upper-class churches, which instead approached the masses by starting social assistance programs.

In this connection it is important to point out that the Norwegian Lutheran Church never became a church of and for the elite in society, even though, like the American Protestant churches, it had been shaped in a rural situation. Like the Catholic Church, it was to a high degree an immigrant church, and had been organized among people familiar with poverty and need. It had never excluded the working class. Waldemar Ager described the Norwegian Lutheran Church in 1917 as a church of the people. He insisted that in his hometown of Eau Claire 90 percent of the members in the Norwegian Lutheran congregations belonged to the working class. On the other hand, the older Lutheran church in America could, in Ager's opinion, hardly be called a church of the people.

Organizational life among Norwegian Americans commenced in earnest in the 1880s. The large systematic charitable undertakings also had their beginning in this decade. In Chicago the Norwegian Lutheran Tabitha Society was founded in 1885. Dissension split it. But the different organizations that evolved from it all promoted good initiatives on their own. Under the leadership of Dr. N. T. Quales, the Norwegian Lutheran Hospital (Det Norske Lutherske Hospital) was opened in 1894. In 1910 it became an independent institution, and in 1929 it assumed the name The Norwegian-American Hospital (Det Norsk-Amerikanske Hospital). The Tabitha group and the related societies operated a nursing home and an orphanage. The deaconess movement, which had first come to New York, opened a hospital in Chicago in 1897 and trained women for nursing and social work. The new institutions indicated economic growth in the Norwegian-American community. But they could exist only with support from the outside. Bazaars, lotteries, and fund drives provided needed

way in which these problems could be solved.

It was the urban immigrants who built most of the charitable and socially beneficial institutions. In 1887 the pastor Josiah Strong had encouraged the Protestant churches to accept "the challenge of the cities." They should depart from their strong concern for the rural environment and come to terms with the new labor proletariat that had been created by urbanization and industrialization. Washington Gladden, the great

Above: Elizabeth Fedde (1850-1921) came to Brooklyn in 1883 as the first Norwegian deaconess in America.

Right: Deaconesses at the Norwegian Lutheran Deaconess Home and Hospital in Chicago around 1900.

means. At the same time these activities promoted social gatherings and an ethnic group life.

Women Had an Important Role in Charitable Work

In other communities developments ran parallel with those in New York and Chicago. Women played an important role in the voluntary charitable work. They were most frequently from what might be called a Norwegian-American urban middle class. Like their American sisters, married women of this class spent much of their free time outside the home. Women's organizations grew in step with urbanization. In Minneapolis both the Norwegian Christian Assistance Society (Den Norske Kristelige Hjælpeforening), organized in 1892, and the Lutheran Charitable Society (Det Lutherske Velgjørenhedsselskab) from 1893 are evidence of women's contributions. In 1888 a Norwegian deaconess hospital—the second in America—came into being. Fairview Hospital, which was to flourish, opened its doors in 1906. A woman's group, Lyngblomsten (The Heather Flower), which had begun as a reading society in 1902, assumed the task of building a home for the elderly in Minneapolis; and a branch of the same organization was responsible for similar projects in Duluth. With these institutions the Norwegian-American community reached a new and important stage in its development.

The Brooklyn Colony, a Norwegian Suburb

"From Norway—to Norway," wrote Sigurd Folkestad in 1907 about the Norwegian-American colony in Greater New York. The Bay Ridge district in Brooklyn became in time the largest urban colony of Norwegian-born people outside Norway. It has on occasion been facetiously called a suburb of Oslo or Bergen. The Norwegian population in the metropolis in 1930 numbered almost 63,000; of these, 60 percent had been born in Norway. The "nearness" to the homeland, a certain amount of "birds of passage"-migration, the many calls by Norwegian ships in the port, in addition to the many members of the colony who worked in shipping, preserved the connection with Norway. And the colony constantly received visits from prominent Norwegians who participated in programs and celebrations and in this way gave people in the colony a feeling of taking part in Norwegian social life. Simultaneously this weakened the connections to compatriots in the Middle West and moved Norwegians in the East away from the immigrant culture that had been created there.

A few Norwegians settled in New York in the 1830s and 1840s. Johannes Nordboe had traveled through the city in 1832, and in a letter from Illinois in 1837 he advised newcomers in New York to go down to the harbor and shout: *Svedisker Norveisk Mand*. Then the newcomers would immediately get in touch with people they could talk Norwegian to, Nordboe wrote. He mentioned especially Fredrik Wang, a pastor's son from Vågå, who operated a tavern. The core of the early settlement was made up of sailors who had abandoned ship. Attracted by higher American wages for sailors, but also by the opportunity to get employment on shore or cheap land farther west, thousands of Norwegian sailors deserted ship when they landed in New York. From 1846 to 1850 an estimated 500 men deserted. After an interlude with sailings to Quebec, Canada, New York again became the port of debarkation after 1870. The number of deserters continued to increase dramatically: between 1871 and 1915 probably 20,000 men abandoned ship in American ports. From 1870 on, the Norwegian population grew quickly.

The first Norwegians had settled in Lower Manhattan. Here sailors who had deserted, as well as later arrivals, could find employment in shipyards, dock construction, and other forms of work associated with shipping. From the 1870s, as bridges and ferries linked Brooklyn to Manhattan, a movement across to the new districts by the harbor in Brooklyn began. Hamilton Avenue, where the ferry from Manhattan landed, was the main Norwegian street between the 1870s and 1910. Saloons with names like Grimstad and Stavanger enticed Norwegian seamen. Nearby was the Norwegian seamen's church and the Norwegian seamen's home to counterbalance

the influence of the saloons. The depression in Norwegian shipping and the crisis in the 1880s caused the permanent Norwegian population to increase, simultaneously making the passage of sailors through the city decline.

The new shipyards that were built on Staten Island in New York harbor in the 1880s made many Norwegians seek employment on the island. Some shipbuilders even sent recruiters to the Norwegian districts of Brooklyn. A permanent Norwegian colony thus emerged on Staten Island.

On the East Coast Norwegians settled mainly in cities. Even though at mid-century there were Norwegians living in Boston, and gradually also elsewhere in New England and in the mid-Atlantic states, only in New York did they form urban colonies.

The greatest period of growth in the Brooklyn colony, *myostkolonien* (*mysost* being a Norwegian sweet cheese), as they affectionately called it, occurred from 1900 to 1930. Settlement moved from block to block, and in an ethnic neighborhood succession other nationalities moved in as the Norwegians moved out. In the 1890s the main force of Norwegian settlement in Brooklyn was in Park Slope; after 1900 it had moved to the Sunset Park district; and in the 1920s the core of the colony was in Bay Ridge. The moves might be prompted by cultural conflicts between Norwegians and other immigrant groups who settled in the neighborhood, for instance, between Norwegian reticence and lively Italian social activity. The sociologist Christen T. Jonassen explains the Norwegians' desire to move on the basis of their attachment to the sea and nature, and their wish to be surrounded by large open areas. When conditions no longer were satisfactory, they moved. On the basis of definite ecological criteria Jonassen concludes that Norwegians in Brooklyn finally settled in one of the best residential areas of the city.

Working in the Metropolis

The Norwegian colony in time took on an appearance of prosperity. Most people belonged to the solid middle class or to the well-paid part of the working class. Many Norwegian technicians and engineers found employment in the rapidly expanding building activity in the great city. In

1907 there were probably 300 Norwegian technically trained people, according to Sigurd Folkestad, who "were responsible for the construction and maintenance of the tunnels, railroads, bridges, and skyscrapers." In a survey in 1941 *Nordisk Tidende* found that as many as 35 percent of the Norwegian labor force were skilled and only 8 percent unskilled. The construction sector especially employed many Norwegians. In 1927, for instance, 75 percent of all contractors and carpenters on Staten Island were Norwegian.

Shipping continued to be important in the occupational distribution. In the same survey from 1941 *Nordisk Tidende* determined that 27 percent of the Norwegians who were working were employed on ships and in related occupations. Norwegian sailors traveled both on distant waters and along the coast; Knut Gjerset, who made a detailed study of sailors in the East, thinks that they were well regarded, and many were promoted to captain.

The fact that so many workers were skilled produced a strong union movement. In 1941, 60 percent of all Norwegian laborers were organized. The historian Leola Nelson Bergmann sees a rela-

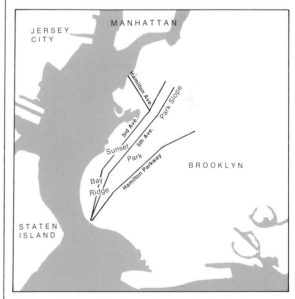

The Bay Ridge district of Brooklyn had the largest Norwegian urban population outside Norway, and it was good-humoredly referred to as a suburb of Bergen or Oslo.

tionship between this circumstance and the weak position that both the church and national Norwegian-American organizations apparently had. The labor unions took their place. Sigurd Folkestad maintained that Norwegians in New York were "frightened of religion and of each other." Despite such contentions, it was the church that formed the major link between Norwegians in the East and elsewhere in America. The pastor H. A. Preus, who visited New York in 1865 and preached in Norwegian for "about 150 listeners" in the church of the Missouri Synod, reported that the Norwegians themselves requested a "servant of the Word" from the Middle West. It was, however, extremely difficult for the Synod pastor O. Juul to get support for the congregation he organized a couple of years later. The Bethel Ship mission of the Methodists also struggled for its existence. It was basically a question of money. In 1941, for instance, the colony supported no fewer than thirty different churches and some missions as well. Most churches were Lutheran, but many other religious convictions were represented.

Many Bonds Existed between East and West

Several other bonds gradually linked Norwegians on the East Coast to Norwegians in the Middle West. For example, Lars W. Boe, president of St. Olaf College, sent the college choir on a tour among Norwegians in the East in 1920. A purpose of the tour was also to recruit students. Knut Gjerset has expressed regret that Norwegians in the East did not possess sufficient resources to establish their own institution of higher learning; such a school would in his opinion have been more Norwegian in both spirit and attitude than the colleges in the Middle West. Through the years, however, Norwegian-American youth in Brooklyn and elsewhere on the East Coast has availed itself of the educational program at the Lutheran institutions, especially St. Olaf College. Such connecting links and personal relationships have strengthened the sense of community among Norwegian Americans.

At its height, the colony in Brooklyn was a strong example of ethnic group life. There were clubs and societies, choirs and temperance

The editorial offices of the Brooklyn newspaper Nordisk Tidende.

lodges, and Norwegian festivals and Norwegian-American events were celebrated. Churches were erected, and institutions like homes for the aged, hospitals, and orphanages got support. Businesses in the colony sold Norwegian goods, and signs with Norwegian names characterized the business district. Norwegian language and Norwegian publications were a part of the colony's life.

All urban colonies were, however, affected by an inescapable development, which may be traced back to their very founding. There was a constant undermining and erosion of the conditions for their existence by movement out and a wandering toward the suburbs. The Norwegian neighborhoods therefore were gradually dissolved, in Brooklyn, Chicago, Minneapolis, and Seattle.

Norwegian America

The Norwegian-American community flourished between 1895 and 1925. During this period organizational life in the cities reached its height, and the *bygdelag*—old-home societies—attracted a following in rural Norwegian-American communities. A unifying impulse was the desire to preserve and cultivate Norwegian language and traditions. Norwegian-American ethnic enthusiasm culminated in 1925 with the centennial celebration of Norwegian immigration to America.

The Voluntary Associations

Voluntary associations were to characterize Norwegian as well as American society in the nineteenth century, though the movement started later in Norway than in America. People joined forces to solve problems, promote specific causes or principles, champion a political view, cultivate special interests, or work for charitable purposes, or simply to socialize. The associations assisted in the adjustment to a society created by industry and the growth of cities. They were a substitute for the old tradition-bound life, for family and kinfolk, and for neighbors in the home community.

In America organizational life flourished in all ethnic groups; they became infected by the associational spirit which had such force in America. They might *joine*, as Norwegian Americans would say, existing societies or form new ones. The American lodge system became a model, and at the same time itself had a strong appeal for many Norwegians. They became members of temperance lodges, the Masonic Order, and other American associations. In the Norwegian-American community the number of organizations was almost endless. "There prevails a veritable organizational mania among us at present," a contributor wrote to the St. Paul newspaper *Nordvesten* (The Northwest) in 1904. He complained that "whenever a few people find out that they have somewhat the same interests they immediately decide to form a society." The newspaperman Lars Siljan was even more critical. In an article in *Skandinaven* the previous year he blamed the great number of societies on the many people who aspired to become officers. Others who deplored the "association madness" and the disunion they thought it brought about accused their compatriots of cliquishness. Carl G. O. Hansen in 1914 estimated that there were fifty secular societies in New York and thirty-four

Grieg Ladies Singing Society of Chicago, Illinois. The choir, which was founded in 1915, is taking part in the May 17 parade dressed in their Hardanger costumes, in 1924.

in Chicago. In Minneapolis, he thought, "there have been innumerable societies that have seen the light of day." Hansen does not include in his survey organizations engaged in church activities, education, or charitable work.

The oldest secular Norwegian society was probably the one established in Boston in 1853. It had mainly a social purpose. There were two active societies in Chicago when Ole Bull visited the city in 1854 on his concert tour. It was not until the 1870s, however, that the idea of organizing became widely accepted; activity increased in the 1880s and attained an absolute high point in the period before World War I. The organizations were carried forward by the final great wave of emigration from Norway after 1900, the one that made the urban colonies swell. Most of the organizations were born in the cities. Newcomers gave life to older societies and filled the membership rosters as the descendants of earlier immigrants were taken up into American society. In these associations the immigrants could satisfy their need to speak Norwegian and retain their traditions. The interests the last arrivals brought with them, impulses from a more developed Norway, also set their mark on organizational life. The youth movement in Norway gave the inspiration for the young people's societies Hugnad in 1895, Norrøna in 1905, and Breidablik in 1906, all in Minneapolis. They were active, writes Hansen, until the members realized that they were no longer young. The established pioneer tradition with its societies and the newer organizational interests coexisted.

In 1906, when all Norwegian consulates submitted reports to the Norwegian foreign office about "Norwegian societies in foreign countries," they stated that there were 237 Norwegian organizations in the United States. The report for the United States has the following to say about the nature and purpose of the societies: "They have especially grown out of the concern for mutual economic aid and support, most frequently in the form of life and health insurance; thereafter it is the national and not least the church-related interests that have promoted organizational life among our countrymen in the United States; but in connection with this are also seen such purposes as song and music, literary activity, charity, health care, sport, temperance, or ordinary social activity, sometimes several of these

simultaneously. Many of the societies have clearly stated in their bylaws that one of their purposes is to preserve Norwegian language, customs, and traditions in their membership."

It was through the last stated purpose—the emphasis on a common cultural background—that the many societies found a certain unity. In general, immigrant activity reflected the belief that a rapid transfer to the use of English was accompanied by cultural loss, which would sweep away the bridges of understanding between parents and children. Between 1895 and 1925 many of the efforts to foster cultural values exceeded all expectations. The organizations flourished, and the immigrant press and efforts to create a Norwegian-American literature also made respectable advances. Many Norwegian Americans had a certain amount of faith in a permanent Norwegian subculture in America. It is therefore this period that may best be described as the Norwegian America.

The Spirit of Nationalism

Several circumstances affected the Norwegian-American community and promoted increased activity. The general economic growth and modernization in the homeland produced a sense of national pride. Norway could no longer be viewed as a backward nation of peasants. Visitors to Norway did not fail to inform the immigrant newspapers of the progress and the enterprise they noticed in the homeland. "As I walked across the fields and saw the American mowing machines do the work that I at one time did with a scythe, I recalled my sore back, when on these same fields I had cut the grain with a scythe for twelve *skilling* per *mål* [0.247 acres]," K. J. Haugen wrote to *Decorah-Posten* after he had visited his home community of Sigdal in 1911. In 1930 Johan Ovren remarked in a travel letter from Fåberg, Norway, that "old houses are gone and new ones have come in their place. And they have been made more convenient and modern. And not to forget the electric light which now is found all over Fåberg, yes, I can say everywhere in Norway, even in the most remote communities."

Feats by individual Norwegians that attracted the attention of the world press strengthened Norwegian-American self-esteem. The Norwegian Club (Den Norske Klub) in San Francisco arranged the welcome for Roald Amundsen, the Norwegian explorer, when the ship *Gjøa* docked in the city in October, 1906, after having sailed through the Northwest Passage. His later explorations, especially his conquest of the South Pole in 1911, and Fridtjof Nansen's expeditions to Greenland and his voyage on the polar vessel *Fram* (Forward) in the 1890s created great enthusiasm. They were magnificent achievements that all Norwegians could take pride in. The name "Fram" was afterward given to publications, choirs, societies, and lodges. In many places monuments, busts, and statues were raised to honor great Norwegians, from Leiv Eiriksson and Gange-Rolv to Henrik Wergeland, Ole Bull, Bjørnstjerne Bjørnson, and Henrik Ibsen. These memorials were to remind later generations of the greatness in the Norwegian people. They also indicated a strong will to mark a Norwegian

Above: At the unveiling of the statue of Leiv Eiriksson in front of the Capitol building in St. Paul, Minnesota, October 9, 1949. In the late nineteenth century the demand to have Leiv Eiriksson, and not Columbus, recognized as the discoverer of America had the support of many Norwegian immigrants. Left: "The World's Largest Viking." The gigantic figure is placed by the Kensington stone museum in Alexandria, Minnesota, and proclaims the town as the "birthplace of America."

presence. Other nationalities were to be made to respect Norway and Norwegians, and children born in America to take pride in the land of their ancestors.

The Cult of Leiv Eiriksson

An ethnic group is frequently judged by how the land they came from is regarded by the American public. It is practically a condition for being well received by the larger society that one's homeland be respectable. The idealization of the Viking Age, a period in history when a heroic life-style existed, was a part of the Norwegian immigrants' self-assertion. It was an expression of the need to feel at home in America and to make a rightful claim on the country. The idealized Vikings possessed qualities that could induce respect; they were both courageous and enterprising. To be known as descendants of these heroes strengthened one's own position. In the second half of the nineteenth century American historians, among them Richmond Mayo Smith, began to differentiate between "colonists"—the "real" Americans whose ancestors had arrived before 1776—and "immigrants." The latter, according to these historians, were in a subordinate position in relation to the "genuine" Americans. Rasmus B. Anderson, in reaction to such views and inspired by New England intellectuals like Henry Wadsworth Longfellow and John Greenleaf Whittier, raised a demand in the late 1860s for recognition of Leiv Eiriksson as America's discoverer. Norwegians had been here long before the Pilgrim fathers; they were thus the first colonists. Anderson's book, *America Not Discovered by Columbus*, was to substantiate this claim. The first statue of Leiv Eiriksson was unveiled in Boston in 1887. Later many more were erected, in places like Chicago, Duluth, St. Paul, and Seattle.

The Kensington Stone

Norwegian America soon found an additional rallying point, a new argument for giving Norwegians their deserved place in the nation's earliest history. It is precisely the need to assume such a place that has produced the persistent efforts to prove the so-called Kensington Stone is authentic. It was discovered by a Swedish farmer, Olof Ohman, in 1898 near the town of Kensington in northern Minnesota, a district of heavy Norwegian settlement. Runic inscriptions on this stone relate the experience of "eight Goths and twenty-two Norwegians on a journey of discovery westward from Vinland" and give a date in the middle of the 1300s. Expert opinions that the inscription is a falsification have never convinced faithful believers. Hjalmar Rued Holand made it a life mission to prove that the stone was authentic. The issue continues to arouse controversy even up to the present time.

Celebration of May Seventeenth

The foremost ethnic symbol has been May 17—*syttende mai*—a commemoration of the signing of the Norwegian constitution at Eidsvoll on May 17, 1814. In 1837 May 17 was celebrated in mid-Atlantic on board the emigrant vessel *Ægir* with cannon salutes and a toast to the fatherland. Ole Rynning read a poem he had written for the occasion. In 1859 *Emigranten* printed an account of

Rasmus B. Anderson's newspaper Amerika *was a one-man enterprise. In this issue, dated January 7, 1921, he attacks, in English, claims of the authenticity of the Kensington stone. The debate about this stone is still lively.*

20455
Published and distributed under Permit No. 411, authorized by the Act of October 6th, 1917, on File at the Post Office, Madison, Wis. By order of the President.
A. S. BURLESON, Postmaster General.

Amerika.

37te aarg.   Madison, Wis., fredag den 7. jan. 1921   No. 1

Kensington Rune a Joke, Anderson Insists; Replies to Peer Stromme

"Amerika's" Editor Likens It to Other Great Fakes; Tells of History of Stone Messages

BY RASMUS B. ANDERSON
(Editor of "America," former U. S. Minister to Denmark and former U. of W. Professor.)

Some of my readers will remember the Cardiff Giant, the supposed fossil giant which was unearthed near Cardiff, Onondaga county, New York, in October, 1869, and exhibited for several months, but was finally proved to be a fraud. This giant was ten and a half feet high and made from a block of gypsum.

The Kensington Rune-stone is, in my judgment, a parallel. One is as much a fake as the other.

A week ago my friend, Peer Stromme, appeared in The Wisconsin State Journal, not exactly in defense of but as one inclined to accept the Kensington rune-stone as genuine and asking for more evidence from those who, repudiate it.

My position is that this runic inscription has already been sufficiently discussed by those who reject it, and that the burden of proof of its genuineness rests wholly upon its advocates. I do not assume to be an authority on the subject of runes. Runology has never been one of my specialties. I know the runes simply as a part of my interest in northern languages, history and literature. What I have shown is that this Kensington rune-stone has been examined and definitely repudiated as a fake, a joke, a fraud, and as a monstrosity by all the most eminent historians, philologists and runologists of Scandinavia, such as Doctor J. H. E. Schueck, Doctor A. G. Noreen, and Doctor M. B. Olsen. On the basis of my interview with Andrew Anderson at Stanley, North Dakota, on the seventeenth of May, 1910, I have shown how the joke could have been made by the knowledge and skill of Mr. Fogelbad, Andrew Anderson and Olof Ohman. While Andrew Anderson did not admit to me that these three had made the inscription, I became entirely convinced in my interviews with him that they were the perpetrators of this very clumsy fake.

IMPORTANT EVIDENCE

I know nothing about the poplar tree under whose roots the stone was found, if these roots by their flattened appearance were important as evidence it is a great pity that they were not preserved by the State Historical Society of Minnesota, or by some similar institution. Mr. Ohman, who is so much interested in Alexander von Humboldt's Cosmos, could not have been blind to the value of this runic inscription, if he believed it to be genuine. He would have saved the roots of the poplar tree and he would no have converted the rune-stone to such sordid use, as a stepping stone to his granary.

Peer Stromme tries to make capital out of the fact that Ohman did not settle on his farm before the year

1892, but he neglects to call attention to a more important fact; viz., that Ohman came from Helsingeland in Sweden in 1875 and that he then settled near Kensington and has lived in that neighborhood continually ever since that time. That is twenty-two years before the unearthing of the rune-stone in 1897.

In speaking of Professor Magnus B. Olsen, the foremost authority in Norway on runology, Peer Stromme says: "Professor Olsen never has examined the stone. He assumed that the thing was an American joke and turned the matter over to one of his young students, who promptly declared the inscription a forgery."

To this, I reply: Professor Magnus B. Olsen did make a careful examination of the inscription on the Kensington stone and decided it to be a forgery, but instead of preparing an opinion himself, he turned the matter over to one of his students in order to give him some practice along this line. The student's report was approved by Magnus Olsen. Does it not frequently happen that the famous Mayo doctors in Rochester, Minn., make a thorough diagnosis of a case and then turn it over to an assistant for operation? Thus Dr. Magnus Olsen made the diagnosis of the rune-

stone and the student performed the operation.

Again, I quote Mr. Stromme: "Then there is the famous Doctor Schueck, the president of Upsala university, quoted at some length by Prof Anderson. His opinion, is, of course of great weight, but we may have some doubt as to the care with which he went into the matter."

QUOTES PROF. SCHUECK

In reply to this, let me quote Professor Schueck himself. He says: "They had had facsimiles of the Kensington rune-stone in Upsala and Dr. A. G. Noreen, the eminent author in Sweden on Northern languages, has studied the inscription. He, like all other historians and linguists of Sweden, was of the opinion that it is a clumsily contrived joke."

Thus, it would appear that the matter was investigated with due care.

Naturally Scandinavian scholars would approach the Kensington rune-stone in a most friendly and hospitable spirit for, if it should be found genuine, it would redound to the honor and glory of the North of Europe. The stone, if genuine, would be worth a million, nay, its weight in gold, and the owner would not have to be im-

portuning historical societies to purchase it for the paltry sum of five thousand dollars. I think it was in 1912 that the present owner of the stone took it with him to the Scandinavian countries and submitted it to the scholars over there, but as Stromme admits, all of them merely laughed at it. If one of these authorities had recognized the stone as genuine, the present owner would not have failed to keep megaphoning this fact throughout the length and breadth of this country. And, it may be that such endorsement, if he had secured it, might have helped him to obtain the five thousand dollars which, I understand, is the price he is asking for the Kensington rune-stone.

May I not ask the defenders of this rune fake why they prate so much about the eight Goths and 22 Norwegians coming up the Red river from Hudson Bay, while the makers of the runic joke claim they came from Vinland, which we all know was somewhere on the Atlantic coast? Why not rather argue that they came up the St. Lawrence river and the great lakes to Duluth and thence penetrated the country to the present Kensington? This would seem to be indicated by the inscription itself.

SUBJECT OF INQUIRY

While comparatively little attention has been paid to runes by American scholars, runology has long been the subject of much investigation in Europe and particularly in Denmark, Sweden and Norway. A collection of all the books, pamphlets and essays on the runes would make a formidable library. In the three northern countries, there have for several centuries been scholars who have made the study of runes their specialty. Over two thousand runic inscriptions on monuments have been found in Sweden alone, about three hundred in Denmark and not a few in Norway. A runic inscription was found in the graveyard of St. Paul's church in London; runes were also found on a grave-stone in Orleans, France, and in the Viking period, runes were carved on a marble lion in the harbor of Athens, Greece. This lion covered with runes may still be seen at the Arsenal of Venice, Italy. Above, I have given a typical specimen of a runic monument found in Sweden. I have taken it from the great history of Sweden by Oscar Montelius. It illustrates the most common use made of the runes.

And, now, for the edification of my readers, I am going to close this discussion of the Kensington rune-stone with the story of an interesting runic fake in Sweden.

From pre-historic times we have a tradition of a Danish king, by name, Harald Hildetand. In his old age, his kingdom began to have bad luck. He decided to die as a hero in battle and sent a message to his nephew, King Sigurd Ring in Sweden. He challenged him to meet him in combat with as large an army as possible. For seven years the two kings prepared for war and when they finally had gathered large hosts from all over the north, the armies of these two kings met on Braavalla Heath in Sweden. This greatest of all battles in the pre-historic wars, King Harald fell with untold thousands of his men. The date of this battle is usually given by historians as approximately 740 after the birth of Christ.

"MAKE FINE TRIO"

On a rock in Hoby Parish in Bleking, in the Southwest part of Sweden, according to Saxo Grammaticus, the father of Danish history, King Harald Hildetand had caused a runic in-

The runes transcribed: Shanmals auk Olauf leta Kiara Merki thausi efter Suain fathus sin. Than Kuth hialbi Salu haus.

Translation: Shanmals and Alauf (names of women) had these monuments made after Swain, their father. God help his soul.

Above: The Norwegian Constitution Day, Syttende Mai, *is celebrated with a children's parade in Wicker Park in Chicago in 1907. May 17 has been the foremost Norwegian-American ethnic symbol.*

Right: May 17 celebration in the mid-1870s. The Norwegian flag has the device marking the union with Sweden in the upper left-hand quarter. The photograph was taken by Andrew Dahl in Winequaw in the vicinity of Madison, Wisconsin.

how the day had been celebrated that year on board the emigrant ship *Norge*. It was an event in which the singing of "national songs was frequently interrupted by the firing of salutes." Still, not until after the Civil War was the day regularly observed in the Norwegian settlements in the Middle West; the observance of May 17 among the immigrants kept pace with the practice in Norway. There a greater celebration of it began in the 1870s as a consequence of Bjørnstjerne Bjørnson's initiative in arranging children's parades. *Emigranten* describes a May 17 celebration in Madison in 1864. The first commemoration of the day in Minneapolis was in 1869. Both were private parties, arranged by the local Scandinavian society. The society in Minneapolis had been organized for the purpose of receiving Ole Bull on his concert tour that year. The occasions were evidence of an "idyllic Scandinavianism," Carl G. O. Hansen writes.

Public celebrations of May 17 became common

during the following years. Scandinavianism had to give way to Norwegian nationalism, and celebrations of the day became an integral part of Norwegian-American folk life. Norwegians came together everywhere on May 17, in towns and in the country, in church and lodge, under open sky and in large halls, to honor the homeland's day of independence. It required time, however, to establish a firm tradition. In 1882 *Skandinaven* complained that "the May Seventeenth festival in Chicago was . . . of a private character." Participation was therefore limited. In time all the

Norwegian societies cooperated in arranging a joint celebration of this day. In Chicago the Norwegian National League (Det norske nasjonalforbund) has thus been responsible since 1900 for a colorful folk festival with children's parades, athletic competitions, choirs, and other musical contributions, and a large program in Humboldt Park, close to Chicago's statue of Leiv Eiriksson. A similar cooperative body has functioned in New York since 1905, and it has attracted large crowds to its magnificent festivals. In 1925 *Nordisk Tidende* reported that 10,000 Norwegians marched down Fourth Avenue in Brooklyn carrying banners and flags. This particular celebration to honor May 17 included the dedication of an open place which the city fathers had decided to call Leiv Eiriksson Square.

The greatest inspiration for commemorating the day came with the dissolution of the Swedish-Norwegian union in 1905. National fervor reached new heights among the immigrants. The thought of a completely independent Norway with its own consulates and a separate identity aroused an almost passionate patriotism. The act of national liberation and the exultation it produced can be said to be at the base of the flowering that took place in the Norwegian-American subculture at that time. The Norwegian university student singing society's tour in America the same year was a highly celebrated event. In 1914, during the centennial jubilee of the Norwegian constitution, the Norwegian Singers Association of America reciprocated, and under the leadership of Emil Biorn of Chicago went on a tour to Norway.

In the year 1914 "the great homecoming" occurred. An estimated 20,000 Norwegian Americans visited the homeland to take part in the centennial celebrations. The large exposition in Frogner Park in Oslo had a display devoted to "the emigrated Norway." Governor Mark Hanna of North Dakota personally delivered a bust of Abraham Lincoln as a gift from his state. Norwegian-American participation in the exposition had been brought about by the efforts of a new organization, Nordmanns Forbundet – the Norsemen's Federation – which in an ethnic connection was a somewhat unique development, for the federation had its headquarters in Norway at the same time as it recruited members among emigrated Norwegians. The Norsemen's Federation had been established in 1907, inspired by the national liberation in 1905 and by the constant visits by Norwegian Americans. These visitors included a coronation delegation in 1906, when Haakon VII was crowned king, and the visit the same year by the St. Olaf College Band, which gave thirty concerts in different parts of the country. The purpose of the Norsemen's Federation was to unite all Norwegians in and outside Norway. It was at that time that Norway discovered a Norwegian America in earnest and began to take an interest in the community that Norwegians had built in their new homeland.

The Eidsvoll Jubilee in America

The Eidsvoll centennial was commemorated wherever Norwegians had settled in America. The celebration in the Twin Cities, Minneapolis and St. Paul, was the largest. A festival lasting three days, with probably as many as 50,000 participants from the cities and the districts around them, marked the occasion. This celebration took on a great symbolic value in ensuing years; it demonstrated the immigrants' strength and their contributions to American society.

Festivities were introduced on May 16 with two processions, one from Minneapolis and one from St. Paul. Thousands of people lined the parade routes; the many colorful peasant costumes (*bunader*) made a great impression. There were both choirs and bands, and there were floats that presented the constituent assembly at Eidsvoll, bearded Vikings in Viking ships, and even one for the women's cause that proclaimed, "Women can vote in Norway." The two processions con-

At the centenary jubilee exposition in Oslo in 1914:
The journalist: Well, what do you think of the exposition?
The Norwegian American: Well, to be in Norway it is not too bad, you know.
(Hvepsen, October 3, 1914.)

vened on the fairgrounds between the two cities, and there the main celebration was conducted. Various entertainment was offered, reunions of the local community societies, the *bygdelag*, were held, and a group of twenty-six veterans from the famous Fifteenth Wisconsin Regiment met. The gray-haired men attracted much attention and respect. The churches took note of the day in their services, colleges and academies of immigrant origin provided musical entertainment, and there were speeches and greetings. The two senators Knute Nelson of Minnesota and Asle Grønna of North Dakota, the two most prominent Norwegian-American politicians, added luster to the festivities by their presence. During the three days of the celebration the Twin Cities were infected with a jubilee spirit.

The *Bygdelag* Movement

The *bygdelag* had assumed major responsibility for the celebration of the Eidsvoll centennial in the Twin Cities. These societies, or *lag*, are a unique organizational development among the immigrants. The name itself reveals the folk roots of these organizations. A Norwegian-American *bygdelag* may be defined as a society of immigrant families from a specific Norwegian *bygd* (rural community), valley, district, or fjord area. These societies intended to gather in one organization immigrants from their district in Norway, regardless of where they lived in America. Especially immigrants residing in agricultural communities, and those who cherished a rural Norwegian orientation, had a great need to assert themselves against city arrogance and proponents of a refined Norwegian high culture. Many immigrants in the cities, on the other hand, feared that the rural traditions would have too much influence in the shaping of a Norwegian-American culture. They did not wish to reinforce the widespread view of Norwegians as being country folk. None of them desired to belong to "a nation of peasants." The *bygdelag* were as a consequence frequently attacked with a bitterness that the *bygdelag* leader and pastor L. M. Gimmestad found reminiscent of the religious "warfare of the nineteenth century." The growth of the *bygdelag*

The Norwegian Old Settlers Society on an outing near Chicago in 1890. The society met annually, in the same manner as the bygdelag *did later. It cultivated memories from the pioneer period and from the land that had been left behind.*

movement was therefore associated with strong tensions. The movement revealed many of the pressures and interests that existed among Norwegian Americans.

The major motivation of the *bygdelag* was strong immigrant attachment to the local Norwegian community; the immigrants possessed a great ability to preserve emotional ties to their past and to re-create familiar conditions in a new environment. They retained a feeling for kinship and the home community, and for the intimate aspects of their cultural heritage, for language and for old traditions and customs. The early patterns of settlement reveal the force of these relationships. Entire groups from a specific rural community or parish had emigrated together, and in America they settled close to each other.

They might re-create the Norwegian community, even to a degree where people who had been neighbors in Norway again became neighbors in America. Later immigrants settled among people from their home community. It is therefore correct to speak about Halling settlements, Trønder settlements, and Sogning settlements. Other people with different local roots in Norway were, however, not excluded. Such regional designations rather indicate that one specific local culture was dominant in the area and gave it its special characteristics. The majority of Norwegians lived scattered among immigrants from many parts of Norway, or among people of other nationalities.

As Norwegians moved westward, the pattern of settlement became more mixed; but even so, people still tended to take land close to former neighbors in the old country. Toward the end of the century local patriotism weakened, and the *bygdelag* movement became a defensive operation; it was a means of reviving "the slumbering *bygd* patriotism," as one man in the movement said. Simultaneously the *bygdelag* wished to preserve a National Romantic and idealized view of

the old homeland: a picture of Norway before industry and economic growth had dissolved and transformed the tradition-bound peasant society. The *bygdelag* belonged in an older immigrant tradition. Their most important purpose was to arrange an annual reunion or *stevne*—often in June after the spring planting or following the harvest season in September—which might assemble folk from the same Norwegian home community now living scattered throughout the great Middle West. The *stevne* provided a framework in which the old *bygd* could be re-created; it was like a visit to the homeland, where precious memories of the land they had left behind could be brought to mind again, and with former neighbors they could revive popular cultural traditions and entertain themselves in the local vernacular. Actually, the reunions were the only place outside the home where the peasant dialects were fully accepted and honored. The *bygdelag* thus strengthened the immigrants' self-esteem and their regard for their modest peasant origin.

Organizing the *Bygdelag*

Immigrants from Valdres, Norway, convened the very first *bygdelag* assembly on June 25, 1899, on the banks of the Mississippi River in Minnehaha Park in Minneapolis. The idea of arranging a *stevne* was not completely new. In both the 1880s and the 1890s old settlers had come together to reminisce about pioneer days. And the different church groups had long had their excursions and picnics. At the first *bygdelag* reunion in 1899 about eight hundred Valdres folk "entertained themselves in their own resounding and rugged Valdres tongue," as the newspaper *Nordvesten* reported. Thomas Lajord had taken the initiative through this weekly to call a gathering of people from Valdres for "a little fun" (*ai liti Moro*). The leading figure, however, both in the Valdres society and in the movement as a whole, was Professor Andrew A. Veblen, who was born in America. He typified many of the more successful second-generation immigrant leaders who had learned the *bygd* vernacular in an immigrant home and who treasured their parents' national background. In 1902, at the fourth annual *stevne*, a society was organized and given the name Val-

184

Andrew A. Veblen (1848-1932) became the leading personality among the people from Valdres as well as in the bygdelag *movement in general. Even though he was born in America, "on this side of the great water," as he himself said, he possessed an abiding interest in his Norwegian background. Veblen was a professor of physics at the state university in Iowa City, Iowa.*

dres Samband (Valdres Union). Veblen was elected president.

Localism was emphasized and strengthened by the formation of this *bygdelag* and by accounts of its activities in the immigrant press. Eventually the individual newspapers carried separate *bygdelag* columns. The regional impulse was also reinforced by a series of articles that Rasmus B. Anderson printed under the heading *Bygdejævning* (*Bygd* Competition) in his newspaper *Amerika* from 1901 to 1903; in these articles different *bygd* groups competed about "being the best in America." This rivalry and the many public urgings to come together bore fruit in 1907, when both Telelaget and Hallinglaget were organized. Thereafter there was growth without pause—a near epidemic spread of organizational activity.

Pacific coast divisions, societies for northwestern North Dakota and the prairie provinces of Canada, organizations for individual states, and many local clubs were formed. The *bygdelag* idea had an exceptional force. Nearly fifty societies with nationwide appeal came into being; in the heyday of the movement at least 75,000 people annually took part in the reunions.

Variety among the *Bygdelag*

The *bygdelag* had their major support in farming communities and small towns. There the church had a strong hold on people, and the entire *bygdelag* movement therefore was permeated with a church-centered and pious spirit. Many *bygdelag* fell into the hands of the Lutheran clergy, one critic claimed. There might even be religious testimonials and prayer meetings at some reunions, most commonly at those that gathered people from the southwestern districts of Norway. It was said of C. J. Eastvold, who served as president of Stavanger Amt Laget for a long time and as a pastor and president of Hauge's Synod, that "many an eye was wet during his sermons, and prodigal sons and daughters turned to their heavenly Father at our reunions."

It was of course natural for church people to find leaders in the Lutheran clergy. But in spite of the generally pious background against which the *bygdelag* operated, some societies were to a large extent able to free themselves from a pietism that regarded all entertainment as sin. This was most frequently the case in *bygdelag* that bore the names of Norwegian mountain valleys with a rich folk culture, such as Hallinglaget, Telelaget, and Setesdalslaget. Under the leadership of Bjørgulv Bjørnaraa, who perhaps was the most original personality in the movement, the Setesdøls retained the traditions from Setesdal. There were contests in *stevjing* (making improvised verses), fiddle playing, and folk dancing, and the *stevne*-goers told anecdotes and stories. Prizes were awarded for the best peasant costumes, and the society sponsored exhibits of home crafts, *rosemaling* (rose painting), and woodcarving.

Most *bygdelag* placed themselves somewhere between these two extremes. There was, however, a strong sentimental strain in all the societies, regardless of their degree of pietism, and during the two or three days the *stevne* lasted,

it found expression in speeches and other programs. It is perhaps most clearly illustrated by Hardangerlaget's annual reenactment of the romantic painting "The Bridal Procession in Hardanger" by Adolph Tidemand and Hans Gude. "The whole bridal party were in boats and came rowing along the shore, exactly as the song says," or a fiddler led the bridal procession into the meeting hall. Every time, the gathering revealed strong emotions; many wept. The reunions represented what O. E. Rølvaag has called "a first love"—"the beauty that surrounds one's childhood home." There were memories and emotions that could be used to nurture interest in Norway in children born in America.

The *bygdelag* stressed traditional Norwegian food at their banquets, dubbed *gjestebø, veitler,* or *sexa* in the various dialects of home. The food was frequently prepared by ladies aid groups in local Lutheran congregations. A spirit of friendliness and kinship prevailed to a degree that can hardly be overstated. The most precious activity might be, as stated in one *bygdelag* publication, "to sit in a circle of friends and talk about the little hut on the shore, the homestead in the valley, the church on the point—yes, and about that time and that time and that . . ."

Sentimentality, nostalgia, and the pietistic attitude, however, prevented a genuine flourishing of the folk culture. But aspects of it were cultivated, and the *bygdelag* were sensitive to the old Norwegian peasant life and the cultural expressions attached to it. In 1914 a unique organization was formed in Ellsworth, Wisconsin; this was Spelemannslaget af Amerika (Harding Fiddlers Society of America), which was a direct result of *bygdelag* activity. It cultivated appreciation of the familiar Norwegian instrument, the Harding fiddle, and had more than one hundred members. Until World War II it arranged contests (*kappleik*), with players competing for a silver cup. Good performers gained an audience in this way. Among the many who appeared, Dagny Andrea Quisling became a well-known and highly regarded player on the Harding fiddle.

The Relationship with the Home Community

The *bygdelag* conflicted with the development of a common Norwegian-American identity. For this reason, many people opposed the rivalry

Above: A reenactment of the "Bridal Procession in Hardanger" at a wedding at Mercer Island in Washington.

> *There quivers a glittering summer air,*
> *Warm over Hardangerfjord's fountains,*
> *Where high 'gainst the heavens, so blue and so bare,*
> *Are tow'ring the mighty mountains;*
> *The glacier shines bright, the hillside is green,*
> *All nature responds, with beauty serene;*
> *Behold, o'er the blue billows rowing,*
> *The wedding folks homeward going.*
>
> *Andreas Munch*
> *(trans. Rasmus B. Anderson)*

Right: A section of the famous painting by Adolph Tidemand and Hans Gude. It was completed in 1848 and is one of the best-known paintings in the Norwegian National Romantic tradition.

organs, baptismal fonts, and monuments, and to build homes for the aged. Nordlandslaget presented a rescue vessel which would be put into service in the treacherous waters off the Lofoten Islands. These gifts brought the *bygdelag* into contact with local Norwegian youth societies (*ungdomslag*), which in turn collected money to buy banners (*faner*) with motifs from the home district and sent them to America. They were dedicated with great ceremony, and the solemn occasion might, as one observer wrote in 1912, awaken "a strange, inexplicable mood in the congregation—there were tears of joy and enthusiasm." At colorful processions the banners were displayed and the *bygd* folk assembled around their emblems.

Interest in History

Interest in their Norwegian home district and the people from this locality, in addition to the interest in history produced by the Eidsvoll jubilee, is evident in the *bygdelag* constitutions. Gudbrandsdalslaget had as its purpose "to collect material for an historical account of the emigrated Gudbrandsdøls' life and activity, circumstances and accomplishments in this country." Many societies published yearbooks, which present significant biographical information and source material from the pioneer era. A few *bygdelag* managed to issue periodicals. *Valdris Helsing* (Valdres Greeting) was published from 1903; in 1910 the name was changed to *Samband* (Union). Knut A. Rene, a tireless collector of the Vossings' history, edited *Vossingen* (The Vossing), which came out from 1920 until 1950. Rene considered the magazine to be a continuation of the remarkable early journal *Wossingen*, which had been published in Leland, Illinois, between 1857 and 1860. Hadelandslaget put out *Brua* (The Bridge) from 1921 until 1951; *Hallingen* (The Halling) has appeared since 1912; and *Nord-Norge* (North Norway) since 1914. The most engrossing *bygdelag* magazine is probably *Telesoga* (The Telemarkings' Saga), edited by Torkel Oftelie. Between 1909 and 1924 Oftelie prepared fifty-three issues, filled with information about the Telemarkings and their settlements, personally collected by Oftelie. The history of the Norwegian-American people could hardly be fully told without these modest publications. In some of them the local attach-

between local groups. The tensions were clearly visible in the grandiose effort to collect money for a memorial gift (*minnegave*) to Norway in 1914, the centennial of the Eidsvoll constitution. The many *bygdelag* collected money for their respective Norwegian home districts to the detriment of a common Norwegian-American undertaking. Several societies had even been formed for the express purpose of sending a gift back "home." They supported "deserving needy" in the home community, gave money to purchase ment is underscored by the use of dialect. This occurred especially in groups where a folk tradition in the Norwegian home district gave support to the local vernacular, as in Sogn, Voss, Valdres, Telemark, and Hallingdal. But in the *bygdelag* there was not much appreciation for efforts to create a new Norwegian national language, "the distorted *landsmaal*," as a man in the movement disapprovingly described New Norse in 1913.

A Joint Council for the *Bygdelag*

In order to celebrate the 1914 centennial, the *bygdelag* had to establish joint action; a cooperative body, the Council of *Bygdelag* (Bygdelagenes Fellesraad), which is still active, was formed. Many *bygdelag* folk feared that the council would interfere in the activities of member societies. There was no desire to have a union, far less a fusion. It was the local patriotism that many guarded jealously—"the Norwegian self," as a critic called regional exclusiveness. "Hallings can get along quite well by themselves and one does

Above: A Halling reunion (stevne) in Spring Grove, Minnesota, as the cartoonist P. J. Rosendahl perceived it.

Left: Nordfjordlaget's banner (fane). The banners of the various bygdelag *were frequently gifts from the Norwegian home communities, and they were displayed at all reunions.*

not travel many miles to listen to Strils and Sognings," a local Halling patriot wrote to *Decorah-Posten*.

It is, however, important to bear in mind that the individual *bygdelag* pulled into organized activity many people who otherwise would never have joined a secular society. They thereby became a factor in the preservation of "the ancestral heritage." The *bygdelag* were also gradually accepted as an expression of Norwegian culture in America. In addition, church historians think, they contributed to creating religious tolerance

in the fractured Norwegian-American community. The main concern of the *bygdelag* was that "one is of the same local origin," wrote the historian John S. Johnson, "without thought of what one is politically, or in church relationship or school activity." The *bygdelag* were thus a factor in preparing for the great church union in 1917, and they became a permanent and popular part of Norwegian-American organizational life.

Sons of Norway— Sociability and Life Insurance

Comfort, sociability, and the company of fellow Norwegians were also to be found in the gatherings of the many lodges. "Lodge night," in the temperance cause or in other connections, satisfied an important need in the lives of many immigrants.

Sons of Norway became by far the largest secular organization. In this organization Norwegian Americans in the cities found a strong institutional base. Both the church and the *bygdelag* had a marked rural orientation. Like the *bygdelag*, Sons of Norway represented a grass-roots movement, but in contrast with the *bygdelag*, this organization evoked the enmity of the Lutheran clergy. It was held to be a secret society, analogous to the Masonic Order. The church harbored antagonism to Freemasonry and to societies that "work in the main in the same direction," as the United Church wrote in 1893 in a pamphlet to warn Christians against becoming members of lodges. The Good Templar lodges were also viewed as competitors of the church.

Sons of Norway was organized as a fraternal order, inspired by American fraternalism. Like the Masons, the order adopted secret membership ceremonies and passwords to the meetings, and the members called each other brothers. The brotherhood began as a society for mutual aid, which was the most common form of ethnic organization. It is not difficult to understand why Sons of Norway emerged during the depression of the 1890s among workers in the Norwegian colony in North Minneapolis. They were the most vulnerable in bad times. The idea of a society may also have been encouraged by their knowledge of workers' societies in Norway. Several of the early leaders were influenced by Unitarianism, and they thereby infused a liberal humanistic spirit into the brotherhood.

Organization and Growth

On January 16, 1895, eighteen young men, fourteen of them Trønders, came together and established the Sons of Norway. Bersvend O. Draxten was elected secretary. In 1900 a supreme lodge was formed, and the original lodge then assumed the name Nidaros. Draxten became the order's first president and an important force in its later growth. The first year three dollars a week was paid to members in unemployment benefits and fifty dollars for funeral expenses. By the end of 1895, eighty-one men were members of the fraternity and there was $700 in the treasury. From this modest beginning came a great

expansion in insurance activity. By 1914, policies with a combined value of $2.3 million had been issued. The order then had 12,000 members in 155 subordinate lodges from coast to coast. In 1897 a sister association, Daughters of Norway, was formed in North Minneapolis. In 1914 the members of Sons of Norway were divided into social and insurance categories, and two years later women were admitted to membership in the order "where Daughters of Norway does not have a chapter." At the time of the full merger in 1950, the women's order had 3,500 members and the brotherhood 32,000. In the early 1980s Sons of Norway had more than 100,000 members distributed among nearly 350 lodges. The headquarters of Sons of Norway remains in Minneapolis.

The founding group attracted attention by taking part in May 17 celebrations and other Norwegian affairs in Minneapolis. Thus the lodge idea spread to other parts of the city. In 1899 the Oslo lodge was formed in South Minneapolis, and the following year the Dovre lodge. The power of example made itself felt also on the West Coast. In 1903 a lodge, Leif Erikson, was organized in Seattle, and thereafter lodges were formed in other cities on the West Coast. In 1910 they joined the supreme lodge in the Middle West as subordinate lodges. The next year the order came to the East Coast, where Færder lodge was organized in Brooklyn. Sons of Norway is a result of the efforts that were made from the 1890s on to form regional and nationwide associations. There existed a strong wish to unite all Norwegians, regardless of where in America they had settled.

Its Activities

Socializing was in time probably accorded greater importance than the opportunity to purchase insurance. In 1914 as many as 47 percent of the members of Sons of Norway had not availed themselves of this opportunity; they had obviously joined for other reasons. Secret rituals and the building of lodge halls nurtured the fraternal idea; the work in the lodge was a source of satisfaction for the individual member. Participation in ceremonies, election to offices, whether as president of a lodge or as outer guard by the entrance door, gave status to people who other-

wise had a modest social position. It was the ordinary Norwegian Americans who filled the lodge halls. Some lodges had male choirs; many had drill teams which performed at conventions of the supreme lodge as well as in the local lodge hall. Lectures, frequently by well-known Norwegians visiting America or by prominent Norwegian Americans, were common; a major purpose was "to foster and preserve the Norwegian language among our members." Other kinds of entertainment were enjoyed as well, but always with strict abstinence from alcohol.

Who Joined the Movement?

No systematic analysis has been made of the social background of the members; conclusions are therefore subjective. It is, however, quite obvious that the mass of members came from the common people. Among the leaders in the early years, one frequently finds men who were active in political reform movements, such as the socialist Laurits Stavnheim. For a long time Stavnheim edited the monthly *Sønner af Norge* (Sons of Norway), which began publication in 1904, while continuing to put out socialistic journals and serving as supreme secretary for the order. The leaders of Sons of Norway belonged to an urban intellectual class, over which the Lutheran Church had less influence. John C. Huseby, supreme president of Sons of Norway for several years, was president of a Unitarian congregation in Minneapolis. Draxten was also influenced by Unitarianism.

Church people naturally stayed away from the order for a time. But criticism lessened as Sons

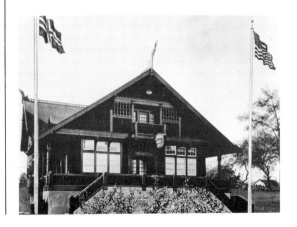

The lodge of the Sons and Daughters of Norway in Seattle was built in 1915 by Leif Erikson lodge of Sons of Norway and Valkyrien lodge of Daughters of Norway. It was called Norway Hall and was the scene of many gatherings. The picture above shows one of the lodge rooms.

of Norway made progress, and many were in time members of both a lodge and a Lutheran church. When a special burial ritual, which had never been used, was abolished in 1909, H. G. Stub, then president of the Norwegian Synod, found cause to express his satisfaction. He hoped for further developments that would make the order worthy of greater goodwill and recognition from all quarters. The church, all the same, clung to its suspicion of the order for a long time. Its

misgivings also reflected social distance. "Somewhat akin to snobbishness," writes Carl G. O. Hansen, many people who did not wish to mix with "the ordinary man" remained aloof from Sons of Norway. But a movement that so clearly satisfied important needs could obviously not be overlooked forever.

Sport Was Popular in Both Town and Country

Sport and athletics might unite everyone; they were neutral interests that could be pursued whether one lived in town or in the country. Some Norwegian Americans, like the famed football coach Knute Rockne at Notre Dame, succeeded in American sports activities. Others gained recognition in sports that were also practiced in Norway; best known is the figure skater Sonja Henie, who also established herself as a film star.

Within the Norwegian-American community, the large number of young men who immigrated led to a flowering of athletic activity. *Turnforeninger* (gymnastic societies) were formed in 1885, following the German model, both in Minneapolis and in Chicago. In the 1890s these societies cooperated with a similar group in Brooklyn to arrange contests. Rifle clubs existed from the 1880s. Hansen relates that in Minneapolis on summer evenings one could watch the members march down Washington and Cedar avenues. Impudent observers along the route might heckle them as the *hyre Venstrum*, a distortion of the Norwegian for "right face" and "left face."

Winter Sports

Winter sports on snow and ice were natural for Norwegians, and they cultivated both. The gymnastic society in Chicago added skating and track sports to its program, and as the Norwegian-American Athletic Society it erected its own building. This organization considered itself to be the largest Norwegian athletic society outside Norway. The ski club "Norge" was organized in Chicago in 1905, and on the East Coast the Norsemen Ski Club was formed in 1921. All the way up to the 1920s Norwegian Americans dominated skiing in America. As interest spread, ski clubs were established in many places. These set up meets for cross-country skiing and jumping. "'Ski jumper' has become a permanent nickname for Norwegians," Bjarne Gukild, writing in *Norden*, claimed in 1930, and "ski jumpers" became a new term in the American language. A Norwe-

Knute Rockne (1888-1931) revolutionized American football and became a legend in the American sport world. In this photograph he is standing as a coach in front of his football team at Notre Dame.

Right: Aurora Ski Club was organized in Red Wing, Minnesota, in 1886. The immigrant brothers Mikkel and Torjus Hemmestvedt from Morgedal were among the founders. The club built the ski jump at Carlson Hill and arranged competitions. From left to right: Paul Henningstad, Mikkel and Torjus Hemmestvedt, and B. L. Hjermstad in 1890.

Below right: Skating party on Silver Lake in Scandinavia, Wisconsin. The picture was taken in 1908.

gian-American company produced 200,000 pairs of skis in 1924.

The sport of skiing had deep roots. In pioneer days skis were used as a means of transportation. "When the first snow had fallen that autumn another Norwegian and I went on skis over the prairie to Beloit to buy flour," a pioneer relates in 1841. He adds that "Americans later saw our tracks in the snow, and no one could figure out what kind of animal might have left them." Sondre Norheim himself, the pioneer of modern skiing, moved from Telemark in Norway to North Dakota in 1884, when he was nearly sixty years old. Well known also is the legendary "Snowshoe Thompson," whose Norwegian name was Jon Thoresen Rue, from Tinn in Tele-

A ski-jumping competition near Duluth, Minnesota, in 1910.

mark. For nearly twenty years from 1856 on, he carried the mail on skis across the wild Sierra Nevada mountains. Thompson "towered . . . above most of his contemporaries in physical perfection and courage," wrote Holand.

Much immigrant romanticism and national self-praise surrounded the growth of skiing as a sport; it was well suited to hero worship. "Where manliness and indefatigable courage are tested Norwegians have made their mark in the American sport world," claimed Aksel Holter proudly. Holter himself was a skier and an enthusiastic writer about the sport. The two brothers Torjus and Mikkel Hemmestvedt, who came to Red Wing, Minnesota, in 1883, contributed much to this development. They were held to be the best skiers of their day in Norway, and in America they became pioneer ski jumpers. Many others did well. In 1913 Ragnar Omtvedt of Chicago set a new world record in ski jumping. Torger Tokle, who came to Brooklyn in 1939, was for American ski sport, writes Frank Elkins, the ski editor of *The New York Times*, what Babe Ruth was for baseball and Jack Dempsey for boxing.

A ski club was organized by Norwegian immigrants in Berlin, New Hampshire, in 1882, and in 1886 a club was founded in Eau Claire, Wisconsin. In that decade skiing was developed as a sport. Interest in skiing decreased in the 1890s, but the rising tide of emigration after the turn of the century produced new enthusiasm for the

sport. In 1904 Carl Tellefsen in Ishpeming, Michigan, succeeded in organizing the National Ski Association; before World War I the association had twenty-eight member clubs. In the 1920s there were 20,000 members in clubs all over the country. National meets were spectacular events. Many people were assembled, and "the same old skiing enthusiasm" as in the contests at the famed Norwegian ski jump at Holmenkollen prevailed, says Gukild. In the 1930s skiing caught the fancy of the American public in earnest, and it has since been a popular American sport. Austria and other nations with traditions in skiing have influenced the growth of this sport. The Norwegian strain is, however, still much in evidence. "This winter's fad on American ski hills is telemarking," *Nordisk Tidende* announced in March, 1982, and *Time* magazine told simultaneously about "the sound of telemarking." The point of this sport is "to make it down a slalom hill using Telemark turns on specially made cross-country tour skis, so that it becomes a mixture of cross-country and alpine skiing." At the end of March, 1982, the World Telemark Championships were arranged in Colorado.

The legendary pioneer Snowshoe Thompson was born in Telemark in 1827 and given the name Jon Thoresen. The family emigrated in 1837. In 1851 Thompson joined the gold rush in California. Because the postal service across the Sierra Nevada mountains from the east was inadequate during the winter months, he himself carried the mail across this mountain range for nearly 20 years. He thereby ensured postal connection between the Territory of Utah and the young state of California. Thompson was already a legend when he died in 1876 on his ranch in the Diamond Valley in California.

Culture and the Elite

The elite among the immigrants usually socialized with people within their own nationality; this was a reflection of the fact that they had still not gained full admission to higher social circles in America. A development toward social exclusiveness resulted from the economic progress many immigrants made. But people in comfortable economic circumstances also came together to promote cultural interests. The Norsemen's Federation appealed mostly to this group of Norwegians, even though membership was open to everyone. Other organizations made a conscious effort to establish an exclusive character by limiting their membership.

Men's clubs were a common form of organization. Their primary purpose was to engage in social activities. One of the oldest clubs was the Scandinavian Society (Det Skandinaviska Sällskapet) in San Francisco, organized in 1859. In 1898 a Norwegian society, the Norwegian Club, was formed in that city. The occasion for its organization was an expected visit by the Norwegian explorer Fridtjof Nansen. Nansen's tour was cancelled, but through the years the club hosted an array of prominent Norwegians who added luster to the society and gained it recognition far beyond the Norwegian-American community. Men's banquets were the most common social activities in this and similar clubs. On occasion women were invited as guests; frequently the women formed an auxiliary society. The Norwegian Club in San Francisco was open to "any man of Norwegian origin of good reputation." It assembled exclusively men of similar taste and lifestyle, however, recruited from the more successful and professionally educated Norwegian Americans.

A Scandinavian "High Life" in the Cities

In Minneapolis, Carl G. O. Hansen records, efforts were made from 1886 on to create a Scandinavian "high life" by arranging exclusive banquets at the West Hotel. For this purpose, a Scandinavian club was formed. These efforts aroused great interest. In 1898 the club was succeeded, also on a joint Scandinavian basis, by the Odin Club, organized for business and professional men. Until 1930 the Odin Club entertained important guests and cultivated social activity. The club at one time had as many as three hundred members. In 1933 another men's club, Torskeklubben, which was a purely Norwegian undertaking, assumed the role the Odin Club had played. The members came together to celebrate their Norwegianness and their worldly success, while consuming boiled cod and drinking aquavit. There were few other aims. It is, however, not without significance that societies of businessmen emerged in the Great Depression; it was a time when solidarity among individuals of a common ethnic background became essential. In Seattle the Norwegian Commercial Club was organized in 1932 by Norwegian businessmen to assist and give support to each other during that troubled time. It continues today as a social club for men.

The first social organization with a strong elitist and exclusive character, The Pioneer Social Club, was formed in Chicago in 1878. Membership was limited to twelve men of Norwegian birth who were admitted by invitation. The original members were shipmasters and businessmen. The society, still active, was described by Birger Osland, himself a prominent businessman in Chicago, as an oasis of friendship. Osland emigrated from Stavanger in 1888, and in his memoirs he gives a fascinating and detailed impression of the growth of societies among a cultivated immigrant elite. In 1891 Osland was one of the founders of the Norrøna Literary Society, which also was limited to twelve men. They were young men of similar educational background from Norway, and they took turns introducing a topic for debate. After about a year, Osland relates, the coming to Chicago of "a much breezier and more modern flock of young intellectuals" caused the membership to be expanded, and the society changed its name to the Arne Garborg Club. In 1893 this exclusive group entertained well-known Norwegian guests, among them the president of the Storting, Viggo Ullman, who was visiting the Chicago World's Fair.

When the Arne Garborg Club was dissolved after some years, the Norwegian Quartet Club became the most select society, Osland continues. In 1911 it merged with the Norwegian Club (Den Norske Klub), a social organization founded in Chicago in 1905 by young Norwegian technicians and engineers. A separate clubhouse was built on Logan Square, and it became the center of an elegant Norwegian social and cultural life.

In New York the Norwegian Club (Det Norske Selskab) came into being after engineers and architects had attempted to form a society in 1902. Two years later the club was started, and other professional groups were then included, but it was still an elite organization with social activities of many kinds. However, it also had as a purpose the promotion of Norwegian language and culture. The name *det norske selskab*—the Norwegian society—was used by groups in many Norwegian environments; the name comes from Det Norske Selskab (The Norwegian Society) in Copenhagen in the 1770s. That club was also nationalistic and elitist in its outlook.

The Norwegian Society in America

The most ambitious effort of all was the Norwegian Society in America (Det Norske Selskab i Amerika), formed in Minneapolis in January, 1903. The society set itself the goal of uniting all Norwegians in a national organization for the advancement of Norwegian culture on a broad front. The leaders of this program even attempted to place the *bygdelag* movement under the control of the society, which was then to function as an umbrella organization. The weight the society gave to the more refined national cultural expressions, especially in literature, prevented it, however, from gaining broad popular support. The Norwegian Society therefore remained an organization for academics and other intellectuals. Waldemar Ager was a major force in the society. A fund established in memory of Sigvald Quale (1890-1909) enabled Ager to arrange declamatory contests among young people in high schools and colleges. The Norwegian Society continued for many years to awaken young people's interest in Norwegian language and literature through these annual speech competitions which awarded medals as prizes.

Strong American Nativism during World War I

The world war called forth, the historian John Higham writes in his *Strangers in the Land*, "the most strenuous nationalism and the most pervasive nativism that the United States has known." The entire society became intolerant and demanded 100 percent support for America. Anything tasting of "hyphen-mentality" and emotional attachment to non-American cultures – German-American, Norwegian-American, or whatever – was challenged. America's quest for national solidarity gave rise to proscriptive legislation and active measures against non-English-speaking groups in the population. This represented an attempt to do away with everything that seemed foreign to English-speaking Americans. Actions intended to secure cultural uniformity had a decisive and destructive impact on the many immigrant cultures that were not of English origin, and they hastened the process of assimilation, even though scholars cannot agree on the extent of their effect.

The immigrant communities had from the beginning been received with a shifting attitude, moving from mild acceptance and fascination to condemnation and demands for restriction on immigration. This ambivalent view of the immigrants persisted throughout the first three-quarters of the nineteenth century. A generally friendly attitude had been altered by anti-Catholic crusades by nativistic groups in the 1830s and 1840s, and by the Know-Nothing party in the 1850s. The 1880s then heralded a long period of increasing xenophobia, though varying in intensity. From the 1890s on, the growing numbers of Jews and Catholics from eastern and southern Europe who came to America produced constant fear and intolerance. Prejudices were aggravated by economic bad times. Both the older American stock and established immigrant groups accused the newcomers of political radicalism, of creating social unrest, and of being a threat to American institutions. Some Norwegian Americans also harbored such suspicions. "The Norsemen have made basic contributions and have participated

During World War I the foreign-language press was subjected to suspicion and control. The artist P. J. Rosendahl drew this cartoon in defense of the press to show its bridge-building role between the immigrants and American society. The drawing appeared in the newspaper Fremtiden in St. Paul, Minnesota.

in the building of America," *Decorah-Posten* wrote in 1924, maintaining on the other hand that "South and East Europeans have come here to benefit from what already has been accomplished." The new immigrant groups, which mainly settled in America's cities, were held to be the cause of political corruption and of alcohol problems, and they were blamed when American workers feared that their standard of living would decline, since the new groups were thought to bring about lower wages for all laborers. There was in addition tension and suspicion between the different new immigrant groups, which also contributed to intolerance and prejudice.

Even though nativism during World War I most directly affected Americans of German origin, no ethnic group was spared. In May, 1918, the governor of Iowa, William L. Harding, issued a proclamation that prohibited the use of anything but the English language as a medium of instruction, in conversations in public places, over the telephone, in public addresses, and at church services. In at least fifteen states the governors introduced legislation to restrict the use of non-English languages to private religious meetings in the homes. Kristine Haugen wrote from Sioux City to accuse Governor Harding of wanting to "combat Prussianism in Europe and to practice it in the homeland." His famous proclamation was also denounced at the meeting of

the supreme lodge of the Sons of Norway in Great Falls, Montana. In a resolution sent to Governor Harding the assembly protested against "unwarranted and unlawful attempts to curtail the rights and liberties of free, loyal American citizens." Foreign-language newspapers were censored. N. A. Grevstad was assigned the responsibility for policing the Scandinavian-American press; the socialistic journal published by Emil L. Mengshoel, *Gaa Paa* (Forward), was among those suspended. Political radicalism was associated with disloyalty to American war objectives. American patriotism demanded unity in political as well as cultural expression.

In spite of protests from several quarters against infringements on civil rights, the immigrant communities made a great effort to display loyalty to the new homeland. They feared that they would arouse suspicion if they were lukewarm in their Americanism. The *bygdelag* published lists of names of young men from their ranks who served in the armed forces; churches adopted loyalty declarations. Gatherings in societies and lodges frequently became demonstrations of American patriotism. As long as the war lasted, there was little appreciation of the injustice that was done against American citizens of non-English origin. The prevailing fear in the American people of anything foreign allowed little room for argument.

Left: The Norse-American Centennial in 1925. The picture shows the crowds on Nicollet Avenue in Minneapolis following the grand Centennial parade. Above: A choir of children forms the Norwegian flag as it sings the Norwegian national anthem. The Centennial celebration was a magnificent undertaking. President Coolidge spoke on this occasion, and he gave his support to efforts to have Leiv Eiriksson recognized as the discoverer of America.

The Last Rally—an Ethnic Counterreaction

Anti-Catholic and antiforeign forces united in the Ku Klux Klan. After the war the secret order gained a large following. It also entered the prairie states, and in North Dakota, for instance, one finds Norwegian names in the leadership of the Klan. Anti-Catholic sentiments were strong, and the self-assertion of older immigrant groups against the more recent arrivals might manifest itself in racial and religious prejudice.

During the war Norwegian and other immigrant groups had experienced a downgrading and humiliation of their ancestral heritage and national background. They had been compelled to take a defensive position and endure disdain for their ethnic identity on the part of the dominant English-speaking group. It was therefore natural that a forceful reaction would express itself when freedom of speech and organization was restored. "We demand recognition as a part of the nation, and we will not tolerate being viewed as a flock of strange foreigners because we speak a language besides English," Knut Løkensgaard wrote in an article against discrimination. Spokesmen for cultural pluralism, like Waldemar Ager, O. E. Rølvaag, and others, introduced comprehensive efforts to unite and strengthen the Norwegian forces. In 1919 American xenophobia reached a new level under the influence of the "Red Scare," a hysterical antiradical nativism. As a kind of protest against the bigotry that swept the country, a new organization, For Fædrearven (For the Ancestral Heritage), was founded that year in Eau Claire. The name of the society carried a declaration of its purpose. Rølvaag became the leading person in this organization as long as it existed. When forces within the Norwegian Lutheran Church of America tried to remove "Norwegian" from its name, protest drives forced the church leaders to make a retreat. This victory is yet another example of the postwar reaction against onslaughts on Norsedom and the ancestral heritage.

The Norse-American Centennial

In 1925 Norwegian forces united around the celebration of the centennial of the first Norwegian immigration, the dramatic voyage of the sloop *Restauration* in 1825. The occasion provided a grand rallying point for the Norwegian-American organizations struggling to gain momentum and recapture some of the lost ground of the preceding years. Newcomers from Norway simultaneously gave renewed life to organizational growth and festivities. As in 1914, it was the *bygdelag*, under the direction of the Council of *Bygdelag*, that assumed responsibility for the Centennial celebration. There was also a separate women's group to present the contributions of Norwegian-American women, which had been overlooked in 1914.

The festivities lasted from June 6 to June 9, 1925, and as in 1914 the main celebration took place on the fairgrounds between Minneapolis and St. Paul. The affair attracted great interest, perhaps especially because President Calvin Coolidge would be present to honor the Norwegians' festival. This lent prestige to the undertaking and encouraged the participation of other dignitaries, Norwegian as well as American, with official representation from the Norwegian Church, cabinet, and Storting.

The high point of the celebration came on June 8. In the morning the Reverend John Atwater and his sister Jane, who were children of the "sloop baby," Margaret Larsen, born during the Atlantic crossing in 1825, spoke to the gathering.

The president was, of course, the main attraction. Calvin Coolidge spoke to an estimated 100,000 people at the open-air meeting on the fairgrounds. In his address he praised the Norwegians, reminded them of what good citizens they had become, and endorsed the claim that Leiv Eiriksson had been the first European to discover America. The message was well received, and an American journalist reported: "The great roar that rose from Nordic throats to Thor and Odin above the lowering gray clouds told that the pride of the race had been touched."

Norwegian ethnic enthusiasm was great.

From the Centennial pageant written for this occasion. 1,000 actors took part.

Among the many musical contributions, there was a children's chorus of five hundred voices that, while singing the two national anthems, formed the Norwegian and American flags. The following day the festivities were concluded by an impressive pageant centering on the life of the Civil War hero Colonel Hans Christian Heg, with one thousand actors in twenty-four scenes.

The grand festival was a magnificent expression of Norwegian ethnicity, and it was long recalled and spoken of by those who took part in it. But it did not place major emphasis on the concept of a lasting Norwegian-American subculture, as the 1914 celebration had done. Instead it underscored the primacy of adjustment and material progress. Most of the program was in English. People were apparently satisfied with having made a place for themselves in their new homeland; from simple immigrant circumstances they had moved toward integration and a privileged place in the nation. The festival was a nostalgic retrospective view. Many spoke warmly of what Norwegian Americans had achieved, but the prospects for a flourishing Norwegian-American culture were dim. The 1920s therefore represent a final mustering of strong Norwegian ethnic forces.

Americans—with Ties to Norway

Assimilation with American society has been an inevitable and natural development. Nevertheless, Norwegians in America cherish and celebrate their Norwegian origin. A consciousness of a common historical past and an ethnic bond between Norwegian Americans and their kinsfolk in Norway is still apparent, expressing itself in various forms of enthusiasm for things Norwegian.

Assimilation, an Inescapable Development

In the home, in organized work, in the church, in the neighborhood, and in publications of many kinds there is evidence of a strong will to preserve the national cultures. Scholars, who have been preoccupied with the process of assimilation, have frequently overlooked such countercurrents. Many immigrants eagerly guarded the homeland's speech and transferred it to children born in America. Riverda Harding Jordan found in 1921 that after a period of more than thirty years in America, Norwegian was still the language used in 19 percent of the Norwegian homes in Minneapolis and St. Paul.

The most striking feature of immigrant history is, however, social mobility—the gradual improvement of the immigrants' standard of living and social status. The change might at times be extremely slow; the second generation might live in much the same circumstances as the previous one. Social mobility in addition varied greatly from one nationality to another, depending on the possibilities that time and place provided. Internal ethnic conditions, cultural and religious factors that were peculiar to the group, were other determining influences. The historian Stephan Thernstrom has shown that in Boston occupational mobility was more rapid among Swedish immigrants than among either the Italians or the Irish, in spite of the fact that the latter were English-speaking. Thernstrom suggests that the Catholic background of both these groups had a greater bearing on their occupational adjustment than did their nationality. The Catholic Church stressed individual advancement less than many Protestant and Jewish groups did. Protestant or Jewish affiliation appears to have led to quicker improvement in social status, both among the immigrants themselves and among their American-born children. For most people, economic considerations had been the basis for

Norwegian Constitution Day in Seattle, Washington, 1982.

their decision to go to America. The idea of doing well was therefore impressed upon the second generation. But among the Catholics, personal ambition might to a certain extent be neutralized by family considerations. Upward mobility might take the children away from the home and, besides, early entrance into the work force was held to be important. Education thus had little intrinsic value. Thernstrom suggests that the Catholic parochial schools were not able to instill personal aspirations: the church set boundaries for the individual. On the other hand, the school became a significant road to social progress for Jewish immigrants. In Boston Thernstrom found that 75 percent of the children of East European Jews had moved from the laboring class into the middle class, a higher percentage than for any other nationality.

Social advancement was a part of the process of assimilation. Individual choice of occupation and social progress gradually became acceptable also to the descendants of Catholic immigrants. Especially from the 1920s, with a rapid improvement in communications, radio, and film, and a strong emphasis on American nationalism in the schools and in public debate, ethnic differ-

In the 1920s American nationalism greatly affected public education and debate; it encouraged the dissolution of ethnic boundaries. The photograph shows a group of immigrants taking the oath of citizenship around 1925."Here you stand, good folk, think I, when I see them at Ellis Island, here you stand in your fifty groups, with your fifty languages and histories, and your fifty blood hatreds and rivalries. But you won't be long like that, brothers, for these are the fires of God. A fig for your feuds and vendettas! Germans and Frenchmen, Irishmen and Englishmen, Jews and Russians—into the Crucible with you all! God is making the American." (Israel Zangwill, The Melting Pot, 1908.)

ences became less visible. Personal advancement loosened the bonds that tied a person to a specific ethnic group and produced an adjustment to the norms established by the dominant society. American biases, which made anything foreign seem suspect, stimulated the new generations to escape into the American environment.

The Immigrants' Alternatives

There were three different ideas about how the immigrants should adjust to American society. The "melting pot" theory held that the immigrants should face the new society by mixing with other immigrant groups and with the older American population in order to bring forth a new type of citizen. For the historian Frederick Jackson Turner, the frontier, the vast uninhabited region, was the gigantic melting pot that would transform the immigrants and produce a common and unique American civilization. Americanization, letting oneself be assimilated as quickly as possible into the large society, was the second alternative. Groups and individuals, often with the best interests of the immigrants in mind, worked to teach the newcomers American ways, to persuade them to abandon their ethnic cultural identity and acquire an American one. Implicit in their activity was the notion that there existed a separate definable American culture that was superior to the culture the immigrants represented. Cultural pluralists, frequently idealists within the ethnic communities, spoke for yet another possibility. They advocated preserving as much as possible of the culture of the old country. They wished to maintain ethnic subcultures in America. Only by honoring one's own cultural background and not discarding it as inferior, they claimed, could the immigrants retain their self-respect, become useful citizens, and contribute to an evolving American culture.

From the day the immigrants stepped onto American soil, however, they faced the inevitable demand to adjust and to lay aside some of the old culture. For many people it was a painful process. Most of the immigrants could speak from experience about their "dog years" in America — the early period of hard physical labor on the lowest rung of the social ladder, in agriculture, in railroad construction, in the mines, and in the forests. Many Scandinavian women worked as domestic servants in the homes of others. Here they came into close contact with Americans; they learned American ideas about housework and conventional American middle-class gentility. "By the time they were married — usually to Scandinavian men — they had become convinced apostles of Americanism," writes H. Arnold Barton in an article on this topic. Men, of course,

It was especially the women who preserved traditional skills and maintained customs and traditions of Norwegian origin. In this photograph from 1921 Barbro Hegdahl is showing her granddaughter Lillian Seljevoll the art of spinning.

also learned new ways and developed new loyalties in their work. With an improved economic position the "dog years" came to an end. But these years were a period of learning and an experience the immigrants viewed in retrospect as essential. Even though the immigrants did not renounce all aspects of their cultural background, the will to adjust was obvious. It revealed itself, among other things, in name-changes, an Americanization that would ease the relationship with the English-speaking majority. As Einar Haugen has shown, the farm name Seim — used as a proper name — might become Sime, Ris changed to Reese, and Strøm to Strum. Greater alterations occurred when Skau became Scow or Skjelderup became Sheldrew. Some people translated the name directly, for instance from Bjørkehaugen to Birchill, and from Brarik to Goodrich.

What Is an Ethnic Group?

The question then becomes to what extent one can speak of an ethnic group. In other words,

what is an ethnic subculture and who can be said to belong to it? Is national background sufficient basis for determining ethnic attachment? How far can one go in the process of assimilation before a sense of ethnic solidarity is lost? The sociologist Orlando Patterson defines an ethnic subculture as a cultural group that provides its members with their primary identity outside the family. When this loyalty conflicts with other interests, occupational considerations, or social class, the ethnic identity is weakened. Norwegian-American newspapers commonly noted it as praiseworthy that a man had not lost interest in his Norwegian heritage in spite of great success in America. He was in this respect an exception to the rule. The need to develop new loyalties outside the ethnic group thus varied from individual to individual. The ethnologist Milton M. Gordon sees assimilation in two stages: a cultural assimilation, or acculturation, where one moves toward the goal of mastering the cultural pattern of the host society; and a structural assimilation, or complete integration, which manifests itself in membership in social organizations, friendship circles, and intermarriage.

The cultural heritage of the old country, Norwegian language, Norwegian dishes, customs, and traditions, was usually preserved and cherished in the home by the women. Their traditional role was as carriers of culture, but circumstances might also cast them in the role of Americanizers. The degree of contact with the larger society was decisive. Both patterns of settlement and congregational life isolated and delimited the local community; this contributed to a maintenance of familiar cultural modes. In many cases Norwegian was used only in the church. As long as Norwegian was the language of religious worship, church membership might segregate Norwegians. The cultural conflict that existed with the host society was gradually resolved by a weakening of ethnic consciousness and the dissolution of a separate Norwegian-American subculture. The inescapable development was an absorption into mainstream American society. Social mobility became the most effective factor in this process. The Norwegian-American people can hardly be described any longer as an ethnic group, according to Orlando Patterson's definition. However, attitudes, norms, and values associated with a specific national and religious tradition still exist. It is also important to bear in mind that to be "American" is to a certain extent to be "ethnic." It is a part of American self-definition to be a nation of immigrants. Norwegian cultural expressions and Norwegian symbols are therefore persistent and visible aspects of American life.

In Search of the American Dream

Social mobility within the Norwegian-American population may be studied by consulting the federal census reports. The statistical information these give is summarized and analyzed by E. P. Hutchinson in *Immigrants and Their Children, 1850-1950.*

The great waves of immigration after 1880 had the consequence that in 1910 immigrants of all nationalities and their children accounted for an impressive 45 percent of the total American labor force. "Each of the many immigrant peoples," writes Hutchinson, "contributed to their adoptive land a collection of native and learned skills." They found their separate niche in the economic life, with specialization in distinct lines of work, and frequently had a unique occupational distribution. The second generation, however, did not as a rule follow the occupational concentration of their parents but became integrated into the labor force in general. The American-born Norwegians, Dutch, and Swiss, however, form an exception; they continued, like their parents, to prefer work in farming.

Occupational Distribution and Integration of Norwegian Men

From 1880 to 1890 the number of employed men from Sweden and Norway more than doubled. In 1890 most of these men were still employed in agriculture, but there was a clear tendency toward owning a farm rather than working as farm laborers. Those in fishing are included as a subcategory to farming. With the growth of American industry came an increase in employment in that sector, especially in the building trade. Not

Top: Workers at the Wm. Lindeke Roller Mills in St. Paul, photographed at the mill around 1900. Many Norwegian men found employment in the flour mills in the Twin Cities.

Bottom: Many Norwegian women were seamstresses. This is a fashionable dressmaking shop in Minneapolis in 1890.

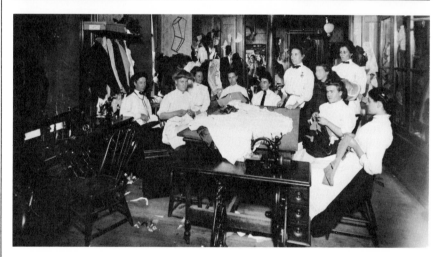

many Norwegian men entered the field of transportation, although there were a number of seamen. A large group were occupied in commerce and clerical work, and the number of engineers and architects increased rapidly. During the same decade there was a doubling of pastors, lawyers, and men in public service.

Further changes can be suggested by looking at the occupational picture in 1950. Norwegians, of both the first and the second generation, still revealed a strong preference for farming. Men born in Norway were overrepresented in construction work. In the second generation, however, there was little occupational concentration

outside the agricultural sector. The sons of the immigrants were distributed over all occupations. Many more of them than their fathers had professional training. The number of unskilled workers was diminishing. Viewed as a whole, the advances in social status are striking. A gradual entrance into the middle class was occurring.

The Position of Women

Industrialization and the growth of cities increasingly created new employment opportunities for women as well. In the course of the nineteenth

Both men and women worked in the woolen mills. This was a strenuous form of labor, with many hazards, low pay, and a long working day. Statistics indicate that relatively few Norwegian women sought employment in factories, in contrast to the number of women from southern and eastern Europe. The photograph is from North Star Woolen Mills in Minneapolis about 1905.

century higher education became accessible to women and opened up new possibilities for them in the professions. Women were well represented in occupations offered by telephone and telegraph companies, and they became teachers and nurses and found employment in offices and in commerce. Gradually they also began to move into specialized professions. Women became more independent and self-confident as they became less dependent for support on a father or a husband.

For a young single woman, the resolve to emigrate might in itself be seen as a feminist statement, a declaration of independence. The U.S. census for 1880 indicates, however, that Norwegian women who worked outside the home were mainly employed in domestic and personal services. As previously stated, this continued to be the major occupation for these women and for their daughters born in America. But the picture changed gradually. It was, of course, the immigrant daughters who could best take advantage

of the various possibilities; in comparison to the immigrant generation, they had made great progress in skilled occupations by 1900. Immigrant women from Eastern and Southern Europe were much more likely to enter American industry than Scandinavian women. In the decades after 1900 Scandinavian women continued to work in agriculture and in different forms of domestic service. But the second generation showed a gradual occupational mobility, and women of this generation moved toward integration into American economic life.

Norwegian Americans Made Good in America

As early as 1925 O. M. Norlie assumed, without substantial evidence, that the distribution of Norwegians in the specialized professions was proportionate to their share of the American population—in other words, that a complete integration had occurred at all occupational levels. Even though his calculations are indefensible, it is a significant fact that education provided quick improvement in social status and moved many people from poor immigrant circumstances to relative prosperity.

Immigrants who upon arrival possessed university training in professions that could be practiced in America had an enormous advantage over those who were not so well prepared. In *Saga in Steel and Concrete*, Kenneth O. Bjork depicts

such an elite among the immigrants, consisting of young men with technical training from Norwegian institutions. They were attracted to America by its insatiable need for technical expertise in the rapidly expanding fields of transportation, mining, and construction.

The great cities demanded bridges, tunnels, subways, and skyscrapers. New York provided employment and challenging tasks for many Norwegian engineers. Ole Singstad, educated at the technical university in Trondheim, was a specialist in tunnel construction; as the chief engineer he designed the Holland Tunnel under the Hudson River. This special tunnel to carry the automobile had an advanced system of ventilation and was completed in 1926 as the first of its kind. Olaf Hoff, who emigrated from Østfold in 1879, gained fame for his sunken-tube method of tunneling and developed time- and labor-saving methods that later were adopted by American engineers.

In Chicago Joachim Giaever, who emigrated in 1882, was assistant chief engineer for the 1893 Chicago World's Fair; his consulting firm also made significant contributions to skyscraper development. Giaever was active in the Norwegian colony and for many years was president of the Norwegian Club. In the 1890s a brilliant Norwegian-educated chemical engineer, E. A. Cappelen-Smith, came to Chicago. In time he became co-owner and director of the world-renowned engineering firm Guggenheim Brothers in New York.

Tinius Olsen from Kongsberg developed new machines to test the quality of different materials and industrial products. In 1869, at age twenty-four, he came to Philadelphia, where he founded the firm that in time became the largest commercial testing company in America. In the Middle West, Magnus Swenson of Madison, born in Larvik, Norway, and trained as a chemical engineer in America, became known as an inventor in the sugar-refining industry.

Several of those who made contributions to American industry were self-taught men. Ole Evinrude, or Eivindrud, was born in Toten, Norway, but grew up on a farm in Wisconsin. He worked as an apprentice in an agricultural machine shop in Madison, and in 1901 he constructed an outboard motor for boats. Later, in an improved version, it was marketed under the

Ole Singstad from Lensvik in South Trøndelag designed the Queens Midtown Tunnel, which is seen here. This automobile tunnel was completed in 1940. Singstad was also responsible for the Holland Tunnel, finished in 1926, and the Brooklyn-Battery Tunnel, opened in 1940.

Norwegian-born engineers established a reputation in the construction of large buildings. To the right is the Woolworth building in New York, which was completed in 1913 and gained recognition at a time when the skyscraper technique was developing. The engineers responsible for this technical feat were Gunvald Aus from Haugesund and Kort Berle from Halden. The Wabash Avenue Bridge across the Chicago River (below) is one of the 56 bridges that Thomas G. Pihlfeldt, originally from Vadsø, built as chief engineer of bridges from 1901 until 1940.

Below: Telephone and telegraph provided new employment opportunities for women. This telephone operator from Washington Island, Wisconsin, is Jossie (Josephine) Jepson, whose mother was Norwegian and father Danish (1906).

company name Evinrude. Nelson Olson Nelson had little contact with the Norwegian-American community. He lived his life among Americans and from 1877 he built up in St. Louis one of the largest companies in the world for the manufacture of building and plumbing supplies.

Production of Agricultural Machinery

Norwegians' heavy involvement in farming and agricultural production called upon inventiveness and enterprise; Norwegians built shops to make plows and factories for the production of more sophisticated farm machinery and implements. Targe G. Mandt from Telemark, who had learned the blacksmith trade in his father's smithy on their farm in Dane county, Wisconsin, constructed the well-known Stoughton wagon, a farm wagon that was much used in the Middle West in the decades after the Civil War.

From Telemark John A. Johnson emigrated with his parents in the 1840s. He was then twelve years old. In 1899 Johnson founded the Gisholt

203

Evinrude is today a worldwide trademark for outboard motors. This is the man behind the name, Ole Evinrude (1877-1934). The original form is Eivindrud, which is the name of a farm in Toten, where he was born. Evinrude grew up on a farm in Wisconsin. His own motor construction was in time mass-produced.

Machine Company for the production of agricultural equipment. He grew up in Wisconsin among Norwegian immigrants and contributed to Norwegian magazines and newspapers, among them *Billed-Magazin*. In later years, however, Johnson became very critical of Norwegian Americans who held on to their old cultural identity instead of becoming assimilated.

White-Collar Workers

Norwegians also founded banks. They frequently began modestly by selling foreign bank notes and steamship tickets. In Minneapolis in 1870, for instance, Rambusch & Christensen announced that "we sell notes on the best banks in Norway, Sweden, and Denmark at the lowest prices." They transferred money to Scandinavian countries and served as agent for several steamship companies.

In bookkeeping and accounting positions Norwegians were well represented. The census of 1950 actually shows a certain concentration of second-generation Norwegian men in this line of work. Some went further. Arthur Andersen, born in Illinois in 1885, was professor of accounting and auditing at Northwestern University and founded in Chicago the nationally known firm that bears his name.

Victor F. Lawson, the son of Ivar Lawson who

had cooperated with John Anderson in founding *Skandinaven* in 1866, became famous as publisher of the *Chicago Daily News*. He followed a cautious and conservative editorial line and has been called "the dean among American newspapermen." Farther west, in Madison, William Evjue gained recognition and influence as editor of the progressive and reform-minded *Madison Capital Times*.

Long lists of persons who achieved eminence in their professions can be set up without difficulty. Ethnic groups actually competed to make the longest ones; these would show which nationality had contributed most to the building of the new land, and would perhaps simultaneously gain the approval of the host society. O. M. Norlie's cataloglike history of the Norwegian-American people, published in 1925, is a good example. It is Norway's claim to historic greatness in immigrant circumstances that is set forth there.

Political office was an avenue to rapid advancement. The candidates frequently owed their success to the support of their own compatriots. Special talents in athletics or the arts made it possible to escape poverty and pursue a successful career. Olive Fremstad, for example, was from 1903 until 1914 a celebrated singer at the Metropolitan Opera in New York. But for Norwegians, as for other ethnic groups, success in these fields has been the exception rather than the rule. Most Norwegian Americans sought respectability in the middle class and security through its occupations. Relatively few really excelled in a larger context. They functioned, for the most part, in intermediate positions. Great industrialists and capitalists were extremely rare among the immigrants, as well as among their children.

Few Great Capitalists

Scholars have pondered why Norwegian Americans have asserted themselves only to an insignificant degree as financiers and masters of industry. Both Leola Nelson Bergmann and Jon Wefald point to a strong sense of solidarity and communal spirit as explanatory factors. Norwegians avoided capitalistic and speculative ventures and revealed a certain distrust of the power of money. This same attitude might also make them reform-minded. In addition, they lacked the ambition that marked Yankee capitalists. Wefald suggests that the Lutheran belief in justification by faith supported an egalitarian view. This situation was perhaps most evident in the pietistic low-church congregations, where the fellowship in the church was considered sufficient. The Calvinistic concept of "the elect of God," which promoted the principle of competition, was missing in the Lutheran congregations.

W. Lloyd Warner, in his investigation of Norwegians in Illinois, also emphasizes the strong

Right: Norwegian-American farmers in Dane county in Wisconsin gathered around the latest in plowing implements. The photograph was taken in the mid-1870s. These farmers subscribed to Norwegian-American newspapers, which carried notices and articles about agricultural tools and machinery. Norwegians were also producers of modern farm implements and owned machine shops and factories.

This photograph from Milwaukee Avenue in Chicago in 1890 shows the offices of the newspaper Norden, *the Scandinavian bookstore (Skandinavisk bokhandel), and a bank in the same building.*

Norwegians in Academic Professions

Thorstein Veblen was the most original thinker among Norwegians in America; the economist John Kenneth Galbraith, among others, considers him to be one of the great philosophers and social critics of the last hundred years. His unorthodox ideas separated him sharply from his contemporaries. Veblen's merciless treatment of the life-style of the wealthy in his main work, *Theory of the Leisure Class* (1899), was a refreshing contribution to American social debate, and it had considerable influence. Veblen has been called the spiritual father of the New Deal.

Some Norwegian Americans gained recognition and success in artistic careers. This is Olive Fremstad (1868-1951), an internationally renowned Wagnerian opera singer, in her starring role as Isolde, New York, 1913. Olive Fremstad emigrated from Oslo to St. Peter, Minnesota, at the age of 12.

communal spirit among Norwegians and their reluctance to regard social advancement as a goal in itself. Wefald in addition called attention to the fact that Norwegian-American industrialists disclosed a similar attitude by introducing cooperative practices with their employees. Both John A. Johnson and Haakon Romnes, who advanced from lineman to president of the giant A.T.&T. in 1965, adopted reforms beneficial to the workers. Nelson Olson Nelson was perhaps the one among Norwegian industrialists who best realized "the American dream"; he became the kind of hero the American novelist Horatio Alger has immortalized. But still he rejected cold capitalistic principles and provided his workers with profit-sharing programs and joint ownership plans.

Norwegians strongly endorsed the principle of equality, and many of them rejected American materialism. This attitude was strengthened by the Lutheran ethic of renouncing worldly pleasures. Perhaps it is against such a background that one can best understand the social criticism of Thorstein Veblen, his attacks on "conspicuous consumption" and the corrupting greed for wealth. Veblen remained somewhat outside the Norwegian-American community and opposed Lutheranism and the clergy. But still he was a product of this subculture and affected by its values and beliefs.

Thorstein Veblen (1857-1929) has been called the spiritual father of the New Deal. He was probably the most original thinker among Norwegians in America. Whereas his brother Andrew Veblen became a leader in the bygdelag *movement, Thorstein Veblen kept aloof from the Norwegian-American community. The photograph was taken ca. 1907.*

But as a group, Laurence M. Larson lamented in 1937, Norwegian Americans had not distinguished themselves intellectually. (Larson himself was an eminent scholar.) The Norwegian people in America had been a peasant folk in transition; their intellectual horizon had been limited to the church. Norwegian Americans had therefore been unable up to that time to produce men and women who gained fame in the scientific world. Larson, however, viewed the future with confidence. Thousands of young people were being admitted to institutions of higher learning, and it was possible already to find some outstanding Norwegian-American scholars. In 1931 John A. Hofstead made a list of nearly four hundred women and men who taught or had taught at American colleges and universities. In addition, there were those positions that were gradually being generated by Norwegian-American colleges.

Larson went on to praise academics who in his opinion were especially deserving. He mentioned the mathematician Oswald Veblen at Princeton University, Thorstein Veblen's nephew, and the well-known physician Ludvig Hektoen at the University of Chicago. He might well have included Ingeborg Rasmussen who, after completing her training in 1892, practiced medicine in Chicago. At the college of dentistry in the University of Minnesota Alfred Owre contributed to the field, and at the same university Owen H. Wangensteen distinguished himself as a surgeon and scholar. Larson also listed the well-known Norwegian-American astronomer John August Anderson and the historian Theodore C. Blegen. In the first edition of *Who's Who in America*, in 1899, only a dozen Norwegian names had been deemed worthy of inclusion, and of these only Rasmus B. Anderson was a productive scholar and author.

Norwegian as an Academic Subject

Anderson worked to make Norwegian especially, and Scandinavian language and culture in general, a university subject in American institutions. Such an endeavor would be of greater interest to the Norwegian-American community than the academic careers of individual persons, though the immigrant press did inform its readers of compatriots who had been a credit to their nationality in the field of scholarship. In 1869 efforts to establish a Scandinavian Department at the University of Wisconsin in Madison succeeded. It was the first one in America, and Anderson was appointed professor. In 1884 he was succeeded by Julius E. Olson, and the third holder of the position was the eminent linguist Einar Haugen, later professor at Harvard. George T. Flom, who also was a well-known philologist, taught at the University of Illinois from 1909. Olaus J. Breda in 1884 filled a professorship in Scandinavian at the University of Minnesota. Norwegians in North Dakota went a step further and, showing their political clout, in 1889 were able to insert into the state constitution a clause guaranteeing that the state university at Grand Forks would offer in perpetuity instruction in Norwegian, "the Scandinavian language," as the law defines it. In 1891 a professorship in Norwegian was established. Right before World War I, students at eight universities and nine colleges in the United States could study Norwegian; every year approximately five hundred students took advantage of this offer. In 1911 professional students of Scandinavian founded their own organization, the Society for the Advancement of Scandinavian Study.

The outstanding American linguist Einar Haugen was born of Norwegian parents in Iowa in 1906. Now retired, he was from 1964 Professor of Scandinavian languages at Harvard University, and he has been especially concerned with Norwegian linguistic developments and the Norwegian language in America.

Americanization of the Immigrants' Institutions

Instruction in Norwegian Expands

The campaign to introduce Norwegian and Swedish into the American educational system intensified just before World War I. This demand indicated a strengthened ethnic self-consciousness. As a result of their work, instruction in Scandinavian languages increased from offerings at five high schools in 1910 to twenty-eight four years later. The expansion took place mainly in the two states of North Dakota and Minnesota; in 1914, 1,190 students in high schools received instruction in either Swedish or Norwegian. Some primary schools also offered instruction. According to an incomplete report, Norwegian was taught at 103 primary schools in Minnesota during the school year 1913-14. J. N. Lenker, who was a champion of foreign-language study, claimed that the introduction of Norwegian into the public school curriculum had encouraged greater interest in the study of language in the Lutheran congregational schools during the summer months. Since pioneer days these schools had given the immigrant children a rudimentary knowledge of Norwegian language and culture in addition to their religious instruction. What was occurring was an inspiration to everyone who dreamed and spoke of a culturally pluralistic America. The magazine *Ungdommens Ven* (The Friend of Youth) in Minneapolis characterized developments as a triumphal march for the Norwegian language.

Difficulties in Preserving an Ethnic Culture

The flourishing activities in a Norwegian America during the period before World War I obviously proved all predictions of early assimilation to be false. It had surprised Ole Munch Ræder as early as 1847 how rapidly his compatriots in America learned English and how quickly they forgot their mother tongue. He thought developments here were analogous to what had happened in the Norse settlement of Normandy during the Viking Age. The pioneer pastor and presi-

dent of Luther College, Laur. Larsen, expressed the opinion in 1857 that the fusion of Norwegians into American society would soon be completed. The industrialist John A. Johnson predicted that by 1900 it would be impossible to distinguish Scandinavian students from American ones at the universities. But they had not considered sufficiently the strength of ethnocentric forces; they could not, of course, have foreseen that the Norwegian impulse would in addition be reinforced by large new waves of immigrants.

Expectations of a permanent Norwegian-American subculture were, however, unrealistic. The ancestral heritage people, those who worked for Norsedom and had faith in its future in America, can best be described as voices in the wilderness. The immigrants themselves for the most part, if they reflected on the problem, considered integration to be natural and inescapble. On the other hand, they had not supposed that settlement in America would oblige them to give up the life-style and cultural identity they had brought with them from Norway. The emigration experience actually fortified the wish to retain specific aspects of the old life. The immigrants lived a natural ethnic existence, and they took it for granted that it should be so. At the same time the American environment intruded into their lives. In politics and in the workplace new loyalties were created, perhaps across national lines. The changes thereby weakened a separate ethnic life-style. Not even the immigrants' two most important institutions, the church and the press, can have regarded the preservation of an ethnic culture as a major purpose. Carl H. Chrislock has made the interesting observation that the Lutheran Church was, however, paradoxically, more ethnic in 1900 than fifty years earlier. By then it had moved away both from Scandinavian cooperation and from the older American Lutheran churches.

Americanization of the Lutheran Church

The Americanization of the Lutheran Church proceeded rapidly following the great union in 1917 that created the Norwegian Lutheran Church in America. The start can, of course, be traced to the very transition from a state-church principle to the establishment of a church within the American free-church tradition. Develop-

ments can be followed by looking at the change-over to the English language. Furthermore, Americanization reveals itself in an increasing contact with broad Lutheran cooperative endeavors and with other denominations. There is also a new openness to theological reevaluation, and the earlier confessionalism is slowly weakened.

The Lutheran Church among the immigrants gradually lost its strong rural orientation, and its influence was no longer limited to the Middle West. The transition to English reflected a wish to minister to an English-speaking generation, to exercise its mission among the young. An American-born generation of pastors appeared on the scene and demanded greater emphasis on the so-called English work. Between the English work and the Norwegian work, tension and controversy inevitably arose. In the different Lutheran synods the percentage of services in English increased from *none* in 1900 to 22 percent in 1915. Of the young in Sunday school and confirmation classes in 1915, 27 percent received their instruction in English. A difficult transitional period ensued. Pastors trained to preach in Norwegian had to adjust to English as the language of the church. To begin with, there was usually one service in English per month. Young people might be amused to hear the old parson struggle through a sermon in English. He preached with a heavy Norwegian accent and made strange blunders that were quoted and produced merriment at the expense of the pastor. One pastor who could not immediately remember how to ask the congregation in English to remain standing until the end of the service announced with great solemnity: "And the audience will be standing till we all pass away." One man who could not help himself whispered to the person next to him: "That could take a long time."

In 1912 the president of the United Church, T. H. Dahl, had realized what direction developments were taking, and in his annual report he encouraged greater concern for the English work and the appointment of English-speaking ministers in the congregations. At the time of the union in 1917, all three synods disclosed similar tendencies, although the number of services in Norwegian varied from 83 percent in Hauge's Synod to 72 percent in the Norwegian Synod. The intolerance and agitation for "100 percent Americanism" during World War I resulted, as

Einar Haugen has shown, in 9,000 services in the Norwegian Lutheran churches being changed from Norwegian to English in the course of only one year, a reduction from 73.1 to 62.2 percent. This was in 1918. The reduction in Norwegian services thereafter followed the death rate in the older generation, and in 1925 there were approximately an equal number of services in the two languages. The loss of Norwegian was naturally greatest in the cities and least in the remote and compact Norwegian farm communities. It is evident that an English-speaking generation had emerged, and in the 1930s all attempts to give young people religious instruction in Norwegian were abandoned in the congregations. Toward the end of World War II less than 7 percent of all services in the Lutheran churches were conducted in Norwegian.

Ethnic identity was tied to the language. When Norwegian was no longer used in the churches, a national Norwegian separatism was also lost. The change to English in addition opened the way for mission work among immigrants other than Norwegians, facilitated cooperation with other denominations, and promoted closer relations with American Protestantism. The church lost its Lutheran fundamentalism and was pulled into a more liberal Lutheran theology. The Norwegian Lutheran Church in America dropped "Norwegian" from its name in 1946. In 1960 it united with German and Danish Lutherans to form the American Lutheran Church. Three years later the Lutheran Free Church joined. The new church organization has displayed an ecumenical position and a will to unite all American Lutherans into one religious body. Norwegian-American religious life has thus become completely integrated, but many congregations still maintain old traditions. Norwegian inscriptions on pulpit and church bell are lasting reminders of the Norwegian attachment.

Norwegian Language in Secular Organizations

The church could, of course, give its message as easily in English as in Norwegian. There were, however, in the Norwegian-American community divided opinions about the role of the language in other connections. A debate was carried on about how much of Norwegian cultural identity could be preserved if the language disappeared.

The idealist Waldemar Ager thought that everything would be lost if the Norwegian language was no longer spoken in America. As the prime mover in the Norwegian Society, he therefore made the preservation of the Norwegian language the main cause. Sons of Norway was concerned with the same problem. In 1914 the order rejected the notion of English-speaking lodges, for it was feared that they would thwart efforts to promote Norsedom. A recommendation to accept such lodges was voted down also in 1918. That year, however, under the pressure of wartime hysteria, the brotherhood approved English-speaking lodges in principle, and from 1919 they became a reality. In 1942 all official reports from Sons of Norway were written in English, and in 1943 the order's official periodical was given the English name *Sons of Norway* (since November, 1963, *The Viking*). Sons of Norway was obviously not dependent on Norwegian in the conduct of its business and in its social functions. The individual lodges could continue to use Norwegian, and did so in many instances, at least in some types of entertainment.

It is the *bygdelag* that retained Norwegian longest in their publications and in their meetings. Not until the 1950s did a gradual transition to English occur. The diminishing number who visited the annual reunions belonged mainly to the older generation of immigrants. There was little desire for change among them. To the contrary, the will to keep the *stevne* the same was a strong force in the preservation of the *bygdelag* idea. Even though there was much talk about reaching the young people, the *bygdelag*, unlike the Sons of Norway and the Lutheran Church, did not try to adjust to the taste of the American-born generations. Hallinglaget still prints much of the material in its magazine *Hallingen* in Norwegian, and Nordlandslaget does the same in *Nord-Norge*. These are the two *bygdelag* magazines from the early years of the movement that are alive today. Valdres Samband has issued *Budstikken* in English since 1970.

A Tenacious Norwegian-American Press

It was not possible for the immigrant newspapers to continue without a sufficient Norwegian-speaking public to write for. These newspapers could not be replaced with publications in English. There had been early attempts to reach young people of Norwegian descent through periodicals in English, such as *Scandinavia* in Chicago from 1883, and *The North* in Minneapolis from 1889, but these efforts had failed. The publications were too special and could not compete with the more attractive and colorful American magazines.

Norwegian-language newspapers, including church publications, came out as long as they found sufficient support. The most successful kept going by acquiring the subscription lists of discontinued newspapers. *Decorah-Posten* had more than 4,000 subscribers at the time of its demise in 1972; it had absorbed *Normanden* in 1954, *Skandinaven* in 1941, *Minneapolis Tidende* in 1935, and several other newspapers. It can be said that the last voice of an older immigrant tradition was silenced when *Decorah-Posten* was discontinued. The newspaper's distribution in the Middle West more or less identified those who were in tune with the immigrant culture that had prospered among Norwegians in America. The fact that the newspaper folded indicated the weakened position of this culture. As editor of this journal, Kristian Prestgard had previously said accurately of the immigrant press that "when it ceases, it will cease of itself just as quietly as it came into being."

Nordisk Tidende, still published in Brooklyn, may be viewed as a voice for the most recent immigrants. In linguistic form as well as layout it is unlike the newspapers that came out in the Middle West. On the West Coast *Western Viking* is published in Seattle and *Norrøna* in Vancouver, British Columbia. Perhaps their most important function is to serve as announcement sheets for Norwegian-American organizations. *Western Viking* in addition embodies features of both *Decorah-Posten* and *Washington-Posten*, being a direct continuation of the latter weekly. In Chicago yet another attempt is being made to put out an English-language newspaper, *Vinland*. One of its purposes is to interest coming generations of Norwegian Americans in their immigrant background.

The Need to Preserve Memories of the Immigrants

With the sudden and steep decline in immigration from 1930 on, a Norwegian-American subculture was doomed. It could have survived only by infusions of new contingents of immigrants who would give life and content to organizations and institutions. Another possibility might have been a massive transfer of cultural interests to the descendants of the immigrants. This did not occur. The flight into the larger society persisted. The 1930s therefore stand as a break, a decisive generational change, where the immigrant generation passed away without their descendants taking up to any appreciable extent the work that earlier in the century had borne such rich fruit. The aging generation of immigrants deplored the loss of accustomed practices in the church and in secular connections. It had a strong sense that an era was approaching its end.

The Norwegian-American Historical Association

Written evidence could be preserved to tell coming generations about the Norwegian people in America, and strong interest in the past was associated with the collection of pioneer history by the *bygdelag*. This work gave hope that a folk literature like the one created in Norway by P. C. Asbjørnsen and Jørgen Moe more than half a century before could evolve in America. The founding of state and local societies reflected a need to record and understand what had gone before.

Inspired by the Slooper anniversary in 1925, a group of people convened at St. Olaf College, and on October 6, 1925, they organized the Norwegian-American Historical Association. A longtime dream was thereby realized. As managing editor, Theodore C. Blegen became a dominant force in the new learned society. The association took it upon itself to collect and write the history of the immigrants, free it from church influence and from an exaggerated piety toward the immi-

grant forebears, and work at a high scholarly and artistic level. The Historical Association was headed by professional historians, and it was the first completely professional historical society founded by any immigrant group. Nearly seventy volumes have so far been published. With some justification, it can be claimed that no immigrant people possesses a richer body of information about its period in America than the Norwegian Americans. Prominent persons with cultural interests, such as the businessmen Magnus Swenson and Arthur Andersen, have been presidents of the association. The current president, Lawrence O. Hauge, is a well-known businessman in Minneapolis and an enthusiastic promoter of Norwegian-American affairs.

Vesterheim, the Norwegian-American Museum

The centennial enthusiasm also resulted in a permanent Norwegian-American museum in Decorah. The museum had been started in 1877 at Luther College, and after 1925 Knut Gjerset became a driving force. He was responsible for an exhibit in twenty-two sections at the Slooper celebration. The displays had such headings as pioneer life, church, school, agriculture, women's arts and crafts, and Norwegian Americans in the world war. This exhibition of artifacts and photographs was a valuable stimulus to the further development of the museum collection.

The development of the museum according to professional standards and guidelines has since 1965 been led by Marion Nelson, professor of art history at the University of Minnesota. Under the name Vesterheim (The Home in the West), the Norwegian-American Museum has become a modern institution with a large collection of objects and an open-air museum. Financial support has come from interested Norwegian Americans. In Seattle there has in recent years been an effort to build a similar collection, but on a broader Scandinavian basis, by the Nordic Heritage Museum.

For determined cultural pluralists in the 1920s, both the museum in Decorah and the historical society were disturbing signs of the demise of Norsedom. They indicated for some that an active Norwegian America would be no more. The

Lawrence O. Hauge, the current president of the Norwegian-American Historical Association. The association was established in 1925 as the first completely professional historical society organized by an immigrant group in America.

memories of it could only be collected and viewed in a museum or be surrendered to the historians.

"Relief for Norway" and for Norwegians in America

Ethnic groups pull together during difficult times; then a sense of kinship and a feeling of mutual responsibility arise with renewed strength. Collections of money to assist newcomers in straitened circumstances and mutual aid societies are expressions of such concerns.

The Great Depression of the 1930s thus brought people of a common national background together. At a time when the process of assimilation was gaining added speed, this circumstance was a counterweight. A consequence was increased ethnic activity. *Skandinaven* reported in 1931 great support for "the charity bazaar in Logan Square Masonic Temple" in Chicago, and *Nordisk Tidende* told readers under the heading "How long will the need last?" that in New York there were in 1931 "at least 800 Norwegian families who now find themselves in a desperate situation." Collections, bazaars, concerts, and theater performances to give aid to the needy produced increased unity and activity in the Norwegian colonies.

Reports of disasters and need in Norway had a similar effect. Collection drives and assistance programs of various kinds were started without delay. "The ruins after the Ålesund fire were still smoking when Norwegians over here began to collect money," Waldemar Ager claimed. Aside from the help given following this destructive fire in 1904, there were numerous other actions. An especially strong impression was made by the natural catastrophes in Loen, where mountain avalanches both in 1905 and in 1937 caused great loss of life.

No calamity called more intensely on the Norwegian Americans' sympathy and assistance than the German attack on the old homeland on April 9, 1940, and the following five long years of occupation. The situation filled Norwegians in America with indignation and sorrow, A. N. Rygg tells in his account of the relief effort. A large-scale relief effort was mounted on a nationwide basis—from New York to San Francisco—among people of Norwegian birth and ancestry. The coordinating organization called itself American Relief for Norway, and J. A. Aasgaard, president of the Norwegian Lutheran Church in America, became its chairman. It was an undertaking to assist "the fair, free land of our race in the North," Aasgaard wrote in soliciting donations to the relief fund.

Clothing, food, medicine, and money were collected and sent through Sweden and Denmark; after the war aid was sent directly. In total the relief drive produced in goods and money more than $8 million. The American press and public opinion were very sympathetic toward Norway. It was a situation that would benefit the Norwegian Americans as well.

There was a romantic aura over the training of Norwegian pilots at Camp Little Norway near Toronto in Canada. Young Norwegian men who had made their way to England were based at this camp. Many Norwegian seamen who sailed in Norway's large merchant fleet and men in the whaling fleet operating in the Antarctic came to America during the war. Some of these enlisted in a Norwegian-speaking military unit, the 99th Battalion. But to a large extent, the men in this battalion were recruited from the immigrant community. In case of an Allied invasion of Norway, the battalion would be a great value. It went to Norway, however, only following the war, after having participated in the battles on the Continent.

The Immigrant Tradition and Norway

The attention that was directed toward Norway during the difficult war years stimulated Norwegian-American activity in many areas. The early postwar years experienced a certain blossoming of organizational life and added support to Norwegian-American institutions. The immigrant contingents of the 1920s are now the most visible participants, as members and leaders, and they are the ones who mainly have sustained Norwegian-language churches in Brooklyn, Chicago, and Minneapolis.

The main building of Vesterheim, the Norwegian-American Museum in Decorah, Iowa. The museum has established high professional standards, and it has collected a great number of cultural artifacts from the Norwegian-American heritage.

The Role of the Postwar Immigrants

The postwar immigrants have been judged variously. They were undoubtedly in many ways a fresh breath of air from the homeland to societies and organizations, and they encouraged the use of the Norwegian language at meetings and other gatherings. Still, there was to some degree tension between the newcomers and the Norwegian Americans, between immigrants and colonists. Similar disparity had of course also been evident earlier, but the distance in time to the older immigration and the long gap in regular departures from Norway made the situation more intense. Antagonism found its way into the newspapers. The theologian Sverre Norborg discharged a powerful salvo in *Nordisk Tidende* against what he called "egocentric Norwegians." "We who are 'old in this country' cannot recall such egocentric self-centeredness among the newcomers of the twenties," Norborg complained. The postwar immigrants were accused of stinginess and a "savings bank mentality" which kept them from giving financial support to immigrant institutions such as hospitals and homes for the aged. In *Duluth Skandinav* one who called himself "Ola" found this situation to be completely normal, for he believed that the experiences of the newcomers were basically different from the National Romantic relationship Norwegian Americans had to Norway. The newcomers "do not thrive . . . in Norwegian-American meeting halls," he wrote. The editor of *Washington-Posten*, Ole J. Ejde, maintained, however, that the group of newcomers in Seattle "feel at home in Norwegian-American surroundings and are for us a pure unadulterated joy."

Seattle and Brooklyn received a substantial postwar stream of immigrants, and it was therefore possibly easier for newcomers to be comfortable in existing organizations and churches there than in the older settlements in the Middle West. Norborg's complaint about the newcomers was based on his experience in Chicago. In Minneapolis a separate club for newcomers, Kontakt, was formed. According to *Nordisk Tidende*, it gave "Norwegian young people something that the numerous other societies in that city could not provide; the genuine Norwegian coziness and friendly atmosphere that we find in youth societies in Norway." In its commentary *Nordisk Ti-dende* explained that the newcomer club emerged quite naturally "in the city where Norwegian culture in America is oldest and the split between it and the most recent arrivals greatest."

The Older Immigrant Tradition Continued

The older immigrant tradition endured in the Middle West. When the Norwegian sociologist P. A. Munch came to Wisconsin after World War II, he discovered to his delight that the Norwegian dialects were still spoken in the old rural settlements. He was, like others directly from Norway, surprised at this phenomenon. The Norwegian author Sigrid Undset visited her compatriots in the Middle West in 1941 and shared her impressions in an article in *Common Ground*. "Recent arrivals from Norway are frequently reminded in a strange way of the world of their grandparents when they attend social functions among Norwegian Americans or read American newspapers in the Norwegian language," she said. What she saw made Undset think of pressed flowers in an album.

The Norwegian-American rural neighborhoods were affected by a growing geographic mobility that removed many young people from the community. But even so, in the 1980s one still meets people like Orville Bakken in Northwood, North Dakota. He speaks the Halling dialect, even though one of his grandmothers was born in America of Norwegian parents and the three other grandparents had all emigrated. In Otter Tail county, Minnesota, Morris Baasen explains in Eggedøl speech that he has never heard his American-born mother speak anything but Norwegian. Farther south in Minnesota, in the Trønder settlement in Wanamingo, Thorny B. Thoreson relates that he and his wife have always communicated in Norwegian, although both are of the third generation. His family has been in America since 1858. It may also still happen that in bars and restaurants in small towns where Norwegians have settled one will come across groups of men who entertain themselves in a language they learned in an immigrant home as children. But they are generally men in their seventies and older, and there are hardly any younger than fifty in this group. The generation after them did not learn Norwegian.

Generations thus grew up in America learning Norwegian as the first language. English was confronted in the public school, and many spoke English with a special accent. Norwegian in this way influenced the speech also of those who learned only English. Many who grew up in an immigrant environment can tell of the role played by schoolteachers in the Americanization process; some teachers even made children who transgressed against strict enforcement of English by speaking Norwegian in the classroom stand in the corner as punishment. But on the playground the children shouted and clamored in the language that was natural for them. At home and in the neighborhood they spoke Norwegian. But to be able to speak Norwegian did not bestow any status. To the contrary, children who spoke English with a Norwegian accent were ridiculed. Following World War I little importance was attached to instruction in foreign languages; an entire generation was in fact deprived of such instruction. Still, Norwegian and other immigrant languages continued to be used when they were the natural medium. Many of those who spoke Norwegian at home knew little about the efforts to create a Norwegian-American high culture. Perhaps knowledge of such endeavors might have resulted in greater respect and appreciation for their Norwegian background.

Language Assimilation and Intermarriage

One generally considers linguistic assimilation to be complete in the course of three generations. For the Norwegian group as a whole, the linguist Joshua A. Fishman has shown that as many as half of the second generation did not learn Norwegian in the period 1940-60. Statistics for the next generation also indicate a sharp decline. But in 1960 there were still 40,000 people of the third generation who had learned Norwegian. Compared with Swedes and Danes, Norwegians in Minnesota had a language preservation rate that was about three times as high; the pattern of settlement of Norwegians, with a large percentage living in farm communities, gives a partial explanation of this situation.

Even after the language was lost, Norwegians to a lesser degree than other Scandinavians abandoned unique cultural qualities. "The decisive test of the degree of assimilation is intermar-

In Search of Roots

In the rural communities investigated by Munch, celebration of May 17 had been discontinued; it was one of the special national traditions that had been abandoned in order to be accepted by American neighbors. This was of course not the case in all regions of Norwegian settlement. It is important also to bear in mind that the 1950s, when these communities were studied, did not encourage cultural pluralism; the emphasis was on national consensus and solidarity, which was reinforced by the agitation against radical political movements to the left. But not all established customs were discarded. Out in the country the women in the congregations assembled to prepare the traditional *lutefisk* suppers and to bake *lefse*. It was, however, organizations and societies in a city environment that took care of ethnic symbols, for instance the May 17 festivities.

It is naturally the simplest and most easily understood aspects of an ethnic culture that survive and are stressed after a separate subculture has disappeared. Especially representative symbols and cultural expressions are embraced, perhaps most by people who may be described as "Norwegians for a day." The social participation is frequently more important than the cultural traits. In Sons of Norway lodges and at so-called heri-

riage," writes the sociologist Lowry Nelson. Albert Jenks has found that in 1910 as many as 70 percent of Norwegian men in Minneapolis had wives of the same nationality. Julius Drachsler has shown that of 330 Norwegian men in New York in 1921, 65 percent had married endogamously (within the ethnic group). In an investigation in 1941 *Nordisk Tidende* found that in Brooklyn 41 percent of the second generation had married persons of Norwegian origin. These are high figures. Marriage within the ethnic group promoted the preservation of the Norwegian language and of special cultural traditions. Endogamy was an even more highly regarded norm outside the cities. Lowry Nelson investigated two rural communities in Minnesota and found a percentage of marriage between Norwegians that is twice as high as one would expect by chance. When Norwegians found a spouse outside their nationality, they generally married a Dane, Swede, or German Protestant.

The investigations confirm that ethnic solidar-

Above: With "Greetings from Hallingdal" on his automobile on July 4, Orville Bakken from Northwood, North Dakota, sits at the wheel.

ity functioned also after the language was gone. Group loyalty was reinforced by the fellowship of the Lutheran congregation. P. A. Munch has indicated that as recently as 1950 Lutheran and Norwegian were synonymous terms in several rural communities in Wisconsin and that during the same period 90 percent of social visiting was confined to others of Norwegian descent. Because status distinction within these communities was no longer based on nationality, as it had been at an earlier time, even prosperous Norwegians sought the company of their own people. Measured in terms of social intercourse, Norwegian Americans were clearly not structurally assimilated in these communities. The cultural assimilation, on the other hand, was nearly completed.

The chest was rose-painted in the Halling style by Judith Nelson of Minnesota in 1981. The chest has placed in the Norwegian-American Museum's gold medal category.

tage week activities a comprehension of Norwegian culture is often limited to folk dancing and rose-painting. The images of a National Romantic Norway in a simplified version are allowed to live on; in the *bygdelag* as well, the appreciation of a genuine folk tradition is gone. There is, for instance, great distance between the faithfulness to old traditions at the annual bridal procession in the early history of Hardangerlaget and the improvised representations at recent reunions.

On the other hand, rose-painting and folk art have attracted capable practitioners among latter-day Norwegian Americans—a separate Norwegian-American tradition has become evident. The *bygdelag* had early inspired a greater appreciation of the value of folk art. In recent years the Norwegian-American Museum in Decorah has, through instruction and exhibitions, contributed much to preserving the quality of the folk art. At Stoughton High School in Stoughton, Wisconsin, a folk dance group has had great success since 1953 and has performed throughout the

The Norwegian Dancers of Stoughton, Wisconsin, are a well-known folk dance group. The young dancers stress authentic traditions and give professional performances.

Right: Lutefisk *became a popular Norwegian dish among Norwegian Americans when Norwegian-American fish dealers were able to offer this product, which is prepared of dried Norwegian cod. Some people treated this fish themselves by soaking it in a lye (*lut*) solution, as at the home of Mr. and Mrs. Andrew Olsen in St. Paul, Minnesota, in December, 1936. Mrs. Olsen tests the quality of the fish she had begun to prepare two weeks before.*

Above: Examples of commercial exploitation of the ethnic renaissance. Buttons with ethnocentric, generally humorous slogans are worn by many people.

Right: Traditions live on among Norwegian Americans. Here three generations are baking for Christmas in Seattle, Washington.

Middle West. This nearly professional group visited Norway in 1972.

All such activity bears evidence of a search for roots. An indication of how far most Norwegian Americans have moved away from their roots is that before any meaningful search can begin it is often necessary first to learn the language. The desire to acquire Norwegian is made apparent by the thousands of people who every year sign up for language courses sponsored by Sons of Norway, church groups, and public agencies.

A White Ethnic Renaissance

From the 1960s public opinion began to shift to a greater acceptance of ethnic diversity; America rediscovered that it is a pluralistic society, and this became a sign of strength rather than a weakness. Black Americans, Afro-Americans, gave the signal, demanding social justice and respect for their race. Their example was contagious. White ethnic groups stood up to be counted, and in addition to the slogan "Black Power," there were calls for "Italian Power," "Polish Power," and for recognition of other minorities. The melting-pot theory was viewed as a myth, a false conception of the forces at work in American society. Perhaps the picture of a "salad bowl"—a mixing together of different ingredients without a melting together—was more accurate. From under a superficial mass culture an ethnic cultural pluralism was again brought to light.

Influential books like *The Rise of the Unmeltable Ethnics* by Michael Novak in 1971 called attention to the ethnicity of Poles, Italians, Greeks, and Slavs. These were the real ethnics. They constituted the principal component of the great army of common workers; the demand for recognition of ethnic characteristics therefore had a strong social basis. In the preface to a later edition Novak maintained that everyone now wanted to belong to an ethnic group. It had come in vogue. The ethnic assertion took on a political cast in many groups, partly in competition with the political gains the black population had made.

Just as the 1960s was the decade of black consciousness, the following decade has been declared the decade of white ethnic groups, an ethnic renaissance. Novak views ethnicity more as a cultural transfer from parents to children than as a genetic inheritance. The so-called new

ethnicity is defined by him as a historical consciousness that raises the question of who we are, what history we belong to, and where we are headed. Some, among others the sociologist Stephen Steinberg, have viewed the white ethnic upsurge of the 1970s as an episode in the creation of an "ethnic mythology." He thinks of the movement as the "dying gasp" of white ethnic groups and communities, many of which had achieved a nearly complete assimilation into modern American society and had common American middle-class values and behavior.

The debate has produced a rich body of scholarly literature. At colleges and universities courses are offered on "white ethnic history," alongside courses about the black population. A new historical interpretation is attempted, in which the individual immigrant groups are considered in the total sweep of American history. The immigrants had assumed a position of inferiority in relationship to the host society. Norwegians might view themselves as "guests" in the new land; this feeling of servility was attacked by cultural pluralists in the Norwegian-American community. As early as 1847 Ole Munch Ræder wrote about Norwegians in America that "they must to a greater degree than they do learn to respect their own nationality and infuse others with respect for it." A desire to be recognized and a protest against disrespect might be at the base of much of the ethnic mobilization of the 1970s.

Norwegian Ethnic Consciousness

These considerations might be motivating forces for a greater ethnic awareness also among Norwegian Americans, but they are obviously not as strong here as in other nationalities with a shorter history in America. The modest beginnings of their presence in the new land and the consciousness of having hailed from a backward and poor peasant society can now be regarded with some detachment. But other impulses are present. New encounters with Norway, encouraged by inexpensive charter flights, have generated enthusiasm. Perhaps the greater determination and self-consciousness of a prosperous postwar Norway infect those who visit the country. The most valuable evidence of a renewed interest in Norwegian origins is the revival of concern for family history. For many, it might be

important to establish descent from the Viking king Harold Hairfair, but even if this cannot be arranged, Norwegian Americans study their family trees, look up relatives in Norway, restore kinship ties, and burden overworked personnel at Norwegian archives and libraries with inquires about family connections. In America *bygdelag* that have introduced workshops and that give assistance in tracing family trees have attracted new members. Among other societies, Valdres Samband has created interest in genealogy, and under the auspices of the Norwegian-American Museum in Decorah Gerhard Naeseth heads a genealogical center.

In 1975 Norwegian Americans commemorated the sesquicentennial of the arrival of the Sloopers in 1825, and they did so under the influence of the increasing sensitivity to ethnic diversity. Relations with Norway were strengthened as well, symbolized by the official visit of King Olav V of Norway at a series of grand affairs from coast to coast in America. The celebrations, however, took on an elitist emphasis, through the mustering of famous Americans of Norwegian descent, awarding of royal decorations, and exclusive banquets. All this created festivity, but no significant new institutions were produced by the jubilee enthusiasm.

An interest in things Norwegian thus is cultivated as a pastime or on special occasions. Perhaps Steinberg is correct when he regards what transpired in the 1970s as a phase in the creation of an ethnic mythology, in this instance an idealized notion of Norwegian ethnicity, the group's cultural values and history. No rebirth of a Norwegian ethnic consciousness in any traditional sense is anticipated. Concern for family background and Norwegian cultural expressions may in many cases be a passing curiosity. But even if this is so, it is significant to note that the expanding exchange of people and cultural impulses between America and Norway in recent years has given the American public a greater awareness of the culture and society with which Norwegian Americans have historical ties.

Organized Norwegian-American Life

Norwegian-American activities have in recent years attracted greater support, and some organizations have been given new life. In 1982 there

King Olav V of Norway came to the United States in 1975 in connection with the sesquicentennial celebration of Norwegian emigration. He visited many Norwegian-American institutions, and his presence stimulated a renewed interest in retaining ties between Norway and Norwegian Americans. The Norwegian monarch was everywhere greeted with Norwegian flags, as in this photograph taken during his visit to the Knute Nelson monument in front of the State Capitol in St. Paul, Minnesota. The statue of Nelson is seen in the background. "We are in the throes of an ethnic revival in this country. . . . They [students] see in ethnicity alternative values to middle-class materialism. They are finding a way of life in tune with nature, especially in Norwegian ethnicity's emphasis on the predominance of nature." (J. R. Christianson, professor of history at Luther College, Decorah, Iowa, as quoted in Telegraph Herald, *Dubuque, Iowa, October 12, 1975.)*

Greetings like this one, which says "Welcome to Poulsbo," painted on a wall in Poulsbo, Washington, are not uncommon in small towns and regions of Norwegian settlement, and they serve to remind visitors that the residents are proud of their Norwegian origin. After a certain decline in Norwegian-American ethnic consciousness, there are now signs indicating an increasing interest in "roots."

were at least ten *bygdelag* reunions in the Middle West, involving nineteen *bygdelag* groups. The *bygdelag* idea, a gathering around regional Norwegian backgrounds, has been strengthened, and some societies that have been inactive for several years have been revived; several have younger Norwegian Americans at the helm. But, in general, decline is more evident than growth. The reunions are shadows of their former greatness; solutions have been to arrange joint reunions with other societies or to unite without giving up a specific local Norwegian identity. In 1979 Vestlandslaget united people whose roots were in Sogn, Voss, Hardanger, and Nordhordland. As regional attachments weaken, such a union is a practical and unsurprising development. On the West Coast as well there is *bygdelag* activity; in 1982 Vestkystens Nordlandslag reported that 146 members had taken part in that year's reunion.

Other efforts enjoy larger participation. In Minneapolis "Norway Day"—a summer afternoon festivity in one of the city's parks—is a popular annual event. Many thousand people each summer attend a magnificent and colorful folk festival, called Nordic Fest, in Decorah. There are

May 17 parades in cities like Brooklyn, Chicago, Seattle, and Minneapolis, but also in small towns with Norwegian-American people. The little town of Spring Grove, Minnesota, arranged a celebration of May 17 in 1982 lasting three days, with an extensive program, Norwegian food, a parade, a play, and a dance.

With renewed force the observance of May 17 in Minneapolis has become a festival for the entire state of Minnesota. Persons of Norwegian descent come together. A notable feature is that many people lacking Norwegian ancestors also participate, march in the parade, line the parade route, and have at least as much fun as those of Norwegian origin. In this manner May 17 may become an ordinary American folk festival, much like the Irish St. Patrick's Day, when all Americans, regardless of national background, feel a little Irish and wear something green. In a society composed of many national strains, it is not unreasonable to predict that at least in certain regions of the United States May 17 will simply become another American day of celebration. The ethnic emphasis in some Norwegian-American towns, for instance in Westby, Wisconsin, is actually spearheaded by Americans with no Norwegian forebears. They emphasize what makes the town distinctive and arrange local festivals. This is, to be sure, an American small-town tradition. Such festivals can, of course, be motivated by commercial interests, but they are part of American folk life. The annual reunion of Setes-

The bygdelag *represent a unique organizational development among the immigrants. The first* bygdelag *reunion occurred in 1899, when immigrants from Valdres arranged a* stevne *(reunion) on the banks of the Mississippi River in Minneapolis. The idea behind the* bygdelag *movement was to strengthen the attachment to the local Norwegian home community and to gather people from a specific Norwegian district wherever they might be now living in America. Close to half a hundred national organizations came into being, and during the heyday of the movement at least 75,000 people participated in the many annual reunions. The notice to the right is from May, 1983, and indicates continued* bygdelag *activity as the individual organizations announce the location and time of that year's get-together.*

NATIONAL COUNCIL
NORWEGIAN-AMERICAN BYGDELAGS
(𝔅𝔶𝔤𝔡𝔢𝔩𝔞𝔤𝔢𝔫𝔢𝔰 𝔉𝔢𝔩𝔩𝔢𝔰𝔯𝔞𝔞𝔡, 𝔍𝔫𝔠.)

7 MAY 1983 — ANNUAL MEETING AT MINDEKIRKEN, MINNEAPOLIS, MINNESOTA

1983 SCHEDULE OF BYGDELAG ANNUAL MEETINGS:

AGDER: October 1 — Luverne, MN., at Blue Mounds Inn
Contact: Ms. John G. Johnson, Secy, 119 E. Barck Ave., Luverne, MN. 56156

GUDBRANDSDAL: (National): August 12 - 13 — La Crosse, Wis.
Contact: Ms. Hjordis Helgestad, Pres., 2426 Hengel Ct., No. 208, La Crosse, WI. 54601

GUDBRANDSDAL: (Northwest). Tentative July 5 - 6 at Devils Lake, N.D.
Contact: Ms. Tillie Overlie, Pres., Battle View, N.D. 58714

HADELAND: July 15 - 16 — Marshall, MN., at S. W. State University
Contact: Morgan Olson, Pres., 3416 Parkview Blvd., Mpls., MN. 55422

HALLINGDAL: June 16 - 19 — Fergus Falls, MN. at Community College
Contact: Bill O. Larson, Pres., 317 W. Gustavus Ave., Fergus Falls, MN. 56537

HARDANGER: June 10 - 11 — Northfield, MN., at St. Olaf College
Contact: Ms. Stella Peterson, Pres., Wittenberg, WI. 54499

LAND: July 15 - 16 — Marshall, MN. at S. W. State University
Contact: Calvin Pederson, Pres., Rt. No. 2 — Box No. 92, Starbuck, MN. 56381

NORDFJORD: June 10 - 11 — Swift Falls, MN.
Contact: Ms. Melvin Skarsten, Pres., Rt. No. 3, Benson, MN. 56215

NORDHORDALAND: June 10 - 11 — Northfield, MN., at St. Olaf College
Contact: Sam Bergaas, Pres., 5816 Zenith Ave. S., Mpls., MN. 55401

NORDLAND: June 24 - 25 — Fargo, N.D., at N.D. State University
Contact: Stanley Anderson, Pres., Rt. No. 2 — Box No. 333, Superior, WI. 54880

SETESDAL: June 24 - 25 — Oklee, MN.
Contact: Ms. Orlando Chervestad, Secy., Rt. No. 1 — Box No. 32, Oklee, MN. 56742

SIGDAL: July 29 — Decorah, IA. at Luther College (Nordic Fest weekend)
Contact: Ms. Marilyn Somdahl, Pres., 10129 Goodrich Circle, Bloomington, MN. 55437

SOGN: June 10 - 11 — Northfield, MN. at St. Olaf College
Contact: Ms. Doreen Ness, Pres., 907 W. 2nd St., Northfield, MN. 55057

SOLOR: July 15 - 16 — Fergus Falls, MN. at Community College
Contact: Aleck Gunderson, Chr., 4515 — 29 Ave. S., Mpls., MN. 55406

SUNNFJORD: June 17 - 18 — Decorah, IA., at Luther College
Contact: Ms. Paul Grimsbo, Secy., Rt. No. 1 — Box No. 67, Lake Mills, IA. 50450

TELEMARK: July 15 - 16 — Marshall, MN., S. W. State University
Contact: Glenn Nelson, Pres., Rt. No. 1 — Box No. 47, Louisburg, MN. 56254

TOTEN: July 15 - 16 — Marshall, MN., at S. W. State University
Contact: Dr. L. J. Opsahl, Pres., 326 W. 3rd St., Willmar, MN. 56201

TRONDHEIM: July 15 - 16: Fergus Falls, MN., Community College
Contact: Ms. Mable Vaala, Co-Chr., 224 E. Sorenson, Appleton, MN. 56208

VALDERS: June 17 - 18 — Mt. Horeb, WI.
Contact: Ms. Hilda Kringstad, Pres., 3633 Vera Cruz Ave. N., Mpls. MN. 55422

VESTLAND: June 10 - 11 — Northfield, MN., at St. Olaf College
Contact: Ms. Ann Urness Gesme, M'ship Secy., 2119 Lincolnshire Dr. S. E., Cedar Rapids, IA. 52403

VOSS: June 10 - 11 — Northfield, MN., at St. Olaf College
Contact: Ms. Ann Urness Gesme, Secy., 2119 Lincolnshire Dr. S. E., Cedar Rapids, IA. 52403

dalslaget in Oklee, Minnesota, has for instance become a celebration for the whole population in and around the small town. Many old Norwegian areas of settlement hoist ethnic colors by placing welcoming signs in Norwegian by roads leading into town. Examples are the small towns of Spring Grove, Minnesota, Mount Horeb, Wisconsin, and Poulsbo, Washington.

Geographic Mobility

The Ancestry Group survey in the 1980 census indicates that the 3,454,000 Americans who claimed Norwegian ancestry are still concentrated in the traditional regions of settlement: 55 percent in the North Central states and 31.1 percent in the West. However, from these areas they have moved to all parts of the country. This is an aspect of the process of assimilation. They have also joined the movement to the sunbelt, and like other Americans have retired to the southern United States. Norwegian settlement in Texas is, however, of an early date, and Norwegians made their way to southern California before 1880. San Francisco Bay has been the main area of Norwegian settlement in that state, but from census to census after 1880 the percentage of Norwegians in the counties farther south has increased. Those who have moved have taken with them their social customs and organizations. Sons of Norway lodges have, for instance, sprung up in keeping with Norwegian movement to the sunbelt; between 1961 and 1977 as many as eleven lodges were established in Florida.

In 1981 Norwegians in the state of Hawaii commemorated an episode in Norwegian emigration history, the arrival of the barque *Beta* in February, 1881, and the sister ship *Musca* in May. A monument that was raised at the celebration tells of the vessels that "brought more than six hundred Norwegians, Swedes, and Danes to work in the sugar cane fields and mills of the Hawaiian Kingdom." They came as contract laborers, and most of them were Norwegian, from Drammen, Oslo,

When the Norwegian king visited Decorah, Iowa, in 1975, folk dancers performed in his honor. At Luther College and the Vesterheim museum, both in Decorah, the Norwegian heritage is honored.

In 1982-83 a grand cultural exhibition, called Scandinavia Today, was arranged in several parts of the United States. The various programs, exhibits, and presentations were mainly financed by the respective Scandinavian countries, and they attracted the attention of the American public to the small nations in the North. To give festivity and luster to the various events, Scandinavian heads of state and royalty crossed the Atlantic to be present. The photograph shows the Norwegian crown prince and crown princess, their royal highnesses Harald and Sonja, upon their arrival at the airport in Minneapolis/St. Paul, where they are greeted by two little Norwegian Americans with flowers in the Norwegian national colors.

and other parts of East Norway. But they adjusted poorly to the strict working discipline and unaccustomed living conditions, and as soon as they saw a way out they fled. Most ended in the United States.

The Norwegian Society of Texas came into being at the time of the sesquicentennial celebration in 1975. In 1982 this society assumed responsibility for an observance of the two-hundredth anniversary of the birth of Cleng Peerson, the "father of Norwegian emigration." Thus the occa-

sion was the immigrants' own history, but they still faced Norway and found inspiration from a progressive and modern Norwegian society. The presence of the Norwegian monarch was again an eloquent expression of this orientation toward the ancestral land. That St. Olaf College establishes a King Olav V Professorship with a gift from the Norwegian state and arranges conferences on "Norway Today" is evidence of the role Norway plays in a growing awareness among Norwegian Americans of a Norwegian cultural

heritage. Sons of Norway has expanded its activity to include Norway: lodges have been formed in Skien, Tønsberg, and Kristiansand. The order is now the best organized group of Norwegian Americans.

An Integrated Pluralism

A description like the one above of organized Norwegian-American activity and jubilee observances might easily overshadow the fact that the vast majority of Americans of Norwegian descent have no direct contact with these undertakings. Many might have a vague idea that great-grandfather, or some other ancestor, came from Norway, but even more are what John Higham describes as "nonethnics"; they possess little or no sense of a specific ethnic identity. Higham views American society as a mosaic of ethnic nuclei, consisting of people who uphold an ethnic group life and preserve the group's cultural values. He suggests what he calls "pluralistic integration" as a sensible solution to the relationship between ethnic groups. By this he means that people can relate to the numerous ethnic nuclei as they wish, participate in activities, and identify with one or more, but also if they wish avoid loyalty to any specific group. This will, Higham thinks, preserve ethnic boundaries, but not make them impenetrable, and promote appreciation for ethnic diversity. Such a situation, Higham maintains, will support the validity of seeking a common American culture and national solidarity without doing injustice to any cultural group.

There are signs that Higham's model of pluralistic integration approximates current developments. Higham had feared that ethnic activism would create antagonism and new fragmentation along ethnic and racial lines. With the possible exception of separatistic tendencies among Spanish-speaking Americans in the Southwest, this has not occurred. In the 1980s Americans are again mounting a quest for national unity. It was rejected by many in the turbulent 1970s, when the idea of cultural pluralism was rarely challenged. A reaction against preoccupation with ethnic cohesion is now evident also at the scholarly level, and researchers are again concerned with the process of assimilation. American patriotism has become acceptable over the entire political spectrum; people are seeking an American nationality and identity, and are rediscovering traditional American values.

Social injustice and prejudice have not disappeared. But the civil rights legislation of the 1960s, state and federal actions in the social and

Right: The Viking ship replica Hjemkomst *on her way to Norway under full sail.*

221

political area and in education, as well as the visible ethnic assertiveness, have resulted in a greater sensitivity in the American population to ethnic dissimilarities and an increased tolerance of other peoples. The idea of equality has gained ground through legislative measures and through economic advances made by underprivileged segments of the population. Minorities and people of various national origins who wish to retain aspects of their cultural background, traditions, and customs may do so, and adjust them so that they are in harmony with the dominant culture and promote the notion of a common American identity.

But even if assimilation should eventually erase all traces of ethnic cultural diversity, there is reason to believe that American society will continue to have nerve-endings to virtually every nation in the world and to every nationality group. The lines of communication need not be broken; personal contacts can persist, as well as a consciousness of historical ties. The situation can make one think of the old Norwegian possessions in the North Sea, such as the Shetland Islands, where a consciousness of a Norwegian homeland was preserved for many generations and a sense of kinship with Norwegians still can be discerned. The western expansion in the Age of the Vikings has furthermore provided Norwegian Americans with their most cherished distinguishing mark. Not only has the Viking symbolism been a means of self-assertion, it has to an equal degree signified a historical and spiritual unity of all Norwegians. "The Viking Spirit" has become a firm expression of courage and desire for adventure. In Minnesota the state's professional football team bears the name "The Vikings," and an examination of the telephone directories for the two cities of St. Paul and Minneapolis reveals that the name "Viking" is used by about one hundred business enterprises.

Hjemkomst—the Ties to Norway Are Strengthened

Viking ships and exhibitions of objects from the Viking period fascinate and create interest. In 1893 a replica of a Viking ship sailed from Norway to the World's Fair in Chicago, where there now are efforts to restore the ship and place it so that it can be viewed by the public. Another ship was built for the Alaska-Yukon-Pacific Exposition in Seattle in 1909. In May of 1982 a Viking ship, a replica of the Gokstad ship, sailed from Duluth, Minnesota, for Norway. It had been built by Robert Asp in Hawley in western Minnesota, a region of Norwegian pioneer settlement. In such a ship he had dreamed of sailing to the land of his ancestors, and he significantly called it *Hjemkomst*—Homecoming. Asp died before his dream could be realized; it was the next generation that set out for the coast of Norway. The dramatic voyage caught the interest of both America and Norway, and it became an eloquent statement of bridge-building between Norway and the immigrants' descendants in America. It draws a picture that conveys the rustle of history, and is a reminder of the thousands of bonds that unite people of a common heritage on both sides of the Atlantic.

Selected Bibliography

With the creation of the Norwegian-American Historical Association (NAHA) in 1925, a systematic scholarly investigation of the Norwegian-American experience was launched. Theodore C. Blegen's *Norwegian Migration to America, 1825-1860* (1931) and his *Norwegian Migration: The American Transition* (1940) are classics in Norwegian immigration history. The series *Norwegian-American Studies* now comprises twenty-nine volumes that present articles and translated documents dealing with Norwegian-American life. Individual works about settlement published by NAHA include Carlton C. Qualey's *Norwegian Settlement in the United States* (1938) and Kenneth O. Bjork's *West of the Great Divide: Norwegian Migration to the Pacific Coast, 1847-1893* (1958).

Saga in Steel and Concrete: Norwegian Engineers in America (1947) by Bjork discusses the contributions of Norwegian engineers to the economic life of America. The standard treatment about the Norwegian Lutheran church in America is the two-volume work *The Lutheran Church among Norwegian-Americans* (1960) by E. Clifford Nelson and Eugene L. Fevold. Arlow W. Andersen interprets the role of Norwegian-Danish Methodism in *The Salt of the Earth: A History of Norwegian-Danish Methodism in America* (1956). *A Folk Epic: The Bygdelag in America* (1975) by Odd S. Lovoll provides insights into the growth of a popular organizational movement. In individual biographical studies, such as *Rasmus Bjørn Anderson: A Pioneer Scholar* (1966) by Lloyd Hustvedt and *Kristofer Janson in America* (1976) by Nina Draxten, there is considerable information about Norwegian-American cultural developments. A basic work is Einar Haugen's *The Norwegian Language in America: A Study in Bilingual Behavior* (1969).

In Norway Ingrid Semmingsen pioneered in the field with her two main works *Veien mot vest: Utvandringen fra Norge til Amerika*, volume one in 1942 and volume two in 1950. They remain the most significant historical studies of Norwegian emigration. In 1978 Semmingsen published a brief study in English, *Norway to America: A History of the Migration*, that incorporates material from the two larger works. A number of Norwegian academic theses have in recent years been investigations of emigration from individual communities. *Tinns emigrasjonshistorie, 1837-1907* (1972) by Andres Svalestuen may serve as a model for similar examinations.

The best short treatment of general American immigration is still Maldwyn Allen Jones, *American Immigration* (1946). *The Distant Magnet: European Emigration to the U.S.A.* (1972) by Philip Taylor is a thorough work by a European scholar.

Emigration

Åkerman, Sune. "Theories and Methods of Migration Research." *From Sweden to America*. Ed. Harald Runblom and Hans Norman. University of Minnesota Press, Minneapolis, 1976.

Blegen, Theodore C. "The Norwegian Government and the Early Norwegian Emigration." *Minnesota History*, 6, 1925.

——. *Norwegian Migration to America, 1825-1860*. NAHA, Northfield, 1931.

De Pillis, Mario S. "Cleng Peerson and the Communitarian Background of Norwegian Immigration." *Norwegian-American Studies*, vol. 21. NAHA, Northfield, 1962.

——. "Still More Light on the Kendall Colony: A Unique Slooper Letter." *Norwegian-American Studies and Records*, vol. 20. NAHA, Northfield, 1959.

Engen, Arnfinn. "Oppbrot og omlegging. Utvandring og økonomisk utvikling i Dovre på 1800-talet." Thesis, University of Oslo, 1973.

——, ed. *Utvandringa—det store oppbrotet*. Det Norske Samlaget, Oslo, 1978.

Gjævenes, Martin. *Utvandrarane frå Sykkylven*. Sykkylven Sogenemnd, Oslo, 1957.

Gran, Johan E. "En amerikareise i 1872." *Samband*, November 1916.

Guillet, Edwin C. *The Atlantic Crossing by Sailing-Ship since 1770*. Thomas Nelson and Sons, New York, 1937.

Hodne, Fritz. "Growth in a Dual Economy—The Norwegian Experience, 1814-1914." *Economy and History*, 16, 1973.

Hvidt, Kristian. *Flight to America: The Social Background of 300,000 Danish Emigrants*. Academic Press, New York, 1975.

——, ed. *Emigration fra Norden indtil 1. verdenskrig. Rapporter til det nordiske historikermøde i København 1971 9-12 august*. Copenhagen, 1971.

Jacobson, Clara. "En amerika-reise for seksti aar siden." *Symra*, 1913.

Janson, Florence F. *The Background of Swedish Emigration, 1840-1930*. University of Chicago Press, Chicago, 1931.

Jerome, Harry. *Migration and Business Cycles*. National Bureau of Economic Research, New York, 1926.

Johnsen, Arne Odd. "Johannes Nordboe and Norwegian Immigration: An 'America Letter' of 1837." *Norwegian-American Studies and Records*, vol. 8. NAHA, Northfield, 1934.

Leirfall, Jon. "Hegra before and after the Emigration Era." Trans. C. A. Clausen. *Norwegian-American Studies*, vol.

27, NAHA, Northfield, 1977.

Lindberg, John S. *The Background of Swedish Emigration to the United States. An Economic and Sociological Study in the Dynamics of Migration*. University of Minnesota Press, Minneapolis, 1930.

Lovoll, Odd S. "From Norway to America. A Tradition of Immigration Fades." *Contemporary American Immigration*. Ed. D. L. Cuddy. Twayne, Boston, 1982.

Malmin, Gunnar J. "Bishop Jacob Neumann's Word of Admonition to the Peasants." *Norwegian-American Studies and Records*, vol. 1. NAHA, Northfield, 1926.

Mangalam, J. J. *Human Migration. A Guide to Migration Literature in English, 1955-1962*. University of Kentucky Press, Lexington, 1968.

Moe, Thorvald. "Demographic Developments and Economic Growth in Norway, 1740-1940: An Econometric Study." Ph.D. dissertation, Stanford University, 1970.

Ore, Oystein. "Norwegian Emigrants with University Training, 1830-1880." *Norwegian-American Studies and Records*, vol. 19. NAHA, Northfield, 1956.

Petersen, William. *Population*. 3rd ed. Macmillan, New York, 1975.

Sandaker, Arvid. "Emigration from Land Parish to America, 1866-1875." *Norwegian-American Studies*, vol. 26. NAHA, Northfield, 1974.

Seip, Jens Arup. *Fra embedsmannsstat til ettpartistat og andre essays*. 2nd ed. Universitetsforlaget, Oslo, 1974.

Semmingsen, Ingrid. "The Dissolution of Estate Society in Norway." *The Scandinavian Economic History Review*, 11, 1954.

——. *Norway to America: A History of the Migration*. University of Minnesota Press, Minneapolis, 1978.

——. *Veien mot vest. Utvandringen fra Norge til Amerika*. 2 vols. Aschehoug, Oslo, 1942 and 1950.

[Semmingsen] Gaustad, Ingrid. "Utvandringen til Amerika, 1866-1873." *Historisk Tidsskrift*, 31, 1937-40.

Sunde, Rasmus. "Ei undersøking av utvandringa til Amerika frå Vik i Sogn, 1839-1915," Thesis, University of Trondheim, 1974.

Svalestuen, Andres A. "Om statistisk grunnmateriale til utvandringshistorien." *Heimen*, 15, 1970.

——. *Tinns emigrasjonshistorie, 1837-1907*. Universitetsforlaget, Oslo, 1972.

Thistlethwaite, Frank. "Migration from Europe Overseas in the Nineteenth and Twentieth Century." *Reports, vol. V, XIth International Congress of Historical Sciences*. Uppsala, 1960.

Thomas, Brinley. *Migration and Economic Growth: A Study*

of Great Britain and the Atlantic Economy. University Press, Cambridge, 1954.

——. *Migration and Urban Development. A Reappraisal of British and American Business Cycles.* Methuen, London, 1972.

Thomas, Dorothy Swaine. *Research Memorandum on Migration Differentials.* Social Science Research Council, New York, 1938.

Tveiten, Helge. "Sosial uro og utvandring frå Nedenes fogderi." *Thranerørsla i norske bygder.* Ed. Tore Pryser. Det Norske Samlaget, Oslo, 1977.

Surveys and Collections

Adamic, Louis. *A Nation of Nations.* Harper & Brothers, New York, 1945.

Ander, O. Fritiof, ed. *In the Trek of the Immigrants: Essays Presented to Carl Wittke.* Augustana College Library, Rock Island, Ill., 1964.

Andersen, Arlow W. *The Norwegian-Americans.* Twayne, Boston, 1975.

Anderson, Rasmus B. *The First Chapter of Norwegian Immigration, 1821-1840.* Published by the author, Madison, 1906.

Babcock, Kendric Charles. *The Scandinavian Element in the United States.* University of Illinois, Urbana, 1914.

Bergmann, Leola N. *Americans from Norway.* Lippincott, Philadelphia, 1950.

Blegen, Theodore C. *Norwegian Migration: The American Transition.* NAHA, Northfield, 1940.

Commager, Henry S., ed. *Immigration and American History: Essays in Honor of Theodore C. Blegen.* University of Minnesota Press, Minneapolis, 1961.

Evjen, John O. *Scandinavian Immigrants in New York, 1630-1674.* Holter, Minneapolis, 1916.

Flom, George T. *A History of Norwegian Immigration to the United States: From the Earliest Beginning down to the Year 1848.* Privately published, Iowa City, Iowa, 1909.

Hansen, Marcus Lee. *The Immigrant in American History.* Harper Torchbooks, New York, 1964.

Jones, Maldwyn Allen. *American Immigration.* University of Chicago Press, Chicago, 1960.

Kälvemark, Ann-Sofie, ed. *Utvandring. Den svenska emigrationen till Amerika i historiskt perspektiv.* Wahlström & Widstrand, Stockholm, 1973.

Keilhau, Wilhelm. *Vår egen tid*, vol. 10. *Det norske folks liv og historie.* Aschehoug, Oslo, 1938.

Klavenes, Thoralv. *Det norske Amerika. Blandt udvandrede nordmænd, vore landsmænds liv og vilkaar i den nye verden.* Alb. Cammermeyers Forlag (Lars Swanstrøm). Christiania, 1904.

Langeland, Knud. *Nordmændene i Amerika. Nogle optegnelser om de norskes udvandring til Amerika.* John Anderson, Chicago, 1889.

Langholm, Sivert, and Sejersted, Francis, eds. *Vandringer. Festskrift til Ingrid Semmingsen.* Aschehoug, Oslo, 1980.

Larson, Laurence. *The Changing West and Other Essays.* NAHA, Northfield, 1937.

Lindmark, Sture. *Swedish America, 1914-1932: Studies in Ethnicity with Emphasis on Illinois and Minnesota.* Läromedelsförlagen, Stockholm, 1971.

Norlie, Olaf Morgan. *History of the Norwegian People in America.* Augsburg Publishing House, Minneapolis, 1925.

Robinson, Elwyn B. *History of North Dakota.* University of Nebraska Press, Lincoln, 1966.

Scott, Franklin D. *The United States and Scandinavia.* Harvard University Press, Cambridge, 1952.

Sejersted, Francis. *Den vanskelige frihet, 1814-1851. Norges historie*, vol. 10. Ed. Knut Mykland. J. W. Cappelens Forlag, Oslo, 1978.

Skard, Sigmund. *The United States in Norwegian History.* Greenwood Press, Westport, Conn., 1976.

Solhaug, Trygve. *De norske fiskeriers historie.* 2 vols. Universitetsforlaget, Oslo, 1976.

Sondresen, S. *Norsk-amerikanerne.* A. S. Lunde, Bergen, 1938.

Steen, Sverre. *Det gamle samfunn. Det frie Norge*, vol. 4. Oslo, 1957.

Stephenson, George M. *A History of American Immigration.* University of Minnesota Press, Minneapolis, 1926.

Strand, A. E., compiler and ed. *A History of the Norwegians of Illinois.* John Anderson, Chicago, 1905.

Sundby-Hansen, Harry, ed. *Norwegian Immigrant Contributions to America's Making.* International Press, New York, 1921.

Takla, Knut. *Det norske folk i de forenede Stater.* J. M. Stenersen, Christiania, 1913.

Taylor, Philip. *The Distant Magnet: European Emigration to the U.S.A.* Harper Torchbooks, New York, 1972.

Try, Hans. *To kulturer—en stat. Norges historie*, vol. 11. Ed. Knut Mykland. J. W. Cappelens Forlag, Oslo, 1979.

Ulvestad, Martin. *Vikings and Their Descendants. Norsk-amerikaneren.* Privately published, Seattle, 1928.

Wittke, Carl. *We Who Built America.* Prentice-Hall, Englewood Cliffs, N.J., 1939.

Letters, Diaries, Memoirs, and Guidebooks

Benson, Adolph B. *America of the Fifties: Letters of Fredrika Bremer.* The American-Scandinavian Foundation, New York, 1924.

Blegen, Theodore C., ed. *Frontier Parsonage: The Letters of Olaus Fredrik Duus. Norwegian Pastor in Wisconsin, 1855-1858.* NAHA, Northfield, 1947.

——, ed. *Land of Their Choice: The Immigrants Write Home.* University of Minnesota Press, Minneapolis, 1955.

——, trans. and ed. *Ole Rynning's True Account of America.* NAHA, Northfield, 1927.

——, trans. and ed. *Peter Testman's Account of His Experience in North America.* NAHA, Northfield, 1929.

Clausen, C. A., ed. *The Lady with the Pen: Elise Wærenskjold.* NAHA, Northfield, 1961.

——, and Elviken, Andreas, trans. and ed. *A Chronicle of Old Muskego: The Diary of Søren Bache, 1839-1847.* NAHA, Northfield, 1951.

Farseth, Pauline, and Blegen, Theodore C., trans. and ed. *Frontier Mother: The Letters of Gro Svendsen.* NAHA, Northfield, 1950.

Haugen, Eva, and Haugen, Einar, trans. and ed. *Land of the Free: Bjørnstjerne Bjørnson's America Letters, 1880-1881.* NAHA, Northfield, 1978.

Malmin, Gunnar J. *America in the Forties: The Letters of Ole Munch Ræder.* NAHA, Northfield, 1929.

——. "The Disillusionment of an Immigrant: Sjur Jørgensen Haaeim's Information on Conditions in North America." *Norwegian-American Studies and Records*, vol. 3. NAHA, Northfield, 1928.

Munch, Helene, and Munch, Peter A. *The Strange American Way: Letters of Caja Munch from Wiota, Wisconsin, 1855-1859.* Southern Illinois University Press, Carbondale, 1970.

Nelson, David T., trans. and ed. *The Diary of Elisabeth Koren, 1853-1855.* NAHA, Northfield, 1955.

Paulson, O. *Erindringer af Pastor O. Paulson. Efter hans død gjennemseet af Prof. Sven Oftedal.* The Free Church Book Concern, Minneapolis, 1907.

Preus, Diderikke Margrethe, and Keyser, Johan Carl. *Linka's Diary: On Land and Sea, 1845-1864.* Augsburg Publishing House, Minneapolis, 1952.

Reiersen, Johan Reinert. *Pathfinder for Norwegian Emigrants.* Trans. Frank G. Nelson. NAHA, Northfield, 1981.

Strømme, Peer. *Erindringer. Efter hans død utgit av en komite.* Augsburg Publishing House, Minneapolis, 1923.

Settlement History

Beijbom, Ulf. *Swedes in Chicago.* Läromedelsförlagen, Stockholm, 1971.

Benson, Thomas I. "Gold, Salt Air, and Callouses." *Norwegian-American Studies*, vol. 24. NAHA, Northfield, 1970.

Bergman, Hans. *History of Scandinavians in Tacoma and Pierce County.* Privately published, Tacoma, 1926.

Bjork, Kenneth O. *West of the Great Divide: Norwegian Migration to the Pacific Coast, 1847-1893.* NAHA, Northfield, 1958.

Clausen, C. A., trans., *A Chronicler of Immigrant Life: Svein Nilsson's Articles in Billed-Magazin.* NAHA, Northfield, 1982.

Clausen, Otto. "Det norske Chicago." *Nordmanns-Forbundet*, March, 1934.

Curti, Merle. *The Making of an American Community: A Case Study of Democracy in a Frontier County.* Stanford University Press, Stanford, 1959.

Dahlie, Jorgen. "Old World Paths in the New: Scandinavians Find Familiar Homes in Washington." *Pacific Northwest Quarterly*, April 1970.

——. *A Social History of Scandinavian Immigration, Washington State, 1895-1910.* Arno Press, New York, 1980.

Davis, Eleanor H., and Davis, Carl D. *Norwegian Labor in Hawaii—the Norse Immigrants.* University of Hawaii, Honolulu, 1962.

Drache, Hiram M. *The Challenge of the Prairie: Life and Times of Red River Pioneers.* North Dakota Institute for Regional Studies, Fargo, 1970.

Essex, Alice. *The Stanwood Story.* Stanwood News, Stanwood, Wash. 1971.

Folkestad, Sigurd. "Norske i Brooklyn—New York." *Symra*, 1907.

Grose, I. F. "A Pioneer Boy's Experience in a Corner of Goodhue County." *Jul i Vesterheimen*, 1919.

Hansen, Carl G. O. *My Minneapolis*. Privately published, Minneapolis, 1956.

Holand, Hjalmar Rued. *Coon Valley*. Augsburg Publishing House, Minneapolis, 1922.

———. "Muskego." *Symra*, 1907.

———. *De norske settlementers historie*. 4th rev. ed. John Anderson, Chicago, 1912.

———. *Den sidste folkevandring: Sagastubber fra nybyggerlivet i Amerika*. Aschehoug, Oslo, 1930.

Hoover, Knight. "Norwegians in New York." *Norwegian-American Studies*, vol. 24. NAHA, Northfield, 1970.

Iverson, O. B. "From the Prairie to Puget Sound." Ed. Sverre Arestad. *Norwegian-American Studies and Records*, vol. 16. NAHA, Northfield, 1950.

Jahr, Torstein. "Oleana." *Symra*, 1910.

Janson, Kristofer. *Hvad jeg har oplevet*. Gyldendalske Boghandel, Nordisk Forlag, Christiania, 1913.

Jervell, Hans A. *Nordmænd og norske hjem i Amerika, samt kirker, skoler, hospitaler, alderdomshjem og lignende institutioner reist væsentlig av nordmænd*. Hans Jervell Publishing, Fargo, 1916.

Johnson, J. S. *Minnesota. En kortfattet historie av nordmændenes bebyggelse av staten. Med avsnit om den norske kirkes historie. I anledning Minnesotas deltagelse i Norges jubilæumsutstilling*. Minnesota-Norway 1914 Centennial Exposition Association, St. Paul, 1914.

———. "Rock Prairie." *Samband*, November 1911.

Jonassen, Christen T. "Cultural Variable in the Ecology of an Ethnic Group." *American Sociological Review*, February 1949.

———. "The Norwegians in Bay Ridge: A Sociological Study of an Ethnic Group." Ph.D. dissertation, New York University, 1947.

Kjølås, Gerhard. *Gull. Kampen om gullet i Alaska*. 2nd ed. Bergen, 1948.

Ljungmark, Lars. *For Sale—Minnesota: Organized Promotion of Scandinavian Immigration, 1866-1873*. Akademiförlaget, Gothenburg, 1971.

Nelson, Oley. *En kort historie af det første norske settlement i Story og Polk counties, Iowa, 1855-1905*. Privately published, Chicago, 1905.

Nordstrom, Byron. "The Sixth Ward: A Minneapolis Swede Town in 1905." *Perspectives on Swedish Immigration*. Ed. Nils Hasselmo. University of Minnesota, Duluth, 1978.

Norsving, G. K. "Noget om indvandringen til Vang i Goodhue County." *Samband*, March 1911.

Oftelie, Torkel. "Blant sofabøndane i Goodhue County." *Telesoga*, December 1917.

Pooley, William Vipond. *The Settlement of Illinois from 1830 to 1850*. University of Wisconsin, Madison, 1908.

Qualey, Carlton C. *Norwegian Settlement in the United States*. NAHA, Northfield, 1938.

Rasmussen, C. A. *A History of Goodhue County Minnesota*. Privately published, 1935. (No place of publication given.)

Redal, Olav. *En norsk bygds historie. Norske i Bottineau County, North Dakota*. Privately published, 1917. (No place of publication given.)

Raaen, Aagot. *Grass of the Earth: Immigrant Life in the Dakota Country*. NAHA, Northfield, 1950.

Rygg, A. N. *Norwegians in New York, 1825-1925*. The Norwegian News Company, Brooklyn, N.Y., 1925.

Sartz, R. S. N. "Fra Washington D.C." *Nordmands-Forbundet*, February 1909.

Schmid, Calvin F. *Social Trends in Seattle*. University of Washington Press, Seattle, 1944.

Söderström, Alfred. *Minneapolis minnen. Kulturhistorisk Axplockning från quarnstaden vid Mississippi*. Svenska Folkets Tidning Förlag, Minneapolis, 1899.

Stine, Thos. Ostenson. *Scandinavians on the Pacific, Puget Sound*. Press of Denny-Coryell Company, Seattle, 1900.

Storseth, John. "Pioneering on the Pacific Coast." *Norwegian-American Studies and Records*, vol. 13. NAHA, Northfield, 1943.

———. "Stemninger og minner." *Trønderlagets Aarbok, 1940-1941*.

Tallaksen, Th., and Wiig, Paul H. *Norske paa Staten Island*. Nordisk Tidendes Forlag, Brooklyn, N.Y., 1927.

Thuland, C. M. "Norske pioneer paa Amerikas vestkyst." *Nordmands-Forbundet*, June 1912.

Tingelstad, Gertrude. *Scandinavians in the Silverton County: Their Arrival and Early Settlement*. Silverton Appeal Tribune, Corvallis, Oreg., 1978.

Wahlgren, Erik. *The Kensington Stone: A Mystery Solved*. University of Wisconsin Press, Madison, 1958.

Welfling, Mary E. *The Ole Bull Colony in Potter County: One Hundredth Anniversary Observed July 31-August 1, 1952*. (No publisher, no date.)

Wilson, Aaste. "Live blant nybyggjarane." *Telesoga*, September 1917.

Religious Life and Schools

Andersen, Arlow W. "Norwegian-American Methodism on the Pacific Coast." *Norwegian-American Studies and Records*, vol. 19. NAHA, Northfield, 1956.

———. *The Salt of the Earth: A History of Norwegian-Danish Methodism in America*. Norwegian-Danish Methodist Historical Society, Nashville, Tenn., 1962.

Anderson, Charles H. *White Protestant Americans: From National Origins to Religious Group*. Prentice-Hall, Englewood Cliffs, N.J., 1971.

Benson, William C. *High on Manitou: A History of St. Olaf College*. St. Olaf College Press, Northfield, Minn., 1949.

Bergh, J. A. *Den norsk lutherske kirkes historie i Amerika*. Augsburg Publishing House, Minneapolis, 1914.

Bjork, Kenneth O. "A Covenant Folk, with Scandinavian Colorings." *Norwegian-American Studies*, vol. 21. NAHA, Northfield, 1962.

Bleken, M. K. "De norsk-amerikanske skoler." *Norsk-amerikanernes festskrift, 1914*. Ed. Johs. B. Wist. The Symra Company, Decorah, 1914.

Bogstad, Rasmus. *The Early History of Concordia College: A Record of the School from 1891 to 1910*. (No place or year given.)

Cadbury, Henry J. "The Norwegian Quakers of 1825." *Norwegian-American Studies and Records*, vol. 1. NAHA, Northfield, 1926.

Cartford, Gerhard M. "Music in the Norwegian Lutheran Church. A Study of Its Development in Norway and Its Transfer to America, 1825-1917." Ph.D. dissertation, University of Minnesota, 1961.

Chrislock, Carl H. *From Fjord to Freeway: 100 Years, Augsburg College*. Augsburg College, Minneapolis, 1969.

Draxten, Nina. *Kristofer Janson in America*. Twayne Publishers for NAHA, Boston, 1976.

Erpestad, Emil. "A History of Augustana College." Typescript, Sioux Falls, S. Dak., 1955.

Fevold, Eugene L. "The Norwegian Immigrant and His Church." *Norwegian-American Studies*, vol. 23. NAHA, Northfield, 1967.

Flom, George T. "Norwegian Language and Literature in American Universities." *Norwegian-American Studies and Records*, vol. 2. NAHA, Northfield, 1927.

Franzén, Gösta. "The Development of Scandinavian Studies in the United States." *Scandinavica*, 3, May 1964.

Gjerde, Jon. "The Effect of Community on Migration: Three Minnesota Townships 1885-1905." *Journal of Historical Geography*, 5, no. 4, 1979.

Haagensen, A. *Den norsk-danske methodismes historie paa begge sider havet*. Den norsk-danske boghandel's officin, Chicago, 1894.

Hamre, James S. "Georg Sverdrup and the Augsburg Plan of Education." *Norwegian-American Studies*, vol. 26. NAHA, Northfield, 1974.

———. *Norwegian Immigrants Respond to the Common School: A Case Study of American Values and the Lutheran Tradition*." *Church History*, September 1981.

Hansen, Marcus L. "Immigration and Puritanism." *Norwegian-American Studies and Records*, vol. 9. NAHA, Northfield, 1936.

Hassing, Arne. "Methodism from America to Norway." *Norwegian-American Studies*, vol. 28. NAHA, Northfield, 1979.

Hetle, Erik. *Lars Wilhelm Boe: A Biography*. Augsburg Publishing House, Minneapolis, 1949.

Hodnefield, Jacob. "Erik L. Petersen." *Norwegian-American Studies and Records*, vol. 15. NAHA, Northfield, 1949.

Hofstead, John Andrew. *American Educators of Norwegian Origin: A Biographical Dictionary*. Augsburg Publishing House, Minneapolis, 1931.

Hustvedt, Lloyd. *Rasmus Bjørn Anderson: Pioneer Scholar*. NAHA, Northfield, 1966.

Janson, Kristofer. *Amerikanske forholde. Fem foredrag*. Gyldendalske Boghandels Forlag, Copenhagen, 1881.

Knaplund, Paul. "Rasmus B. Anderson, Pioneer and Crusader." *Norwegian-American Studies and Records*, vol. 18. NAHA, Northfield, 1954.

Kverndal, Roald. "Bethelship 'John Wesley': A New York Ship Saga from the Mid-1800's with Reverberations on Both Sides of the Atlantic Ocean." *Methodist History*, July 1977.

Larsen, Karen. *Laur. Larsen: Pioneer College President*. NAHA, Northfield, 1936.

Larson, Laurence M. "The Norwegian Pioneer in the Field of American Scholarship." *Norwegian-American Studies and Records*, vol.2. NAHA, Northfield, 1927.

Lenker, J. N. *A Popular Appeal in Three Languages for a Three-Language Education, English, Scandinavian, German*. Luther Press, Minneapolis, 1914.

Lien, A. L. "Kirke og skole i Bluemounds settlementet." *Samband*, June 1913.

Lindberg, Duane Rodell. *Men of the Cloth and the Social Cultural Fabric of the Norwegian Ethnic Community in North Dakota*. Arno Press, New York, 1980.

Mamen, Hans C. "Prestegårdsliv blant nybyggere." *Prestegårdsliv*. Ed. Elisabeth Christie. Oslo, 1969.

Molland, Einar. *Church Life in Norway, 1800-1950*. Augsburg Publishing House, Minneapolis, 1957.

Mulder, William. *Homeward to Zion: Mormon Migration from Scandinavia*. University of Minnesota Press, Minneapolis, 1957.

Munch, P. A. "Authority and Freedom: Controversy in Norwegian-American Congregations." *Norwegian-American Studies*, vol. 28. NAHA, Northfield, 1979.

Narveson, B. H. "The Norwegian Lutheran Academies." *Norwegian-American Studies and Records*, vol. 14. NAHA, Northfield, 1944.

Nelson, David T. *Luther College, 1861-1961*. Luther College Press, Decorah, 1961.

Nelson, E. Clifford. *The Rise of World Lutheranism: An American Perspective*. Fortress Press, Philadelphia, 1982.

——, ed.; Kaasa, Harris, and Rosholt, Malcolm, trans. *A Pioneer Churchman: The Narrative and Journal of J. W. C. Dietrichson*. NAHA, Northfield, 1973.

——, and Fevold, Eugene L. *The Lutheran Church among Norwegian-Americans*. 2 vols. Augsburg Publishing House, Minneapolis, 1960.

Nelson, Frank C. "The School Controversy among Norwegian Immigrants." *Norwegian-American Studies*, vol. 26. NAHA, Northfield, 1974.

Norlie, O. M. *Norsk lutherske menigheter i Amerika, 1843-1916*, 2 vols. Augsburg Publishing House, Minneapolis, 1918.

——. *Norsk lutherske prester i Amerika, 1843-1913*. Augsburg Publishing House, Minneapolis, 1914.

——. *School Calendar, 1824-1924: A Who's Who among Teachers in the Lutheran Synods of America*. Augsburg Publishing House, Minneapolis, 1924.

Nyholm, Paul C. *The Americanization of the Danish Lutheran Churches in America*. Institute for Danish Church History, Copenhagen, 1963.

Olsson, Karl A. *By One Spirit*. Covenant Press, Chicago, 1962.

Paulson, Arthur C. "Bjørnson and the Norwegian-Americans, 1880-81." *Norwegian-American Studies and Records*, vol. 5. NAHA, Northfield, 1930.

Preus, Herman A. *Syv foredrag over de kirkelige forholde blandt de Norske i Amerika*. Christiania, 1867.

Qualey, Carlton C. "Thorstein Bunde Veblen, 1857-1929." *Makers of an American Immigrant Legacy*. Ed. Odd S. Lovoll. NAHA, Northfield, 1980.

Ristad, D. G. "Om de norsk-lutherske høiskoler i Amerika." *Symra*, 1906.

Rohne, J. Magnus. *Norwegian-American Lutheranism up to 1872*. Macmillan, New York, 1926.

Rolfsrud, Erling Nicolai. *Cobber Chronicle: An Informal History of Concordia College*. Concordia College, Moorhead, Minn., 1966.

Schafer, Joseph. "Scandinavian Moravians in Wisconsin." *Wisconsin Magazine of History*, 24, 1940-41.

Schnackenberg, Walter C. *The Lamp and the Cross: Sagas of Pacific Lutheran University from 1890 to 1965*. Pacific Lutheran University Press, Parkland, Wash., 1965.

Shaw, Joseph M. *History of St. Olaf College, 1874-1974*. St. Olaf College Press, Northfield, 1974.

Stephenson, George M. *The Religious Aspects of Swedish Immigration: A Study of Immigrant Churches*. University of Minnesota Press, Minneapolis, 1932.

Stiansen, P. *History of the Norwegian Baptists in America*. The Norwegian Baptist Conference in America and The American Baptist Publication Society, Wheaton, Ill., 1939.

Swansen, H. F. "The Quakers of Marshall County, Iowa." *Norwegian-American Studies and Records*, vol. 10. NAHA, Northfield, 1938.

Sweet, William Warren. *Methodism in American History*. Abingdon Press, New York, 1961.

Language and Literature

Ager, Waldemar. "Norsk-amerikansk skjønliteratur." *Norsk-amerikanernes festskrift, 1914*. Ed. Johs. B. Wist. The Symra Company, Decorah, 1914.

Blegen, Theodore C. "The Ballad of Oleana: A Verse Translation." *Norwegian-American Studies and Records*, vol. 14. NAHA, Northfield, 1944.

——, and Ruud, Martin B. *Norwegian Emigrant Songs and Ballads*, University of Minnesota Press, Minneapolis, 1936.

Buckley, Joan N. "Martha Ostenso: A Norwegian-American Immigrant Novelist." *Norwegian-American Studies*, vol. 28. NAHA, Northfield, 1979.

Christianson, J. R. "Literary Traditions of Norwegian-American Women." *Makers of an American Immigrant Legacy*. Ed. Odd S. Lovoll. NAHA, Northfield, 1980.

Flom, George T. "Det norske sprogs bruk og utvikling i Amerika." *Nordmands-Forbundet*, 5, 1912.

Folkestad, Sigurd. "Den norsk-amerikanske skjønliteratur." *Nordmands-Forbundet*, 18, 1925.

Glasrud, Clarence A. *Hjalmar Hjorth Boyesen*. NAHA, Northfield, 1963.

Gvåle, Gudrun Hovde. *O. E. Rølvaag. Nordmann og amerikaner*. Universitetsforlaget, Oslo, 1962.

Haugen, Einar. "Language and Immigration." *Norwegian-American Studies and Records*, vol. 10. NAHA, Northfield, 1938.

——. *The Norwegian Language in America: A Study in Bilingual Behavior*. 2 vols. Indiana University Press, Bloomington, 1969.

——. "O. E. Rølvaag: Norwegian-American." *Norwegian-American Studies and Records*, vol. 7, NAHA, Northfield, 1933.

——. "The Struggle over Norwegian." *Norwegian-American Studies and Records*, vol. 17. NAHA, Northfield, 1952.

Heitmann, John. "Julius B. Baumann: A Biographical Sketch." *Norwegian-American Studies and Records*, vol. 15. NAHA, Northfield, 1949.

Hoidahl, Aagot D. "Norwegian-American Fiction, 1880-1928." *Norwegian-American Studies and Records*, vol. 5. NAHA, Northfield, 1930.

Hustvedt, Lloyd. "Ole Amundsen Buslett, 1855-1924."

Makers of an American Immigrant Legacy. Ed. Odd S. Lovoll. NAHA, Northfield, 1980.

Jorgenson, Theodore, and Solum, Nora O. *Ole Edvart Rølvaag: A Biography*. Harper & Brothers, New York, 1939.

Kilde, Clarence. "Dark Decades: The Declining Years of Waldemar Ager." *Norwegian-American Studies*, vol. 28. NAHA, Northfield, 1979.

Kimmerle, Marjorie M. "Norwegian-American Surnames." *Norwegian-American Studies and Records*, vol. 12. NAHA, Northfield, 1941.

Larson, Laurence M. "Tellef Grundysen and the Beginnings of Norwegian-American Fiction." *Norwegian-American Studies and Records*, vol. 8. NAHA, Northfield, 1934.

Mannsåker, Jørund. *Emigrasjon og dikting. Utvandringa til Nord-Amerika i norsk skjønnlitteratur*. Det Norske Samlaget, Oslo, 1971.

Naess, Harald S. *Knut Hamsun og Amerika*. Gyldendal, Oslo, 1969.

Paulson, Kristoffer. "What Was Lost: Ole Rølvaag's *The Boat of Longing*." *Melus*, Spring 1980.

Ratner, Marc L. "The Romantic Spencerian." *Norwegian-American Studies*, vol. 23. NAHA, Northfield, 1967.

Reigstad, Paul. *Rølvaag: His Life and Art*. University of Nebraska Press, Lincoln, 1972.

Semmingsen, Ingrid. "A Pioneer: Agnes Mathilde Wergeland, 1857-1914." *Makers of an American Immigrant Legacy*. Ed. Odd S. Lovoll. NAHA, Northfield, 1980.

Skårdal, Dorothy Burton. *The Divided Heart: Scandinavian Immigrant Experience through Literary Sources*. University of Nebraska Press, Lincoln, 1974.

Thorson, Gerald H. "America Is Not Norway: The Story of the Norwegian-American Novel." Ph.D. dissertation, Columbia University 1957.

——. "First Sagas of the New World: A Study of the Beginnings of Norwegian-American Literature." *Norwegian-American Studies and Records*, vol. 17. NAHA, Northfield, 1952.

——. "Norwegian Immigrant Novels Set in Chicago." *Midamerica*, 4, 1977.

——. "The Novels of Peer Strømme." *Norwegian-American Studies and Records*, vol. 18. NAHA, Northfield, 1954.

——. "Pressed Flowers and Still-Running Brooks: Norwegian-American Literature." *Ethnic Literature since 1776: The Many Voices of America*. Texas Tech University, Lubbock, Tex., 1978.

——. "Tinsel and Dust: Disenchantment in Two Minneapolis Novels from 1880." *Minnesota History*, Summer 1977.

Zempel, Solveig. "Language Use in the Novels of Johannes B. Wist: A Study of Bilingualism in Literature." Ph.D. dissertation, University of Minnesota, 1980.

Associations and Societies

Bergh, Martin. "Det norske nationalforbund og 17de mai i Chicago." *Norden*, April-May 1929.

——. "Det norske sangerforbund i Amerika." *Nordmands-Forbundet*, 18, 1925.

Eckers, H. A. "Gymnastikk og idrett: Norwegian-American Athletic Association." *Norden*, February-March 1929.

Elkins, Frank. "Norwegian Influence on American Skiing." *American-Scandinavian Review*, December 1947.

Foss, H. A., Johson, Simon, and Olson, B. *Trediveaarskrigen mod Drikkeondet. Kort oversigt over avholds og forbudsarbeidet særlig blandt skandinaver i Nord Dakota*. Nord Dakota Totalavholdsselskab, Minot, 1922.

Fuglum, Per. *Kampen om alkoholen i Norge 1816-1904*. Universitetsforlaget, Oslo, 1972.

Furnas, J. C. *The Life and Times of the Late Demon Rum*. G. P. Putnam's Sons, New York, 1965.

Gukild, Bjarne. "Skiklubben 'Norge,' 1905-1930." *Norden*, December 1930.

Hambro, Johan, ed. *De tok et Norge med seg. Nordmanns Forbundets saga gjennom 50 år*. Nordmanns Forbundet, Oslo, 1957.

Hansen, Carl G. O. *History of Sons of Norway*. Sons of Norway Supreme Lodge, Minneapolis, 1944.

——. "Det norske foreningsliv i Amerika." *Norsk-amerikanernes festskrift, 1914*. Ed. Johs. B. Wist. The Symra Company, Decorah, 1914.

——. "Northern Music in America." *American-Scandinavian Review*, January-February 1916.

Hodnefield, Jacob. "Norwegian-American Bygdelags and Their Publications." *Norwegian-American Studies and Records*, vol. 18. NAHA, Northfield, 1954.

Holter, Aksel H. "Nordmænds indflydelse i Amerikas sportsliv." *Nordmands-Forbundet*, 18, 1925.

Lovoll, Odd S. *A Folk Epic: The Bygdelag in America*. Twayne Publishers for NAHA, Boston, 1975.

Naeseth, Gerhard B. "Hender over havet. Norsk-amerikansk slektsforskning." *Norsk slektshistorisk tidsskrift*, 24, 1974.

Norborg, C. Sverre. *An American Saga*. Sons of Norway, Minneapolis, 1970.

"Norske foreninger i fremmede lande." *Nordmands-Forbundet*, 1, 1908.

Nydahl, J. L. *Afholdssagens historie*. Forfatterens forlag, Minneapolis, 1896.

Nyquist, Gerd. *Bataljon 99*. Aschehoug, Oslo, 1981.

Osland, Birger. *A Long Pull from Stavanger. The Reminiscences of a Norwegian Immigrant*. NAHA, Northfield, 1945.

——. "Norwegian Clubs in Chicago." *Norwegian-American Studies and Records*, vol. 12. NAHA, Northfield, 1941.

Rygg, A. N. *American Relief for Norway*. American Relief for Norway, Chicago, 1947.

Steen, Sverre. "De frivillige sammenslutninger og det norske demokrati." *Historisk Tidsskrift*, 34, 1946-48.

Wetterman, August. *The History and Review of the Scandinavian Society of San Francisco, California*. R and E Research Associates, San Francisco, 1970.

Wilt, Napier, and Naeseth, Henriette C. Koren. "Two Early Norwegian Dramatic Societies in Chicago." *Norwegian-American Studies and Records*, vol. 10. NAHA, Northfield, 1938.

Politics and the Press

Andersen, Arlow W. *The Immigrant Takes His Stand: The Norwegian-American Press and Public Affairs, 1847-1872*. NAHA, Northfield, 1953.

——. "Knud Langeland: Pioneer Editor." *Norwegian-American Studies and Records*, vol. 14. NAHA, Northfield, 1944.

Barone, Michael. "The Social Basis of Urban Politics: Minneapolis and St. Paul, 1890-1905." Honors thesis, Harvard University, 1965.

Barton, Albert Olaus. "The Beginnings of the Norwegian Press in America." *The State Historical Society of Wisconsin. Separate No. 174. From the Proceedings of the Society for 1916*. Madison, Wis., 1916.

Brye, David L. "Wisconsin Scandinavians and Progressivism, 1900-1950." *Norwegian-American Studies*, vol. 27. NAHA, Northfield, 1977.

Capps, Finis Herbert. *From Isolationism to Involvement: The Swedish Immigrant Press in America, 1914-1943*. Swedish Pioneer Historical Society, Chicago, 1966.

Carlsson, Sten. "Scandinavian Politicians in Minnesota Around the Turn of the Century. A Study in the Role of the Ethnic Factor in an Immigrant State." *Americana Norvegica*, vol. 3. Universitetsforlaget, Oslo, 1971.

Chrislock, Carl H. *Ethnicity Challenged: The Upper Midwest Norwegian-American Experience in World War I*. NAHA, Northfield, 1981.

——. "The Norwegian-American Impact on Minnesota Politics: How far 'Left-of-Center'?" *Norwegian Influence on the Upper Midwest*. Ed. Harald S. Naess. University of Minnesota, Duluth, 1976.

——. *The Progressive Era in Minnesota, 1899-1918*. Minnesota Historical Society, St. Paul, 1971.

Dennis, Charles H. *Victor Lawson: His Time and His Work*. University of Chicago Press, Chicago, 1935.

Dieserud, Juul. "Nordmænd i det offentlige og politiske liv." *Norsk-amerikanernes festskrift, 1914*. Ed. Johs. B. Wist. The Symra Company, Decorah, 1914.

——. "Den norske presse i Amerika. En historisk oversigt." *Nordmands-Forbundet*, April 1912.

Evjue, William T. *A Fighting Editor*. Wells Printing Company, Madison, Wis., 1968.

Fite, Gilbert Courtland. *Peter Norbeck: Prairie Statesman*. University of Missouri, Columbia, 1948.

Fjærtoft, Torgeir. "Knute Nelson's Political Career, 1878-1905. From Ethnic Politician to Political Independence." Thesis, University of Oslo, 1980.

Gieske, Millard L. *Minnesota Farmer-Laborism: The Third-Party Alternative*. University of Minnesota Press, Minneapolis, 1979.

Hansen, Carl G. O. "Den norsk-amerikanske presse før borgerkrigen." *Symra*, 1907.

——. "Pressen til borgerkrigens slutning." *Norsk-amerikanernes festskrift, 1914*. Ed. Johs. B. Wist. The Symra Company, Decorah, 1914.

Hansen, Jean Skogerboe. "*Skandinaven* and the John Anderson Publishing Company." *Norwegian-American Studies*, vol. 28. NAHA, Northfield, 1979.

Haugen, Nils P. *Pioneer and Political Reminiscences*. State Historical Society of Wisconsin, Madison, 1930.

Larson, Agnes M. "The Editorial Policy of *Skandinaven*,

1900-1903." *Norwegian-American Studies and Records*, vol. 8. NAHA, Northfield, 1934.

Larson, Laurence M. "The Convention Riot at Benson Grove, Iowa, in 1876." *Norwegian-American Studies and Records*, vol. 6. NAHA, Northfield, 1931.

Lindberg, Duane R. "Pastors, Prohibition and Politics: The Role of Norwegian Clergy in the North Dakota Abstinence Movement, 1880-1920." *North Dakota Quarterly*, Autumn 1981.

Lovoll, Odd S. "*Decorah-Posten*: The Story of an Immigrant Newspaper." *Norwegian-American Studies*, vol. 27. NAHA, Northfield, 1977.

——. "The Norwegian Press in North Dakota." *Norwegian-American Studies*, vol. 24. NAHA, Northfield, 1970.

"Marie Vognild Lund og *Washington-Posten*." *Trønderlagets Aarbok*, 1940-1941.

Marzolf, Marion Tuttle. *The Danish-Language Press in America*. Arno Press, New York, 1979.

Mattson, Hans. *Reminiscences: The Story of an Emigrant*. D. D. Merrill Company, St. Paul, 1892.

Maxwell, Robert S. *La Follette and the Rise of the Progressives in Wisconsin*. State Historical Society of Wisconsin, Madison, 1956.

Mayer, George H. *The Political Career of Floyd B. Olson*. University of Minnesota Press, Minneapolis, 1951.

Morlan, Robert L. *Political Prairie Fire*. University of Minnesota Press, Minneapolis, 1955.

Norlie, O. M. *Norwegian-American Papers, 1847-1946*. Eilron Mimeopress, Northfield, 1946.

Odland, Martin W. *The Life of Knute Nelson*. Lund Press, Minneapolis, 1926.

Park, Robert E. *The Immigrant Press and Its Control*. Harper & Brothers, New York, 1922.

Roedder, Karsten. *Av en utvandreravis' saga*. 2 vols. Norwegian News, Brooklyn, N.Y., 1966 and 1968.

Smith, Donnal V. "The Influence of the Foreign-Born of the Northwest in the Election of 1860." *Ethnic Voters and the Election of Lincoln*. Ed. Frederick C. Luebke. University of Nebraska Press, Lincoln, 1971.

Soike, Lowell Jerome. "Norwegian-Americans and the Politics of Dissent, 1880-1924." Ph.D. dissertation, University of Iowa, 1979.

Søyland, Carl. *Skrift i sand*. Gyldendal, Oslo, 1954.

Wefald, Jon. *A Voice of Protest: Norwegians in American Politics, 1890-1917*. NAHA, Northfield, 1971.

Weintraub, Hyman. *Andrew Furuseth: Emancipator of the Seamen*. University of California Press, Los Angeles, 1959.

Wist, Johs. B. "Pressen efter borgerkrigen." *Norsk-amerikanernes festskrift, 1914*. Ed. Johs. B. Wist. The Symra Company, Decorah, 1914.

Professions and Occupations

Andrews, Ralph W., and Larssen, A. K. *Fish and Ships*. Bonanza Books, New York, 1959.

Arestad, Sverre. "The Norwegians in the Pacific Coast Fisheries." *Pacific Northwest Quarterly*, January 1943.

Bjork, Kenneth O. "Ole Evinrude and the Outboard

Motor." *Norwegian-American Studies and Records*, vol. 12. NAHA, Northfield, 1941.

——. *Saga in Steel and Concrete: Norwegian Engineers in America*. NAHA, Northfield, 1947.

Gimnes, Trygve. "Norske ingeniører i New York." *Nordmanns-Forbundet*, 25, 1932.

Gjerset, Knut. *Norwegian Sailors in American Waters: A Study in the History of Maritime Activity on the Eastern Seaboard*. NAHA, Northfield, 1933.

——. *Norwegian Sailors on the Great Lakes: A Study in the History of American Inland Transportation*. NAHA, Northfield, 1928.

——, and Hektoen, Ludvig. "Health Conditions and the Practice of Medicine among the Early Norwegian Settlers." *Norwegian-American Studies and Records*, vol. 1. NAHA, Northfield, 1926.

Guttersen, Alma A., and Christensen, Regina Hilleboe, eds. *Souvenir "Norse-American Women," 1825-1925*. Lutheran Free Church Publishing Company, St. Paul, 1926.

Hall, Prescott F. *Immigration and Its Effect upon the United States*, Holt, New York, 1906.

Harstad, Peter T. "Disease and Sickness on the Wisconsin Frontier." *Wisconsin Magazine of History*, 43, 1959-60.

Hougen, Olaf. "Magnus Swenson, Inventor and Engineer." *Norwegian-American Studies and Records*, vol. 10. NAHA, Northfield, 1938.

Hoverstad, T. A. *The Norwegian Farmers in the United States*. Hans Jervell Publishing, Fargo N. Dak., 1915.

Klaveness, E. *Norske læger i America, 1840-1942*. Privately published, St. Paul, 1943.

Knaplund, Paul. *Moorings Old and New: Entries in an Immigrant's Log*. University of Wisconsin Press, Madison, 1963.

Larson, Agnes M. *John A. Johnson: An Uncommon American*. NAHA, Northfield, 1969.

Lokken, Harold. "The Halibut Fishing, an Important Industry Developed by Norwegians." *Trønderlagets Aarbok*, 1940-41.

Midelfort, Christian Fredrik. "Non-Migration and Migration in Twenty-Five Hundred Families." Manuscript in NAHA's archives.

Nelson, O. N. *History of the Scandinavians and Successful Scandinavians in the United States*. 2 vols. 2nd rev. ed. O. N. Nelson, Minneapolis, 1900.

——. "The Nationality of Criminal and Insane Persons in the United States." Nelson, O. N., ed. *History of the Scandinavians and Successful Scandinavians in the United States*, vol. 2. O. N. Nelson, Minneapolis, 1900.

Ødegaard, Ørnulv. *Emigration and Insanity: A Study of Mental Disease among the Norwegian-born Population of Minnesota*. Copenhagen, 1932.

Wong, Johs. *Norske utvandrere og forretningsdrivende i Amerika*. J. Burner, New York, 1927.

Assimilation and Ethnic Life

Ager, Waldemar. "Norskhetsbevægelsen i Amerika." *Nordmands-Forbundet*, 18, 1925.

Anderson, Harry H. "Scandinavian Immigration in Milwaukee Naturalization Records." *Milwaukee History*, Spring and Summer 1978.

Chrislock, Carl H. "Name Change and the Church, 1918-1920." *Norwegian-American Studies*, vol. 27. NAHA, Northfield, 1977.

Drachsler, Julius. *Intermarriage in New York City*. Columbia University Press, New York, 1921.

Dybvig, Philip S. "Facts about the Language Question." *Lutheran Church Herald*, May 20, 1930.

Fishman, Joshua A. *Language Loyalty in the United States: The Maintenance and Perpetuation of Non-English Mother Tongues by American Ethnic and Religious Groups*. Mouton, The Hague, 1966.

Gordon, Milton M. *Assimilation in American Life: The Role of Race, Religion, and National Origins*. Oxford University Press, New York, 1964.

Handlin, Oscar. *The American People in the Twentieth Century*. Harvard University Press, Cambridge, 1954.

——, ed. *Immigration as a Factor in American History*. Prentice-Hall, Englewood Cliffs, N.J., 1959.

Higham, John. *Send These to Me: Jews and Other Immigrants in Urban America*. Atheneum, New York, 1975.

——. *Strangers in the Land: Patterns of American Nativism, 1860-1925*. 19th ed. Atheneum, New York, 1977.

——, ed. *Ethnic Leadership in America*. Johns Hopkins University Press, Baltimore, 1978.

Hollingshead, A. B. *Elmtown's Youth and Elmtown Revisited*. John Wiley, New York, 1975.

Hutchinson, E. P. *Immigrants and Their Children, 1850-1950*. Russell & Russell, New York, 1956.

Jenks, Albert. "Ethnic Census in Minneapolis." *American Journal of Sociology*, May 1912.

Jordan, Riverda Harding. "Nationality and School Progress. A Study in Americanization." Ph.D. dissertation, University of Minnesota, 1921.

Lovoll, Odd S., ed. *Cultural Pluralism versus Assimilation: The Views of Waldemar Ager*. NAHA, Northfield, 1977.

Munch, Peter A. "Segregation and Assimilation of Norwegian Settlements in Wisconsin." *Norwegian-American Studies and Records*, vol. 18. NAHA, Northfield, 1954.

Nelson, Lowry. *The Minnesota Community: Country and Town in Transition*. University of Minnesota Press, Minneapolis, 1960.

Novak, Michael. *The Rise of the Unmeltable Ethnics: Politics and Culture in the Seventies*. Macmillan, New York, 1971.

Patterson, Orlando. "Context and Choice in Ethnic Allegiance: A Theoretical Framework and Caribbean Case Study." *Ethnicity: Theory and Experience*. Ed. Nathan Glazer and Daniel P. Moynihan. Harvard University Press, Cambridge, Mass., 1975.

Steinberg, Stephen. *The Ethnic Myth: Race and Class in America*. Atheneum, New York, 1981.

Stephenson, George M. "The Mind of the Scandinavian Immigrant." *Norwegian-American Studies and Records*, vol. 4. Northfield, 1929.

Thernstrom, Stephan. *Poverty and Progress: Social Mobility in a Nineteenth Century City*. Harvard University Press, Cambridge, Mass., 1964.

——. *The Other Bostonians: Poverty and Progress in the American Metropolis, 1880-1970*. Harvard University Press, Cambridge, Mass., 1973.

Warner, W. Lloyd. *Democracy in Jonesville: A Study in Quality and Inequality*. Harper & Row, New York, 1949.

Credits for
Illustrations

Andrew Dahl, landscape photographer, was a part of the Norwegian-American cultural picture. Several of his photographs are reproduced in the present volume, and they represent documentary photography at its best.

Andreas Larsen Dahl (1844-1923) came from Skrautvål in Østre Slidre. He emigrated to America in 1869 and supported himself as an itinerant photographer with Norwegian-American milieus as his most important field.

p. 196 Minnesota Historical Society.

p. 198 Photo by Scotty Sapiro. In Kristina Veirs, ed., *Nordic Heritage Northwest*, Seattle: The Writing Works, 1982.

p. 199 Minnesota Historical Society.

p. 200 Minnesota Historical Society.

p. 201 Minnesota Historical Society.

p. 202 Minnesota Historical Society

p. 203 Below left: In Thallaug and Erickson, *Our Norwegian Immigrants*.
Above and right: In Kenneth O. Bjork, *Saga in Steel and Concrete*, Northfield, Norwegian American Historical Association, 1947.

p. 204 Hedmarksmuseet og Domkirkeodden.

p. 205 Photo by Andrew Dahl. State Historical Society of Wisconsin.

p. 206 Left: In Thallaug and Erickson, *Our Norwegian Immigrants*.
Right: Sons of Norway Collection.

p. 207 Left: Norwegian-American Historical Association.
Right: Privately owned.

p. 210 Haga Photography (Minneapolis).

p. 211 Norwegian-American Museum.

p. 213 Above: Hedmarksmuseet og Domkirkeodden.
Below: Norwegian-American Museum.

p. 214 Above: Photo by Wendt Studio. Stoughton High School (Stoughton, Wisconsin).
Below: Minnesota Historical Society.

p. 215 Photo: by Scotty Sapiro. In Veirs, *Nordic Heritage Northwest*.

p. 217 Left: *Minneapolis Star and Tribune Picture Magazine*, November 9, 1975.
Right: Photo by Odd Lovoll.

p. 219 *Telegraph Herald*, October 12, 1975 (Dubuque, Iowa).

p. 220 In possession of Scandinavia Today organizers in Minneapolis.

p. 221 Photo by Mike Zerby. *Minneapolis Star and Tribune*.

Index